Officer
Candidate Tests

Officer Candidate Tests

Solomon Wiener • *Edited by Scott A. Ostrow*

THOMSON

PETERSON'S

Australia • Canada • Mexico • Singapore • Spain • United Kingdom • United States

An ARCO Book

ARCO is a registered trademark of Thomson Learning, Inc., and is used herein under license by Peterson's.

About The Thomson Corporation and Peterson's

With revenues of US$7.8 billion, The Thomson Corporation (www.thomson.com) is a leading global provider of integrated information solutions for business, education, and professional customers. Its Learning businesses and brands (www.thomsonlearning.com) serve the needs of individuals, learning institutions, and corporations with products and services for both traditional and distributed learning.

Peterson's, part of The Thomson Corporation, is one of the nation's most respected providers of lifelong learning online resources, software, reference guides, and books. The Education Supersite℠ at www.petersons.com—the Internet's most heavily traveled education resource—has searchable databases and interactive tools for contacting U.S.-accredited institutions and programs. In addition, Peterson's serves more than 105 million education consumers annually.

For more information, contact Peterson's, 2000 Lenox Drive, Lawrenceville, NJ 08648; 800-338-3282; or find us on the World Wide Web at: www.petersons.com/about

Editor: Theresa C. Moore; Production Editor: Teresina Jonkoski;
Manufacturing Manager: Ray Golaszewski; Composition Manager: Melissa Ignatowski

ISSN: International Standard Serial Number information available upon request.

ISBN: 0-7689-1701-8

Printed in the United States of America

10 9 8 7 6 5 4 3 2 1   06 05 04

Seventh Edition

ACKNOWLEDGMENTS

I wish to express my gratitude and appreciation to:

The Officer Recruiting Offices and the Offices of Public Affairs of the Air Force, Army, Coast Guard, Marines, and Navy for making available the most recent officer recruiting brochures and for providing guidance on current requirements and qualifications for programs leading to a commission, career fields for officers, and other pertinent areas.

U.S. Department of Defense, Washington, D.C. for

Military Careers
ASVAB [18/19] Student and Parent Guide
ASVAB [18/19] Educator and Counselor Guide

Bureau of Naval Personnel, Washington, D.C. for

Tools and Their Uses
Basic Machines

ARCO for making available its vast test item bank from which questions were selected to formulate many of the practice exercises and specimen tests.

Special thanks to Col. Scott Ostrow of the United States Air Force for his invaluable advice and support of this project.

Solomon Wiener
New York, New York

Petersons.com/publishing

Check out our Web site at www.petersons.com/publishing to see if there is any new information regarding the tests and any revisions or corrections to the content of this book. We've made sure the information in this book is accurate and up-to-date; however, the format or content of your test may have changed since the time of publication.

CONTENTS

Acknowledgments iii

PART I   **CAREER OPPORTUNITIES AS A
                COMMISSIONED OFFICER IN THE
                ARMED FORCES OF THE UNITED STATES** 1

Career Opportunities for Officers 3
    Military Officer Occupations 3
    General Qualification Requirements for a Commission 6
    Pathways to Becoming an Officer...8
    Basic Officer Training 10
    Rank, Pay, and Benefits 11

PART II   **EARNING YOUR COMMISSION
                IN THE ARMED FORCES** 17

Earning a Commission in the U.S. Army 19
    Officer Candidate School (OCS) 19
    Career Fields 20
    Requirements and Qualifications 21
Earning a Commission in the U.S. Navy 25
    Officer Candidate School and Technical Training 25
    Career Fields 28
    Requirements and Qualifications 29
Earning a Commission in the U.S. Air Force 33
    Officer Training School (OTS) 34
    Tour of Duty 35
    Requirements and Qualifications 35
Earning a Commission in the U.S. Marine Corps 39
    Officer Candidate School and Basic Training 39
    Career Fields 40
    Requirements and Qualifications 41
Earning a Commission in the U.S. Coast Guard 43
    Officer Candidate School 43
    Career Fields 43
    Requirements and Qualifications 44

PART III   MILITARY TESTS AND TESTING 47

Historical Background 49
    World War I 49
    World War II 49
    After World War II.. 50
    Armed Services Vocational Aptitude Battery (ASVAB) 51
    Scholastic Assessment Test (SAT) 53
    ACT Assessment 53
    Air Force Officer Qualifying Test (AFOQT) 53
    Army Officer Candidate Test (OCT) 55
    Alternate Army Flight Aptitude Selection Test (AFAST) 55
    Navy and Marine Corps Aviation Selection Test Battery 55
    Composite Scoring 57

**PART IV   MULTIPLE-CHOICE TESTS AND
MACHINE-SCORED ANSWER SHEETS 59**

Multiple-Choice Tests 61
    Alphabetical Options 62
    Numerical Options 62
    Chronological Options 63
    Length of Option 63
    Random Options 63
Machine-Scored Answer Sheets 65
    Filling Out the Heading 68
    Marking Your Answers 71

PART V   PREPARING FOR AND TAKING THE TEST 73

Test-Taking Strategies 75
    Applying for the Test 75
    Preparing for the Test 75
    Guessing 77
    Taking the Test 79
Types of Questions Used for Selecting Officer Candidates..................... 81
    Synonyms 81
    Verbal Analogies 83
    Reading Comprehension 87
    Paragraph Comprehension 90
    Sentence Comprehension 93
    Arithmetic Reasoning 96
    Math Knowledge... 99
    Data Interpretation 108
    General Science 111
    Electronics Information 113
    Mechanical Comprehension 115

PART VI   SUGGESTED STUDY PLAN FOR TEST PREPARATION **119**

How to Use the Practice Exercises and Specimen Tests 121
    U.S. Air Force 121
    U.S. Army 123
    U.S. Navy 124
    U.S. Marine Corps 125
    U.S. Coast Guard 126

PART VII   PRACTICE EXERCISES **127**

Answer Sheet for Practice Exercises 129
Practice Exercise 1: Synonyms 133
Practice Exercise 2: Verbal Analogies 141
Practice Exercise 3: Reading Comprehension 147
Practice Exercise 4: Arithmetic Reasoning 161
Practice Exercise 5: Math Knowledge 171
Practice Exercise 6: Data Interpretation 181
Practice Exercise 7: General Science 195
Practice Exercise 8: Electronics Information 199
Practice Exercise 9: Mechanical Comprehension 205

PART VIII   KEY ANSWERS AND RATIONALE FOR PRACTICE EXERCISES **215**

Key Answers and Rationale for Practice Exercise 1: Synonyms 217
Key Answers and Rationale for Practice Exercise 2: Verbal Analogies 221
Key Answers and Rationale for Practice Exercise 3: Reading Comprehension 225
Key Answers and Rationale for Practice Exercise 4: Arithmetic Reasoning 231
Key Answers and Rationale for Practice Exercise 5: Math Knowledge 239
Key Answers and Rationale for Practice Exercise 6: Data Interpretation 245
Key Answers and Rationale for Practice Exercise 7: General Science 249
Key Answers and Rationale for Practice Exercise 8: Electronics Information 253
Key Answers and Rationale for Practice Exercise 9: Mechanical Comprehension ... 259

PART IX   UNITED STATES AIR FORCE OFFICER QUALIFYING TEST **263**

Part 1: Verbal Analogies 267
Part 2: Arithmetic Reasoning 271
Part 3: Reading Comprehension 277
Part 4: Data Interpretation 285
Part 5: Word Knowledge 293
Part 6: Math Knowledge 297
Key Answers and Rationale for Subtests 1 through 6 301

PART X   ARMED SERVICES VOCATIONAL
**   APTITUDE BATTERY (ASVAB)** **321**

Part 1: General Science 325
Part 2: Arithmetic Reasoning 329
Part 3: Word Knowledge 333
Part 4: Paragraph Comprehension 337
Part 5: Mathematics Knowledge 343
Part 6: Electronics Information 347
Key Answers and Rationale for ASVAB Test Items 351

PART XI   UNITED STATES NAVY AND MARINE CORPS
**   AVIATION SELECTION TEST BATTERY** **371**

Test 1: Math/Verbal Test 375
Test 2: Mechanical Comprehension Test 381
Key Answers and Rationale for Navy and Marine Corps
    Aviation Selection Test Battery 387

PART I

Career Opportunities as a Commissioned Officer in the Armed Forces of the United States

CAREER OPPORTUNITIES FOR OFFICERS

Commissioned officers in the Armed Forces of the United States—Air Force, Army, Coast Guard, Marines, and Navy—enjoy a diversified professional career interwoven with adventure and travel plus a variety of assignments geared to challenge and develop individual skills and expertise. In addition, opportunities for promotion are excellent.

Commissioned officers enjoy a combination of privileges, benefits, opportunities, and responsibilities rarely offered elsewhere. Currently, about 225,000 men and women are serving as officers either on active duty or in reserve components of the Armed Forces. They have found rewarding careers in the service of our country.

Among the many advantages of a military career are the following:
- Responsibility and an opportunity to exercise leadership at an early age
- Opportunity for advanced education through tuition assistance programs
- Excellent pay
- Opportunity for travel
- Opportunity to gain personnel and management experience
- Unmatched job and financial security
- Low-cost life insurance of up to $250,000
- Medical and dental care
- Government-paid moving expenses when changing duty stations
- 30 days annual leave with pay
- Shopping privileges at military commissaries and exchanges
- Periodic promotions based on performance
- Membership privileges at officers' clubs
- Outstanding retirement benefits
- Thrift Savings Plan that provides tax-deferred savings

The following are some of the major disadvantages of military life:
- Occasional family moves
- Separation from family when on certain assignments
- Slightly greater hazard than in some other occupations
- Working hours not always constant
- Desired job assignment or duty station not always available

MILITARY OFFICER OCCUPATIONS

Military officers work in a variety of managerial, professional, and scientific occupations. Of course, officers are leaders in all of the combat specialty areas, such as special forces, infantry, armored assault vehicles, missiles and artillery, and combat mission support.

Together, the five services offer employment opportunities in more than 1,500 officer job specialties. To help you visualize the scope and breadth of the many military officer careers available, these specialties are divided into 58 occupations in nine broad groups.
- Executive, administrative, and managerial occupations
- Human resource development occupations

- Support services occupations
- Media and public affairs occupations
- Health-care occupations
- Engineering, science, and technical occupations
- Protective service occupations
- Transportation occupations
- Combat specialty occupations

A tabulation of the officer occupational areas listing the nine broad groups and 58 occupations appears on the following pages. Note that the military services offering employment and training opportunities in each occupation are shown by an X.

Figure 1 (page 6) shows the distribution of officers across the nine occupational groups. About 88 percent of all military occupations have counterparts in the civilian world of work. For example, there are personnel managers, optometrists, electronics engineers, and music directors in both the military and civilian work forces.

The Commissioned Corps of the Public Health Service, an agency within the Department of Health and Human Services, and the National Oceanic and Atmospheric Administration, an agency within the Department of Commerce, are also members of the uniformed services. However, these two agencies are not part of the Armed Forces of the United States.

The Commissioned Corps of the Public Health Service is made up of men and women who are highly trained medical personnel and research scientists. The Commissioned Corps of the National Oceanic and Atmospheric Administration consists of men and women who have engineering or science degrees with specialization in mathematics, physics, oceanography, meteorology, or other physical, geophysical, or biological disciplines.

OFFICER OCCUPATIONAL AREAS

Officer Occupations	Army	Navy	Air Force	Marine Corps	Coast Guard
Executive, administrative, and managerial occupations					
Administrative officers		X	X	X	X
Finance and accounting managers	X	X	X	X	X
Health services administrators	X	X	X		X
International relations officers	X	X	X	X	X
Logisticians	X	X	X	X	
Management analysts and planners	X	X	X	X	X
Purchasing and contracting managers	X	X	X	X	X
Recruiting managers	X	X	X	X	X
Store managers	X	X	X	X	X
Supply and warehousing managers	X	X	X	X	X
Human resource development occupations					
Personnel managers	X	X	X	X	X
Recruiting managers	X	X	X	X	X
Teachers and instructors	X	X	X	X	X
Training and education directors	X	X	X	X	X

Officer Occupations	Army	Navy	Air Force	Marine Corps	Coast Guard
Support services occupations					
Chaplains	X	X	X		
Food service managers	X	X	X	X	X
Social workers	X	X	X		
Media and public affairs occupations					
Audiovisual and broadcast directors	X	X	X	X	
Music directors	X	X	X	X	X
Public information officers	X	X	X	X	X
Health-care occupations					
Dentists	X	X	X		X
Dietitians	X	X	X		
Optometrists	X	X	X		
Pharmacists	X	X	X		X
Physical and occupational therapists	X	X	X		X
Physician assistants	X	X	X		X
Physicians and surgeons	X	X	X		X
Psychologists	X	X	X		
Registered nurses	X	X	X		X
Speech therapists	X	X	X		X
Engineering, science, and technical occupations					
Aerospace engineers		X	X	X	X
Civil engineers	X	X	X	X	X
Communications managers	X	X	X	X	X
Computer systems officers	X	X	X	X	X
Electrical and electronics engineers	X	X	X	X	X
Environmental health and safety officers	X	X	X	X	X
Industrial engineers	X	X	X	X	X
Intelligence officers	X	X	X	X	X
Lawyers and judges	X	X	X	X	X
Life scientists	X	X	X		
Marine engineers		X			X
Nuclear engineers	X	X		X	
Ordnance officers	X	X	X	X	X
Physical scientists	X	X	X	X	X
Space operations officers	X	X	X	X	
Protective service occupations					
Emergency management officers	X	X	X	X	X
Law enforcement and security officers	X	X	X	X	X

Officer Occupations	Army	Navy	Air Force	Marine Corps	Coast Guard
Transportation occupations					
Air traffic control managers	X	X	X	X	
Airplane navigators	X	X	X	X	X
Airplane pilots	X	X	X	X	X
Helicopter pilots	X	X	X	X	X
Ship and submarine officers	X	X			X
Ship engineers	X	X			X
Transportation maintenance managers	X	X	X	X	X
Transportation managers	X	X	X	X	X
Combat specialty occupations					
Armored assault vehicle officers	X			X	
Artillery and missile officers	X	X	X	X	
Combat mission support officers	X	X	X	X	
Infantry officers	X	X			
Special officers	X	X	X	X	

Figure 1 Distribution of Officers by Occupational Group

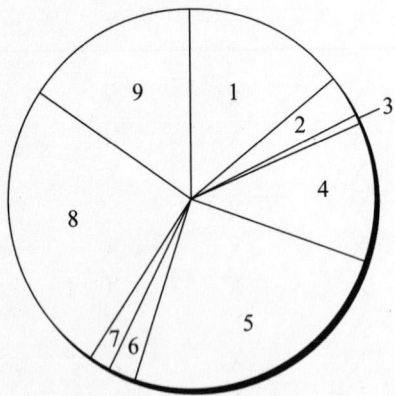

1. Executive, administrative, and managerial
2. Human resource development
3. Media and public affairs
4. Health care
5. Engineering, science, and technical
6. Protective services
7. Support services
8. Transportation
9. Combat specialty

GENERAL QUALIFICATION REQUIREMENTS FOR A COMMISSION

The men and women who become commissioned officers in the Armed Forces serve at the will of Congress. The term "commissioned" refers to the certification that officers receive upon meeting all qualification requirements. The certification confers military rank, authority, and obligation. To join the military as a commissioned officer, applicants generally must have a four-year college degree. The general qualification requirements are presented below. Specific requirements vary by service.

GENERAL QUALIFICATIONS*

Age	Must be between 19 and 29 years for OCS/OTS; 17 and 21 years for ROTC; 17 and 22 years for the service academies.
Citizenship Status	Must be U.S. citizen.
Physical Condition	Must meet minimum physical standards listed below. Some occupations have additional physical standards.

Height—Males: Maximum—6'5"

                           Minimum—5'0"

         Females: Maximum—6'5"

                           Minimum—4'10"

Weight—There are minimum and maximum weights, according to age and height, for males and females.

Vision—There are minimum vision standards.

Overall Health—Must be in good health and pass a medical exam. Certain diseases or conditions may exclude persons from enlistment, such as diabetes, severe allergies, epilepsy, alcoholism, and drug addiction.

Education	Must have a four-year college degree from an accredited institution. Some occupations require advanced degrees or four-year degrees in a particular field.
Aptitude	Must achieve the minimum entry score on an officer qualification test (or SAT, ACT Assessment, or ASVAB, depending on service).
Moral Character	Must meet standards designed to screen out persons unlikely to become successful officers. Standards cover court convictions, juvenile delinquency, arrests, and drug use.
Marital Status and Dependents	May be either single or married for ROTC, OCS/OTS, and direct appointment pathways. Must be single to enter and graduate from service academies. The number of dependents allowable varies by the branch of service.
Waivers	On a case-by-case basis, exceptions (waivers) are granted by individual services for some of the above qualification requirements.

Each service sets its own qualification requirements for officers.

Figure 2 Pathways to Newly Commissioned Officers

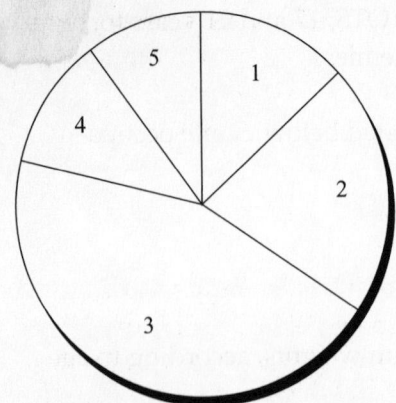

1. Service academies
2. Officer Candidate School (OCS) and Officer Training School (OTS)
3. Reserve Officers' Training Corps (ROTC)
4. Direct appointment
5. Other

PATHWAYS TO BECOMING AN OFFICER

There are four main ways to become a commissioned officer:

- Service academies
- Officer Candidate School (OCS) and Officer Training School (OTS) (depending on branch of service)
- Reserve Officers' Training Corps (ROTC)
- Direct appointment

Figure 2 shows the percentages of new officers who become officers through these pathways. Descriptions of these pathways are found in the following sections.

Service Academies

The four service academies are

- United States Military Academy (Army) West Point, New York 10996 www.usma.edu
- United States Naval Academy (Navy and Marine Corps) Annapolis, Maryland 21402 www.usna.edu
- United States Air Force Academy (Air Force) USAFA, Colorado 80840 www.usafa.edu
- United States Coast Guard Academy (Coast Guard) New London, Connecticut 06320 www.cga.edu

In addition, the Merchant Marine Academy (www.usmma.edu) located in King's Point, New York, prepares individuals for commissioning in the Naval Reserve (although many graduates apply for Active Duty commission in other services).

The competition for entry into the academies is keen. Among candidates who meet all of the eligibility requirements, the academies offer admission to only the most qualified. To be eligible for admission to any of the academies, a person must be at least 17 years of age, a citizen of the United States, of good moral character, and academically and physically qualified. In addition, candidates for the Army, Navy, Merchant Marine, and Air Force academies must have a congressional nomination to be considered for admission. (Nominations are not necessary for admission to the Coast Guard Academy.) It is not necessary to know senators or representatives personally to receive a nomination. The recommended time to apply for nomination is the spring of the junior year in high school.

The academies all offer four-year programs of study leading to a Bachelor of Science degree in one of many disciplines. Students, called cadets or midshipmen, receive free tuition, room, board, medical and dental care, and a monthly allowance. Graduates receive commissions as military officers and must serve on active duty for at least five years. Each year, about 13 percent of the military's new officers are graduates of these four academies.

Officer Candidate/Training School

Each service offers a program for college graduates with no prior military training who want to become military officers. These programs are called Officer Candidate School (OCS) or Officer Training School (OTS), depending on the service. Interested candidates should apply through a local recruiter as early as the fall of their senior year of college or anytime after graduation. Young men and women selected for OCS/OTS join the military as enlisted members for the duration of their OCS/OTS training. Depending on the service, OCS/OTS lasts up to 20 weeks. After successful completion, candidates are commissioned as military officers. Each year, about 21 percent of the military's new officers are commissioned through OCS/OTS.

Each branch of service has its own eligibility requirements and selection procedure. More detailed information regarding the OCS/OTS programs of the U.S. Air Force, U.S. Army, U.S. Coast Guard, U.S. Marines, and U.S. Navy is contained in subsequent sections. Background material will be given about the length and type of training received at the school, career fields open to OCS/OTS graduates, requirements and qualifications for admission into the OCS/OTS programs, and service obligations after being commissioned.

Unlike enlisted members of the Armed Forces, officers are not required to re-enlist to extend their service beyond the initial service commitment.

Written tests are an essential part of the selection process for all OCS/OTS programs. Because test scores play a significant role in determining who is accepted and rejected, it is important to prepare for such tests in order to obtain the highest possible score.

This book is intended as a practical guide to preparing applicants for such tests. It provides basic information on military testing, describes the general areas covered in these tests, delineates techniques to increase your test-taking sophistication and improve your test scores, discusses the specific subject matter contained in each test, and supplies practice exercises in each of these subject areas, as well as specimen tests and subtests.

A major portion of this book consists of practice exercises that contain a sampling of multiple-choice questions similar to those generally found on military tests used to select candidates for training for commissioned status in the Armed Forces. Use the answer sheets on pages 129-132 to record your answers to these practice questions.

Check your answers against the key answers following the practice exercises. Read the explanations for those questions you did not answer correctly. It is essential that you review each question answered incorrectly and that you understand why your answer was wrong and how to arrive at the correct answer. It is an important training technique for developing know-how in test-taking and will aid materially in improving your test scores.

The specimen tests and subtests included in this book give you a real idea of what the tests are like and provide practice for taking these tests under actual test conditions. Answer all questions in these specimen tests within the allotted time on the sample answer sheets furnished for each test. Key answers and explanations are provided for all specimen tests and subtests to aid in increasing your knowledge, broadening your understanding, and improving your test sophistication so that you can be more at ease when taking the real test and achieve the maximum score within your capability.

Reserve Officers' Training Corps

Undergraduate students in public or private colleges or universities may receive training to become military officers under the Reserve Officers' Training Corps (ROTC). ROTC programs for the Army, Navy, Air Force, and Marine Corps are available in over 1,400 colleges and universities nationwide.

Depending on the service and ROTC option selected, students train for two, three, or four years. Commissioning, however, only takes place after a four-year degree is earned. Often, they receive scholarships for tuition, books, fees, uniforms, and a monthly allowance. In addition to their military and college course work, ROTC candidates perform drills for several hours each week and participate in military training exercises for several weeks each summer.

Graduating ROTC candidates become commissioned as military officers and either go on active duty or become members of Reserve or National Guard units. Each year, about 44 percent of the military's new officers are gained through ROTC programs. For information on the colleges and universities that offer ROTC programs for a particular service, contact a recruiter from that service.

Direct Appointments

Medical, legal, engineering, and religious professionals who are fully qualified in their fields may apply to receive direct appointments as military officers. These individuals enter military service and begin practicing their profession with a minimum of military training. Each year, direct appointments make up about 11 percent of the military's new officers.

Other

In addition to the four main pathways described above, the services have programs for qualified enlisted personnel to earn commissions as officers. These programs are exclusive, as they account for only 10 percent of newly commissioned officers each year. Essentially, these programs allow enlisted personnel to compete for entrance into the four main pathways.

BASIC OFFICER TRAINING

An important part of every pathway leading to officer commissioning is training on the basic knowledge required to become a military officer. The topics covered in this training include the following:

- The role and responsibilities of the officer
- Military laws and regulations
- Service traditions and military history
- Military customs and courtesies
- Leadership

- Career development
- Military science
- Administrative procedures

In addition, most commissioning pathways involve physical conditioning, consisting of calisthenics, running, and drills. The duration and timing of officer training may vary with the commissioning pathway followed. For example, ROTC candidates receive basic officer training over the course of their two- to four-year ROTC programs. The same is true for cadets or midshipmen at the service academies. In contrast, OCS/OTS candidates receive their basic officer training in the 12- to 20-week OCS/OTS programs they attend after graduation from college.

RANK, PAY, AND BENEFITS

Ranks and Insignia

The comparable commissioned ranks and insignia for the various military services are shown in Figure 3 (page 13).

Pay and Benefits

Military officers in all five services are paid according to the same pay scale and receive the same basic benefits. Military pay and benefits are set by Congress, which normally grants a cost-of-living pay increase once each year, usually on January 1. In addition to pay, the military provides many of life's necessities, such as food, clothing, and housing, or pays monthly allowances for them. The following sections describe officer pay, allowances, and benefits in more detail.

Officer Pay Grades

Officers can progress through 10 officer pay grades during their careers. Pay grade and length of service determine an officer's pay. Figure 3 illustrates the insignia for the ranks in each service. Figure 4 contains information on the relationship between pay grade, rank, and years of service.

Most newly commissioned officers begin at pay grade 0–1 (Second Lieutenant or Ensign). Those who have certain professional qualifications and receive a direct appointment may enter at a higher pay grade. After two years, officers usually move up to 0–2 (First Lieutenant or Lieutenant Junior Grade). After an additional two years, the military generally promotes officers to 0–3 (Captain or Lieutenant) if job performance is satisfactory and other requirements are met. Promotions to 0–4 (Major or Lieutenant Commander) and above are based on job performance, leadership ability, years of service, and time in present pay grade. Officers are generally eligible for promotion to 0–4 in the 9th or 10th year of service and to 0–5 in the 15th or 16th year of service. Each promotion, of course, is accompanied by a substantial pay raise. Because the number of officers at advanced pay grades is limited by Congress, the competition for promotion at these levels is intense.

Basic Pay

The major part of an officer's paycheck is basic pay. Pay grade and total years of service determine an officer's basic pay. Figure 4 (page 14) contains information on annual basic pay as of January 2004. Cost-of-living increases generally occur once a year. At the time of publication, a 3.5 percent increase in base pay is expected as of January 1, 2005.

Incentives and Special Pay

The military offers incentive and special pay (in addition to basic pay) for certain types of duty. For example, incentives are paid for submarine and flight duty. Other types of hazardous duty with monthly incentives include parachute jumping, flight deck duty, and explosives demolition. In addition, the military gives special pay for sea duty, diving duty, duty in some foreign countries, and duty in areas subject to hostile fire.

Allowances

Many officers and their families live free of charge in military housing on the base where they are assigned. Those living off base receive a quarters (housing) allowance in addition to their basic pay. In 2004, the monthly housing allowance ranged from $473 to $3,441, depending on pay grade, location, and whether or not the officer had dependents. Each officer also receives a subsistence (food) allowance of $175.23 per month. Because allowances are not taxed as income, they provide a significant tax savings in addition to their cash value. For detailed information on pay and allowances, visit www.dfas.mil.

Figure 3

SERVICE / PAY GRADE	ARMY	NAVY	AIR FORCE	MARINE CORPS	COAST GUARD
O-10	GENERAL	ADMIRAL	GENERAL	GENERAL	ADMIRAL
O-9	LIEUTENANT GENERAL	VICE ADMIRAL	LIEUTENANT GENERAL	LIEUTENANT GENERAL	VICE ADMIRAL
O-8	MAJOR GENERAL	REAR ADMIRAL (UPPER HALF)	MAJOR GENERAL	MAJOR GENERAL	REAR ADMIRAL (UPPER HALF)
O-7	BRIGADIER GENERAL	REAR ADMIRAL (LOWER HALF)	BRIGADIER GENERAL	BRIGADIER GENERAL	REAR ADMIRAL (LOWER HALF)
O-6	COLONEL	CAPTAIN	COLONEL	COLONEL	CAPTAIN
O-5	LIEUTENANT COLONEL	COMMANDER	LIEUTENANT COLONEL	LIEUTENANT COLONEL	COMMANDER
O-4	MAJOR	LIEUTENANT COMMANDER	MAJOR	MAJOR	LIEUTENANT COMMANDER
O-3	CAPTAIN	LIEUTENANT	CAPTAIN	CAPTAIN	LIEUTENANT
O-2	FIRST LIEUTENANT	LIEUTENANT JUNIOR GRADE	FIRST LIEUTENANT	FIRST LIEUTENANT	LIEUTENANT JUNIOR GRADE
O-1	SECOND LIEUTENANT	ENSIGN	SECOND LIEUTENANT	SECOND LIEUTENANT	ENSIGN

Figure 4

BASIC PAY – EFFECTIVE JANUARY 1, 2004

Rank	O-1	O-2	O-3	O-4	O-5	O-6	O-7	O-8	O-9	O-10
<2	$2264.40	$2608.20	$3018.90	$3433.50	$3979.50	$4773.60	$6440.70	$7751.10	$0.00	$0.00
>2	2356.50	2970.60	3422.40	3974.70	4482.90	5244.30	6739.80	8004.90	0.00	0.00
>3	2848.50	3421.50	3693.90	4239.90	4793.40	5588.40	6878.40	8173.20	0.00	0.00
>4	2848.50	3537.00	4027.20	4299.00	4851.60	5588.40	6988.50	8220.60	0.00	0.00
>6	2848.50	3609.90	4220.10	4545.30	5044.80	5609.70	7187.40	8430.30	0.00	0.00
>8	2848.50	3609.90	4431.60	4809.30	5161.20	5850.00	7384.20	8781.90	0.00	0.00
>10	2848.50	3609.90	4568.70	5137.80	5415.90	5882.10	7611.90	8863.50	0.00	0.00
>12	2848.50	3609.90	4794.30	5394.00	5602.80	5882.10	7839.00	9197.10	0.00	0.00
>14	2848.50	3609.90	4911.30	5571.60	5844.00	6216.30	8066.70	9292.80	0.00	0.00
>16	2848.50	3609.90	4911.30	5673.60	6213.60	6807.30	8781.90	9579.90	0.00	0.00
>18	2848.50	3609.90	4911.30	5733.00	6389.70	7154.10	9386.10	9995.70	0.00	0.00
>20	2848.50	3609.90	4911.30	5733.00	6563.40	7500.90	9386.10	10379.10	10954.50	12524.70
>22	2848.50	3609.90	4911.30	5733.00	6760.80	7698.30	9386.10	10635.30	11112.30	12586.20
>24	2848.50	3609.90	4911.30	5733.00	6760.80	7897.80	9386.10	10635.30	11340.30	12847.80
>26	2848.50	3609.90	4911.30	5733.00	6760.80	8285.40	9433.50	10635.30	11738.40	13303.80

Note: Basic pay for O-7 to O-10 is limited to $12,050.00 by Level III of the Executive Schedule. Basic pay for O-6 and below is limited to $10,608.30 by Level V of the Executive Schedule.

Employment Benefits

Military officers receive substantial benefits in addition to their pay and allowances. While they are in the service, officers' benefits include health care, vacation time, legal assistance, recreational programs, educational assistance, and commissary/exchange (military store) privileges. Families of officers also receive some of these benefits.

Retirement Benefits

For individuals who joined the U.S. military on or after August 1, 1986, there are two retirement options. After fifteen years of service, such a member must decide which of the two retirement plans he or she would prefer:

1. The first option is to receive a lump sum payment of $30,000 at this point, and then receive a pension after twenty years of service at the rate of 40 percent of the *average* of the highest three years' pay.
2. The second option is *not* to receive the cash bonus at fifteen years, but to wait and receive a pension after twenty years of service at the rate of 50 percent of the *average* of the highest three years' pay.

With either option, the percentage of pay increases if retirement is delayed beyond 20 years. The maximum percentage for retirement pay is 75 percent.

Today's military members may also contribute to a separate retirement plan in addition to the standard military retirement plan. Members contribute to the Thrift Savings Plan using "Pre-Tax" dollars. Unlike some plans, however, there are no matching funds from the government.

Veterans' Benefits

Veterans of military service are entitled to certain veterans' benefits set by Congress and provided by the Department of Veterans Affairs (formerly the Veterans Administration). In most cases, these include guarantees for home loans, hospitalization, survivor benefits, educational benefits, disability benefits, and assistance in finding civilian employment.

Opportunities in the Guard and Reserve

Besides a career as an active duty officer, you may choose to pursue a career in the Reserve or National Guard.

In general, the only pathway to a commission through the Guard or Reserve is through Officer Candidate School or Officer Training School. The Air Force also commissions enlisted members through the Deserving Airman Program. Additionally, Merchant Marine Academy graduates are commissioned as ensigns in the Naval Reserve.

Reserve and Guard officers generally serve in most career fields as their Active Duty counterparts but on a part-time basis. Reserve officers usually serve one weekend a month and one two-week active duty tour per year.

Reserve officers enjoy some of the same benefits as their Active Duty counterparts, including; Commissary and Exchange privileges, membership in officers' clubs, a military retirement plan, and, in some cases, tuition assistance.

Because most officers join the Guard and Reserve fully trained by their "sister" Active Duty branches, the competition for these positions is keen.

If you want more information on Reserve and National Guard opportunities, contact:

Air Force
www.afreserve.com
(800) 257-1212
Army
www.goarmy.com
(800) 872-2769, ext. 181
Coast Guard
www.uscg.mil/reserve
(800) 438-8724
Marine Corps
www.marforres.usmc.mil
(800) 552-8762

Navy
www.navalreserve.com
(800) 872-8767
Air National Guard
www.goang.mil
(800) 864-6264
Army National Guard
www.1800goguard.com
(800) 464-8273

PART II

Earning Your Commission in the Armed Forces

EARNING A COMMISSION IN THE U.S. ARMY

The Officer Candidate School (OCS) is an important source of officers for the various branches of the active Army. There are two ways to gain admission into OCS: as an in-service applicant and as a college option enlistee. Qualified active-duty soldiers with at least two years of college training are encouraged to apply. Civilian men and women who possess baccalaureate degrees and are otherwise qualified may enlist in the Army to attend OCS. The Army is unique, however, in that it requires all applicants without prior Army service to attend basic training before attending OCS.

OFFICER CANDIDATE SCHOOL (OCS)

This fourteen-week course, given at Fort Benning, Georgia, serves as the active Army's only officer candidate school. It provides commissioned officers for all branches of the Army except the Judge Advocate General Corps, the Chaplain Corps, the Army Medical Corps, the Army Dental Corps, the Army Nurse Corps, the Medical Specialist Corps, and the Army Veterinary Corps.

When all candidates have been selected for a particular class, the OCS Selection Board assigns each selectee to either a combat arms, combat support, or combat service support specialty. In designating specialty assignments, the OCS Selection Board uses the following criteria:
- Army needs for new officers in the different specialties
- Candidate's personal preferences
- Physical qualifications
- Candidate's education and experience
- Prior military training and experience

Officer candidate training is divided into three phases:
1. **Basic Phase (7 weeks):** Training is centered on basic military skills.
2. **Intermediate Phase (3 weeks):** The standards of discipline and personal conduct become more stringent. Additional academic training is received.
3. **Senior Phase (4 weeks):** Training is centered on tactical field exercises and subjects basic to all branches (i.e., military justice, methods of instruction, etc.).

Leadership development is accomplished through practical application of leadership principles, constructive counseling, and other appropriate instructional media. Evaluations of leadership are made by using observation reports on demonstrated performance, leadership ratings, graded examinations, and other pertinent information.

Academic instruction consists of both classroom work and field exercises. Topics include squad drill, land navigation, maintenance, communication, weapons, tactics, combat support subjects, staff functions, and oral presentations. Professional skill in land navigation and physical training are emphasized in this course.

Passing grades in leadership, academics, land navigation, and physical fitness are required for graduation and commissioning as a second lieutenant. The top third of the class is eligible to compete for Regular Army appointment upon successful completion of the officer basic course. The other two thirds are commissioned in the U.S. Army Reserve.

Female candidates have the same academic curriculum of military science subjects, the same leadership development training, and the same land navigation instructions and testing as the male candidates. However, the physical fitness standards have been modified to reflect physiological differences between men and women. The Army Physical Readiness Test (APRT) for Men and Women is given to candidates during the first week of the course. The test is composed of the following three events:

1. **Push-ups—2 minutes:** Measures strength of shoulder and arm muscles
2. **Sit-ups—2 minutes:** Measures abdominal muscle strength
3. **Two-mile run:** Measures endurance and ability to complete a prolonged run

This test is given again prior to the completion of the tenth week of training. A prerequisite for graduation is scoring at least 180 points with a minimum of 60 points in each event.

Male candidates in the 17- to 21-year age group must complete at least 42 push-ups in 2 minutes, at least 52 sit-ups in 2 minutes, and a 2-mile run in 15 minutes, 54 seconds. Male candidates in the 22- to 26-year age group must complete at least 40 push-ups in 2 minutes, at least 47 sit-ups in 2 minutes, and a 2-mile run in 16 minutes, 36 seconds.

Female candidates in the 17- to 21-year age group must complete at least 18 push-ups in 2 minutes, at least 50 sit-ups in two minutes, and a 2-mile run in 18 minutes, 54 seconds. Female candidates in the 22- to 26-year age group must complete at least 16 push-ups in 2 minutes, at least 45 sit-ups in 2 minutes, and a 2-mile run in 19 minutes, 36 seconds.

For candidates in higher age groups, these standards are lowered slightly.

To prepare for the Army Physical Readiness Test and for the rigorous physical training program at the Branch Immaterial Officer Candidate Course, it is suggested that, before arriving at Fort Benning, candidates engage in a personal physical fitness program that includes practicing push-ups and sit-ups, running 2 to 3 miles per day, and taking conditioning hikes of 10 to 15 miles wearing boots.

CAREER FIELDS

Those who successfully complete OCS next attend an officer basic course for the Army branch in which the individual was commissioned. Such basic courses are generally about four months in length and prepare newly commissioned officers for their first assignment.

OCS graduates are commissioned in the following branches of the Army:

Infantry	Aviation
Air Defense Artillery	Field Artillery
Armor	Signal Corps
Ordnance	Adjutant General Corps
Military Intelligence	Quartermaster
Corps of Engineers	Transportation
Military Police	Medical Service Corps
Chemical Corps	Finance

REQUIREMENTS AND QUALIFICATIONS

Age

Applicants must be at least $19\frac{1}{2}$ years and not more than 29 years of age at time of enrollment (a waiver may be granted up to 32 years of age).

Citizenship

Applicants must be citizens of the United States.

Character

Applicants must be of high moral character. Persons who have been convicted by a military or civilian court for an offense involving a fine or forfeiture of $100 or more are ineligible (a waiver may be granted in certain instances).

Physical

Vision: Individuals being initially appointed or assigned as officers in Armor, Field Artillery, Infantry, Corps of Engineers, Military Intelligence, Military Police, and Signal Corps must possess uncorrected distance visual acuity of any degree that corrects with spectacle lenses to at least 20/20 in one eye and 20/100 in the other eye within 8 diopters of plus or minus refractive error, and be able to identify without confusion the colors vivid red and vivid green.

Height: Male applicants—5'0" to 6'10"
Female applicants—4'10" to 6'10"

Weight: Weight must be proportional to height and within standards for age.

Dental: Teeth must be in good condition without excessive cavities.

General: Applicants must be in good health with no abnormalities or chronic illnesses.

The maximum weight for height table appearing in Army Regulation 600-9, used by the Army in screening individuals for physical fitness for military duty, may serve as a useful guide.

WEIGHT FOR HEIGHT TABLE (SCREENING TABLE WEIGHT)

Height (in inches)	Male Age				Female Age			
	17-20	21-27	28-39	40+	17-20	21-27	28-39	40+
58	—	—	—	—	109	112	115	119
59	—	—	—	—	113	116	119	123
60	132	136	139	141	116	120	123	127
61	136	140	144	146	120	124	132	137
62	141	144	148	150	125	129	132	137
63	145	149	153	155	129	133	137	141
64	150	154	158	160	133	137	141	145
65	155	159	163	165	137	141	145	149
66	160	163	168	170	141	146	150	154
67	165	169	174	176	145	149	154	158
68	170	174	179	181	150	154	159	164
69	175	179	184	186	154	158	163	168
70	180	185	189	192	158	163	168	173
71	185	189	194	197	163	167	172	177
72	190	195	200	203	167	172	177	183
73	195	200	205	208	172	177	182	188
74	201	206	211	214	178	183	188	194
75	208	212	217	220	183	188	194	200
76	212	217	223	226	189	194	200	206
77	215	223	229	232	193	199	206	211
78	223	229	235	238	198	204	210	216
79	229	235	241	244	203	209	215	222
80	234	240	247	250	208	214	220	227

Notes:

1. The height will be measured in stocking feet (without shoes), standing on a flat surface with the chin parallel to the floor. The body should be straight but not rigid, similar to the position of attention. The measurement will be rounded to the nearest inch with the following guidelines:

   a. If the height fraction is less than $\frac{1}{2}$ inch, round down to the nearest whole number in inches.

   b. If the height fraction is $\frac{1}{2}$ inch or greater, round up to the next highest whole number in inches.

2. The weight should be measured and recorded to the nearest pound within the following guidelines:

   a. If the weight fraction is less than $\frac{1}{2}$ pound, round down to the nearest pound.

   b. If the weight fraction is $\frac{1}{2}$ pound or greater, round up to the next highest pound.

3. All measurements will be in a standard PT uniform (gym shorts and T-shirt, without shoes).

4. If the circumstances preclude weighing soldiers during the APFT, they should be weighed within 30 days of the APFT.

5. Add 6 pounds per inch for males over 80 inches and 5 pounds for females for each inch over 80 inches.

Academic

College option enlistees must have a baccalaureate degree from an accredited college or university.

Active-duty soldiers must have completed two years of a four-year college degree program or have a two-year college equivalency evaluation. In addition, both male and female applicants must obtain an aptitude area General Technical (GT)* score of 110 or higher on the Armed Services Vocational Aptitude Battery (ASVAB).

Those interested in flight training are referred to the companion book, ARCO *Military Flight Aptitude Tests.*

*The GT aptitude area consists of arithmetic reasoning, word knowledge, and paragraph comprehension. It is derived from the academic ability composite on the Armed Services Vocational Aptitude Battery (ASVAB).

Service Commitment

A three-year service obligation from the date of graduation and commission is required of all Army officers.

Additional information and guidance regarding a commission in the U.S. Army may be obtained by contacting any Army recruiting office, company commander, battalion commander, or by contacting:

www.goarmy.com
1-800-USA-ARMY

EARNING A COMMISSION IN THE U.S. NAVY

There are many roads leading to a commission as a Naval officer for men and women with a college degree. The basic commissioning program, other than the U.S. Naval Academy and NROTC, is the Officer Candidate School (OCS) in Pensacola, Florida, which is open only to college graduates. However, college students within one year of graduation may submit their applications.

Officers who receive a direct commission in medicine or law attend a different school. The Officer Indoctrination School (OIS) is located in Newport, Rhode Island.

OFFICER CANDIDATE SCHOOL AND TECHNICAL TRAINING
Officer Candidate School (OCS)

The Navy Officer Candidate School (OCS), located at Naval Air Station (NAS) in Pensacola, Florida, provides an intensive training program of approximately 13 weeks. Both aviation and non-aviation candidates train together. The course has been designed to give candidates for training a basic knowledge of the naval establishment afloat, in the air, and ashore, and the traditions of the naval service. This precommissioning training includes naval science (naval operations, naval orientation, and naval administration), human relations, management, and physical conditioning. Successful completion of OCS leads to a commission as ensign.

Physical training standards are high. The objectives of the physical training classes at OCS are to develop stamina and endurance and to improve the overall physical condition of candidates so that they can meet minimum physical fitness standards.

These objectives are accomplished primarily through the use of a running program augmented by calisthenics, an obstacle course, an aquatic program, and participation in various competitive sports.

Swimming. Students must take the third-class swimmers test during the second week. It includes the following: jumping from a 12-foot tower, treading water or floating for 5 minutes, and swimming the length (50 yards) of a pool using any stroke(s). Students unable to pass the test are placed in swim instruction.

Physical Training. Students must pass these minimum requirements each semester to graduate.
Men:
   Push-ups: 29 in 2 minutes
   Sit-ups: 40 in 2 minutes
   1.5 mile run: 13 minutes, 45 seconds maximum
Women:
   Push-ups: 11 in 2 minutes
   Sit-ups: 33 in 2 minutes
   1.5 mile run: 16 minutes, 45 seconds maximum

Failure to perform any portion of these requirements constitutes an unsatisfactory performance for the entire test. Failure causes the student to be placed in a remedial physical training program added to the normal daily routine.

Officer candidates removed voluntarily or involuntarily for academic failure, unsatisfactory military aptitude, or failure to meet physical standards are discharged from the Navy unless they have obligated service remaining.

Technical Training

Navy officers go through specialized or technical training before their initial assignments. Initial advanced training after being commissioned as officers usually takes place at the Navy specialty school that pertains to an officer's major field of education or for which he or she qualified when entering the Navy. Here new officers learn how to apply the specialty to naval operations. Technical training programs can last from several weeks to more than a year. Specialty training schools include:

Surface warfare officer: Surface Warfare Officer School

Cryptology officer: Naval Security Group orientation course

Civil Engineer Corps officer: Civil Engineer Corps School

Intelligence officer: Navy and Marine Corps Intelligence School

Supply Corps officer: Navy Supply School

Nuclear propulsion officer: Nuclear Power School, followed by Surface Warfare Officer School or Submarine Officer Basic Course

CAREER FIELDS

In general, Navy officer occupations are in two major categories:

Operations and management: Includes practically every type of executive and managerial position with both the fleet and the shore establishment.

Scientific and technical: Includes many areas of professional expertise, such as engineering, mathematics, physical science, psychology, medicine, dentistry, nursing, law, chaplaincy, comptrolling, and personnel and supply specialization.

Other occupations are designated as "unrestricted line," "restricted line," and "staff corps." *Unrestricted line officers* are trained to command the Navy's ships, submarines, aircraft, squadrons, operational staffs, and fleets. *Restricted line officers* perform specialized duties in technical fields, such as ship engineering, cryptology, meteorology, and oceanography/hydrography. *Staff corps officers* serve in areas such as civil engineering, law, medicine, dentistry, and chaplaincy.

Designated Navy Officer Occupations

Unrestricted Line Officers

Aviation maintenance duty officer
General unrestricted line officer
Naval aviator
Naval flight officer
Nuclear power instructor
Special operations officer
Special warfare officer
Submarine warfare officer
Surface warfare officer

Restricted Line Officers

Civil Engineer Corps officer
Cryptology officer
Engineering duty officer
Intelligence officer
Oceanography officer
Public affairs officer
Supply Corps officer

Staff Corps Officers

Chaplain Corps officer
Dental Corps officer
Judge Advocate General Corps officer
Medical Corps officer
Medical Service Corps officer
Nurse Corps officer

Women officers are assigned to shore duty, but may also be called on to serve on combatant or noncombatant ships or aircraft.

REQUIREMENTS AND QUALIFICATIONS

Age

Non-aviation applicants must generally be at least 19 and no more than 29 years of age on the date of appointment to commissioned grade. Stricter age requirements apply for several naval occupations, such as nuclear propulsion officer, who must be 19 to 27 years of age at the time of commissioning.

The age requirement for Civil Engineer Corps officer, cryptology officer, intelligence officer, and oceanography officer is 19 to 35 years at time of commissioning.

Citizenship

Applicants must be citizens of the United States.

Character

Applicants must be of good moral character.

Physical

Vision: *Correctable to 20/20 with normal color vision:*

> Engineering duty officer
> Nuclear propulsion officer
> Special warfare officer
> Submarine warfare officer
> Surface warfare officer

Correctable to 20/20 with normal color vision and depth perception:

> Intelligence officer

82 percent Binocular Vision Efficiency; spherical not more than 8.0; cylindrical not more than 3.0:

> Civil Engineering Corps officer
> Cryptology officer
> Oceanography officer (also normal color vision)
> Supply Corps officer

Correctable to 20/20:

> Most other non-aviation officers

Height: For non-aviation male officers—4'10" to 6'6"

For non-aviation female officers—4'10" to 6'6"

Dental: Teeth must be in good condition without excessive cavities.

General: Applicants must be in good health with no abnormalities or chronic illnesses.

The following table shows the weight standards, in pounds, used at OCS. Failure to meet these standards could jeopardize your chance to become a naval officer.

Height	Weight (Men)		Weight (Women)	
(Inches)	Min.	Max.	Min.	Max.
58	98	130	90	124
59	99	134	92	127
60	100	139	94	131
61	102	143	96	135
62	103	148	98	138
63	104	152	100	142
64	105	157	102	145
65	106	162	104	149
66	107	167	106	153
67	111	172	109	156
68	115	176	112	160
69	119	182	115	163
70	123	187	118	167
71	127	192	122	171
72	131	197	125	175
73	135	202	128	178
74	139	208	132	181
75	143	213	136	185
76	147	219	139	189
77	151	224	143	192
78	153	230	147	196

Academic

Applicants must have a baccalaureate degree to qualify for the Officer Candidate School. However, for the more highly specialized naval occupations, there are additional educational requirements. For example:

Nuclear power instructor: A baccalaureate degree in engineering, physics, mathematics, or chemistry, including one year of calculus.

Nuclear propulsion officer: A baccalaureate degree with a minimum of one year of college physics and mathematics through integral calculus.

Engineering duty officer: A baccalaureate degree in engineering or science.

Oceanography geophysics officer: A baccalaureate degree in meteorology, oceanography, or other field of earth science, physical science, or engineering.

All Staff Corps officers require a professional, scientific, or highly technical background.

In addition to needing a college degree to qualify for the Officer Candidate Schools, applicants must also achieve a qualifying score on the Officer Aptitude Rating (OAR), a composite exam formed from the following two tests of the U.S. Navy and Marine Corps Aviation Selection Test Battery: the Math/Verbal Test and the Mechanical Comprehension Test.

The Math/Verbal Test measures quantitative aptitude (arithmetic reasoning, general mathematics, algebra, and plane geometry) and verbal aptitude (sentence comprehension).

The Mechanical Comprehension Test measures mechanical aptitude (understanding of the principles involved in the operation of mechanical devices, basic physics, and so on).

The complete U.S. Navy and Marine Corps Aviation Selection Test Battery must be taken by those applying for flight training. Scores on the five tests comprising this battery are used to construct six composite ratings that are used in evaluating aviation candidates.

Those interested in flight training are referred to the companion book, ARCO *Military Flight Aptitude Tests*.

Service Commitment

This varies with the program applied for and the training received. Nuclear propulsion officers incur a five-year active-duty obligation upon commissioning. Non-aviation officers generally incur a four-year active-duty obligation upon commissioning.

Additional information and guidance regarding a commission in the U.S. Navy may be obtained by contacting www.navy.com or 1-800-USA-NAVY.

EARNING A COMMISSION IN THE U.S. AIR FORCE

There are three commissioning sources for earning a commission as an Air Force officer: the U.S. Air Force Academy, the Air Force Reserve Officers' Training Corps (AFROTC), and the Officer Training School (OTS). Individuals who are fully qualified in the medical profession, the legal profession, or the religious field may obtain direct commissions without attending one of the above commissioning programs.

The Officer Training School program was developed to meet the Air Force's growing requirements for qualified commissioned officers. Applicants for Officer Training School (OTS)—civilians or active-duty airmen—must be college graduates. Applications may be submitted by men and women in their senior year of college or by engineering students in their junior year.

Non-rated applicants (those not applying for flight training) may apply for any three of the major career areas in non-flying specialties.

Accounting and Finance	Engineering	Public Affairs
Acquisition Services	Electronics	Scientific Analysis
Administrative Services	Finance	Security
Aerial Recon Weather	Food Service	Space Systems
Aeronautical Engineering	Geodetic	Special Investigations
Aircraft Maintenance	Industrial Engineering	Supply Services Sales
Architectural Engineering	Intelligence	Systems Program
Astronautical Engineering	Logistics	Data Management
Audio-Visual	Management Analysis	Transportation
Behavioral Science	Management Engineering	Weather
Budget	Manpower Management	
Cartography	Mathematics	
Chemistry	Mechanical Engineering	
Civil Engineering	Metallurgy	
Communications Electronics	Missile Maintenance	
Computer Systems	Nuclear Research	
Cost Analysis	Personnel	
Data Automation Development	Procurement Management	

All applications are reviewed by a board of Air Force officers. The Air Force offers you a career field based on careful consideration of your desires, scholastic record, experience, and the needs of the Air Force. Each application is evaluated for character, academic accomplishments, and community service, as well as leadership potential.

OFFICER TRAINING SCHOOL (OTS)

An intensive 12-week training program known as Basic Officer Training Program is conducted at Maxwell Air Force Base, Alabama. Candidates are taught the fundamental military knowledge and skills needed for effective performance as second lieutenants in the U.S. Air Force. They are constantly evaluated for personal appearance, conduct, and how well they apply the principles of military discipline, customs, and courtesies. The concepts of leadership, discipline, competition, physical fitness, and moral character are fundamental to OTS training.

Four major study areas comprise the academic program:

Communication skills

Leadership and management

Professional knowledge

Defense studies

All officer trainees are required to participate in physical training and sports activities. Physical standards are the same for men and women except for the time limits for the $1\frac{1}{2}$-mile run, height and weight scales, and the minimum passing score on physical fitness tests.

A series of written tests and subjective measuring techniques is used to evaluate officer trainees' potential for commissioned service. Trainees must pass all tests and meet all criteria to be graduated and commissioned. Trainees are evaluated on the following:

1. **Run Test:** Trainees must run $1\frac{1}{2}$ miles within the following time limits:

   Men: Under 30 years—11 minutes 45 seconds

               30 years and over—12 minutes 30 seconds

   Women: Under 30 years—13 minutes 40 seconds

               30 years and over—14 minutes 30 seconds

2. **Physical Fitness Test:**
   (a) Pull-ups (for men)

         Flexed arm hang (for women)

   (b) Standing long jump

   (c) Push-ups

   (d) Sit-ups

   (e) 600-yard run

   Trainees are required to pass all five events, or pass four of the events along with achieving a specified total score.

3. **Drill Performance Rating:** Each trainee is required to command a group of officer trainees on the drill pad and lead it through a series of maneuvers.

4. **Verbal Communications:** Each trainee must give graded briefings and conduct counseling sessions.

5. **Written Communications:** Each trainee is required to complete several letter-writing assignments, culminating in the preparation of a graded military letter.

6. **Officer Trainee Effectiveness Reports:** Two written evaluations of trainee's military and personal qualifications are made by the flight commander. Trainees are evaluated in these categories:
   (a) Leadership and fellowship
   (b) Adaptability to military training
   (c) Professional qualities
   (d) Adaptability to stress
   (e) Written communication
   (f) Oral communication
   (g) Judgment and decisions
   (h) Duty performance
   (i) Personal relations

7. **Consolidated Written Tests:** Trainees are required to take five tests over the OTS academic subject areas. A score of 80 percent or better is required in each academic area to pass these tests.

8. **Trainees are also tested periodically on student directives.** These publications are the guidance that the trainees use to run the student wing.

TOUR OF DUTY

All officer trainees are assigned a specific career field before arriving at OTS. Upon graduation from OTS, most newly commissioned non-rated officers attend a technical school. Technical training varies in length according to the specialty, ranging from five weeks to more than a year. Some newly commissioned officers go directly to their first duty assignment and attend a technical school at a later date.

At various points during a career as an Air Force officer, there is an opportunity to participate in professional military education. Such educational programs prepare officers for the increasing responsibilities associated with career progression and provide the command and staff knowledge required to be a professional officer.

REQUIREMENTS AND QUALIFICATIONS
Age

Applicants must be at least 18 years of age at the time of commissioning and not have reached age 30 by the initial selection board convening date. Applicants should be commissioned before reaching age 30, though this requirement may be waived to allow commissioning up to age 35 in outstanding and deserving cases based on the needs of the Air Force.

Citizenship

Applicants must be citizens of the United States.

Character

Applicants must be of good moral character. All offenses or infractions pertaining to character are evaluated on a case-by-case basis.

Physical

Physical requirements are more stringent for rated (pilot or navigator) applicants.

Vision: Correctable with glasses to 20/20 in one eye and 20/30 in the other eye. Normal color vision is required for some technical job skills.

Height: 5'0" to 6'8"

Weight: Weight must be proportional to height. Applicants must meet the weight standards specified in Air Force Instruction 40-502, shown below.

HEIGHT AND WEIGHT CHART*

Height (inches)	Men Minimum	Men Maximum (MAW)	Women Minimum	Women Maximum (MAW)
58	98	149	88	132
59	99	151	90	134
60	100	153	92	136
61	102	155	95	138
62	103	158	97	141
63	104	160	100	142
64	105	164	103	146
65	106	169	106	150
66	107	174	108	155
67	111	179	111	159
68	115	184	114	164
69	119	189	117	168
70	123	194	119	173
71	127	199	122	177
72	131	205	125	182
73	135	211	128	188
74	139	218	130	194
75	143	224	133	199
76	147	230	136	205
77	151	236	139	210
78	153	242	141	215
79	157	248	144	221
80	161	254	147	226

* For every inch under 60 inches, subtract 2 pounds from the MAW standards. For every inch over 80 inches, add 6 pounds to the MAW standards. Individuals over, at, or within 10 pounds below MAW are given a body fat measurement (BFM). Those who exceed BFM are disqualified. Individuals, who have failed BFM previously, remain disqualified regardless of weight unless they meet BFM standards.

Dental: Teeth must be in good condition without excessive cavities.

General: Applicants must be in good health with no abnormalities or chronic illness.

Academic

Applicants must possess a baccalaureate degree to enroll in the OTS program. In addition, applicants must complete the Air Force Officer Qualifying Test (AFOQT).

The AFOQT measures aptitudes used in selecting candidates for officer commissioning programs and specific commissioned officer training programs. The AFOQT consists of sixteen subtests. Subtest scores are combined to generate one or more composite scores used to help predict success in certain types of Air Force training programs.

The Pilot composite measures some of the knowledge and abilities considered necessary for successful completion of pilot training.

The Navigator-Technical composite measures some of the knowledge and abilities considered necessary for successful completion of navigator training.

The Academic Aptitude composite measures verbal and quantitative knowledge and abilities. The verbal subtests measure the ability to reason and recognize relationships among words, the ability to read and understand paragraphs on diverse topics, and the ability to understand synonyms. The quantitative subtests measure the ability to understand and reason with arithmetic relationships, interpret data from graphs and charts, and to use mathematical terms, formulas, and relationships. The Academic Aptitude composite measures some of the knowledge and abilities considered necessary for successful completion of training to become an Air Force officer.

The Air Force uses the Academic Aptitude composite score as one of the factors in selecting applicants for OTS. Those interested in flight training are referred to the companion book, ARCO *Military Flight Aptitude Tests*.

Service Commitment

Non-rated officers incur a four-year active-duty obligation from the date of commission.

Pilots incur eight-year active duty terms of service and navigators six. Additional information and guidance regarding a commission in the U.S. Air Force can be obtained by contacting any Air Force recruiting office or by contacting:

www.afoats.af.mil

1-800-423-USAF

EARNING A COMMISSION IN THE U.S. MARINE CORPS

The Marine Corps's mission is unique among the five services. Marines serve on U.S. Navy ships, protect naval bases, guard U.S. embassies abroad, and serve as an ever-ready strike force to quickly protect the interests of the United States and its allies everywhere in the world.

Virtually all paths to a Marine Corps commission require a bachelor's degree. The major commissioning programs other than the U.S. Naval Academy and the NROTC Marine Option are

Officer Candidates Class (OCC): For seniors and college graduates

Platoon Leaders Class (PLC): For freshmen, sophomores, and juniors

OFFICER CANDIDATE SCHOOL AND BASIC TRAINING

No matter which program is entered, Marine officer candidates must undergo training, generally for a ten-week period, at the Officer Candidates School at Quantico, Virginia. This pre-commission training comprises physical training, leadership, and military academics, including basic Marine tactics and weapons. Successful completion of training at the Officer Candidates School leads to a commission as a second lieutenant.

Newly commissioned officers are provided a twenty-one-week basic professional education at The Basic School at Quantico, Virginia. Instruction is given in the following:

Leadership	Data processing utilization	Command and ceremonies
Techniques of military instruction	Patrolling	Military law
	Combat intelligence	Logistics
Marksmanship	Vertical envelopment operations	Tank-infantry operations
Map reading		Aviation and air support
Communications	Marine Corps history and tradition	Amphibious operations
Infantry tactics on a small-unit level		Contemporary operations
	First aid	Physical training and conditioning techniques
Infantry weapons and supporting arms	Field engineering	
Company personnel administration	Marine Corps organization and staff functions	
	Drill	

At The Basic School, students are evaluated in three general areas. Relative performance in these areas determines class standing at graduation:

Academic: Military knowledge of areas listed on page 39 is measured by written examinations of the multiple-choice type. There are ten to twelve such examinations given during the training period.

Military skills: Students are graded on the practical application of military training, such as land navigation, techniques of military instruction, rifle and pistol qualification, and physical fitness.

Leadership: Leadership evaluation is determined by two command evaluations and a written examination. Students are rated by their instructors in terms of acceptance of responsibility, attention to duty, use of authority, attitude, judgment, common sense, cooperation, initiative, and command presence.

CAREER FIELDS

Those who successfully complete training at The Basic School are selected for various career paths. The occupational fields assigned will be based on the needs of the Marine Corps, class standing, company commander's recommendation, and personal preference. Approximately 90 percent of all graduates from The Basic School are assigned to the occupational field of their choice. The Marine Corps non-aviation occupational fields are as follows:

Infantry	Tracked Vehicles	Special Support	
Field Artillery	Communications	–Military Police	–Ground Supply
Engineer	Data Processing	–Public Affairs	–Aviation Supply
Legal	Air Control	–Logistics	
Intelligence	Motor Transport	–Personnel and Administration	
		–Signals Intelligence/Ground Electronic Warfare	
		–Auditing/Finance/Accounting	

There is also a special law option in the commissioning programs for law school students and graduates that enable them to postpone active duty until they are admitted to the bar. Upon successful completion of training at Officer Candidates School and The Basic School, they are guaranteed placement in legal work and an opportunity for a rewarding law career.

REQUIREMENTS AND QUALIFICATIONS

Age

Ground applicants must be at least 18 years and less than 30 years of age on the date of appointment to commissioned grade.

Citizenship

Applicants must be citizens of the United States.

Character

Applicants must be of high moral character. Persons convicted of any felony or misdemeanor involving moral turpitude are disqualified. Addiction to narcotics or history of such addiction is disqualifying. All other offenses or infractions pertaining to character are evaluated on a case-by-case basis.

Physical

Vision: Applicants must be correctable to 20/20 with glasses (waiver may be granted up to 20/400).

Height: Male applicants—5′6″ to 6′6″ (waiver may be granted down to 5′4″)
Female applicants—5′1″ to 6′0″ (waiver may be granted down to 4′10″ and up to 6′1″)

Weight: Weight must be proportional to height, as shown in the table on page 42.

Dental: Teeth must be in good condition without excessive cavities.

General: Applicants must be in good health with no abnormalities or chronic illness. Male applicants must pass a physical fitness test that consists of pull-ups or chin-ups, bent-knee crunches, and a 3-mile run. Female applicants must pass a physical fitness test that consists of the flexed arm hang, bent-knee crunches, and a 3-mile run.

WEIGHT STANDARDS FOR MARINES

Male Marines (regardless of age)
Height (inches)

64	65	66	67	68	69	70	71	72	73	74	75	76	77	78

Weight (pounds)

	64	65	66	67	68	69	70	71	72	73	74	75	76	77	78
Min.	105	106	107	111	115	119	123	127	131	135	139	143	147	151	153
Max.	160	165	170	175	181	186	192	197	203	209	214	219	225	230	235

Female Marines (regardless of age)
Height (inches)

58	59	60	61	62	63	64	65	66	67	68	69	70	71	72	73

Weight (pounds)

	58	59	60	61	62	63	64	65	66	67	68	69	70	71	72	73
Min.	90	92	94	96	98	100	102	104	106	109	112	115	118	122	125	128
Max.	121	123	125	127	130	134	138	142	147	151	156	160	165	170	175	180

Academic

Applicants must be full-time students or college graduates to qualify for the Officer Candidates Class (OCC) or the Platoon Leaders Class (PLC). A bachelor's degree is required for a commission.

Marine Corps officer applicants are no longer required to take a specific officer candidate test. Instead, applicants must have: (1) a minimum combined score of 1000 on the verbal and math sections of the Scholastic Aptitude Test (SAT); (2) a minimum combined math and verbal score of 45 on the American College Test (ACT); or (3) must obtain an acceptable score on the Armed Services Vocational Aptitude Battery (ASVAB).

The complete U.S. Navy and Marine Corps Aviation Selection Test Battery must be taken by those applying for flight training. Scores on the five tests comprising this battery are used to construct six composite ratings that are used in evaluating aviation candidates.

Those interested in flight training are referred to the companion book, ARCO *Military Flight Aptitude Tests*.

Service Commitment

For non-aviation officers there is a $3\frac{1}{2}$-year active-duty obligation from commencement of active duty after commissioning.

Additional information and guidance regarding a commission in the Marine Corps can be obtained by contacting any of the Marine Corps officer selection officers who travel the college circuit on a regular basis, any Marine Corps recruiting office, any major Marine Corps installation, or by contacting

www.marines.com/officer

1-800-MARINES

EARNING A COMMISSION IN THE U.S. COAST GUARD

The Coast Guard is a part of the U.S. Department of Homeland Security. In time of war it may be placed under the command of the Navy Department. Coast Guard officers perform in many different occupations to support the missions of the Coast Guard.

The Coast Guard has many missions. It is the foremost maritime law enforcement agency in America. It carries out search and rescue operations, maintains a worldwide network of navigational aids, collects and analyzes oceanographic and meteorological data, opens ice-blocked shipping lanes, administers a merchant marine safety program, enforces maritime conservation laws, acts to prevent maritime pollution, patrols the 200-mile fishing conservation zone, and carries out other related missions.

Assignments might be ashore at duty stations that run the gamut from a small station in Alaska or Hawaii to port safety units in major ports; at bases, district offices, or headquarters; or at sea on Coast Guard ships that operate from the tropics to the ice masses at both poles.

Civilian applicants for a commission in the Coast Guard must possess a baccalaureate degree to be admitted to Officer Candidate School. The Coast Guard Academy is located in New London, Connecticut.

OFFICER CANDIDATE SCHOOL

Candidates must undergo training, generally for seventeen weeks, at the Coast Guard Leadership Development Center located at the Coast Guard Academy in New London, Connecticut. This pre-commission training includes Coast Guard orientation, leadership, seamanship, navigation, law enforcement, and military subjects. Practical training is given in maneuvering ships, tracking unidentified surface contacts, communications, damage control, gunnery, rescue, and law enforcement. Physical education, military drill, and sports are also included in the curriculum. Successful completion of training leads to a commission as ensign in the U.S. Coast Guard.

CAREER FIELDS

Those who successfully complete Officer Candidate School training and receive a commission are assigned to various career paths. The type of duty and location assigned are based on the needs of the Coast Guard, educational background, prior experience, and personal preference. Candidates with degrees in areas such as biology, chemistry, computer science, economics, engineering (civil, electrical, electronic, industrial, marine, mechanical, or ocean), financial management, industrial management, marine science, mathematics, operations research, and statistics do receive preference in assignments relating to their areas of specialization. All career fields are open to both female and male applicants.

The following are some of the career fields to which graduates of Officer Candidate School might be assigned:

Aviation	Merchant Marine Safety
Civil Engineering	Military Readiness
Civil Rights	Naval Engineering
Communications Management	Personnel Administration
Environmental Protection	Personnel Recruitment
Financial and Supply Management	Port Safety/Law Enforcement
Industrial Management	Public Affairs
Intelligence	Research and Development
Legal Assistance	Reserve Administration

After the initial assignment, an officer is encouraged to apply for postgraduate education or specialized training. The Coast Guard provides training in a range of career areas. Many courses are provided to instruct officers in specific skills needed for a particular assignment. In addition, there is an opportunity to participate in professional military education such as the Armed Forces Staff College, the Industrial College of the Armed Forces, or one of the colleges run by another branch of the service.

Each Coast Guard officer is given a new assignment, or tour, as it is called, every few years. Every effort is made to match personal desires with the needs of the Coast Guard. An assignment may be in the officer's chosen field, or it may be in a different field where there is a need.

REQUIREMENTS AND QUALIFICATIONS

Age

Applicants must be at least 21 years and under 26 years of age at the convening date of the Officer Candidate School class for which application is made (a waiver may be granted in certain instances).

Citizenship

Applicants must be citizens of the United States.

Character

Applicants must be of good moral character. Persons who have been convicted of a felony are ineligible.

Dependent

Applicants may not have more than three dependents. Any single individual who has sole/primary custody of another individual or relinquishes custody of another individual solely for the purpose of applying for appointment may not apply.

Swimming

Applicants are required to pass extensive swimming tests.

Physical

Vision: Applicants must have a minimum distant visual acuity of 20/400 or better, corrected to 20/20. Color vision must be normal.

Height: 5′0″ to 6′6″ for both male and female applicants

Weight: Weight must be proportional to height. The weight-height standards used are available at U.S. Coast Guard recruiting offices.

Dental: Teeth must be in good condition without excessive cavities.

General: Applicants must be in good health with no abnormalities or chronic illnesses.

Academic

Applicants must have a baccalaureate degree to qualify for Officer Candidate School. Applicants are no longer required to take the Officer Aptitude Rating (OAR). However, SAT or ACT Assessment scores are considered in the "whole person" application concept.

The complete U.S. Navy and Marine Corps Aviation Selection Test Battery must be taken by those applying for flight training. Scores on the five tests comprising this battery are used to construct six composite ratings that are used in evaluating aviation candidates.

Those interested in flight training are referred to the companion book, ARCO *Military Flight Aptitude Tests*.

Service Commitment

Graduates of OCS have a three-year active-duty obligation from the date of commission.

Additional information and guidance regarding a commission in the Coast Guard can be obtained by contacting the military recruiting officer at any major Coast Guard installation or by contacting:

www.cga.edu

(Once online, select **LDC**—Leadership Development Center—for OCS information)

1-800-438-8724

PART III

Military Tests and Testing

HISTORICAL BACKGROUND

Military testing in the United States began in the early part of the nineteenth century when tests were first administered to applicants seeking admission to the Naval Academy and West Point. Until World War I, the military used academic-style tests in selecting officer candidates.

WORLD WAR I

Army Alpha and Beta Tests

Early in World War I, the U.S. Army designed the Army Alpha Test, a group test used in the selection of draftees and the assignment of recruits. This written test, assembled from a number of general intelligence tests then in use, consisted of 212 multiple-choice and true-false items. Test areas included vocabulary, sentence structure, arithmetic problems, number series, general knowledge, and "common sense."

When it became apparent that many applicants could not read or write English, and therefore could not be tested adequately with the Army Alpha, the military developed the Army Beta Test. This paper-and-pencil group test minimized verbal knowledge and used only pictures and diagrams. Test items consisted of mazes, cube counting, noticing missing parts of pictures of familiar objects, number comparisons, and so on.

Nearly 2 million men were given the Alpha or Beta tests during World War I. Scores on these tests became part of each recruit's personnel record and were available for use when making assignments to specific duties and in selecting men for advancement to the noncommissioned ranks. Unfortunately, these test scores played only a minor role in making personnel assignments. The Army and Navy discontinued these testing programs in 1919.

WORLD WAR II

In 1940, the War Department began to develop tests to measure aptitude for specific skills, to measure knowledge of specific trades, and to select officer candidates.

Army General Classification Test (AGCT)

By late 1940, the Army General Classification Test was prepared and standardized. This test of general mental ability was used during World War II to measure "trainability" and to classify men and women according to their ability to learn military duties.

Because many military skills were of a technical nature, emphasis was placed on verbal comprehension, quantitative reasoning, and spatial perception. The test items used to measure these aptitudes were a composite of vocabulary, arithmetic problems, and block counting (the ability to determine the number of blocks in a series of pictured piles).

The 150 items composing this test were presented in spiral form—a group of vocabulary items, then a group of arithmetic problems, and then a group on block counting. This sequence was repeated a number of times, with each group being more difficult than the previous one. Raw scores were converted to standardized scores and subsequently changed into percentile ratings.

This test was given to more than 9 million recruits in World War II. Unlike the World War I Army Alpha and Beta Test, whose results were generally ignored, the Army General Classification Test formed the foundation for Army selection and classification procedures.

AFTER WORLD WAR II
Armed Forces Qualification Test (AFQT)

The Armed Forces Qualification Test (AFQT) was originally developed to meet a congressional requirement for procedures to screen selective service registrants for military trainability. From 1950 until the mid-1970s, the AFQT was the primary selection test used by all military services to ascertain enlistment eligibility.

The AFQT, a group test consisting of 100 multiple-choice items, covered the following subjects:

Vocabulary
Arithmetic
Spatial relations
Mechanical ability

There were five categories of scores based on percentile rating of a standard reference group.

Category	Raw Score	Percentile Range
I	89-100	93rd to 99th
II	74-88	65th to 92nd
III*	53-73	31st to 64th
IV	25-52	10th to 30th
V	1-24	9th and below

* Category Ill may be subdivided into Category IIIA and Category IIIB. The percentile range for IIIA is 50-64; the range for IIIB is 31-49. Those in Categories I-IIIA compose the upper half of the distribution; those in Categories IIIB-V compose the lower half.

Each service established its minimum standards for selection and assignment unless directed otherwise by the Secretary of Defense or by legislation. The Selective Service Act of 1958 provided that services must accept AFQT Category IV and above in time of war.

Determination of AFQT score minimums are based on two important considerations:

1. The ability levels considered essential for successful performance in training and general adjustment to military service.
2. Supply-and-demand considerations in meeting training quotas.

Although the services could accept Category V personnel, they found it necessary to exclude them because there were too few jobs that they could be trained to perform in the limited time available for training.

The AFQT was replaced by the Armed Services Vocational Aptitude Battery (ASVAB). With the implementation of the ASVAB in the mid-1970s, the AFQT became a composite of several ASVAB tests and is no longer a separate screening test. The AFQT composite is now formed from the following four ASVAB tests:

Arithmetic Reasoning
Paragraph Comprehension
Word Knowledge
Mathematics Knowledge

The number correct on Arithmetic Reasoning + twice the number correct on Word Knowledge + twice the number correct on Paragraph Comprehension + the number correct on Mathematics Knowledge = the AFQT raw score, which is then converted into a percentile score.

ARMED SERVICES VOCATIONAL APTITUDE BATTERY (ASVAB)

ASVAB, Form 1, was developed in the late 1960s for use in the Department of Defense High School Testing Program. Two subsequent ASVAB forms were constructed in the early 1970s. Although Form 2 was used only in the High School Testing Program, Form 3 was used by the U.S. Air Force and the U.S. Marines to replace their classification batteries. Form 4, constructed for high school testing, was never used. By 1975, ASVAB Forms 5, 6, and 7 were developed. Form 5, slightly shorter than, but similar in content to, Forms 6 and 7, was used in the student testing program.

Validated subtests from the various service test batteries were consolidated to produce ASVAB Forms 6 and 7. In 1976, these two ASVAB forms were used throughout the Department of Defense by all services as the enlistment screening-and-classification test battery. In 1980, ASVAB Forms 8, 9, and 10 were introduced. They were used not only as common Department of Defense enlisted selection-and-classification test batteries, but they were also used by the U.S. Army and the U.S. Marines in the selection and classification of officer candidates. Forms 11, 12, and 13, similar to and replacing Forms 8, 9, and 10, were introduced in 1984. Form 14, a parallel form, was introduced in 1984 for school use, replacing Form 5. Forms 15, 16, and 17, similar to and replacing Forms 11, 12, and 13 were introduced in 1989. Forms 18/19, similar to and replacing Form 14, were introduced in 1992. Additional changes were made in 2002 and 2004.

The current ASVAB consists of the following nine subjects, which are administered in the order listed.

Order of Administration	Test Subject
Test 1	General Science (GS)
Test 2	Arithmetic Reasoning (AR)
Test 3	Word Knowledge (WK)
Test 4	Paragraph Comprehension (PC)
Test 5	Mathematics Knowledge (MK)
Test 6	Electronics Information (EI)
Test 7	Auto and Shop Information (AS)
Test 8	Mechanical Comprehension (MC)
Test 9	Assembling Objects (AO)

The following table presents the ASVAB tests, the time allowed for the administration of each test, the number of items in each test, and a description of the abilities or knowledge measured.

Time limits for each test are strictly enforced to assure equal opportunity for all test subjects. Moreover, score norms are based on these standardized time limits.

ASVAB CONTENT

Testing Time	**134 minutes**
Administrative Time	**36 minutes**
Total Testing Time	**170 minutes**
Total Number of Items	**200**

Test	Time	Items	Description
General Science	11 minutes	25	Measures knowledge of the physical and biological sciences.
Arithmetic Reasoning	36 minutes	30	Measures ability to solve arithmetic word problems.
Word Knowledge	11 minutes	35	Measures ability to select the correct meaning of words presented in context and to identify the best synonym for a given word.
Paragraph Comprehension	13 minutes	15	Measures ability to obtain information from written passages.
Mathematics Knowledge	24 minutes	25	Measures knowledge of general mathematics principles, including algebra and geometry.
Electronics Information	9 minutes	20	Measures knowledge of electricity, radio principles, and electronics.
Auto and Shop Information	11 minutes	25	Measures knowledge of automobiles, tools, and shop terminology and practices.
Mechanical Comprehension	19 minutes	25	Measures knowledge of mechanical and physical principles and ability to visualize how illustrated objects work.
Assembling Objects	9 minutes	16	Measures spatial aptitude—the ability to perceive spatial relations.

ASVAB results are reported by three academic composite scores—Academic Ability, Verbal Ability, and Math Ability—and the nine Test Scores in the test battery.

Academic Ability measures how well you did on the Verbal Ability and Math Ability sections combined. Verbal Ability measures how well you did on the Word Knowledge and Paragraph Comprehension tests combined. Math Ability measures how well you did on the Arithmetic Reasoning and Mathematics Knowledge tests combined.

The nine ASVAB Test Scores, as well as the three composite scores, are reported as percentiles. Percentile scores show how well you did in relation to others. Two types of percentile scores are reported: same grade/same sex and same grade/opposite sex scores.

Tests 2, 3, and 4 are used to construct the aptitude area General Technical (GT) used by the Army in screening applicants for its OCS program. Tests 1, 2, 5, and 6 are used by the Marine Corps as one of the methods of meeting the academic requirement for its Officer Candidates Class and Women Officer Candidates program.

SCHOLASTIC ASSESSMENT TEST (SAT)

This multiple-choice test, developed by the Educational Testing Service for the College Entrance Examination Board, is a college entrance examination designed to measure general verbal and mathematical reasoning ability.

The verbal section consists of verbal analogies, sentence completions, and items based upon critical reading skills. The subject matter on which the mathematical questions are based includes arithmetic (addition, subtraction, multiplication, and division; properties of odd and even integers; percentages; and averages), algebra, and geometry.

Separate scores are given for the verbal and the mathematical parts of the test. These scores indicate standing on the College Board scale of 200 to 800.

ACT ASSESSMENT

This test, developed by ACT, Inc., is also a college entrance examination designed to measure general verbal and mathematical comprehension. The test battery consists of four parts—English, mathematics, reading, and science reasoning.

Separate scores are given for each part, in addition to a composite score. These scores indicate standing on a standard-score scale of 1 to 36.

Test scores on the SAT and the ACT Assessment are used by the U.S. service academies in their selection process and by the U.S. Navy and the U.S. Air Force in screening for admission to the Reserve Officer Training Corps (ROTC) program. The U.S. Marines and the U.S. Coast Guard use these scores in selecting applicants for Officer Candidate School.

AIR FORCE OFFICER QUALIFYING TEST (AFOQT)

The AFOQT measures aptitudes used to select candidates for officer commissioning programs and specific commissioned officer training programs. It is based on analyses of tasks required for student pilots, navigators, and officers.

The first AFOQT was published in 1953 and has been revised periodically to minimize obsolescence and the possibility of compromise. However, successive forms of the AFOQT have been similar in many respects.

The current AFOQT consists of sixteen multiple-choice subtests. The order in which these subtests are administered, the number of items in each subtest, and the time limit for each subtest are as follows:

Order of Administration	Subtest Subject	Number of Items	Time Limit
Subtest 1	Verbal Analogies	25	8 minutes
Subtest 2	Arithmetic Reasoning	25	29 minutes
Subtest 3	Reading Comprehension	25	18 minutes
Subtest 4	Data Interpretation	25	24 minutes
Subtest 5	Word Knowledge	25	5 minutes
Subtest 6	Math Knowledge	25	22 minutes
	(Break) (10 minutes)		
Subtest 7	Mechanical Comprehension	20	10 minutes
Subtest 8	Electrical Maze	20	10 minutes
Subtest 9	Scale Reading	40	15 minutes
Subtest 10	Instrument Comprehension	20	6 minutes
Subtest 11	Block Counting	20	3 minutes
Subtest 12	Table Reading	40	7 minutes
Subtest 13	Aviation Information	20	8 minutes
Subtest 14	Rotated Blocks	15	13 minutes
Subtest 15	General Science	20	10 minutes
Subtest 16	Hidden Figures	15	8 minutes
		380	208 minutes (3 hrs, 28 min)

The subtest scores are combined to generate one or more of five composite scores used to help predict success in certain types of Air Force training programs. The five AFOQT composites are

Pilot
Navigator-Technical
Academic Aptitude
Verbal
Quantitative

The 5 aptitude composites are formed from the AFOQT subtests as shown in the following table.

CONSTRUCTION OF AFOQT COMPOSITES

Subtest	Pilot	Navigator-Technical	Academic Aptitude	Verbal	Quantitative
1. Verbal Analogies	X		X	X	
2. Arithmetic Reasoning		X	X		X
3. Reading Comprehension			X	X	
4. Data Interpretation		X	X		X
5. Word Knowledge			X	X	
6. Math Knowledge		X	X		X
7. Mechanical Comprehension	X	X			
8. Electrical Maze	X	X			
9. Scale Reading	X	X			
10. Instrument Comprehension	X				
11. Block Counting	X	X			
12. Table Reading	X	X			
13. Aviation Information	X				
14. Rotated Blocks		X			
15. General Science		X			
16. Hidden Figures		X			

The Air Force uses the Academic Aptitude composite to screen non-aviation applicants for OCS. This composite measures verbal and quantitative knowledge and abilities.

ARMY OFFICER CANDIDATE TEST (OCT)

The Officer Candidate Test (OCT), first introduced by the Army in 1967, was used to screen male applicants for Officer Candidate School. The OCT was a multiple-choice test and required approximately 90 minutes of testing time. The test areas included mathematical computations, word knowledge, and scientific and technical subjects. This test was phased out in 1983 and replaced by earlier versions of the Officer Selection Battery. The Army no longer utilizes a specific test for officer candidates but instead uses ACT Assessment, SAT, or ASVAB results.

ALTERNATE ARMY FLIGHT APTITUDE SELECTION TEST (AFAST)

The Alternate Flight Aptitude Selection Test (AFAST) is used to select men and women for training to become Army helicopter pilots. AFAST consists of six multiple-choice subtests designed to measure those special aptitudes and personality/background characteristics that are predictive of success in Army helicopter flight training. It contains 200 test items and requires 70 minutes of test time.

AFAST is not used by the Army to screen applicants for its OCS training program.

NAVY AND MARINE CORPS AVIATION SELECTION TEST BATTERY

This test battery is used by the Navy, the Marine Corps, and the Coast Guard for selecting officer candidates for both their pilot and flight officer training programs. The battery is also used by the

Navy and the Coast Guard for screening officer candidates for their OCS programs. The battery consists of the following tests:

1. Math/Verbal Test (MVT)
2. Mechanical Comprehension Test (MCT)
3. Spatial Apperception Test (SAT)*
4. Aviation/Nautical Information Test (ANT)*
5. Biographical Inventory (BI)*

* Given only to aviation applicants.

The Math/Verbal Test measures quantitative aptitude (arithmetic reasoning, general mathematics, algebra, and plane geometry) and verbal aptitude (sentence comprehension).

The Mechanical Comprehension Test measures mechanical aptitude (understanding of the principles involved in the operation of mechanical devices, basic physics, etc.)

The Spatial Apperception Test is designed to measure ability to recognize simple changes in the position or attitude of an airplane by viewing the ground and horizon from the cockpit.

The Aviation/Nautical Information Test measures knowledge of basic aviation and nautical terminology, principles, and practices.

The Biographical Inventory is designed to obtain essential biographical data, including general background, education, employment experience, skills, values, opinions, and other personal attributes essential for successful performance in pilot and flight officer training.

The table below shows the number of items in each test, testing time, and how the various tests are combined to produce the six composite scores.

TESTING SCHEDULE AND CONSTRUCTION OF COMPOSITES

Tests	No. of Items	Testing Time (minutes)	AQR	PFAR	FOFAR	PBI	FOBI	OAR
Math/Verbal (MVT)	37	35	X	X	X			X
Mechanical Comprehension(MCT)	30	15	X	X				X
Spatial Apperception (SAT)	35	10	X	X	X			
Aviation/Nautical Information (ANT)	30	15	X	X	X			
Biographical Information (BI)	76	20				X	X	
	208	95						

The Academic Qualification Rating (AQR) is a composite derived from a weighted combination of the Math/Verbal (MVT), Mechanical Comprehension (MCT), Spatial Apperception (SAT), and Aviation/Nautical Information (ANT) tests. It predicts academic performance in both the pilot and flight officer training programs.

The Pilot Flight Aptitude Rating (PFAR) is a composite derived from a weighted combination of the same four tests (MVT, MCT, SAT, and ANT). It predicts flight performance in primary in the pilot training program.

The Flight Officer Flight Aptitude Rating (FOFAR) is a composite derived from a weighted combination of the following three tests: Math/Verbal (MVT), Spatial Apperception (SAT), and Aviation/Nautical Information (ANT). It predicts flight performance in basic in the flight officer training program.

The Pilot Biographical Interest (PBI) is the score received on the Biographical Inventory (BI). It predicts attrition through primary in the pilot training program.

The Flight Officer Biographical Interest (FOBI) is the score received in the Biographical Inventory (BI). It predicts attrition through basic in the flight officer training program.

The Officer Aptitude Rating (OAR) is a composite derived from a weighted combination of the Math/Verbal (MVT) and the Mechanical Comprehension (MCT). The OAR is used by the Navy to screen applicants for their Officer Candidate Schools.

Each aviation applicant obtains six scores. Except for the OAR, all obtained scores are on the 1-9 (stanine) scale. The OAR score is a standard score.

The typical aviation applicant scores are:

AQR   7
PFAR   6
FOFAR 5
PBI   8
FOBI   9
OAR   56

For all scores, except the OAR, applicants must obtain at least a 3 to be considered for further processing. Applicants have only two chances to take this test battery. At least 180 days must elapse before a re-take.

COMPOSITE SCORING

If any Air Force Officer Qualifying Test or Armed Services Vocational Aptitude Battery composite or any composite of the Navy and Marine Corps Aviation Selection Test Battery is administered to a large number of examinees for whom it is appropriate, the raw score most frequently encountered will be near the mean of the group, and the least frequently encountered raw scores will be at the extremes. If raw scores are shown on the horizontal axis and frequencies on the vertical axis, a figure is generated that closely approximates Figure 1. Figure 1 is the normal probability curve. Many sets of psychological and biological data assume the form of this curve.

In a normal distribution, the mean score is so located that half of the cases lie above it. Hence, it can also be taken as the median score. The partition of the distribution at this point is shown in Figure 1. Other partitions are shown at one, two, three, and four standard deviations above and below the mean; and the percentages of the total area under the curve and between the partitions are indicated. These percentages also represent the proportions of the total number of cases in the distribution lying within these areas.

The definite mathematical relationships between these properties of the normal probability curve and the stanine scale are used for the Navy and Marine Corps Aviation Selection Test Battery, the percentile scale used for the Air Force Officer Qualifying Test and the Armed Services Vocational Aptitude Battery, and the College Entrance Examination Board (CEEB) scale used for the Scholastic Aptitude Test (SAT). The relationships that exist in a normal distribution among these common types of scoring are shown below the curve in Figure 1.

Figure 1 Relationships Among Common Types of Test Scores in a Normal Distribution

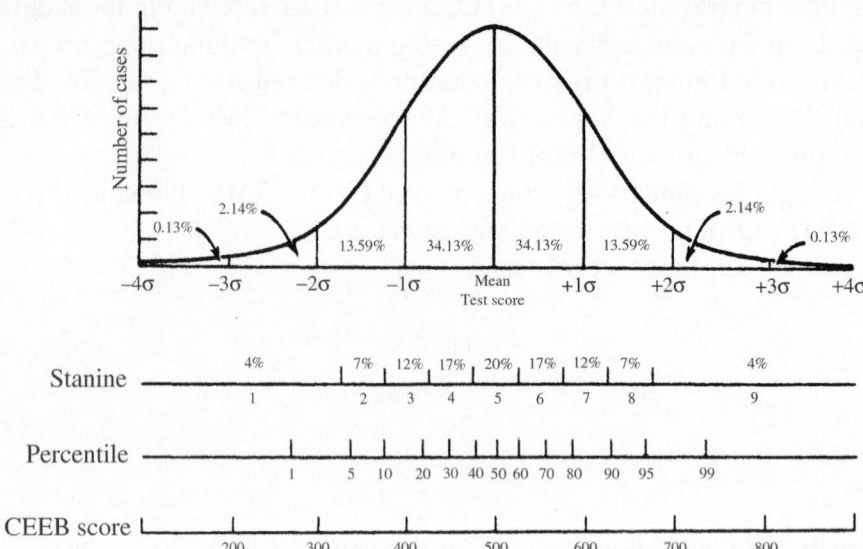

The raw composite scores in the Navy and Marine Corps Aviation Test selection battery, except for the OAR, are converted to normalized standard scores on the stanine scale. Scores on the stanine scale, developed by the Air Force during World War II, run from 1 to 9. Limiting the scores to single-digit numbers simplified certain computations, as each score required only a single column on computer-punched cards. The term *stanine* is actually a contraction form of "standard nine."

On the stanine scale, the median and the mean are 5 and the standard deviation (s) is about 2. To convert to the single-digit system of stanine scores, the lowest 4 percent would be given a value of 1; the next 7 percent, 2; the next 12 percent, 3; the next 17 percent, 4; the next 20 percent, 5; the next 17 percent, 6; the next 12 percent, 7; the next 7 percent, 8; and the highest 4 percent, 9.

Air Force Officer Qualifying Test composite scores, formerly expressed in stanines, are now reported in percentiles. Percentiles serve, as do stanines, to permit meaningful interpretation of test performance.

A percentile score is the rank expressed in percentage terms that indicates what proportion of the group received lower composite raw scores. A person at the 50th percentile would be the "typical" individual. The 50th percentile is known as the median and indicates a score exactly in the middle of the test group. The higher the percentile, the better the individual's standing; the lower the percentile, the poorer the individual's standing. Percentiles above 50 indicate above-average performance; percentiles below 50 indicate below-average performance.

If a score at the 25th percentile or better is required for a certain aviation program, the lowest quarter of the distribution is cut off. If a score at the 75th percentile or better is required, the lowest three-quarters of the distribution are cut off, and only those in the top quarter are accepted.

The scores on the Scholastic Aptitude Test (SAT) of the College Entrance Examination Board, reported on a scale of 200 to 800, are standard scores adjusted to a mean of 500 and a standard deviation of 100.

PART IV

Multiple-Choice Tests and Machine-Scored Answer Sheets

MULTIPLE-CHOICE TESTS

Multiple-choice tests are basic measuring instruments used by industrial organizations, educational institutions, government agencies, and the military. Tens of millions of individuals are examined each year to measure aptitude, achievement, specific knowledge, special abilities, or essential skills in connection with school admissions, school examinations, scholarships, employment in both the public and private sectors, and military testing.

The versatility of these tests, the ease of scoring them, the development of sophisticated test-scoring machines and ancillary equipment, the reliability of the scoring, and the adaptability of the test results for statistical analysis and for research and development have made this test format the one most widely accepted and most commonly used in military testing. This book deals almost entirely with the multiple-choice type of written test in view of its widespread use by the military in personnel selection practice.

Most multiple-choice items in military tests have either four or five options. However, two- or three-option items might be found in a few tests or subtests and in biographical inventories eliciting background information, likes or dislikes, preferences, opinions, and so on.

Two-option items might be TRUE/FALSE, RIGHT/WRONG, CORRECT/INCORRECT, AGREE/DISAGREE, LIKE/DISLIKE, or YES/NO. The forced-choice type of item used to ascertain characteristics or traits—such as opinions, preferences, or interests—is two-option.

An understanding of the form and structure of multiple-choice test items is helpful for all military test-takers. The anatomy of the multiple-choice test item is illustrated below:

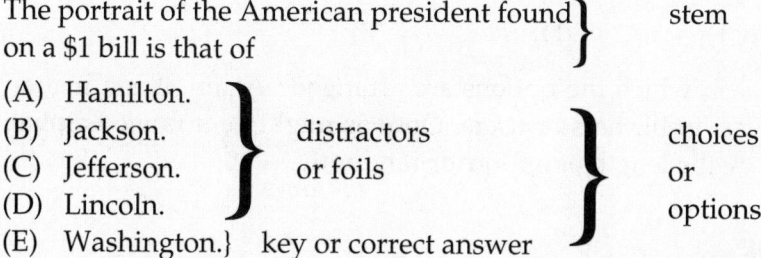

The stem either asks the question or presents the problem with which the test item is concerned. The stem might be written as an incomplete statement that might be completed by any one of the choices or options that follow, as a direct question, or as a command.

Which American president's portrait is found on a $1 bill? (interrogative)

Name the American president whose portrait is on a $1 bill. (imperative)

Options consist of a key or correct answer and foils or distractors that are absolutely incorrect, although they might appear to be plausible to one who is unfamiliar with the right answer.

How are the options that follow the stem of the test item arranged? This depends on the format preferred by the publisher or user. Options in military tests are generally listed vertically. However, in certain instances, they are listed horizontally. For example:

Vertical in One Column

Four-option	*Five-option*
(A)	(A)
(B)	(B)
(C)	(C)
(D)	(D)
	(E)

Vertical in Two Columns

Four-option

(A)	(C)
(B)	(D)

Five-option

(A)	(D)
(B)	(E)
(C)	

Horizontal

Four-option

(A)	(B)	(C)	(D)

Five-option

(A)	(B)	(C)	(D)	(E)

What determines the order in which the options are arranged? Again, it is a matter of style and varies with the different test publishers or users. Options might be arranged alphabetically, numerically, chronologically, by the length of option, or randomly.

ALPHABETICAL OPTIONS

Whether the option consists of one word, several words, or a sentence, the options might be arranged in alphabetical order. For example:

(A) academic	(A)	calcium and carbon
(B) commercial	(B)	hydrogen and nitrogen
(C) general	(C)	iron and oxygen
(D) technical	(D)	manganese and phosphorus
(E) vocational	(E)	potassium and zinc

NUMERICAL OPTIONS

Options for questions dealing with arithmetic reasoning or involving computations that have a numerical answer might be arranged in numerical order. For example:

(A) 3	(B) 9	(C) 27	(D) 36	(E) 81
(A) $4.98	(B) $5.19	(C) $5.49	(D) $5.69	(E) $5.98

CHRONOLOGICAL OPTIONS

Options for questions dealing with time relationships, dates, or historical events might be arranged in chronological order. For example:

(A) January

(B) M

(C) Ju

(D) A

(E) N

(A) 14   (E) 1540

LENG

One te   g order of length. For example:

(A) E   or the correction.

(B) F   t to the deleted sentence.

(C) F   ext to the deleted sentence.

(D) L   correction on the next available line.

(E) V   place the correction on a separate page for
    c

RAND

Rando   r but strictly by chance or haphazardly. For
examp

(A) technical

(B) academic

(C) vocational

(D) commercial

(E) general

Some test-makers claim that arranging the options randomly makes it easier to construct a test with a proper balance of key answers; that is, a test with approximately the same percentage of (A) choices, (B) choices, (C) choices, (D) choices, and so on, as correct answers as would normally occur, based on probability or chance.

On a four-option multiple-choice test, the probability of either an (A), (B), (C), or (D) being the correct answer is 1 in 4. Accordingly, one would expect the correct answers to be approximately 25 percent (A), 25 percent (B), 25 percent (C), and 25 percent (D).

On a five-option multiple-choice test, the probability of either an (A), (B), (C), (D), or (E) being the correct answer is 1 in 5. One would normally expect the correct answers to be approximately 20 percent (A), 20 percent (B), 20 percent (C), 20 percent (D), and 20 percent (E).

There is some merit to this claim, as options put together at random can be rearranged easily to provide the proper ratio of correct or key answers. However, very little effort is required in most instances to change the key answer by either modifying the stem of the question or changing the options or the wording of the options to equalize the number of (A), (B), (C), (D), and so on, choices as key answers.

MACHINE-SCORED ANSWER SHEETS

Before the advent of machine test scoring, the answer sheets used for multiple-choice tests consisted of columns of numbers followed by dotted or solid lines where candidates would record their answers. Answer sheets now in use with the more sophisticated test-scoring machines have response positions indicated by ovals, circles, brackets, or rectangles, which are lettered (A), (B), (C), (D), etc., or numbered (1), (2), (3), (4), etc. Two and three response positions are given for two- and three-option items. The sets of response positions are numbered consecutively to correspond to the number of the questions in the test booklet. Similarly, the ovals, circles, or brackets are labeled to correspond to the designation given to the options in the test items.

Examples of some of the more popular line arrangements and labeling are shown below:

Four-option Items

Five-option Items

Answer sheets are classified as standard answer sheets or special answer sheets. Standard answer sheets are general-purpose forms that can be used in many different kinds of situations. Special answer sheets are printed for the exclusive use of a particular testing organization.

In military testing, special answer sheets are printed for the exclusive use of military organizations that require a particular type of test format or a special answer sheet layout.

The answer sheet for the Army Officer Selection Battery consists of a single page with the heading (upper half of the page) for recording identification and personal data, such as date of test and the candidate's name, college, or university, academic major, academic year, race/ethnic group code, military status, social security number, and sex.

The lower half of the page composes the actual testing section and is used to record the answers to the four-option multiple-choice questions that compose the test battery.

The heading of the Officer Selection Battery (used by Army ROTC) answer sheet is shown on the next page.

The three-page set of answer sheets for the Armed Services Vocational Aptitude Battery (ASVAB) administered to more than 1.5 million young men and women annually is one of the most sophisticated sets of answer sheets currently used in military testing.

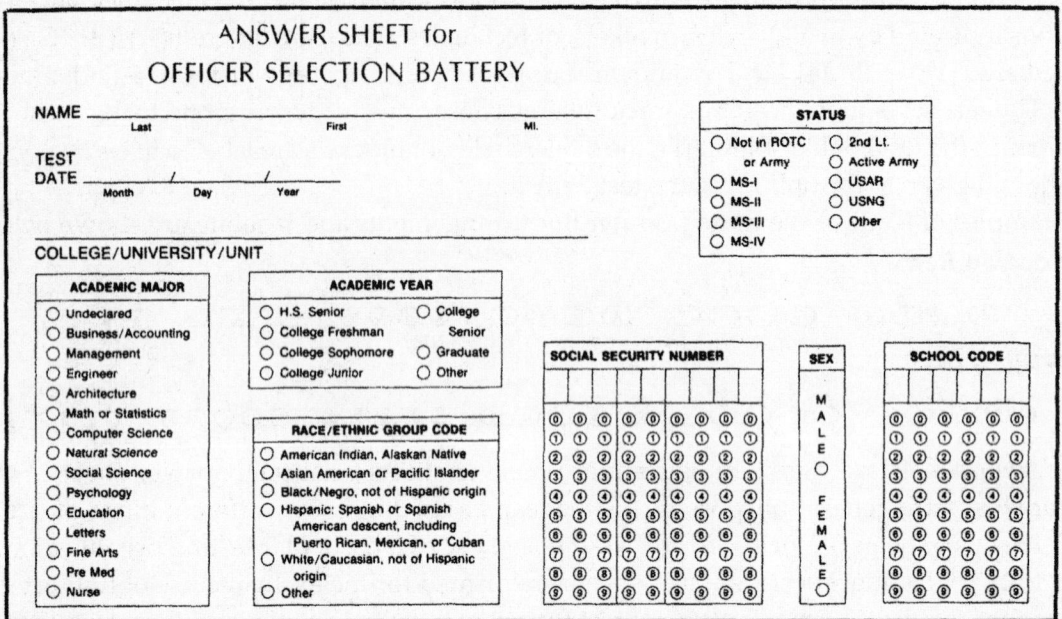

The first page of the set, the heading, is the identification and personal data sheet and provides space for recording by mark sensing the following:

1. Student's Name (last, first, middle initial)
2. Home Mailing Address
3. Home City
4. State
5. ZIP Code
6. Area Code and Phone Number
7. School Code
8. Name of School
9. Educational Level
10. Population (Ethnic) Group
11. Sex
12. Intentions (i.e., future schooling or employment)
13. Test Version
14. Date of Birth (year, month, day)
15. Test Booklet Number

SCHEMATIC SAMPLE

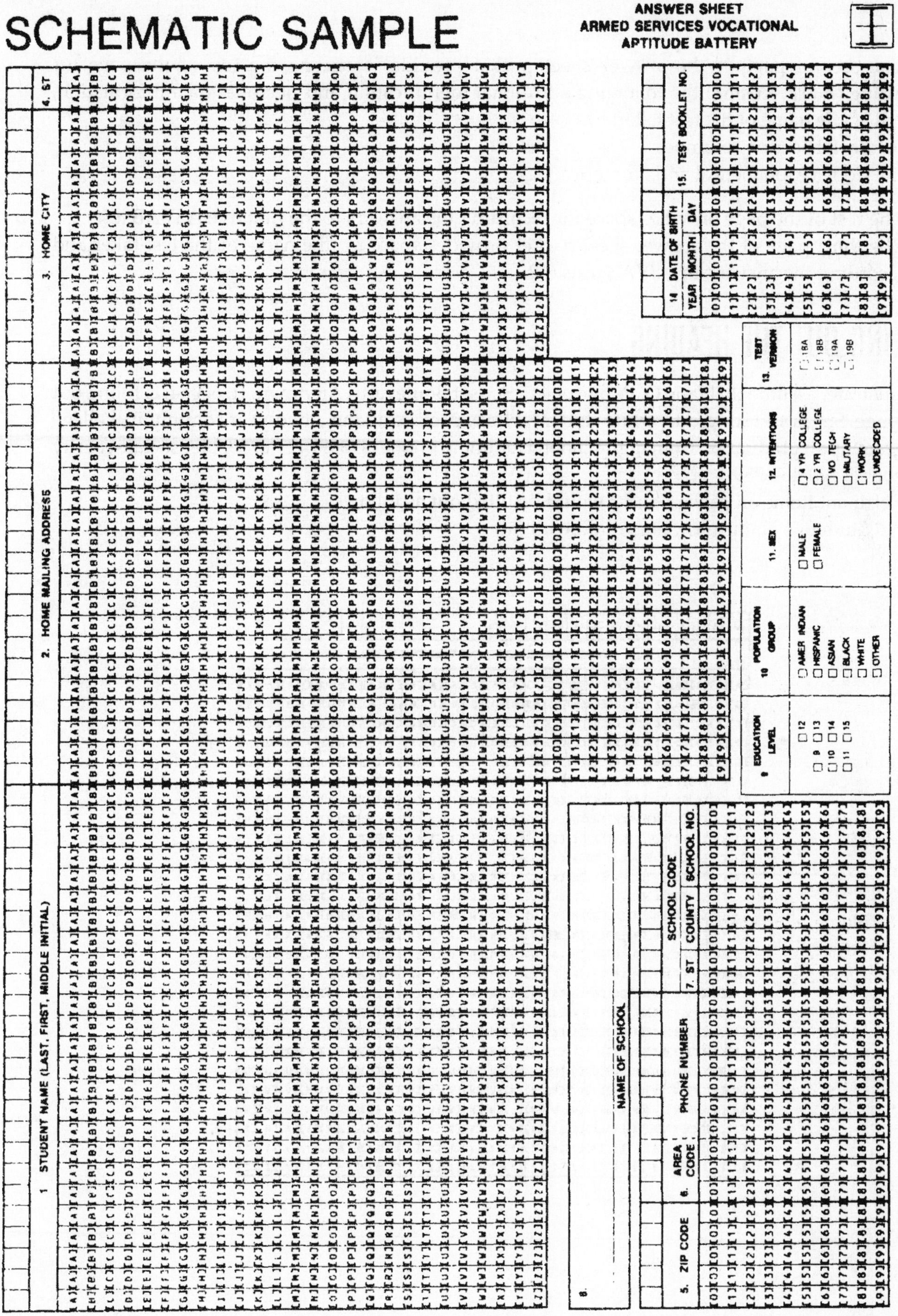

**ANSWER SHEET
ARMED SERVICES VOCATIONAL
APTITUDE BATTERY**

1. STUDENT NAME (LAST, FIRST, MIDDLE INITIAL)

2. HOME MAILING ADDRESS

3. HOME CITY

4. ST

5. ZIP CODE

6. AREA CODE / PHONE NUMBER

7. ST / COUNTY / SCHOOL NO.

SCHOOL CODE

8. NAME OF SCHOOL

9. EDUCATION LEVEL
☐ 12 ☐ B ☐ 13 ☐ 10 ☐ 14 ☐ 11 ☐ 15

10. POPULATION GROUP
☐ AMER INDIAN ☐ HISPANIC ☐ ASIAN ☐ BLACK ☐ WHITE ☐ OTHER

11. SEX
☐ MALE ☐ FEMALE

12. INTENTIONS
☐ 4 YR COLLEGE ☐ 2 YR COLLEGE ☐ VO TECH ☐ MILITARY ☐ WORK ☐ UNDECIDED

13. TEST VERSION
☐ 18A ☐ 18B ☐ 19A ☐ 19B

14. DATE OF BIRTH
YEAR MONTH DAY

15. TEST BOOKLET NO.

The second page of the answer sheet packet provides space on the top of the page for recording (mark sensing) the following additional identification and personal data information, as well as the name of the test taker:

16. Social Security Number
17. Code (Alphabetical and Numerical)

The rest of the page provides space for recording the answers to the first five ASVAB tests.

The third page of the answer sheet packet provides space for the name of the test-taker and for recording the answers to ASVAB tests 6-9.

FILLING OUT THE HEADING

To illustrate, assume that Jane Q. Public of 415 Sunset Boulevard, Anytown, IL 60064, is filling out this page. She is an 11th-grade, white student who expects to attend a two-year community college program upon graduation from high school. Her home phone is (309) 421-6758. Her social security number is 123-45-6789.

Pertinent items on pages 1 and 2 would be filled out as follows:

1. Student's Name (last, first, middle initial)

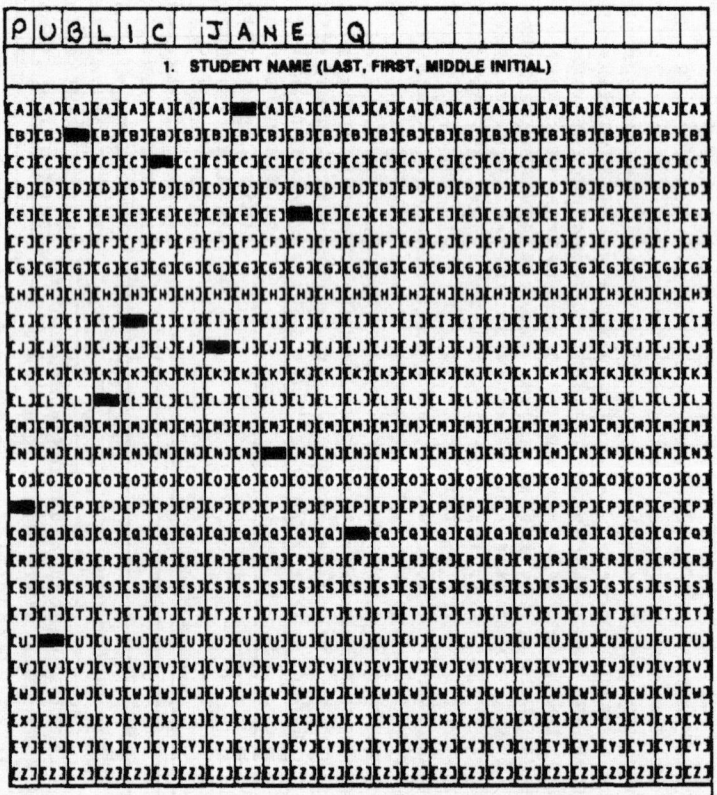

2. Home Mailing Address   3. Home City   4. State

| 4 | 1 | 5 | | S | U | N | S | E | T | | B | L | V | D | | | | | A | N | Y | T | O | W | N | | | | | I | L |

| 2. HOME MAILING ADDRESS | 3. HOME CITY | 4. ST |

5. ZIP Code   6. Area Code and Phone Number

| 6 | 0 | 0 | 6 | 4 | 3 | 0 | 9 | 4 | 2 | 1 | 6 | 7 | 5 | 8 |

| 5. ZIP CODE | 6. AREA CODE | PHONE NUMBER |

9. Educational Level   10. Population Group   11. Sex   12. Intentions

9. EDUCATION LEVEL	10. POPULATION GROUP	11. SEX	12. INTENTIONS	13. TEST VERSION
☐ 12	☐ AMER INDIAN	☐ MALE	☐ 4 YR COLLEGE	☐ 18A
☐ 9 ☐ 13	☐ HISPANIC	■ FEMALE	■ 2 YR COLLEGE	☐ 18B
☐ 10 ☐ 14	☐ ASIAN		☐ VO TECH.	☐ 19A
■ 11 ☐ 15	☐ BLACK		☐ MILITARY	☐ 19B
	■ WHITE		☐ WORK	
	☐ OTHER		☐ UNDECIDED	

16. Social Security Number

MARKING YOUR ANSWERS

The body of the answer sheet is the actual testing section used to record the answers to the questions comprising the test. A soft (No. 2) pencil must be used to record the answers by blackening the space in the marking position with the same letter as the option selected as the best answer. The mark should be dark and cover the entire area of the marking position.

A soft (No. 2) pencil makes marks that are sufficiently dark enough to be picked up by the scoring machine, and yet can be readily erased. A No. 3 pencil does not sufficiently darken the marked position, and a No. 1 pencil makes marks that are difficult to erase.

Choice (E) on a bracketed answer sheet is marked like this:

$$\boxed{\text{A B C D} \ \blacksquare}$$

Remember

NOT	A B C D Ⓔ
NOT	A B C D ✗
NOT	A B C D ✓
NOT	A B C D E *E*
NOT	A B C D E|
NOT	A B C D ♥
NOT	A B C ●
BUT	A B C D ▮

The same principle applies if the response positions are indicated by ovals, circles, rectangles, or any other design.

To change an answer, first erase it completely, then blacken the space in the response position with the same designation as the new answer.

Avoid making stray marks on your answer sheet. Such marks might be read by the test-scoring machine as a second answer to a question, and your answer—even if correct—might not be credited.

PART V

Preparing for and Taking the Test

TEST-TAKING STRATEGIES

APPLYING FOR THE TEST

Are you a college graduate or in your senior year of college? Are you interested in a career as an officer in the Armed Forces of the United States? If the answer to both questions is yes, contact the branch or branches of service in which you are interested to obtain pertinent recruiting information, qualification requirements, and application forms. The first two parts of this book provide general information regarding career opportunities as a commissioned officer, qualification requirements, and guidance on how to enroll in officer training programs for the various services—Air Force, Army, Coast Guard, Marines, and Navy.

But, after reviewing the recruiting brochures, you find that, although you more than meet most of the official requirements, you are slightly deficient in perhaps one or two areas. Should you give up? No! Waivers might be granted in meritorious cases.

Arrange for an interview with the officer in charge of officer recruiting for additional information, guidance, or assistance in filling out and processing your application forms.

In listing your qualifications on the application, be sure to describe fully and accurately all pertinent training, experience, and other personal qualifications.

A college transcript or diploma, documents verifying your date of birth and U.S. citizenship, Social Security card, and other official documents might be needed in connection with processing your application. Make certain that you have them readily available or have arranged to obtain them.

PREPARING FOR THE TEST

Whether it be studying subject matter, reviewing sample questions in practice exercises, or getting into condition for a strenuous physical test, the "test-wise" individual will *immediately* begin preparing for the tests ahead.

Become familiar with the format of multiple-choice test items. These items are used exclusively in written tests given by the military in the selection process for officer candidates.

Become familiar with the layout of machine-scored answer sheets. Know the proper way to record your answers in the spaces provided, whether brackets, rectangles, squares, ovals, or circles. These standard answer sheets are not complicated if you understand the layout and have practiced blackening the answer space in the correct manner.

Ascertain what the test covers. This book, as well as the officer in charge of officer recruiting, is an excellent source for invaluable suggestions and guidance.

Review subject matter covered in the test. Books and other study materials may be borrowed from libraries or purchased in bookstores.

Using the suggested study guide for reviewing practice exercises and taking the specimen test, determine which ones will fulfill your requirements. Answer all questions in these practice exercises. Take the specimen test under actual test conditions. Record your answers on the specimen answer sheet. Keep within the allotted time limits. Work quickly but carefully.

Check your answers with the key answers and rationale. For those questions answered incorrectly, determine why your answers are incorrect. Make certain that you understand the rationale for arriving at the correct answer. This is essential to broaden your background, increase your test sophistication, and prepare you for the real test.

Set aside definite hours each day for concentrated study. Adhere closely to this schedule. Don't waste time with excessive breaks. A cup of coffee, a piece of fruit, or a look out the window are fine—but don't indulge too often.

Study with a friend or a group. The exchange of ideas that this arrangement affords can be very beneficial. It is also more pleasant to get together in study sessions than it is to study alone.

Eliminate distractions. Study efforts will prove more fruitful when there is little or no diversion of attention. Disturbances caused by family and neighbor activities (telephone calls, chitchat, TV programs, etc.) will work to your disadvantage. Study in a quiet, private room.

Use the library. Most colleges and universities have excellent library facilities. Take full advantage of them. The library is free from distractions that might inhibit your home study.

Review each practice exercise and take the specimen test as though you were taking the real test. With this attitude, you will derive greater benefit. Put yourself under strict test conditions. Tolerate no interruptions while you are "taking the test." Work steadily. Do not spend too much time on any one question. If a question seems too difficult, go to the next one. Go back to the omitted questions only after you complete the initial pass through the practice exercise and each subtest or test of the specimen test.

If you are interested in and applying for flight training, be sure to refer to the companion book, ARCO *Military Flight Aptitude Tests*. If you are interested in obtaining a commission in the U.S. Coast Guard, but not interested in flight training, be sure to refer to ARCO *Master the SAT* or ARCO *Master the ACT Assessment*, depending on which test you plan to take.

Keep physically fit. Physical health promotes mental efficiency.

If possible, avoid taking the test under adverse conditions, such as when you are fatigued, ill, injured, emotionally upset, or dispirited; have your mind on other problems; or any other condition that might handicap you physically, mentally, or emotionally.

Go to bed early the night before the test and get a good night's sleep.

Eat a light meal before taking the test. Consuming a heavy meal just before the test can make you somewhat lethargic and might reduce your effectiveness as a test-taker.

Bring along all the supplies you will need for the test—a pen, several No. 2 pencils, an eraser, a ruler, eyeglasses if you need them for reading, and so on.

Bring a watch to help you allocate your time. Be certain that you know the amount of time you have for the test and for each timed test section or subtest. With military tests, you are frequently not permitted to go back and check your answers on test sections or subtests that have already been completed.

Be sure to give yourself plenty of time to get to the test site. Arriving early puts you in a much better frame of mind for taking the exam than does frantically arriving at the last minute.

Last-minute review is inadvisable. Relax before the start of the test.

Refrain from drinking excessive amounts of liquids before the test. Going to the rest room during the test wastes valuable testing time. Use the rest room before or after the test, not during the test.

GUESSING

When you're unsure of an answer to a multiple-choice test item, should you guess? Emphatically yes, if it is to your advantage! If there is no penalty for incorrect answers (the test score is based solely on the number of correct responses), be certain that all questions are answered before handing in your answer sheet to the proctor. If there is a penalty for wrong answers (the test score is determined by subtracting from the number of right answers the number of wrong answers or some fraction of the number of wrong answers), guess only if the odds are in your favor.

On the Air Force Officer Qualifying Test, the Armed Services Vocational Aptitude Battery, and the Navy and Marine Corps Aviation Test Selection Battery, the test scores are based solely on the number of correct responses. There is no penalty for incorrect answers.

To obtain the maximum score possible by guessing, you should understand the differences between *guessing blindly*, *educated guessing*, and *probability*.

To guess blindly is to select at random the correct answer to the question from all of the options given. To make an educated guess is first to eliminate those options that you know to be definitely incorrect and then to make your selection from among the remaining options.

Probability is the likelihood or chance of some event or series of events occurring. When tossing a coin, what is the probability that a head appears? The probability is one out of two. Similarly, the probability of obtaining a tail is also one out of two. Head and tail are equally likely. Such probability is expressed as $\frac{1}{2}$ or .50.

Probability ranges between one and zero. At one, the event will probably occur every time. At zero, the event will probably never occur. The probability of occurring plus the probability of not occurring always equals one.

Assume that there are three marbles in a jar and only one marble is red. What is the probability of picking the red marble strictly by chance? The probability is one out of three, expressed as $\frac{1}{3}$ or .33. Similarly, if there are four marbles in a jar and only one is red, the probability of picking the red marble strictly by chance is one out of four, expressed as $\frac{1}{4}$ or .25. If there are five marbles in a jar and only one is red, the probability of picking the red marble strictly by chance is one out of five, expressed as $\frac{1}{5}$ or .20.

With a true/false or two-option item, the probability of guessing the correct answer when the test-taker knows nothing about the item is one out of two $\left(\frac{1}{2}\right)$. For a three-option multiple-choice item, the probability of guessing the correct answer strictly by chance is one out of three $\left(\frac{1}{3}\right)$. For a four-option multiple-choice item, the probability of guessing the correct answer strictly by chance is one out of four $\left(\frac{1}{4}\right)$. For a five-option multiple-choice item, the probability of guessing the correct answer strictly by chance is one out of five $\left(\frac{1}{5}\right)$. Obviously, the probability of selecting the correct answer increases with every incorrect option eliminated before making that educated guess.

By guessing blindly or picking strictly by chance, the test-taker will probably answer correctly 50 percent of the test items in a true/false or two-option test, 33 percent of the test items in a three-option multiple-choice test, 25 percent of the test items in a four-option test, and 20 percent of the test items in a five-option test.

Is probability important for a test-taker? Definitely! Understanding and applying the principles of probability can increase your test score by a few to many points. It can make the difference between passing or failing a test, and it could make the difference between being reached for appointment or not being reached.

The following two examples illustrate how the principles of probability can influence test scores. In the first example, assume that no deduction is made for incorrect answers and that only the number of correct answers determines the test score. In the second example, assume that deductions are made for incorrect answers and that the number of correct answers minus some fraction of one for each incorrect answer determines the test score.

Example 1: Correct Answers Only

Assume that you are taking a 100-item, five-option multiple-choice test and that test scores are based solely on the number of correct answers. Assume further that there are twenty answers of which you are uncertain. If you do not answer these twenty items, you will receive no credit for them. If you guess blindly by picking any option at random, you will probably answer four out of the twenty items correctly and earn four extra points.

If you are able to eliminate one option that you know is incorrect on each of the twenty items and then pick at random from the remaining four options, you will probably answer five of the twenty items correctly and earn five extra points.

If you are able to eliminate two options that you know are incorrect on each of the twenty items and then pick at random from the remaining three options, you will probably answer seven of the twenty items correctly and earn seven extra points.

If you are able to eliminate three options that you know are incorrect on each of the twenty items and then pick at random from the remaining two options, you will probably answer ten of the twenty items correctly and earn ten extra points.

If scores are based on correct answers only:
- Answer all items.
- When you are unsure of the correct answer, first eliminate options that you know are incorrect and then pick at random from the remaining options.

Example 2: Penalty Scoring

Assume that you are taking a 100-item, five-option multiple-choice test and that the test score is based on the number of correct answers minus $\frac{1}{4}$ point for each incorrect answer. Assume further that there are twenty answers of which you are uncertain.

A penalty of $\frac{1}{4}$ point for each incorrect answer might be used on a five-option multiple-choice test to compensate for guessing blindly by picking an option strictly at random. Similarly, for a four-option multiple-choice test, a penalty of $\frac{1}{3}$ point for each incorrect answer might be used. In a true/false test, the formula items correct minus items incorrect might be used to compensate for guessing blindly.

If you do not answer the twenty items, you will receive no extra points and incur no penalty. If you guess blindly by picking any option at random, you will probably answer four of the twenty items correctly and sixteen of the items incorrectly. You will receive four extra points for the four correct answers and will be penalized four points ($\frac{1}{4}$ of 16) for the sixteen incorrect answers. With this penalty formula, there is no advantage in answering the twenty items by picking options strictly at random over not answering these twenty items.

However, if you are able to eliminate an option that you know is incorrect on each of the twenty items and then select at random from the remaining four options, you will probably select five correct answers and fifteen incorrect answers. You will receive five extra points for the five correct answers and will be penalized $3\frac{3}{4}$ points ($\frac{1}{4}$ of 15) for the fifteen incorrect answers, and you will earn an extra $1\frac{1}{4}$ points ($5 - 3\frac{3}{4}$).

If you are able to eliminate two options that you know are incorrect on each of the twenty items and then select at random from the remaining three options, you will probably select seven correct and thirteen incorrect answers. You will receive seven extra points for the seven correct answers and will be penalized $3\frac{1}{4}$ points ($\frac{1}{4}$ of 13) for the thirteen incorrect answers. You will earn an extra $3\frac{3}{4}$ points ($7 - 3\frac{1}{4}$).

If you are able to eliminate three options that you know are incorrect on each of the twenty items and then select at random from the remaining two options, you will probably select ten correct and ten incorrect answers. You will receive ten extra points for the ten correct answers and will be penalized $2\frac{1}{2}$ points ($\frac{1}{4}$ of 10) for the ten incorrect answers. You will earn an extra $7\frac{1}{2}$ points ($10 - 2\frac{1}{2}$).

If there is a guessing penalty:
- Answer only those items where the probability of gain is greater than the probability of loss.
- For those items where the odds are in your favor, first eliminate options that you know are incorrect and then pick at random from the remaining options.
- An educated guess is better than guessing blindly.

TAKING THE TEST

Arrive early at the test location.

If you have a choice, choose a comfortable seat with good lighting and away from possible distractions such as friends, the proctor's desk, the door, open windows, and so on.

If you are left-handed, inform the proctor of your needs and ask if some arrangements can be made to enable you to compete equally with the other candidates.

If the examination room is too cold, too warm, or not well ventilated, call these conditions to the attention to the person in charge.

Be confident and calm. A certain amount of anxiety is not only normal but desirable. Test-takers are not at their best when they are completely relaxed. If you have prepared faithfully, you will attain your true score—based on your ability, your degree of preparation for the test, and your test sophistication.

Keep an eye on your watch and apportion your time intelligently.

Give the test your complete attention. Blot out all other thoughts, pleasant or otherwise, and concentrate solely on the task before you.

Listen carefully to all oral instructions. Read carefully the directions for taking the test and marking the answer sheet. If you don't understand the instructions or directions, raise your hand and ask the proctor for clarification. Failure to follow instructions or misreading directions can only result in a loss of points.

When the signal is given to begin the test, start with the first question. Don't jump to conclusions. Carefully read the stem of the question and all of the options before selecting the answer.

Answer the question as given in the test booklet, not as you believe the question should be. Work steadily and quickly, but not carelessly.

Do not spend too much time on any one question. If you can't figure out the answer in a few seconds, go on to the next question. If you skip a question, be sure to skip the answer space for that question on the answer sheet. Continue in this fashion through the entire test, answering only those questions that require relatively little time and of which you are sure.

Make certain that the number of the question you are working on in the test booklet corresponds to the number of the question you are answering on the answer sheet. It is a good idea to check the numbers of questions and answers frequently. If you skip a question but fail to skip the corresponding answer blank for that question, all of your answers after that will be wrongly placed.

Go back to the questions you skipped and attempt to answer them. If you are still unsure of the correct answer, eliminate those options that you know are incorrect and make an educated guess as to which one of the remaining options is correct. If there is a penalty for wrong answers, make an educated guess only when the odds are in your favor.

If time permits, recheck your answers for errors. If you find that your initial response is incorrect, change it to the correct answer, making sure to erase your initial response completely on the answer sheet.

Keep working until you have rechecked all of your answers and made all corrections. If necessary, be a "bitter ender" and remain until the signal is given to stop.

TYPES OF QUESTIONS USED FOR SELECTING OFFICER CANDIDATES

SYNONYMS

Synonym questions appear as five-option items in Subtest 5 (Word Knowledge) of the Air Force Officer Qualifying Test. They also appear as four-option items in Subtest 3 (Word Knowledge) of the Armed Services Vocational Aptitude Battery.

Synonyms are commonly used to measure breadth of vocabulary, or word knowledge. For each word given (usually capitalized, underlined, or italicized), you are required to select from among the options the one that is the same or most nearly the same in meaning. The usual dictionary definition is required when only the word is given. If the word appears in a sentence, the meaning of the word as used in the sentence is necessary.

Consider all options before answering the question. Although several options might have some connection with the key word, the closest in meaning to the key word is the correct answer.

Sample Items (5 options)

S1. SUCCUMB means most nearly to

    (A) aid
    (B) be discouraged
    (C) check
    (D) oppose
    (E) yield

To *succumb* means "to cease to resist before a superior strength or overpowering desire or force." Choice (E) is the only one that means almost the same as *succumb*.

S2. SUBSUME means most nearly to

    (A) belong
    (B) cover
    (C) include
    (D) obliterate
    (E) understate

To *subsume* is "to include within a larger class or category." Of all of the options given, choice (C) is closest in meaning to *subsume*.

Sample Items (4 options)

S3.   DEFICIENT means most nearly

    (A) sufficient

    (B) outstanding

    (C) inadequate

    (D) bizarre

Of the options given, *inadequate* is the only one that is synonymous with *deficient*. Choice (C) is the correct answer.

S4.   "The *rear* compartment is locked." The word *rear* as used in the sentence means most nearly

    (A) raised

    (B) upright

    (C) high

    (D) back

As used in the sentence, the word *rear* most nearly means *back*. Choice (D) is the correct answer.

VERBAL ANALOGIES

Verbal analogy questions appear as five-option items in Subtest 1 (Verbal Analogies) of the Air Force Officer Qualifying Test.

Verbal Analogy questions test not only your knowledge of word meanings and your vocabulary level but also your ability to reason—that is, to see the relationships between words and the ideas they represent. To determine such relationships, you must know the meaning of each word in the first given pair. Then you must figure out the precise relationship between these two words. Finally, you must complete the analogy by selecting the pair of words that best expresses a relationship similar to that expressed by the first two paired words.

There are two forms of verbal analogy questions in general use:

1. The first pair of words and the first word of the second pair are given in the stem of the question. This is followed by options, only one of which best expresses a relationship to the third word that is similar to the relationship expressed between the first two words.

    MAN is to BOY as WOMAN is to

    (A) baby
    (B) bride
    (C) child
    (D) girl
    (E) lad

2. Only the first pair of words appears in the stem of the question. It is followed by options, each consisting of a pair of words.

    MAN is to BOY as

    (A) adult is to girl
    (B) bride is to groom
    (C) lass is to child
    (D) woman is to youth
    (E) woman is to girl

Let us analyze the first analogy form given above. What is the relationship of the first two paired words?

MAN—member of the human race, male, mature
BOY—member of the human race, male, young

Both are male members of the human race. MAN is mature; BOY is young.

What is the meaning of the word WOMAN and each of the words appearing in the options?

WOMAN—member of the human race, female, mature
"baby"—member of the human race, either male or female, very young
"bride"—member of the human race, female, about to be married or newly married
"child"—member of the human race, either male or female, young
"girl"—member of the human race, female, young
"lad"—member of the human race, male, young

To complete the analogy with WOMAN as the first word, we need a term denoting a young female member of the human race.

Choice (A) is incorrect because "baby" can be male or female and is very young. Choice (B) is incorrect because "bride" is a special kind of female—one about to be married or newly married. If GROOM had been substituted for BOY in the first half of the analogy, then "bride" would have been the proper choice. Choice (C) is incorrect because "child" might be male or female. Choice (E) is incorrect because "lad" is a male.

Choice (D) is the correct choice because "girl" denotes a young female member of the human race.

Analyzing the second analogy form given above, again we find that the relationship of MAN is to BOY, the paired words in the stem, is that both are male members of the human race—MAN is mature, and BOY is young. Of the choices given, the only similar relationship is WOMAN (member of the human race, female, and mature) to GIRL (member of the human race, female, and young). Choice (E) is the correct answer.

Relationships commonly found in verbal analogies are as follows:

Relationship	Example
synonyms	brochure : pamphlet
antonyms	victory : defeat
homonyms	hale : hail
measurement (time, distance, weight, volume, etc.)	distance : mile
location (in, at, near)	Boston : Massachusetts
numerical	ten : dime
cause : effect	burn : blister
whole : part	ship : keel
object : purpose or function	pencil : write
object : user	saw : carpenter
creator : creation	composer : opera
raw material : final product	cotton : dress
female : male	goose : gander
general : specific	fruit : apple
larger : smaller	river : stream
more : less (degree)	hot : warm
early stage : later stage	larva : pupa

Grammatical Relationships

NOUN

singular : plural   child : children

PRONOUN

singular : plural   she : they

nominative : objective   he : him

first person : third person we : they

VERB

tense   fly : flown

ADJECTIVE

comparative   bad : worse

superlative   little : least

DIFFERENT PARTS OF SPEECH

noun : adjective   dog : canine

adjective : adverb   good : well

Be careful! The order of the two words in the second pair must be in the same sequence as the order of words in the first pair. As in mathematical proportions, reversing the sequence of the members of the second pair breaks the relationship between the two and makes it no longer analogous. The following demonstrates the importance of the order of the words.

2 is to 5 as 4 is to 10 (correct)

2 is to 5 as 10 is to 4 (incorrect)

MAN is to BOY as WOMAN is to GIRL (correct)

MAN is to BOY as GIRL is to WOMAN (incorrect)

Sample Items (5 options)

Each of the following sample items consists of an incomplete analogy. Select the answer that best completes the analogy developed at the beginning of each question.

S1.   BOTANY is to PLANTS as ENTOMOLOGY is to

(A)   animals

(B)   climate

(C)   diseases

(D)   languages

(E)   insects

Botany is the study of *plants; entomology* is the study of *insects.* Choice (E) is the correct answer.

S2.   EPILOGUE is to PROLOGUE as

(A)   appendix is to index

(B)   appendix is to preface

(C)   preface is to footnote

(D)   preface is to table of contents

(E)   table of contents is to index

Epilogue is a closing section added to a novel or a play; *prologue* is an introduction to a novel or a play. *Appendix* is material added after the end of a book; *preface* is an introduction to a book. Choice (B) is the correct answer.

S3.   OCTAGON is to SQUARE as HEXAGON is to

    (A) cube
    (B) military
    (C) pyramid
    (D) rectangle
    (E) triangle

Octagon is an eight-sided figure; *square* is a four-sided figure (one-half of eight). *Hexagon* is a six-sided figure; *triangle* is a three-sided figure (one-half of six). Choice (E) is the correct answer.

S4.   GLOW is to BLAZE as

    (A) compact is to sprawling
    (B) eager is to reluctant
    (C) glance is to stare
    (D) hint is to clue
    (E) wicked is to naughty

Glow is steady subdued light; *blaze* is intensely bright light. *Glance* is to look briefly; *stare* is to gaze intently. Choice (C) is the correct answer.

S5.   WATER is to THIRST as FOOD is to

    (A) famine
    (B) grief
    (C) hunger
    (D) indigestion
    (E) scarcity

Water satisfies *thirst*; *food* satisfies *hunger*. Choice (C) is the correct answer.

READING COMPREHENSION

Paragraph comprehension questions appear as five-option items in Subtest 3 (Reading Comprehension) of the Air Force Officer Qualifying Test and as four-option items in Subtest 4 (Paragraph Comprehension) of the Armed Services Vocational Aptitude Battery.

Sentence comprehension questions appear in the Math/Verbal Test of the Navy and Marine Corps Aviation Selection Test Battery.

The ability to read and understand written or printed material is an important verbal skill. Reading comprehension tests present reading passages that vary in length from one sentence to several paragraphs, followed by one or more questions about each passage. The reading selections are usually samples of the type of material that you would be required to read, whether at school or on the job.

Following are some of the common types of reading comprehension items:

1. *Finding specific information or directly stated detail in the reading passage.*

Although this type is commonly found in elementary-level tests, it is also found in intermediate-level tests such as the Armed Services Vocational Aptitude Battery and in advanced-level tests such as the Air Force Officer Qualifying Test. At the intermediate and advanced levels, the vocabulary is more difficult, the reading passages are of greater complexity, and the questions posed are much more complicated.

Samples:

Helping to prevent accidents is the responsibility of _____.
The principal reason for issuing traffic summonses is to _____.
The reason for maintaining ongoing safety education is that _____.

2. *Recognizing the central theme, the main idea, or concept expressed in the passage.*

Although questions of this type may be phrased in different ways, they generally require that you summarize or otherwise ascertain the principal purpose or idea expressed in the reading passage. In addition to reading and understanding, the ability to analyze and interpret written material is necessary. Some questions require the ability to combine separate ideas or concepts found in the reading passage to reach the correct answer. Other questions merely require drawing a conclusion that is equivalent to a restatement of the main idea or concept expressed in the passage.

Samples:

The most appropriate title for the above passage is _____.
The best title for this paragraph would be _____.
This paragraph is mainly about _____.
The passage best supports the statement that _____.
The passage means most nearly that _____.

3. *Determining the meaning of certain words as used in context.*

The particular meaning of a word as actually used in the passage requires an understanding of the central or main theme of the reading passage, as well as the thought being conveyed by the sentence containing the word in question.

Samples:

The word "......" as used in this passage means _____.

The expression "......" as used in the passage means _____.

4. *Finding implications or drawing inferences from a stated idea.*

This type of item requires the ability to understand the stated idea and then to reason by logical thinking to the implied or inferred idea. *Implied* means not exactly stated but merely suggested; *inferred* means derived by reasoning. Although the terms are somewhat similar in meaning, *inferred* implies being further removed from the stated idea. Much greater reasoning ability is required to arrive at the proper inference. Accordingly, inference items are used principally at the advanced level.

Samples:

Which of the following is implied by the above passage?

Of the following, the most valid implication of the above paragraph is _____.

The author probably believes that _____.

It can be inferred from the above passage that _____.

The best of the following inferences that can be made is that _____.

5. *Sentence-completion items.*

Sentence-completion items are considered to be both vocabulary items and reading comprehension items. They are considered to be vocabulary items as they test for ability to understand and use words. However, they also measure an important phase of reading comprehension—the ability to understand the implications of a sentence or a paragraph.

Sentence-completion items consist of a sentence or paragraph in which one or two words are missing. The omissions are indicated by a blank underlined space (_____). You must read and understand the sentence or paragraph as given and then select the option that best completes the thought in the reading passage. Your choice must also be consistent in style and logic with other elements in the sentence.

Sample:

Select the lettered option that best completes the thought expressed in the sentence.

6. *Word-substitution items.*

Word-substitution items are very similar to sentence-completion items and are also considered to be both vocabulary and reading comprehension items. These items consist of a sentence or paragraph in which a key word has been changed. The changed word is incorrect and it is not in keeping with the meaning that the sentence is intended to convey. Determine which word is used incorrectly. Then select from the choices the word that, when substituted for the incorrectly used word, would best convey the meaning of the sentence or paragraph.

General Suggestions for Answering Reading Comprehension Questions

1. Scan the passage to get the general intent of the reading selection.
2. Reread the passage carefully to understand the main idea and any related ideas. If necessary for comprehension, reread the passage again.
3. Read each question carefully and base your answer on the material given in the reading passage. Be careful to base your answer on what is stated, implied, or inferred. Do not be influenced by your opinions, personal feelings, or any information not expressed or implied in the reading passage.
4. Options that are partly true and partly false are incorrect.
5. Be very observant for such words as *least, greatest, first, not,* etc. appearing in the preamble of the question.
6. Be suspicious of options containing words such as *all, always, every, forever, never, none, wholly,* and so on.
7. Be sure to consider all choices given for the question before selecting your answer.
8. Speed is an important consideration in answering reading comprehension questions. Try to proceed as rapidly as you can without sacrificing careful thinking or reasoning.

PARAGRAPH COMPREHENSION

Sample Items (5 options)

For each of the following sample five-option questions, select the option that best completes the statement or answers the question.

S1.   The rates of vibration perceived by the ears as musical tones lie between fairly well-defined limits. In the ear, as in the eye, there are individual variations. However, variations are more marked in the ear, because its range of perception is greater.

The paragraph best supports the statement that the ear
(A)   is limited by the nature of its variations.
(B)   is the most sensitive of the auditory organs.
(C)   differs from the eye in its broader range of perception.
(D)   is sensitive to a great range of musical tones.
(E)   depends for its sense on the rate of vibration of a limited range of sound waves.

The passage makes the point that individual differences in auditory range are greater than individual differences in visual range because the total range of auditory perception is greater. Although the statements made by choices (D) and (E) are both correct, neither expresses the main point of the reading passage. Choice (C) is the correct answer.

S2.   The propaganda of a nation at war is designed to stimulate the energy of its citizens and their will to win, and to imbue them with an overwhelming sense of the justice of their cause. Directed abroad, its purpose is to create precisely contrary effects among citizens of enemy nations and to assure to nationals of allied or subjugated countries full and unwavering assistance.

The title below that best expresses the ideas of this passage is
(A)   "Propaganda's Failure."
(B)   "Designs for Waging War."
(C)   "Influencing Opinion in Wartime."
(D)   "The Propaganda of Other Nations."
(E)   "Citizens of Enemy Nations and Their Allies."

The theme of this passage is influencing opinion in wartime, both at home and abroad. Choice (C) is the correct answer.

Answer the following two sample questions on the basis of the information contained in the passage below.

S3.   I have heard it suggested that the "upper class" English accent has been of value in maintaining the British Empire and Commonwealth. The argument runs that all manner of folk in distant places, understanding the English language, will catch in this accent the notes of tradition, pride, and authority and so will be suitably impressed. This might have been the case some nine or ten decades ago, but it is certainly not true now. The accent is more likely to be a liability than an asset.

The title below that best expresses the ideas of this passage is
(A)   "Changed Effects of a 'British Accent'."
(B)   "Prevention of the Spread of Cockney."
(C)   "The Affected Language of Royalty."
(D)   "The Decline of the British Empire."
(E)   "The 'King's English'."

S4.   According to the author, the "upper class" English accent

(A)   has been imitated all over the world.
(B)   has been inspired by British royalty.
(C)   has brought about the destruction of the British Commonwealth.
(D)   might have caused arguments among the folk in distant corners of the Empire.
(E)   might have helped to perpetuate the British Empire before 1900.

In S3, the last two sentences of the reading passage indicate that the folk in distant places might have been suitably impressed decades ago, but they are not impressed now. Choice (A) is the correct answer.

In S4, the "upper class" English accent might have been of value in maintaining the British Empire nine or ten decades ago (or before 1900). Choice (E) is the correct answer.

Sample Items (4 options)

For each of the following sample four-option questions, select the choice that best completes the statement or answers the question.

S5.   The view is widely held that butter is more digestible and better absorbed than other fats because of its low melting point. There is little scientific authority for such a view. As margarine is made today, its melting point is close to that of butter, and tests show only the slightest degree of difference in digestibility of fats of equally low melting points.

The paragraph best supports the statement that
(A)   butter is more easily digested than margarine.
(B)   the concept that butter has a lower melting point than other fats is a common misconception, disproved by scientists.
(C)   there is not much difference in the digestibility of butter and margarine.
(D)   most people prefer butter to margarine.

The passage states that the melting points of butter and margarine are similar and that therefore they are about equally digestible. Choice (C) is the correct answer.

Answer the following two sample questions on the basis of the information contained in the passage below.

Science made its first great contribution to war with gunpowder. But because gunpowder can be used effectively only in suitable firearms, science also had to develop the iron and steel that were required to manufacture muskets and cannon on a huge scale. To this day, metallurgy receives much inspiration from war. Bessemer steel was the direct outcome of the deficiencies of artillery as they were revealed by the Crimean War. Concern with the expansion and pressure of gases in guns and combustibility of powder aroused interest in the laws of gases and other matters that seemingly have no relation whatever to war.

S6.   The title below that best expresses the ideas of this passage is

(A) "Gunpowder, the First Great Invention."
(B) "How War Stimulates Science."
(C) "Improvement of Artillery."
(D) "The Crimean War and Science."

S7.   An outcome of the Crimean War was the

(A) invention of gunpowder.
(B) origin of metallurgy.
(C) study of the laws of gases.
(D) use of muskets and cannon.

In S6, the basic theme of the reading passage is that science contributes to the war effort and that war stimulates science research. Choice (B) is the correct answer.

In S7, the last sentence in the reading passage indicates that interest in the laws of gases arose as a direct outcome of artillery deficiencies revealed by the Crimean War. Choice (C) is the correct answer.

S8.   We find many instances in early science of "a priori" scientific reasoning. Scientists thought it proper to carry generalizations from one field to another. It was assumed that the planets revolved in circles because of the geometrical simplicity of the circle. Even Newton assumed that there must be seven primary colors corresponding to the seven tones of the musical scale.

The paragraph best supports the statement that
(A) Newton sometimes used the "a priori" method of investigation.
(B) scientists no longer consider it proper to uncritically carry over generalizations from one field to another.
(C) the planets revolve about the earth in ellipses rather than in circles.
(D) even great men like Newton sometimes make mistakes.

The tone of the passage and the choice of illustrations showing the fallacy of "a priori" reasoning make it evident that scientists no longer carry generalizations automatically from one field to another. Choices (A) and (D) are true statements, but they are only illustrative points. Choice (B) carries the real message of the passage and is the correct answer.

SENTENCE COMPREHENSION

Sample Items (5 options)

Question S9 consists of a sentence with a blank space, indicating that a word has been omitted. Beneath the sentence are five lettered options. Select the option that, when inserted in the sentence, best fits in with the meaning of the sentence as a whole.

S9. If the weather report forecasts fog and smoke, we can anticipate having _____.
   (A) rain
   (B) sleet
   (C) smog
   (D) snow
   (E) thunder

A mixture of fog and smoke is called smog. Of the options listed, choice (C) is the only correct answer.

Question S10 consists of a sentence with two blank spaces, each blank indicating that a word has been omitted. Beneath the sentence are five lettered sets of words. Choose the set of words that, when inserted in the sentence, best fits in with the meaning of the sentence as a whole.

S10. Although the publicity has been _____, the film itself is intelligent, well-acted, handsomely produced, and altogether _____.
   (A) extensive . . . arbitrary
   (B) tasteless . . . respectable
   (C) sophisticated . . . amateurish
   (D) risqué . . . crude
   (E) perfect . . . spectacular

The correct answer should involve two words that are more or less opposite in meaning, as the word *although* suggests that the publicity misrepresented the film. Another clue to the correct answer is that the second word should fit in context with the words "intelligent, well-acted, handsomely produced." Choices (A), (D), and (E) are not opposites. Choice (C) cannot be the correct answer even though the words in it are nearly opposites, because if the film is intelligent, well-acted, and handsomely produced, it is not amateurish. Also, only choice (B), when inserted in the sentence, produces a logical statement. Choice (B) is the correct answer.

Question S11 consists of a quotation that contains one word that is incorrectly used, because it is not in keeping with the meaning that the quotation is intended to convey. Determine which word is incorrectly used. Then select from the lettered options the word that, when substituted for the incorrectly used word, would best help convey the intended meaning of the quotation.

S11.   "College placement officials have frequently noted the contradiction that exists between the public statements of the company president who questions the value of a liberal arts background in the business world and the practice of his recruiters who seek specialized training for particular jobs."

(A) admissions
(B) praises
(C) reject
(D) science
(E) technical

A careful reading of the passage shows no inconsistency until the word *questions* is reached. If a contradiction exists and the recruiters seek specialized training, the company president would accept, endorse, or praise rather than question the value of a liberal arts background. Choice (B) appears to be the proper substitute that would best convey the intended meaning of the quotation. *Contradiction* is used properly, as none of the options can be substituted for it. Although *reject* might appear to be an appropriate substitution for *seek*, it does not help convey the intended meaning of the quotation. Choice (B) is the only correct answer.

Question S12 consists of a sentence in which one word is omitted. Select the lettered option that best completes the thought expressed in the sentence.

S12.   Although her argument was logical, her conclusion was _____.

(A) illegible
(B) natural
(C) positive
(D) unreasonable

When a subordinate clause begins with *although*, the thought expressed in the main clause will not be consistent with that contained in the subordinate clause. If the argument was *logical*, the conclusion would be illogical. Of the options given, *unreasonable* is the only opposite to logical. Therefore, choice (D) is the correct answer.

Question S13 consists of a sentence with two blank spaces, each blank indicating that a word or figure has been omitted. Select one of the lettered options which, when inserted in the sentence, best completes the thought expressed in the sentence as a whole.

S13.   The height of a 5-foot, 10-inch person in the_____ system would be approximately_____ meters.

(A) English . . . 1.78
(B) English . . . 2.00
(C) Metric . . . 1.78
(D) Metric . . . 2.00

Feet and inches are used in the English system; meters are used in the Metric system. Accordingly, choices (A) and (B) are eliminated immediately. A meter is equivalent to a little less than 40 inches, so the correct answer must be around 1.75. The only choice in this range is (C). Choice (C) is the correct answer.

Question S14 consists of a quotation that contains one word that is incorrectly used, because it is not in keeping with the meaning that the quotation is intended to convey. Determine which word is used incorrectly. Then select from the lettered options the word that, when substituted for the incorrectly used word, would best help convey the intended meaning of the quotation.

S14. "In manufacturing a fabric-measuring device, it is advisable to use a type of cloth whose length is highly susceptible to changes of temperature, tension, etc."

(A) decreases
(B) increases
(C) instrument
(D) not

A careful reading of the passage shows no inconsistency until the word *highly* is reached. To give a true measure, the device's length should not change with temperature or tension but should be constant. Choice (D) is the only correct answer.

For Question S15, select the option that best completes the statement or answers the question.

S15. "Look before you leap."

The statement means most nearly that you should
(A) always be alert.
(B) always be cautious.
(C) move quickly but carefully.
(D) proceed rapidly when directed.

This proverb does not state or imply that you should always be alert or cautious, or that you should proceed quickly when directed. It directs that you should proceed rapidly but cautiously. Choice (C) is the correct answer.

ARITHMETIC REASONING

Questions on arithmetic reasoning appear as five-option items in Subtest 2 of the Air Force Officer Qualifying Test and in the Math/Verbal Test of the Navy and Marine Corps Aviation Selection Test Battery. They also appear as four-option items in Subtest 2 of the Armed Services Vocational Aptitude Battery.

Arithmetic reasoning is concerned with solving mathematical problems. It requires the recognition and application of basic mathematical processes and operations in problems encountered in everyday life. Processes or operations required for solution rather than computational complexity are generally emphasized.

Sample questions illustrating some of the types of questions on arithmetic reasoning found on military tests follow.

Sample Items (5 options)

S1.   Which of the following amounts of money has the greatest value?

(A)   3 quarters
(B)   8 dimes
(C)   15 nickels
(D)   1 quarter, 3 dimes, and 4 nickels
(E)   4 dimes, 7 nickels, and 4 pennies

Computing the value of the coins in each option proves that choice (B) has the greatest value.

$3 \times 25¢ = 75¢$
$8 \times 10¢ = 80¢$
$15 \times 5¢ = 75¢$
$25¢ + 30¢ + 20¢ = 75¢$
$40¢ + 35¢ + 4¢ = 79¢$

S2.   Subtract 1 foot, 6 inches from 2 feet, 4 inches.

(A)   8 inches
(B)   10 inches
(C)   1 foot
(D)   1 foot, 2 inches
(E)   1 foot, 4 inches

Two feet, 4 inches is equal to 1 foot, 16 inches. This amount minus 1 foot, 6 inches equals 10 inches, or choice (B).

$$\begin{array}{r} 1'16'' \\ -1'6'' \\ \hline 10'' \end{array}$$

S3. It costs $1.00 per square yard to waterproof canvas. What will it cost to waterproof a canvas truck cover that is 15′ × 24′?

(A) $20.00
(B) $36.00
(C) $40.00
(D) $360.00
(E) $400.00

15′ × 24′ = 5 yards × 8 yards = 40 square yards; 40 square yards × $1.00 = $40.00. Choice (C) is the correct answer.

S4. Mr. Johnson earns $500 per week. If he spends 20% of his income for rent, 25% for food, and puts 10% in savings, how much is left each week for other expenses?

(A) $225
(B) $240
(C) $250
(D) $260
(E) $275

Fifty-five percent goes for rent, food, and savings; 45% is left for other expenses; $500 × .45 = $225. Choice (A) is the correct answer.

S5. A vessel left a port and sailed west at an average rate of 25 mph. Two hours later, a second vessel left the same port and traveled in the same direction at an average rate of 30 mph. In how many hours did the second vessel overtake the first vessel?

(A) 8 hours

(B) $8\frac{1}{2}$ hours

(C) 9 hours

(D) $9\frac{1}{2}$ hours

(E) 10 hours

In 2 hours, the first vessel would be 50 miles out.

Difference in rate is 5 mph. $\frac{50}{5}$ = 10 hours to overtake the first vessel. Choice (E) is correct.

Sample Items (4 options)

S6. Of the 36 students registered in a class, $\frac{2}{3}$ are females. How many males are registered in the class?

(A) 12
(B) 18
(C) 24
(D) 30

Two thirds of 36 is 24, the number of females. This number subtracted from 36 gives the number of males. Choice (A) is the correct answer.

S7.   A team played 24 games, of which it won 18. What percent of the games played did it lose?

(A) 25%
(B) 42%
(C) 50%
(D) 75%

If it won 18 games, it lost 6 games. $\frac{6}{24} = \frac{1}{4} = .25 = 25\%$. Choice (A) is the correct answer.

S8.   A $75 fund is available for a holiday party. If 75% of the available money is spent for food and beverages, how much is left for other expenses?

(A) $18.75
(B) $28.75
(C) $46.25
(D) $56.25

The amount of money spent is .75 times $75, which equals $56.25. $75.00 – $56.25 = $18.75. Choice (A) is the correct answer.

S9.   A certain employee is paid at the rate of $6.74 per hour with time-and-a-half for overtime. The regular work week is 40 hours. During the past week, the employee put in 44 working hours. What was the employee's gross wages for that week?

(A) $269.60
(B) $296.56
(C) $310.04
(D) $444.84

$$1\tfrac{1}{2} \times \$6.74 = \quad \$10.11$$

$$\begin{aligned} \$6.74 \times 40 &= \$269.60 \\ \$10.11 \times 4 &= \underline{40.44} \\ & \$310.04 \end{aligned}$$

Choice (C) is the correct answer.

S10. If one quart of floor wax covers 400 square feet, how many gallons of wax are needed to wax the floor of a 6,400-sq.-ft. office?

(A) 4 gals.
(B) 8 gals.
(C) 12 gals.
(D) 16 gals.

$1:400 :: x:6400$
$400\,x = 6400$
$x = 16$ (16 quarts of wax are needed.)

There are four quarts to a gallon. Therefore, 16 quarts divided by 4 equals 4 gallons. Choice (A) is the correct answer.

MATH KNOWLEDGE

Questions on math knowledge appear as five-option items in Subtest 6 of the Air Force Officer Qualifying Test and in the Math/Verbal Test of the Navy and Marine Corps Aviation Selection Test Battery. Mathematics knowledge questions also appear as four-option items in Subtest 5 of the Armed Services Vocational Aptitude Battery.

Math knowledge involves the application of mathematical principles and measures ability to use learned mathematical relationships. The content area may include equation solving; plane/solid geometry; exponents, roots, and powers; conversion of common fractions, decimals, and percents; least common denominators, greatest common factor, and smallest common multiple; prime numbers and factorials; linear equations; and transforming verbal problems into algebraic symbols.

The review of some basic mathematical concepts that follows should be helpful in reinforcing your math knowledge.

Some Basic Mathematical Concepts

Factors of a Product

When two or more numbers are multiplied to produce a certain product, each of the numbers is known as a factor of the product.

$1 \times 8 = 8$ (1 and 8 are factors of the product)
$2 \times 4 = 8$ (2 and 4 are factors of the product)

Base

A base is a number used as a factor two or more times. $2 \times 2 \times 2$ may be written 2^3, which is read "2 cubed" or "2 to the third power." In the equation $2^3 = 8$, 2 is called the base.

Exponent

An exponent is a number that shows how many times the base is to be used as a factor. 10^2 is a short way of writing 10×10. 10 is called the base in 10^2; 2 is called the exponent.

$a^4 = a \times a \times a \times a$ (a is the base, 4 is the exponent)
$5^3 = 5 \times 5 \times 5$ (5 is the base; 3 is the exponent)

Power

A power is a number that can be expressed as a product of equal factors. 3^2 is the second power of 3 (3×3) and is equal to 9. 2^4 is the fourth power of 2 ($2 \times 2 \times 2 \times 2$) and is equal to 16.

Reciprocal

If the product of two numbers is 1, either number is called the reciprocal of the other number. $4 \times \frac{1}{4} = 1$. Therefore 4 is the reciprocal of $\frac{1}{4}$ and $\frac{1}{4}$ is the reciprocal of 4. $\frac{3}{5} \times \frac{5}{3} = 1$. Therefore, $\frac{3}{5}$ is the reciprocal of $\frac{5}{3}$ and $\frac{5}{3}$ is the reciprocal of $\frac{3}{5}$.

Factorial

The factorial of a natural or counting number is the product of that number and all of the natural numbers less than it. 4 factorial, written as $4! = 4 \times 3 \times 2 \times 1 = 24$.

Prime Number

A prime number is a natural or counting number that is not divisible by any other number except 1 and itself. Examples of prime numbers are 2, 3, 5, 7, 11, 13, and 17.

Roots

- **Square Root:** The square root of a number is a number that, when raised to the second power, produces the given number. For example, the square root of 16 is 4 because $4^2 = 16$. $\sqrt{}$ is the symbol for square root.
- **Cube Root:** Cube root is the procedural inverse of raising to a cube. If $2^3 = 8$, than $\sqrt[3]{8} = 2$. The cube root of $27 = 3$; $3^3 = 27$.

Algebraic Equations

An equation is an equality. The values on either side of the equal sign in an equation must be equal. To learn the value of an unknown in an equation, do the same thing to both sides of the equation so as to leave the unknown on one side of the equal sign and its value on the other side.

$X - 2 = 8$

Add 2 to both sides of the equation.

$X - 2 + 2 = 8 + 2$; $X = 10$

$5X = 25$

Divide both sides of the equation by 5.

$\dfrac{^1\cancel{5}X}{\cancel{5}_1} = \dfrac{25}{5}$; $X = 5$

$Y + 9 = 15$

Subtract 9 from both sides of the equation.

$Y + 9 - 9 = 15 - 9$; $Y = 6$

$A \div 4 = 48$

Multiply both sides of the equation by 4.

$\dfrac{^1\cancel{4}A}{\cancel{4}_1} = 48 \times 4$; $A = 192$

Sometimes more than one step is required to solve an equation.

$6A \div 4 = 48$

First, multiply both sides of the equation by 4.

$$\frac{6A}{{}_1 4} \times \frac{4^1}{1} = 48 \times 4; \; 6A = 192$$

Then, divide both sides of the equation by 6.

$$\frac{{}^1 6A}{{}_1 6} = \frac{192}{6}; \; A = 32$$

Angles

An angle is a geometric figure made by two lines that intersect. The symbol for an angle is $\angle$. The two lines are called sides of the angle.

Types of Angles

A *right angle* is an angle of 90° and is formed by one fourth of a complete revolution ($\frac{1}{4}$ of 360°).

A *straight angle* is an angle of 180° and is formed by one half of a complete revolution ($\frac{1}{2}$ of 360°).

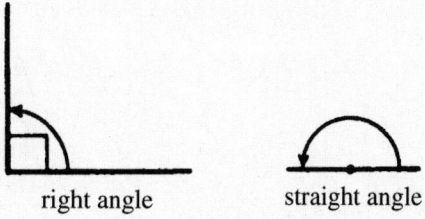

right angle   straight angle

An *acute angle* is an angle that is greater than 0° but less than 90°.

An *obtuse angle* is an angle that is greater than 90° but less than 180°.

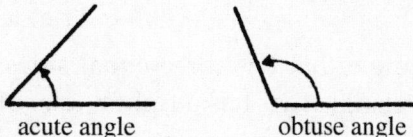

acute angle   obtuse angle

Complementary angles are two angles whose sum is 90°. Each angle is the complement of the other. If an angle contains 30°, its complement contains 60°. If an angle contains $x°$, its complement contains $(90 - x)°$.

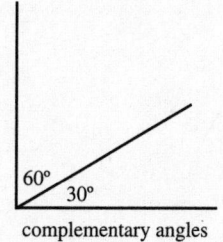

complementary angles

Supplementary angles are two angles whose sum is 180°. Each angle is the supplement of the other. If an angle contains 140°, its supplement contains 40°. If an angle contains x°, its supplement contains $(180 - x)$°.

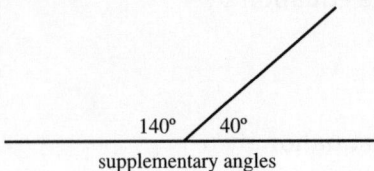

140°   40°

supplementary angles

Triangles

A triangle is a plane figure consisting of three points not on a straight line and the line segments connecting these points.

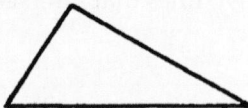

A *scalene triangle* is a triangle with no two sides equal.

An *isosceles* triangle is a triangle that has two equal sides. The equal sides are called legs or arms. The remaining side is called the base. The base angles of an isosceles triangle are equal.

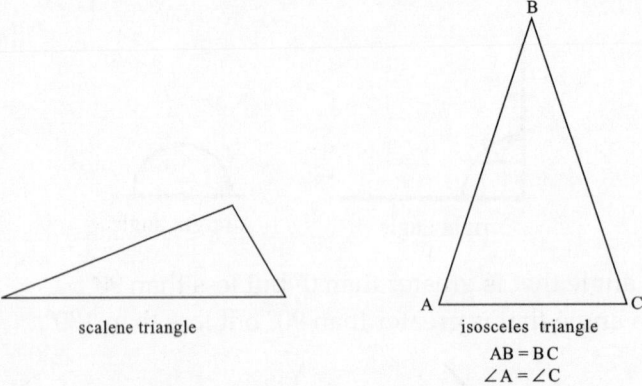

scalene triangle

isosceles triangle

$AB = BC$

$\angle A = \angle C$

An *equilateral triangle* is a triangle that has three equal sides. An equilateral triangle is also equiangular. A *right triangle* is a triangle that has a right angle. The side opposite the right angle is called the hypotenuse.

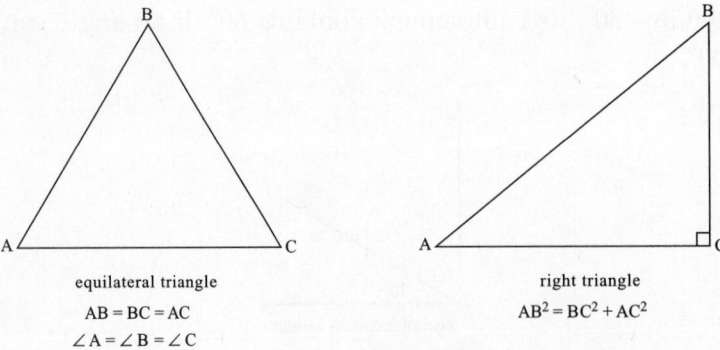

equilateral triangle

$AB = BC = AC$

$\angle A = \angle B = \angle C$

right triangle

$AB^2 = BC^2 + AC^2$

Pythagorean Theorem

In a right triangle, the square of the length of the hypotenuse is equal to the sum of the squares of the lengths of the other two sides: $a^2 + b^2 = c^2$.

Area, Perimeter, and Volume

Area is the space enclosed by a plane (flat) figure. A rectangle is a plane figure with four right angles. Opposite sides of a rectangle are of equal length and are parallel to each other. To find the area of a rectangle, multiply the length of the base of the rectangle by the length of its height. Area is *always* expressed in square units.

3ft.

9ft.

$A = bh$
$A = 9\text{ft.} \times 3\text{ft.}$
$A = 27 \text{ sq.ft.}$

A square is a rectangle in which all four sides are the same length. The area of a square is found by squaring the length of one side, which is exactly the same as multiplying the square's length by its height.

4in.

4in.

$A = S^2$
$A = 4\text{in.} \times 4\text{in.}$
$A = 16 \text{ sq.in.}$

A triangle is a three-sided plane figure. The area of a triangle is found by multiplying the base by the altitude (height) and dividing by two.

5in.

9in.

$A = \frac{1}{2} bh$
$A = \frac{1}{2} (9\text{in.})(5\text{in.}) = \frac{45}{2}$
$A = 22\frac{1}{2} \text{ sq.in.}$

A circle is a perfectly round plane figure. The distance from the center of a circle to its rim is its radius. The distance from one edge to the other through the center is its diameter. The diameter is twice the length of the radius.

Pi (π) is a mathematical value equal to approximately 3.14, or $\frac{22}{7}$. Pi is frequently used in calculations involving circles. The area of a circle is found by squaring the radius and multiplying it by π.

4 cm.

$A = \pi r^2$
$A = \pi (4 \text{ cm.})^2$
$A = 16\pi \text{ sq.cm.}$

You may leave the area in terms of pi unless you are told what value to assign π.

The perimeter of a plane figure is the distance around the outside. To find the perimeter of a polygon (a plane figure bounded by straight lines), just add the lengths of the sides.

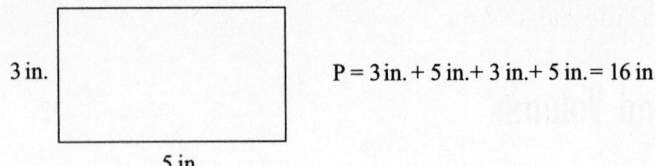

P = 3 in. + 5 in. + 3 in. + 5 in. = 16 in.

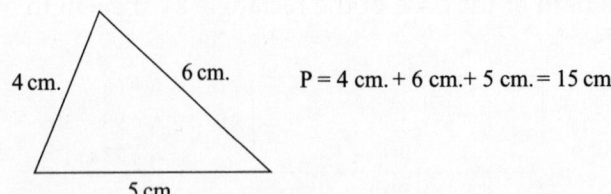

P = 4 cm. + 6 cm. + 5 cm. = 15 cm.

The perimeter of a circle is called the *circumference*. The formula for the *circumference* of a circle is πd or $2\pi r$, which are, of course, the same thing.

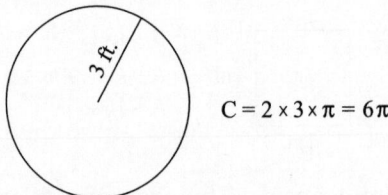

C = 2 × 3 × π = 6π

The volume of a solid figure is the measure of the space within. To figure the volume of a solid figure, multiply the area by the height or depth.

The volume of a rectangular solid is length × width × height. Volume is always expressed in cubic units.

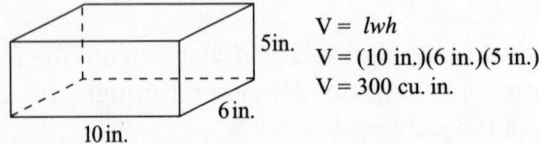

V = *lwh*
V = (10 in.)(6 in.)(5 in.)
V = 300 cu. in.

The volume of a cube is the cube of one side.

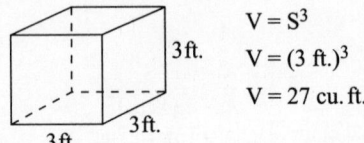

V = S³
V = (3 ft.)³
V = 27 cu. ft.

The volume of a cylinder is π times the square of the radius of the base times the height.

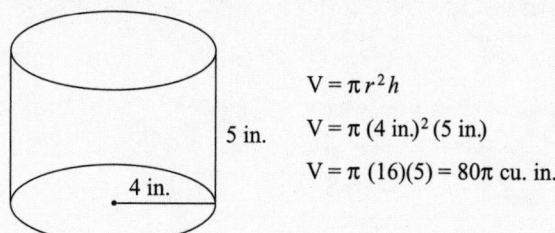

$V = \pi r^2 h$

$V = \pi (4 \text{ in.})^2 (5 \text{ in.})$

$V = \pi (16)(5) = 80\pi$ cu. in.

Sample questions illustrating some of the types of questions on math knowledge found on military tests follow. Solutions to these sample questions are given to show how the correct answers are obtained.

Sample Items (5 options)

S1. If 20% of a number is 8, what is 25% of the number?

(A) 10
(B) 11
(C) 12
(D) 14
(E) 15

$.20 \times x = 8$; $x = 40$; $.25 \times 40 = 10$. Choice (A) is the correct answer.

S2. Which of the following has the greatest value?

(A) $\dfrac{1}{2}$

(B) $\sqrt{.2}$

(C) .2

(D) $(.2)^2$

(E) $(.02)^2$

(A) = .5; (B) = more than .4 but less than .5; (C) = .2; (D) = .04; (E) = .0004. Choice (A) is the correct answer.

S3. Henry needs M hours to mow the lawn. After working for X hours, what part of the job remains to be done?

(A) $M - X$
(B) $X - M$

(C) $\dfrac{M - X}{M}$

(D) $\dfrac{X}{M}$

(E) $\dfrac{M - X}{X}$

M hours to mow lawn; $M - X$ = time still needed to complete lawn. $\dfrac{M - X}{M}$ = part still to be done. Choice (C) is the correct answer.

S4.   A square is equal in area to a rectangle whose length is 9 and whose width is 4. Find the perimeter of the square.

   (A) 24
   (B) 26
   (C) 30
   (D) 34
   (E) 36

   Area of rectangle = $9 \times 4 = 36$; area of square = 36; each side = 6; perimeter of square = 6 + 6 + 6 + 6 = 24. Choice (A) is the correct answer.

S5.   The circumference of a circle whose area is 9π is

   (A) 3
   (B) 3π
   (C) 6
   (D) 6π
   (E) 9

   If area is 9π, the radius is 3 and the diameter is 6. Circumference = πd or 6π. Choice (D) is the correct answer.

Sample Items (4 options)

S6.   80 is $12\frac{1}{2}\%$ of what number?

   (A) 10
   (B) 64
   (C) 100
   (D) 640

   $12\frac{1}{2}\% = \frac{1}{8}$; $80 = \frac{1}{8} \times x$; $x = 640$. Choice (D) is the correct answer.

S7.   If $a = 5b$, then $\frac{3}{5}a =$

   (A) $\frac{5}{3}b$

   (B) $\frac{3}{5}b$

   (C) $3b$

   (D) $\frac{b}{3}$

   $\frac{3}{5} \times 5b = 3b$. Choice (C) is the correct answer.

S8.   A purse contains 28 coins in nickels and dimes. The ratio of nickels to dimes is 3:4. What is the value of the dimes?

(A) 20¢
(B) 60¢
(C) $1.00
(D) $1.60

Let $3x$ = number of nickels and $4x$ = number of dimes. $3x + 4x = 7x$; $7x = 28$; $x = 4$; $4x = 4 \times 4 =$ 16 dimes, worth $1.60. Choice (D) is the correct answer.

S9.   Which of the following sets of angles can be the three angles of a triangle?

(A) 30°, 40°, 50°
(B) 30°, 45°, 90°
(C) 30°, 60°, 80°
(D) 30°, 65°, 85°

The three angles of the triangle must add up to 180°. 30° + 65° + 85° = 180°. Choice (D) is the correct answer.

S10.   Water is poured into a cylindrical tank at the rate of 9 cubic inches a minute. How long will it take to fill the tank if its radius is 3 inches and its height is 14 inches?

(A) 41 minutes
(B) 44 minutes
(C) 47 minutes
(D) 50 minutes

$\pi r^2 \times$ height = volume; $\pi \times 3^2 \times 14$ = volume; volume = $\frac{22 \times 9 \times 14}{7}$ = 396; 396 cubic inches divided by 9 cubic inches per minute = 44 minutes. Choice (B) is the correct answer.

DATA INTERPRETATION

Questions on data interpretation appear in Subtest 4 of the Air Force Officer Qualifying Test. They are designed to measure ability to interpret data from tables and graphs. In general, each table and graph is followed by two, three, or four questions pertaining to that table or graph.

Although numerical ability is not needed to read tables and graphs, their interpretation requires numerical ability plus analytical ability and the ability to draw conclusions. Arithmetic reasoning is involved in the analysis and interpretation of the data presented. The types of graphs generally used in such test questions are bar graphs, line graphs, circle graphs, and pictographs.

Sample questions to illustrate some of the types of questions that appear in the data interpretation subtest follow. Solutions to these sample questions are given to show how the correct answers are obtained.

Sample Items (5 options)

Answer questions S1 and S2 on the basis of the table given below.

POPULATION OF GEOGRAPHICAL CITY

District	1980	1990
Central	14,248	14,717
North	26,273	26,020
South	16,982	15,392
East	18,095	19,871
West	2,219	2,954
Total:	77,817	78,954

S1.   For which district was the change in number of residents greatest between 1980 and 1990?

(A) Central
(B) North
(C) South
(D) East
(E) West

S2.   In 1990, the population of East District was approximately what fraction of the total population of Geographical City?

(A) $\dfrac{1}{8}$

(B) $\dfrac{1}{5}$

(C) $\dfrac{1}{4}$

(D) $\dfrac{1}{3}$

(E) $\dfrac{1}{2}$

For question S1, subtract 1980 population figure from 1990 figure for each district. The greatest difference is in East District, which gained 1,776 (19,871 − 18,095 = 1,776). Choice (D) is the correct answer.

For question S2, the population of East District was approximately 25% of the total population of Geographical City ($\frac{20,000}{79,000}$ = .25). As this is equivalent to $\frac{1}{4}$, choice (C) is the correct answer.

Answer questions S3 through S5 on the basis of the data contained in the following graph.

RAINFALL IN DAMPTOWN (IN INCHES) JANUARY–DECEMBER

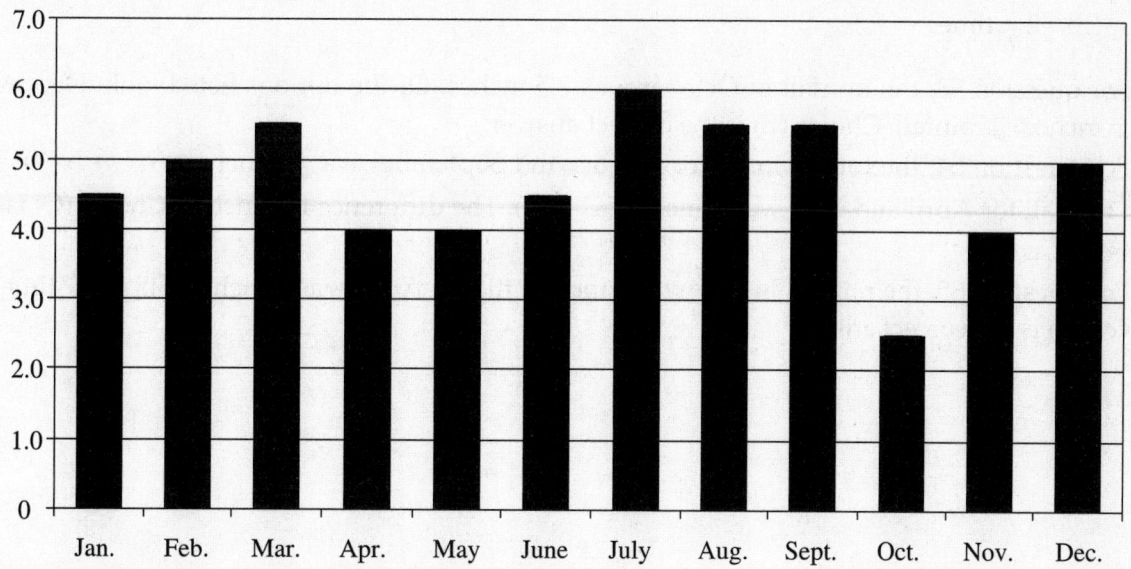

S3. The rainfall in October was one-half the rainfall in

(A) March.
(B) June.
(C) July.
(D) November.
(E) December.

S4. The total rainfall for August and September exceeded the total rainfall for April and May by

(A) 2 inches.

(B) $2\frac{1}{2}$ inches.

(C) 3 inches.

(D) $3\frac{1}{2}$ inches.

(E) 4 inches.

S5.   How many times greater was the rainfall in July than in April?

(A) $1\frac{1}{4}$ times

(B) $1\frac{1}{2}$ times

(C) 2 times

(D) $2\frac{1}{4}$ times

(E) $2\frac{1}{2}$ times

For question S3, the rainfall in October was 2.5 inches. Of the options listed, only December had 5 inches of rainfall. Choice (E) is the correct answer.

For question S4, the total rainfall for August and September was 11 inches ($5\frac{1}{2}''+5\frac{1}{2}''$). The total rainfall for April and May was 8 inches (4″ + 4″). The difference is 3 inches. Choice (C) is the correct answer.

For question S5, the rainfall in July was 6 inches; that in April was 4 inches. Six is $1\frac{1}{2}$ times 4. Choice (B) is the correct answer.

GENERAL SCIENCE

Questions on general science appear as four-option items in Subtest 1 of the Armed Services Vocational Aptitude Battery (ASVAB). Most of the questions deal with life science and physical science. There are also a few questions on earth science.

The life science items deal with basic biology, human nutrition, and health. The physical science items are concerned with elementary chemistry and physics. Fundamentals of geology, meteorology, and astronomy might be included in the earth science area.

Sample questions to illustrate some of the types of questions that appear in the general science subtest follow. Solutions to these sample questions are given to show how the correct answers are obtained.

Sample Items (4 options)

S1. Organisms that sustain their life cycles by feeding off other live organisms are known as
  (A) parasites.
  (B) saprophytes.
  (C) bacteria.
  (D) viruses.

Organisms that live on or in the body of other live organisms from which food is obtained are called parasites. Choice (A) is the correct answer.

S2. Lack of iodine is often related to which of the following diseases?
  (A) Beriberi
  (B) Scurvy
  (C) Rickets
  (D) Goiter

Goiter is a disease of the thyroid gland, the body's storehouse for iodine. It may be caused by insufficient iodine in the diet. Choice (D) is the correct answer.

S3. When two or more elements combine to form a substance that has properties different from those of the component elements, that new substance is known as a (an)
  (A) mixture.
  (B) solution.
  (C) alloy.
  (D) compound.

A compound is a substance composed of two or more different elements that are chemically combined. The correct answer is choice (D).

S4. Photosynthesis is the process by which green plants manufacture carbohydrates from

(A) oxygen and nitrogen.
(B) carbon dioxide and water.
(C) oxygen and water.
(D) glucose and water.

Photosynthesis is the process by which green plants manufacture carbohydrates from carbon dioxide and water in the presence of sunlight and chlorophyll. Choice (B) is the correct answer.

S5. The primary reason designers seek to lower the center of gravity in automobiles is to

(A) reduce wind resistance.
(B) provide smoother riding.
(C) increase stability.
(D) reduce manufacturing costs.

The primary reason for lowering the center of gravity in automobiles is to give the car greater stability. Choice (C) is the correct answer.

S6. A thermometer that indicates the freezing point of water at 0 degrees and the boiling point of water at 100 degrees is called the

(A) Celsius thermometer.
(B) Fahrenheit thermometer.
(C) Reaumer thermometer.
(D) Kelvin thermometer.

With the Celsius or centigrade scale, the fixed points are the freezing and the boiling points of water. The interval is divided into 100 parts, so the freezing point of water is 0°C and the boiling point is 100°C. Choice (A) is the correct answer.

S7. "Shooting stars" are

(A) exploding stars.
(B) cosmic rays.
(C) planetoids.
(D) meteors.

Meteors, or "shooting stars," come into the earth's atmosphere from outer space with high velocity. The resistance offered by the earth's atmosphere makes these meteors incandescent in flight. Choice (D) is the correct answer.

S8. A body in space that orbits around another body is known as a

(A) moon.
(B) planet.
(C) satellite.
(D) comet.

A satellite is a small body that revolves around a planet. The moon is a satellite that revolves around the planet Earth. Choice (B) is the correct answer.

ELECTRONICS INFORMATION

Questions on electronics information appear as four-option items in Subtest 6 of the ASVAB. They are designed to ascertain your knowledge of electrical, radio, and electronics information.

Sample questions to illustrate some of the types of questions that appear in the electronics information subtest follow. Solutions to these sample questions are also given.

Sample Items (4 options)

S1. The safest way to run an extension cord to a lamp is

(A) under a rug.
(B) along a baseboard.
(C) under a sofa.
(D) behind a sofa.

The safest way would be to run it along a baseboard where there would be little likelihood of it being tampered with. Choice (B) is the correct answer.

S2. What does the abbreviation AC stand for?

(A) Additional charge
(B) Alternating coil
(C) Alternating current
(D) Ampere current

AC is a standard electrical abbreviation and stands for alternating current. Choice (C) is the correct answer.

S3. Most electrical problems involving voltage, resistance, and current are solved by applying

(A) Ohm's law.
(B) Watt's law.
(C) Coulomb's law.
(D) Kirchoff's voltage and current laws.

Ohm's law describes the relationship between the voltage, current, and resistance in a circuit: $V = IR$. The watts consumed by a circuit are the product of the voltage times the current. One ampere flowing for 1 second delivers 1 coulomb of electrical charge. Kirchoff's voltage and current laws concern the way voltages and currents around a circuit can be summed up. Choice (A) is correct.

S4. Electronic circuits designed to produce high-frequency alternating currents are usually known as

(A) oscillators.
(B) amplifiers.
(C) rectifiers.
(D) detectors.

Oscillators capable of producing high-frequency AC might include crystals capable of producing particular frequencies, or they might involve electronic components, such as capacitors and inductors, capable of being tuned to various frequencies. Choice (A) is the correct answer.

S5. Which one of the following devices converts heat energy directly into electrical energy?

(A) A piezoelectrical crystal
(B) A photoelectric cell
(C) A steam-driven generator
(D) A thermocouple

Thermocouples usually consist of connections between wires of two dissimilar metals. They are frequently calibrated so that the amount of voltage produced can be directly related to the temperature. They are thus capable of measuring temperatures. Choice (D) is the correct answer.

S6. One use of a coaxial cable is to

(A) ground a signal.
(B) pass a signal from the set to the antenna of a mobile unit.
(C) carry the signal from a ballast tube.
(D) carry grid signals in high-altitude areas.

Coaxial cable consists of an inner conducting wire covered with insulation and run inside a concentric cylindrical outer conductor. TV antenna lead-in wires of the 75-ohm variety are examples of coaxial cables. Coaxial cables are used principally to minimize signal loss between antennas and either receiving or transmitting sets. Choice (B) is the correct answer.

S7. Which of the following has the least resistance?

(A) Silver
(B) Aluminum
(C) Copper
(D) Steel

All of the materials listed are conductors. Silver is the best, although it is not often used because of its high cost. The moving contacts in motor starters, however, are often made of silver, and it is widely used where low-resistance contacts are required. Choice (A) is the correct answer.

S8. In electronic circuits, the symbol shown below usually represents a

(A) transformer.
(B) capacitor.
(C) transistor.
(D) diode.

The symbol shows a semiconductor diode. These usually contain silicon and sometimes germanium. They conduct only in the direction shown by the arrow. Currents flowing in the opposite direction meet with high resistance and are effectively blocked. For these reasons, silicon diodes are often used to rectify AC to DC. Choice (D) is the correct answer.

MECHANICAL COMPREHENSION

Questions on mechanical comprehension are widely used by the military. They appear as three-option items in the Mechanical Comprehension Test of the Navy and Marine Corps Aviation Selection Test Battery. The results on the Mechanical Comprehension Test are combined with the results on the Math/Verbal Test to arrive at the Officer Aptitude Rating (OAR).

Mechanical comprehension test items require an understanding of mechanical principles that comes from observing the physical world, working with or operating mechanical devices, or reading and studying.

Sample questions illustrating some of the types of questions on mechanical comprehension that might be found in this test follow. Solutions to these sample questions are given to show how the correct answers are obtained.

Sample Items (3 options)

Study each diagram carefully and select the choice that best answers the question or completes the statement.

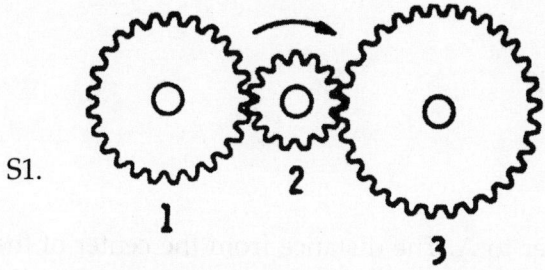

S1.

Which of the other gears is moving in the same direction as gear 2?
(A) Gear 1
(B) Gear 3
(C) Neither of the gears

The arrow indicates that gear 2 is moving clockwise. This would cause both gear 1 and gear 3 to move counterclockwise. Choice (C) is the correct answer.

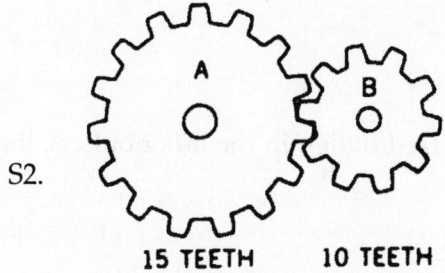

S2.

If gear A makes 30 revolutions, gear B will make
(A) 40
(B) 45
(C) 50

For every revolution made by gear A, gear B will make $1\frac{1}{2}$ times as many. If gear A makes 30 revolutions, gear B will make 45. Choice (B) is the correct answer.

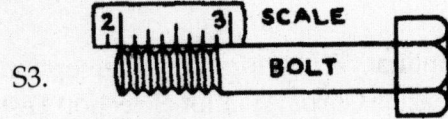

S3.

The number of threads per inch on the bolt is
(A) 7
(B) 8
(C) 10

The bolt thread makes one revolution per $\frac{1}{8}$ inch. Accordingly, it has 8 threads in 1 inch. Choice (B) is the correct answer.

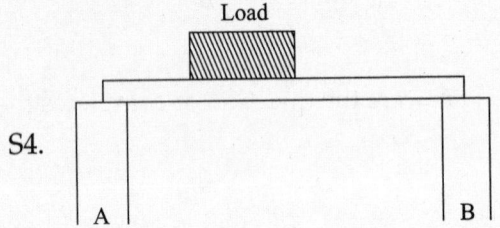

S4.

Which post holds up the greater part of the load?
(A) Post A
(B) Post B
(C) Both are equal

The weight of the load is not centered but is closer to A. The distance from the center of the load to A is less than the distance from the center of the load to B. Therefore, post A would support the greater part of the load. Choice (A) is the correct answer.

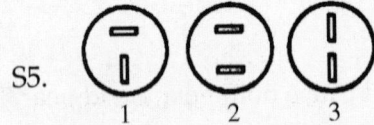

S5.

The convenience outlet that is known as a *polarized* outlet is number
(A) 1
(B) 2
(C) 3

The plug can go into the outlet in only one way in a polarized outlet. In the other outlets, the plug can be reversed. Choice (A) is the correct answer.

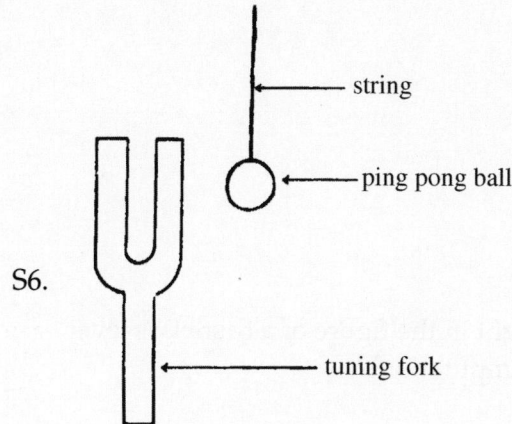

S6.

When the tuning fork is struck, the Ping-Pong ball will
(A) remain stationary.
(B) bounce up and down.
(C) swing away from the tuning fork.

When a tuning fork vibrates, it moves currents of air. This vibrating air would cause the Ping-Pong ball to be pushed away. Choice (C) is the correct answer.

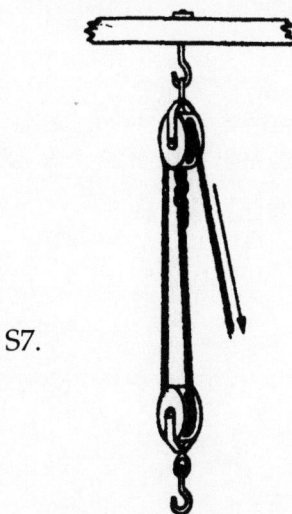

S7.

In the figure shown above, the pulley system consists of a fixed block and a movable block. The theoretical mechanical advantage is

(A) 2
(B) 3
(C) 4

The number of parts of the rope going to and from the movable block indicates the mechanical advantage. In this case, it is 2. Choice (A) is the correct answer.

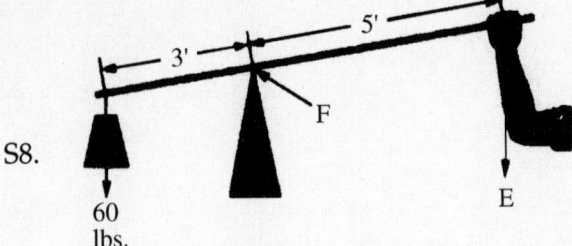

S8.

What effort must be exerted to lift a 60-pound weight in the figure of a first-class lever shown above (disregard weight of lever in your computation)?

(A) 36 pounds
(B) 45 pounds
(C) 48 pounds

Let x = effort that must be exerted.

$60 \times 3 = x \times 5; 5x = 180; x = \frac{180}{5} = 36.$

Choice (A) is the correct answer.

PART VI

Suggested Study Plan for Test Preparation

HOW TO USE THE PRACTICE EXERCISES AND SPECIMEN TESTS

This part contains basic information on the tests used by each branch of service in selecting officer candidates, followed by specific information as to which practice exercises and specimen tests to review for each officer selection test.

Based on the branch of service you are interested in and applying for, determine which practice exercises and specimen tests are pertinent. Do these practice exercises and take the specimen tests, recording your answers as directed in the spaces provided. Work carefully but quickly, simulating actual test conditions as much as possible.

After completing each practice exercise and specimen test or subtest, refer to the key answers to ascertain the number of questions you answered correctly and to note the questions you did not answer correctly and those you are still unsure of despite the fact that you selected the right answer.

Look these questions over carefully. Read the rationale. Be sure you fully understand why your answer was wrong, why the key answer is the correct answer, and the reasoning used to arrive at the correct answer. This is one of the most important benefits to be derived from doing these practice exercises and taking these specimen tests. It will increase your test-taking ability, improve your test sophistication, broaden your knowledge, and enable you to obtain a higher score on the real test.

Those interested in flight training should obtain a copy of the companion book, ARCO *Military Flight Aptitude Tests*.

U.S. AIR FORCE

AIR FORCE OFFICER QUALIFYING TEST (AFOQT)

Subtests	Pilot	AFOQT Composites Navigator-Technical	Academic Aptitude
Verbal Analogies	X		X
Arithmetic Reasoning		X	X
Reading Comprehension			X
Data Interpretation		X	X
Word Knowledge			X
Math Knowledge		X	X
Mechanical Comprehension	X	X	
Electrical Maze	X	X	
Scale Reading	X	X	
Instrument Comprehension	X		
Block Counting	X	X	
Table Reading	X	X	
Aviation Information	X		
Rotated Blocks		X	
General Science		X	
Hidden Figures		X	

The AFOQT, published in several booklets, contains 380 test items and requires a total of $4\frac{1}{2}$ hours of administrative and testing time. The test is administered on a monthly basis. Thousands of applicants are tested each year.

Although applicants are required to take all AFOQT subtests, the Academic Aptitude composite is the relevant composite used in selecting individuals for Officer Training School (OTS).

To prepare for the AFOQT Academic Aptitude composite:

- Complete the following practice exercises:

Practice Exercise	Subject
1	Synonyms
2	Verbal Analogies
3	Reading Comprehension
4	Arithmetic Reasoning
5	Math Knowledge
6	Data Interpretation

Use the sample answer sheet on pages 129–131 for recording your answers to the questions appearing on these subtests.

- Take the specimen subtests in Part IX, Air Force Officer Qualifying Test (AFOQT), on pages 263–300:

Subtest Number	Subject
1	Verbal Analogies
2	Arithmetic Reasoning
3	Reading Comprehension
4	Data Interpretation
5	Word Knowledge
6	Math Knowledge

U.S. ARMY

Test Areas	Aptitude Composites ASVAB General Technical Composite (GT)
General Science	X
Arithmetic Reasoning	X
Word Knowledge	X
Paragraph Comprehension	X
Mathematics Knowledge	
Electronics Information	
Auto and Shop Information	
Mechanical Comprehension	
Assembling Objects	

Test requirements are an aptitude area General Technical (GT)* score of 110 or higher.

* The GT aptitude area consists of Arithmetic Reasoning, Word Knowledge, and Paragraph Comprehension. It is derived from the Academic Ability composite on the Armed Services Vocational Aptitude Battery (ASVAB).

To prepare for Army officer tests:
- Complete the following practice exercises:

Practice Exercise	Subject
1	Synonyms
3	Reading Comprehension
4	Arithmetic Reasoning

- Take the specimen tests in Part X, pages 321–350, Armed Services Vocational Aptitude Battery:

Test Number	Subject
2	Arithmetic Reasoning
3	Word Knowledge
4	Paragraph Comprehension

U.S. NAVY

	Composites					
	Academic Qualification Rating (AQR)	Pilot Flight Aptitude Rating (PFAR)	Flight Officer Flight Aptitude Rating (FOFAR)	Pilot Biograph- ical Interest (PBI)	Flight Officer Biograph- ical Interest (FOBI)	Officer Aptitude Rating (OAR)
Math/Verbal (MVT)	X	X	X			X
Mechanical Comprehension (MCT)	X	X				X
Spatial Apperception (SAT)	X	X	X			
Aviation/Nautical Information (ANT)	X	X	X			
Biographical Information (BI)				X	X	

To qualify for the Officer Candidate Schools, applicants must achieve a qualifying score on the Officer Aptitude Rating (OAR), a composite formed from the scores received on the Math/Verbal Test and the Mechanical Comprehension Test of the Navy and Marine Corps Aviation Selection Test Battery.

The Math/Verbal Test measures quantitative aptitude (arithmetic reasoning, general mathematics, algebra, and plane geometry) and verbal aptitude (sentence comprehension).

The Mechanical Comprehension Test measures mechanical aptitude (understanding of the principles involved in the operation of mechanical devices, basic physics, and so on).

Although applicants are encouraged by the Navy to take all tests comprising the Navy and Marine Corps Aviation Selection Test Battery, those interested in obtaining a commission only and not in flight training are permitted to take only the Math/Verbal Test and the Mechanical Comprehension Test. The Officer Aptitude Rating (OAR) is the relevant composite used in selecting individuals for the Officer Candidate Schools.

To prepare for Navy officer candidate tests:
  • Complete the following practice exercises:

Practice Exercise	Subject
3	Reading Comprehension
4	Arithmetic Reasoning
5	Math Knowledge
10	Mechanical Comprehension

  • Then take the following tests on the specimen Navy and Marine Corps Aviation Selection Test Battery, pages 371–386.

Test Number	Subject
1	Math/Verbal Test
2	Mechanical Comprehension Test

U.S. MARINE CORPS

Tests	Aptitude Composite ASVAB Composite
Arithmetic Reasoning	X
Mathematics Knowledge	X
General Science	X
Electronics Information	X

A bachelor's degree is required for a Marine Corps commission. In addition, applicants must have: (1) a minimum combined score of 1000 on the verbal and math sections of the Scholastic Aptitude Test (SAT), (2) a minimum combined math and verbal score of 45 on the American College Test (ACT), or *(3) a minimum converted score of 120 (a waiver may be granted down to 115) on the composite of the ASVAB*; derived from the scores received on the following ASVAB tests:

Arithmetic Reasoning
General Science
Mathematics Knowledge
Electronics Information

* Those who have the required minimum combined score in the SAT or ACT are not given the ASVAB.

To qualify on the basis of the above composite score on the Armed Services Vocational Aptitude Battery:

- Complete the following practice exercises:

Practice Exercise	Subject
4	Arithmetic Reasoning
5	Math Knowledge
7	General Science
8	Electronics Information

- Take the following tests of the specimen Armed Services Vocational Aptitude Battery on pages 321–350.

Test Number	Subject
1	General Science (GS)
2	Arithmetic Reasoning (AR)
5	Mathematics Knowledge (MK)
6	Electronics Information (EI)

U.S. COAST GUARD

	Composites					
	Academic Qualification Rating (AQR)	Pilot Flight Aptitude Rating (PFAR)	Flight Officer Flight Aptitude Rating (FOFAR)	Pilot Biograph- ical Interest (PBI)	Flight Officer Biograph- ical Interest (FOBI)	Officer Aptitude Rating (OAR)
Math/Verbal (MVT)	X	X	X			X
Mechanical Comprehension (MCT)	X	X				X
Spatial Apperception (SAT)	X	X	X			
Aviation/Nautical Information (ANT)	X	X	X			
Biographical Information (BI)				X	X	

To qualify for Officer Candidate School, applicants must achieve a qualifying score on the SAT or ACT Assessment. Those interested in obtaining a commission only and not in flight training should refer to ARCO *Master the SAT* or ARCO *Master the ACT Assessment*.

Only applicants for flight training are required by the Coast Guard to take the Navy and Marine Corps Aviation Selection Test Battery. Those interested in flight training should refer to ARCO *Military Flight Aptitude Tests*, but may begin preparation for the first two tests of the battery in this book.

To prepare for the Navy and Marine Corps Aviation Selection Test Battery:

- Complete the following practice exercises:

Practice Exercise	Subject
3	Reading Comprehension
5	Arithmetic Reasoning
6	Math Knowledge
13	Mechanical Comprehension

- Then take the following tests on the specimen Navy and Marine Corps Aviation Selection Test Battery, pages 371–386.

Test Number	Subject
1	Math/Verbal Test
2	Mechanical Comprehension Test

PART VII

Practice Exercises

ANSWER SHEET FOR PRACTICE EXERCISES

Practice Exercise 1

1. Ⓐ Ⓑ Ⓒ Ⓓ Ⓔ	21. Ⓐ Ⓑ Ⓒ Ⓓ Ⓔ	41. Ⓐ Ⓑ Ⓒ Ⓓ Ⓔ	61. Ⓐ Ⓑ Ⓒ Ⓓ	81. Ⓐ Ⓑ Ⓒ Ⓓ
2. Ⓐ Ⓑ Ⓒ Ⓓ Ⓔ	22. Ⓐ Ⓑ Ⓒ Ⓓ Ⓔ	42. Ⓐ Ⓑ Ⓒ Ⓓ Ⓔ	62. Ⓐ Ⓑ Ⓒ Ⓓ	82. Ⓐ Ⓑ Ⓒ Ⓓ
3. Ⓐ Ⓑ Ⓒ Ⓓ Ⓔ	23. Ⓐ Ⓑ Ⓒ Ⓓ Ⓔ	43. Ⓐ Ⓑ Ⓒ Ⓓ Ⓔ	63. Ⓐ Ⓑ Ⓒ Ⓓ	83. Ⓐ Ⓑ Ⓒ Ⓓ
4. Ⓐ Ⓑ Ⓒ Ⓓ Ⓔ	24. Ⓐ Ⓑ Ⓒ Ⓓ Ⓔ	44. Ⓐ Ⓑ Ⓒ Ⓓ Ⓔ	64. Ⓐ Ⓑ Ⓒ Ⓓ	84. Ⓐ Ⓑ Ⓒ Ⓓ
5. Ⓐ Ⓑ Ⓒ Ⓓ Ⓔ	25. Ⓐ Ⓑ Ⓒ Ⓓ Ⓔ	45. Ⓐ Ⓑ Ⓒ Ⓓ Ⓔ	65. Ⓐ Ⓑ Ⓒ Ⓓ	85. Ⓐ Ⓑ Ⓒ Ⓓ
6. Ⓐ Ⓑ Ⓒ Ⓓ Ⓔ	26. Ⓐ Ⓑ Ⓒ Ⓓ Ⓔ	46. Ⓐ Ⓑ Ⓒ Ⓓ Ⓔ	66. Ⓐ Ⓑ Ⓒ Ⓓ	86. Ⓐ Ⓑ Ⓒ Ⓓ
7. Ⓐ Ⓑ Ⓒ Ⓓ Ⓔ	27. Ⓐ Ⓑ Ⓒ Ⓓ Ⓔ	47. Ⓐ Ⓑ Ⓒ Ⓓ Ⓔ	67. Ⓐ Ⓑ Ⓒ Ⓓ	87. Ⓐ Ⓑ Ⓒ Ⓓ
8. Ⓐ Ⓑ Ⓒ Ⓓ Ⓔ	28. Ⓐ Ⓑ Ⓒ Ⓓ Ⓔ	48. Ⓐ Ⓑ Ⓒ Ⓓ Ⓔ	68. Ⓐ Ⓑ Ⓒ Ⓓ	88. Ⓐ Ⓑ Ⓒ Ⓓ
9. Ⓐ Ⓑ Ⓒ Ⓓ Ⓔ	29. Ⓐ Ⓑ Ⓒ Ⓓ Ⓔ	49. Ⓐ Ⓑ Ⓒ Ⓓ Ⓔ	69. Ⓐ Ⓑ Ⓒ Ⓓ	89. Ⓐ Ⓑ Ⓒ Ⓓ
10. Ⓐ Ⓑ Ⓒ Ⓓ Ⓔ	30. Ⓐ Ⓑ Ⓒ Ⓓ Ⓔ	50. Ⓐ Ⓑ Ⓒ Ⓓ Ⓔ	70. Ⓐ Ⓑ Ⓒ Ⓓ	90. Ⓐ Ⓑ Ⓒ Ⓓ
11. Ⓐ Ⓑ Ⓒ Ⓓ Ⓔ	31. Ⓐ Ⓑ Ⓒ Ⓓ Ⓔ	51. Ⓐ Ⓑ Ⓒ Ⓓ	71. Ⓐ Ⓑ Ⓒ Ⓓ	91. Ⓐ Ⓑ Ⓒ Ⓓ
12. Ⓐ Ⓑ Ⓒ Ⓓ Ⓔ	32. Ⓐ Ⓑ Ⓒ Ⓓ Ⓔ	52. Ⓐ Ⓑ Ⓒ Ⓓ	72. Ⓐ Ⓑ Ⓒ Ⓓ	92. Ⓐ Ⓑ Ⓒ Ⓓ
13. Ⓐ Ⓑ Ⓒ Ⓓ Ⓔ	33. Ⓐ Ⓑ Ⓒ Ⓓ Ⓔ	53. Ⓐ Ⓑ Ⓒ Ⓓ	73. Ⓐ Ⓑ Ⓒ Ⓓ	93. Ⓐ Ⓑ Ⓒ Ⓓ
14. Ⓐ Ⓑ Ⓒ Ⓓ Ⓔ	34. Ⓐ Ⓑ Ⓒ Ⓓ Ⓔ	54. Ⓐ Ⓑ Ⓒ Ⓓ	74. Ⓐ Ⓑ Ⓒ Ⓓ	94. Ⓐ Ⓑ Ⓒ Ⓓ
15. Ⓐ Ⓑ Ⓒ Ⓓ Ⓔ	35. Ⓐ Ⓑ Ⓒ Ⓓ Ⓔ	55. Ⓐ Ⓑ Ⓒ Ⓓ	75. Ⓐ Ⓑ Ⓒ Ⓓ	95. Ⓐ Ⓑ Ⓒ Ⓓ
16. Ⓐ Ⓑ Ⓒ Ⓓ Ⓔ	36. Ⓐ Ⓑ Ⓒ Ⓓ Ⓔ	56. Ⓐ Ⓑ Ⓒ Ⓓ	76. Ⓐ Ⓑ Ⓒ Ⓓ	96. Ⓐ Ⓑ Ⓒ Ⓓ
17. Ⓐ Ⓑ Ⓒ Ⓓ Ⓔ	37. Ⓐ Ⓑ Ⓒ Ⓓ Ⓔ	57. Ⓐ Ⓑ Ⓒ Ⓓ	77. Ⓐ Ⓑ Ⓒ Ⓓ	97. Ⓐ Ⓑ Ⓒ Ⓓ
18. Ⓐ Ⓑ Ⓒ Ⓓ Ⓔ	38. Ⓐ Ⓑ Ⓒ Ⓓ Ⓔ	58. Ⓐ Ⓑ Ⓒ Ⓓ	78. Ⓐ Ⓑ Ⓒ Ⓓ	98. Ⓐ Ⓑ Ⓒ Ⓓ
19. Ⓐ Ⓑ Ⓒ Ⓓ Ⓔ	39. Ⓐ Ⓑ Ⓒ Ⓓ Ⓔ	59. Ⓐ Ⓑ Ⓒ Ⓓ	79. Ⓐ Ⓑ Ⓒ Ⓓ	99. Ⓐ Ⓑ Ⓒ Ⓓ
20. Ⓐ Ⓑ Ⓒ Ⓓ Ⓔ	40. Ⓐ Ⓑ Ⓒ Ⓓ Ⓔ	60. Ⓐ Ⓑ Ⓒ Ⓓ	80. Ⓐ Ⓑ Ⓒ Ⓓ	100. Ⓐ Ⓑ Ⓒ Ⓓ

Practice Exercise 2

1. Ⓐ Ⓑ Ⓒ Ⓓ Ⓔ	11. Ⓐ Ⓑ Ⓒ Ⓓ Ⓔ	21. Ⓐ Ⓑ Ⓒ Ⓓ Ⓔ	31. Ⓐ Ⓑ Ⓒ Ⓓ Ⓔ	41. Ⓐ Ⓑ Ⓒ Ⓓ Ⓔ
2. Ⓐ Ⓑ Ⓒ Ⓓ Ⓔ	12. Ⓐ Ⓑ Ⓒ Ⓓ Ⓔ	22. Ⓐ Ⓑ Ⓒ Ⓓ Ⓔ	32. Ⓐ Ⓑ Ⓒ Ⓓ Ⓔ	42. Ⓐ Ⓑ Ⓒ Ⓓ Ⓔ
3. Ⓐ Ⓑ Ⓒ Ⓓ Ⓔ	13. Ⓐ Ⓑ Ⓒ Ⓓ Ⓔ	23. Ⓐ Ⓑ Ⓒ Ⓓ Ⓔ	33. Ⓐ Ⓑ Ⓒ Ⓓ Ⓔ	43. Ⓐ Ⓑ Ⓒ Ⓓ Ⓔ
4. Ⓐ Ⓑ Ⓒ Ⓓ Ⓔ	14. Ⓐ Ⓑ Ⓒ Ⓓ Ⓔ	24. Ⓐ Ⓑ Ⓒ Ⓓ Ⓔ	34. Ⓐ Ⓑ Ⓒ Ⓓ Ⓔ	44. Ⓐ Ⓑ Ⓒ Ⓓ Ⓔ
5. Ⓐ Ⓑ Ⓒ Ⓓ Ⓔ	15. Ⓐ Ⓑ Ⓒ Ⓓ Ⓔ	25. Ⓐ Ⓑ Ⓒ Ⓓ Ⓔ	35. Ⓐ Ⓑ Ⓒ Ⓓ Ⓔ	45. Ⓐ Ⓑ Ⓒ Ⓓ Ⓔ
6. Ⓐ Ⓑ Ⓒ Ⓓ Ⓔ	16. Ⓐ Ⓑ Ⓒ Ⓓ Ⓔ	26. Ⓐ Ⓑ Ⓒ Ⓓ Ⓔ	36. Ⓐ Ⓑ Ⓒ Ⓓ Ⓔ	46. Ⓐ Ⓑ Ⓒ Ⓓ Ⓔ
7. Ⓐ Ⓑ Ⓒ Ⓓ Ⓔ	17. Ⓐ Ⓑ Ⓒ Ⓓ Ⓔ	27. Ⓐ Ⓑ Ⓒ Ⓓ Ⓔ	37. Ⓐ Ⓑ Ⓒ Ⓓ Ⓔ	47. Ⓐ Ⓑ Ⓒ Ⓓ Ⓔ
8. Ⓐ Ⓑ Ⓒ Ⓓ Ⓔ	18. Ⓐ Ⓑ Ⓒ Ⓓ Ⓔ	28. Ⓐ Ⓑ Ⓒ Ⓓ Ⓔ	38. Ⓐ Ⓑ Ⓒ Ⓓ Ⓔ	48. Ⓐ Ⓑ Ⓒ Ⓓ Ⓔ
9. Ⓐ Ⓑ Ⓒ Ⓓ Ⓔ	19. Ⓐ Ⓑ Ⓒ Ⓓ Ⓔ	29. Ⓐ Ⓑ Ⓒ Ⓓ Ⓔ	39. Ⓐ Ⓑ Ⓒ Ⓓ Ⓔ	49. Ⓐ Ⓑ Ⓒ Ⓓ Ⓔ
10. Ⓐ Ⓑ Ⓒ Ⓓ Ⓔ	20. Ⓐ Ⓑ Ⓒ Ⓓ Ⓔ	30. Ⓐ Ⓑ Ⓒ Ⓓ Ⓔ	40. Ⓐ Ⓑ Ⓒ Ⓓ Ⓔ	50. Ⓐ Ⓑ Ⓒ Ⓓ Ⓔ

Practice Exercise 3

1. Ⓐ Ⓑ Ⓒ Ⓓ Ⓔ	16. Ⓐ Ⓑ Ⓒ Ⓓ Ⓔ	31. Ⓐ Ⓑ Ⓒ Ⓓ	46. Ⓐ Ⓑ Ⓒ Ⓓ	61. Ⓐ Ⓑ Ⓒ Ⓓ
2. Ⓐ Ⓑ Ⓒ Ⓓ Ⓔ	17. Ⓐ Ⓑ Ⓒ Ⓓ Ⓔ	32. Ⓐ Ⓑ Ⓒ Ⓓ	47. Ⓐ Ⓑ Ⓒ Ⓓ	62. Ⓐ Ⓑ Ⓒ Ⓓ
3. Ⓐ Ⓑ Ⓒ Ⓓ Ⓔ	18. Ⓐ Ⓑ Ⓒ Ⓓ Ⓔ	33. Ⓐ Ⓑ Ⓒ Ⓓ	48. Ⓐ Ⓑ Ⓒ Ⓓ	63. Ⓐ Ⓑ Ⓒ Ⓓ
4. Ⓐ Ⓑ Ⓒ Ⓓ Ⓔ	19. Ⓐ Ⓑ Ⓒ Ⓓ Ⓔ	34. Ⓐ Ⓑ Ⓒ Ⓓ	49. Ⓐ Ⓑ Ⓒ Ⓓ	64. Ⓐ Ⓑ Ⓒ Ⓓ
5. Ⓐ Ⓑ Ⓒ Ⓓ Ⓔ	20. Ⓐ Ⓑ Ⓒ Ⓓ Ⓔ	35. Ⓐ Ⓑ Ⓒ Ⓓ	50. Ⓐ Ⓑ Ⓒ Ⓓ	65. Ⓐ Ⓑ Ⓒ Ⓓ
6. Ⓐ Ⓑ Ⓒ Ⓓ Ⓔ	21. Ⓐ Ⓑ Ⓒ Ⓓ Ⓔ	36. Ⓐ Ⓑ Ⓒ Ⓓ	51. Ⓐ Ⓑ Ⓒ Ⓓ	66. Ⓐ Ⓑ Ⓒ Ⓓ
7. Ⓐ Ⓑ Ⓒ Ⓓ Ⓔ	22. Ⓐ Ⓑ Ⓒ Ⓓ Ⓔ	37. Ⓐ Ⓑ Ⓒ Ⓓ	52. Ⓐ Ⓑ Ⓒ Ⓓ	67. Ⓐ Ⓑ Ⓒ Ⓓ
8. Ⓐ Ⓑ Ⓒ Ⓓ Ⓔ	23. Ⓐ Ⓑ Ⓒ Ⓓ Ⓔ	38. Ⓐ Ⓑ Ⓒ Ⓓ	53. Ⓐ Ⓑ Ⓒ Ⓓ	68. Ⓐ Ⓑ Ⓒ Ⓓ
9. Ⓐ Ⓑ Ⓒ Ⓓ Ⓔ	24. Ⓐ Ⓑ Ⓒ Ⓓ Ⓔ	39. Ⓐ Ⓑ Ⓒ Ⓓ	54. Ⓐ Ⓑ Ⓒ Ⓓ	69. Ⓐ Ⓑ Ⓒ Ⓓ
10. Ⓐ Ⓑ Ⓒ Ⓓ Ⓔ	25. Ⓐ Ⓑ Ⓒ Ⓓ Ⓔ	40. Ⓐ Ⓑ Ⓒ Ⓓ	55. Ⓐ Ⓑ Ⓒ Ⓓ	70. Ⓐ Ⓑ Ⓒ Ⓓ
11. Ⓐ Ⓑ Ⓒ Ⓓ Ⓔ	26. Ⓐ Ⓑ Ⓒ Ⓓ Ⓔ	41. Ⓐ Ⓑ Ⓒ Ⓓ	56. Ⓐ Ⓑ Ⓒ Ⓓ	71. Ⓐ Ⓑ Ⓒ Ⓓ
12. Ⓐ Ⓑ Ⓒ Ⓓ Ⓔ	27. Ⓐ Ⓑ Ⓒ Ⓓ	42. Ⓐ Ⓑ Ⓒ Ⓓ	57. Ⓐ Ⓑ Ⓒ Ⓓ	72. Ⓐ Ⓑ Ⓒ Ⓓ
13. Ⓐ Ⓑ Ⓒ Ⓓ Ⓔ	28. Ⓐ Ⓑ Ⓒ Ⓓ	43. Ⓐ Ⓑ Ⓒ Ⓓ	58. Ⓐ Ⓑ Ⓒ Ⓓ	73. Ⓐ Ⓑ Ⓒ Ⓓ
14. Ⓐ Ⓑ Ⓒ Ⓓ Ⓔ	29. Ⓐ Ⓑ Ⓒ Ⓓ	44. Ⓐ Ⓑ Ⓒ Ⓓ	59. Ⓐ Ⓑ Ⓒ Ⓓ	74. Ⓐ Ⓑ Ⓒ Ⓓ
15. Ⓐ Ⓑ Ⓒ Ⓓ Ⓔ	30. Ⓐ Ⓑ Ⓒ Ⓓ	45. Ⓐ Ⓑ Ⓒ Ⓓ	60. Ⓐ Ⓑ Ⓒ Ⓓ	75. Ⓐ Ⓑ Ⓒ Ⓓ

Practice Exercise 4

1. Ⓐ Ⓑ Ⓒ Ⓓ Ⓔ	16. Ⓐ Ⓑ Ⓒ Ⓓ Ⓔ	31. Ⓐ Ⓑ Ⓒ Ⓓ Ⓔ	46. Ⓐ Ⓑ Ⓒ Ⓓ Ⓔ	61. Ⓐ Ⓑ Ⓒ Ⓓ
2. Ⓐ Ⓑ Ⓒ Ⓓ Ⓔ	17. Ⓐ Ⓑ Ⓒ Ⓓ Ⓔ	32. Ⓐ Ⓑ Ⓒ Ⓓ Ⓔ	47. Ⓐ Ⓑ Ⓒ Ⓓ Ⓔ	62. Ⓐ Ⓑ Ⓒ Ⓓ
3. Ⓐ Ⓑ Ⓒ Ⓓ Ⓔ	18. Ⓐ Ⓑ Ⓒ Ⓓ Ⓔ	33. Ⓐ Ⓑ Ⓒ Ⓓ Ⓔ	48. Ⓐ Ⓑ Ⓒ Ⓓ Ⓔ	63. Ⓐ Ⓑ Ⓒ Ⓓ
4. Ⓐ Ⓑ Ⓒ Ⓓ Ⓔ	19. Ⓐ Ⓑ Ⓒ Ⓓ Ⓔ	34. Ⓐ Ⓑ Ⓒ Ⓓ Ⓔ	49. Ⓐ Ⓑ Ⓒ Ⓓ Ⓔ	64. Ⓐ Ⓑ Ⓒ Ⓓ
5. Ⓐ Ⓑ Ⓒ Ⓓ Ⓔ	20. Ⓐ Ⓑ Ⓒ Ⓓ Ⓔ	35. Ⓐ Ⓑ Ⓒ Ⓓ Ⓔ	50. Ⓐ Ⓑ Ⓒ Ⓓ Ⓔ	65. Ⓐ Ⓑ Ⓒ Ⓓ
6. Ⓐ Ⓑ Ⓒ Ⓓ Ⓔ	21. Ⓐ Ⓑ Ⓒ Ⓓ Ⓔ	36. Ⓐ Ⓑ Ⓒ Ⓓ Ⓔ	51. Ⓐ Ⓑ Ⓒ Ⓓ	66. Ⓐ Ⓑ Ⓒ Ⓓ
7. Ⓐ Ⓑ Ⓒ Ⓓ Ⓔ	22. Ⓐ Ⓑ Ⓒ Ⓓ Ⓔ	37. Ⓐ Ⓑ Ⓒ Ⓓ Ⓔ	52. Ⓐ Ⓑ Ⓒ Ⓓ	67. Ⓐ Ⓑ Ⓒ Ⓓ
8. Ⓐ Ⓑ Ⓒ Ⓓ Ⓔ	23. Ⓐ Ⓑ Ⓒ Ⓓ Ⓔ	38. Ⓐ Ⓑ Ⓒ Ⓓ Ⓔ	53. Ⓐ Ⓑ Ⓒ Ⓓ	68. Ⓐ Ⓑ Ⓒ Ⓓ
9. Ⓐ Ⓑ Ⓒ Ⓓ Ⓔ	24. Ⓐ Ⓑ Ⓒ Ⓓ Ⓔ	39. Ⓐ Ⓑ Ⓒ Ⓓ Ⓔ	54. Ⓐ Ⓑ Ⓒ Ⓓ	69. Ⓐ Ⓑ Ⓒ Ⓓ
10. Ⓐ Ⓑ Ⓒ Ⓓ Ⓔ	25. Ⓐ Ⓑ Ⓒ Ⓓ Ⓔ	40. Ⓐ Ⓑ Ⓒ Ⓓ Ⓔ	55. Ⓐ Ⓑ Ⓒ Ⓓ	70. Ⓐ Ⓑ Ⓒ Ⓓ
11. Ⓐ Ⓑ Ⓒ Ⓓ Ⓔ	26. Ⓐ Ⓑ Ⓒ Ⓓ Ⓔ	41. Ⓐ Ⓑ Ⓒ Ⓓ Ⓔ	56. Ⓐ Ⓑ Ⓒ Ⓓ	71. Ⓐ Ⓑ Ⓒ Ⓓ
12. Ⓐ Ⓑ Ⓒ Ⓓ Ⓔ	27. Ⓐ Ⓑ Ⓒ Ⓓ Ⓔ	42. Ⓐ Ⓑ Ⓒ Ⓓ Ⓔ	57. Ⓐ Ⓑ Ⓒ Ⓓ	72. Ⓐ Ⓑ Ⓒ Ⓓ
13. Ⓐ Ⓑ Ⓒ Ⓓ Ⓔ	28. Ⓐ Ⓑ Ⓒ Ⓓ Ⓔ	43. Ⓐ Ⓑ Ⓒ Ⓓ Ⓔ	58. Ⓐ Ⓑ Ⓒ Ⓓ	73. Ⓐ Ⓑ Ⓒ Ⓓ
14. Ⓐ Ⓑ Ⓒ Ⓓ Ⓔ	29. Ⓐ Ⓑ Ⓒ Ⓓ Ⓔ	44. Ⓐ Ⓑ Ⓒ Ⓓ Ⓔ	59. Ⓐ Ⓑ Ⓒ Ⓓ	74. Ⓐ Ⓑ Ⓒ Ⓓ
15. Ⓐ Ⓑ Ⓒ Ⓓ Ⓔ	30. Ⓐ Ⓑ Ⓒ Ⓓ Ⓔ	45. Ⓐ Ⓑ Ⓒ Ⓓ Ⓔ	60. Ⓐ Ⓑ Ⓒ Ⓓ	75. Ⓐ Ⓑ Ⓒ Ⓓ

Practice Exercise 5

1. Ⓐ Ⓑ Ⓒ Ⓓ Ⓔ	16. Ⓐ Ⓑ Ⓒ Ⓓ Ⓔ	31. Ⓐ Ⓑ Ⓒ Ⓓ Ⓔ	46. Ⓐ Ⓑ Ⓒ Ⓓ Ⓔ	61. Ⓐ Ⓑ Ⓒ Ⓓ
2. Ⓐ Ⓑ Ⓒ Ⓓ Ⓔ	17. Ⓐ Ⓑ Ⓒ Ⓓ Ⓔ	32. Ⓐ Ⓑ Ⓒ Ⓓ Ⓔ	47. Ⓐ Ⓑ Ⓒ Ⓓ Ⓔ	62. Ⓐ Ⓑ Ⓒ Ⓓ
3. Ⓐ Ⓑ Ⓒ Ⓓ Ⓔ	18. Ⓐ Ⓑ Ⓒ Ⓓ Ⓔ	33. Ⓐ Ⓑ Ⓒ Ⓓ Ⓔ	48. Ⓐ Ⓑ Ⓒ Ⓓ Ⓔ	63. Ⓐ Ⓑ Ⓒ Ⓓ
4. Ⓐ Ⓑ Ⓒ Ⓓ Ⓔ	19. Ⓐ Ⓑ Ⓒ Ⓓ Ⓔ	34. Ⓐ Ⓑ Ⓒ Ⓓ Ⓔ	49. Ⓐ Ⓑ Ⓒ Ⓓ Ⓔ	64. Ⓐ Ⓑ Ⓒ Ⓓ
5. Ⓐ Ⓑ Ⓒ Ⓓ Ⓔ	20. Ⓐ Ⓑ Ⓒ Ⓓ Ⓔ	35. Ⓐ Ⓑ Ⓒ Ⓓ Ⓔ	50. Ⓐ Ⓑ Ⓒ Ⓓ Ⓔ	65. Ⓐ Ⓑ Ⓒ Ⓓ
6. Ⓐ Ⓑ Ⓒ Ⓓ Ⓔ	21. Ⓐ Ⓑ Ⓒ Ⓓ Ⓔ	36. Ⓐ Ⓑ Ⓒ Ⓓ Ⓔ	51. Ⓐ Ⓑ Ⓒ Ⓓ	66. Ⓐ Ⓑ Ⓒ Ⓓ
7. Ⓐ Ⓑ Ⓒ Ⓓ Ⓔ	22. Ⓐ Ⓑ Ⓒ Ⓓ Ⓔ	37. Ⓐ Ⓑ Ⓒ Ⓓ Ⓔ	52. Ⓐ Ⓑ Ⓒ Ⓓ	67. Ⓐ Ⓑ Ⓒ Ⓓ
8. Ⓐ Ⓑ Ⓒ Ⓓ Ⓔ	23. Ⓐ Ⓑ Ⓒ Ⓓ Ⓔ	38. Ⓐ Ⓑ Ⓒ Ⓓ Ⓔ	53. Ⓐ Ⓑ Ⓒ Ⓓ	68. Ⓐ Ⓑ Ⓒ Ⓓ
9. Ⓐ Ⓑ Ⓒ Ⓓ Ⓔ	24. Ⓐ Ⓑ Ⓒ Ⓓ Ⓔ	39. Ⓐ Ⓑ Ⓒ Ⓓ Ⓔ	54. Ⓐ Ⓑ Ⓒ Ⓓ	69. Ⓐ Ⓑ Ⓒ Ⓓ
10. Ⓐ Ⓑ Ⓒ Ⓓ Ⓔ	25. Ⓐ Ⓑ Ⓒ Ⓓ Ⓔ	40. Ⓐ Ⓑ Ⓒ Ⓓ Ⓔ	55. Ⓐ Ⓑ Ⓒ Ⓓ	70. Ⓐ Ⓑ Ⓒ Ⓓ
11. Ⓐ Ⓑ Ⓒ Ⓓ Ⓔ	26. Ⓐ Ⓑ Ⓒ Ⓓ Ⓔ	41. Ⓐ Ⓑ Ⓒ Ⓓ Ⓔ	56. Ⓐ Ⓑ Ⓒ Ⓓ	71. Ⓐ Ⓑ Ⓒ Ⓓ
12. Ⓐ Ⓑ Ⓒ Ⓓ Ⓔ	27. Ⓐ Ⓑ Ⓒ Ⓓ Ⓔ	42. Ⓐ Ⓑ Ⓒ Ⓓ Ⓔ	57. Ⓐ Ⓑ Ⓒ Ⓓ	72. Ⓐ Ⓑ Ⓒ Ⓓ
13. Ⓐ Ⓑ Ⓒ Ⓓ Ⓔ	28. Ⓐ Ⓑ Ⓒ Ⓓ Ⓔ	43. Ⓐ Ⓑ Ⓒ Ⓓ Ⓔ	58. Ⓐ Ⓑ Ⓒ Ⓓ	73. Ⓐ Ⓑ Ⓒ Ⓓ
14. Ⓐ Ⓑ Ⓒ Ⓓ Ⓔ	29. Ⓐ Ⓑ Ⓒ Ⓓ Ⓔ	44. Ⓐ Ⓑ Ⓒ Ⓓ Ⓔ	59. Ⓐ Ⓑ Ⓒ Ⓓ	74. Ⓐ Ⓑ Ⓒ Ⓓ
15. Ⓐ Ⓑ Ⓒ Ⓓ Ⓔ	30. Ⓐ Ⓑ Ⓒ Ⓓ Ⓔ	45. Ⓐ Ⓑ Ⓒ Ⓓ Ⓔ	60. Ⓐ Ⓑ Ⓒ Ⓓ	75. Ⓐ Ⓑ Ⓒ Ⓓ

Practice Exercise 6

1. Ⓐ Ⓑ Ⓒ Ⓓ Ⓔ	11. Ⓐ Ⓑ Ⓒ Ⓓ Ⓔ	21. Ⓐ Ⓑ Ⓒ Ⓓ Ⓔ	31. Ⓐ Ⓑ Ⓒ Ⓓ Ⓔ	41. Ⓐ Ⓑ Ⓒ Ⓓ Ⓔ
2. Ⓐ Ⓑ Ⓒ Ⓓ Ⓔ	12. Ⓐ Ⓑ Ⓒ Ⓓ Ⓔ	22. Ⓐ Ⓑ Ⓒ Ⓓ Ⓔ	32. Ⓐ Ⓑ Ⓒ Ⓓ Ⓔ	42. Ⓐ Ⓑ Ⓒ Ⓓ Ⓔ
3. Ⓐ Ⓑ Ⓒ Ⓓ Ⓔ	13. Ⓐ Ⓑ Ⓒ Ⓓ Ⓔ	23. Ⓐ Ⓑ Ⓒ Ⓓ Ⓔ	33. Ⓐ Ⓑ Ⓒ Ⓓ Ⓔ	43. Ⓐ Ⓑ Ⓒ Ⓓ Ⓔ
4. Ⓐ Ⓑ Ⓒ Ⓓ Ⓔ	14. Ⓐ Ⓑ Ⓒ Ⓓ Ⓔ	24. Ⓐ Ⓑ Ⓒ Ⓓ Ⓔ	34. Ⓐ Ⓑ Ⓒ Ⓓ Ⓔ	44. Ⓐ Ⓑ Ⓒ Ⓓ Ⓔ
5. Ⓐ Ⓑ Ⓒ Ⓓ Ⓔ	15. Ⓐ Ⓑ Ⓒ Ⓓ Ⓔ	25. Ⓐ Ⓑ Ⓒ Ⓓ Ⓔ	35. Ⓐ Ⓑ Ⓒ Ⓓ Ⓔ	45. Ⓐ Ⓑ Ⓒ Ⓓ Ⓔ
6. Ⓐ Ⓑ Ⓒ Ⓓ Ⓔ	16. Ⓐ Ⓑ Ⓒ Ⓓ Ⓔ	26. Ⓐ Ⓑ Ⓒ Ⓓ Ⓔ	36. Ⓐ Ⓑ Ⓒ Ⓓ Ⓔ	46. Ⓐ Ⓑ Ⓒ Ⓓ Ⓔ
7. Ⓐ Ⓑ Ⓒ Ⓓ Ⓔ	17. Ⓐ Ⓑ Ⓒ Ⓓ Ⓔ	27. Ⓐ Ⓑ Ⓒ Ⓓ Ⓔ	37. Ⓐ Ⓑ Ⓒ Ⓓ Ⓔ	47. Ⓐ Ⓑ Ⓒ Ⓓ Ⓔ
8. Ⓐ Ⓑ Ⓒ Ⓓ Ⓔ	18. Ⓐ Ⓑ Ⓒ Ⓓ Ⓔ	28. Ⓐ Ⓑ Ⓒ Ⓓ Ⓔ	38. Ⓐ Ⓑ Ⓒ Ⓓ Ⓔ	48. Ⓐ Ⓑ Ⓒ Ⓓ Ⓔ
9. Ⓐ Ⓑ Ⓒ Ⓓ Ⓔ	19. Ⓐ Ⓑ Ⓒ Ⓓ Ⓔ	29. Ⓐ Ⓑ Ⓒ Ⓓ Ⓔ	39. Ⓐ Ⓑ Ⓒ Ⓓ Ⓔ	49. Ⓐ Ⓑ Ⓒ Ⓓ Ⓔ
10. Ⓐ Ⓑ Ⓒ Ⓓ Ⓔ	20. Ⓐ Ⓑ Ⓒ Ⓓ Ⓔ	30. Ⓐ Ⓑ Ⓒ Ⓓ Ⓔ	40. Ⓐ Ⓑ Ⓒ Ⓓ Ⓔ	50. Ⓐ Ⓑ Ⓒ Ⓓ Ⓔ

Practice Exercise 7

1. Ⓐ Ⓑ Ⓒ Ⓓ	11. Ⓐ Ⓑ Ⓒ Ⓓ	21. Ⓐ Ⓑ Ⓒ Ⓓ	31. Ⓐ Ⓑ Ⓒ Ⓓ	41. Ⓐ Ⓑ Ⓒ Ⓓ
2. Ⓐ Ⓑ Ⓒ Ⓓ	12. Ⓐ Ⓑ Ⓒ Ⓓ	22. Ⓐ Ⓑ Ⓒ Ⓓ	32. Ⓐ Ⓑ Ⓒ Ⓓ	42. Ⓐ Ⓑ Ⓒ Ⓓ
3. Ⓐ Ⓑ Ⓒ Ⓓ	13. Ⓐ Ⓑ Ⓒ Ⓓ	23. Ⓐ Ⓑ Ⓒ Ⓓ	33. Ⓐ Ⓑ Ⓒ Ⓓ	43. Ⓐ Ⓑ Ⓒ Ⓓ
4. Ⓐ Ⓑ Ⓒ Ⓓ	14. Ⓐ Ⓑ Ⓒ Ⓓ	24. Ⓐ Ⓑ Ⓒ Ⓓ	34. Ⓐ Ⓑ Ⓒ Ⓓ	44. Ⓐ Ⓑ Ⓒ Ⓓ
5. Ⓐ Ⓑ Ⓒ Ⓓ	15. Ⓐ Ⓑ Ⓒ Ⓓ	25. Ⓐ Ⓑ Ⓒ Ⓓ	35. Ⓐ Ⓑ Ⓒ Ⓓ	45. Ⓐ Ⓑ Ⓒ Ⓓ
6. Ⓐ Ⓑ Ⓒ Ⓓ	16. Ⓐ Ⓑ Ⓒ Ⓓ	26. Ⓐ Ⓑ Ⓒ Ⓓ	36. Ⓐ Ⓑ Ⓒ Ⓓ	46. Ⓐ Ⓑ Ⓒ Ⓓ
7. Ⓐ Ⓑ Ⓒ Ⓓ	17. Ⓐ Ⓑ Ⓒ Ⓓ	27. Ⓐ Ⓑ Ⓒ Ⓓ	37. Ⓐ Ⓑ Ⓒ Ⓓ	47. Ⓐ Ⓑ Ⓒ Ⓓ
8. Ⓐ Ⓑ Ⓒ Ⓓ	18. Ⓐ Ⓑ Ⓒ Ⓓ	28. Ⓐ Ⓑ Ⓒ Ⓓ	38. Ⓐ Ⓑ Ⓒ Ⓓ	48. Ⓐ Ⓑ Ⓒ Ⓓ
9. Ⓐ Ⓑ Ⓒ Ⓓ	19. Ⓐ Ⓑ Ⓒ Ⓓ	29. Ⓐ Ⓑ Ⓒ Ⓓ	39. Ⓐ Ⓑ Ⓒ Ⓓ	49. Ⓐ Ⓑ Ⓒ Ⓓ
10. Ⓐ Ⓑ Ⓒ Ⓓ	20. Ⓐ Ⓑ Ⓒ Ⓓ	30. Ⓐ Ⓑ Ⓒ Ⓓ	40. Ⓐ Ⓑ Ⓒ Ⓓ	50. Ⓐ Ⓑ Ⓒ Ⓓ

Practice Exercise 8

1. Ⓐ Ⓑ Ⓒ Ⓓ	11. Ⓐ Ⓑ Ⓒ Ⓓ	21. Ⓐ Ⓑ Ⓒ Ⓓ	31. Ⓐ Ⓑ Ⓒ Ⓓ	41. Ⓐ Ⓑ Ⓒ Ⓓ
2. Ⓐ Ⓑ Ⓒ Ⓓ	12. Ⓐ Ⓑ Ⓒ Ⓓ	22. Ⓐ Ⓑ Ⓒ Ⓓ	32. Ⓐ Ⓑ Ⓒ Ⓓ	42. Ⓐ Ⓑ Ⓒ Ⓓ
3. Ⓐ Ⓑ Ⓒ Ⓓ	13. Ⓐ Ⓑ Ⓒ Ⓓ	23. Ⓐ Ⓑ Ⓒ Ⓓ	33. Ⓐ Ⓑ Ⓒ Ⓓ	43. Ⓐ Ⓑ Ⓒ Ⓓ
4. Ⓐ Ⓑ Ⓒ Ⓓ	14. Ⓐ Ⓑ Ⓒ Ⓓ	24. Ⓐ Ⓑ Ⓒ Ⓓ	34. Ⓐ Ⓑ Ⓒ Ⓓ	44. Ⓐ Ⓑ Ⓒ Ⓓ
5. Ⓐ Ⓑ Ⓒ Ⓓ	15. Ⓐ Ⓑ Ⓒ Ⓓ	25. Ⓐ Ⓑ Ⓒ Ⓓ	35. Ⓐ Ⓑ Ⓒ Ⓓ	45. Ⓐ Ⓑ Ⓒ Ⓓ
6. Ⓐ Ⓑ Ⓒ Ⓓ	16. Ⓐ Ⓑ Ⓒ Ⓓ	26. Ⓐ Ⓑ Ⓒ Ⓓ	36. Ⓐ Ⓑ Ⓒ Ⓓ	46. Ⓐ Ⓑ Ⓒ Ⓓ
7. Ⓐ Ⓑ Ⓒ Ⓓ	17. Ⓐ Ⓑ Ⓒ Ⓓ	27. Ⓐ Ⓑ Ⓒ Ⓓ	37. Ⓐ Ⓑ Ⓒ Ⓓ	47. Ⓐ Ⓑ Ⓒ Ⓓ
8. Ⓐ Ⓑ Ⓒ Ⓓ	18. Ⓐ Ⓑ Ⓒ Ⓓ	28. Ⓐ Ⓑ Ⓒ Ⓓ	38. Ⓐ Ⓑ Ⓒ Ⓓ	48. Ⓐ Ⓑ Ⓒ Ⓓ
9. Ⓐ Ⓑ Ⓒ Ⓓ	19. Ⓐ Ⓑ Ⓒ Ⓓ	29. Ⓐ Ⓑ Ⓒ Ⓓ	39. Ⓐ Ⓑ Ⓒ Ⓓ	49. Ⓐ Ⓑ Ⓒ Ⓓ
10. Ⓐ Ⓑ Ⓒ Ⓓ	20. Ⓐ Ⓑ Ⓒ Ⓓ	30. Ⓐ Ⓑ Ⓒ Ⓓ	40. Ⓐ Ⓑ Ⓒ Ⓓ	50. Ⓐ Ⓑ Ⓒ Ⓓ

Practice Exercise 9

1. Ⓐ Ⓑ Ⓒ	11. Ⓐ Ⓑ Ⓒ	21. Ⓐ Ⓑ Ⓒ	31. Ⓐ Ⓑ Ⓒ	41. Ⓐ Ⓑ Ⓒ
2. Ⓐ Ⓑ Ⓒ	12. Ⓐ Ⓑ Ⓒ	22. Ⓐ Ⓑ Ⓒ	32. Ⓐ Ⓑ Ⓒ	42. Ⓐ Ⓑ Ⓒ
3. Ⓐ Ⓑ Ⓒ	13. Ⓐ Ⓑ Ⓒ	23. Ⓐ Ⓑ Ⓒ	33. Ⓐ Ⓑ Ⓒ	43. Ⓐ Ⓑ Ⓒ
4. Ⓐ Ⓑ Ⓒ	14. Ⓐ Ⓑ Ⓒ	24. Ⓐ Ⓑ Ⓒ	34. Ⓐ Ⓑ Ⓒ	44. Ⓐ Ⓑ Ⓒ
5. Ⓐ Ⓑ Ⓒ	15. Ⓐ Ⓑ Ⓒ	25. Ⓐ Ⓑ Ⓒ	35. Ⓐ Ⓑ Ⓒ	45. Ⓐ Ⓑ Ⓒ
6. Ⓐ Ⓑ Ⓒ	16. Ⓐ Ⓑ Ⓒ	26. Ⓐ Ⓑ Ⓒ	36. Ⓐ Ⓑ Ⓒ	46. Ⓐ Ⓑ Ⓒ
7. Ⓐ Ⓑ Ⓒ	17. Ⓐ Ⓑ Ⓒ	27. Ⓐ Ⓑ Ⓒ	37. Ⓐ Ⓑ Ⓒ	47. Ⓐ Ⓑ Ⓒ
8. Ⓐ Ⓑ Ⓒ	18. Ⓐ Ⓑ Ⓒ	28. Ⓐ Ⓑ Ⓒ	38. Ⓐ Ⓑ Ⓒ	48. Ⓐ Ⓑ Ⓒ
9. Ⓐ Ⓑ Ⓒ	19. Ⓐ Ⓑ Ⓒ	29. Ⓐ Ⓑ Ⓒ	39. Ⓐ Ⓑ Ⓒ	49. Ⓐ Ⓑ Ⓒ
10. Ⓐ Ⓑ Ⓒ	20. Ⓐ Ⓑ Ⓒ	30. Ⓐ Ⓑ Ⓒ	40. Ⓐ Ⓑ Ⓒ	50. Ⓐ Ⓑ Ⓒ

PRACTICE EXERCISE 1: SYNONYMS

Questions 1–50 are five-option items. For each question, select the option that means the same or most nearly the same as the capitalized word. Answers are on page 217.

1. ABRIDGED
   - (A) alphabetized
   - (B) expanded
   - (C) linked
   - (D) researched
   - (E) shortened

2. ACUMEN
   - (A) caution
   - (B) inability
   - (C) keenness
   - (D) sarcasm
   - (E) strictness

3. ANARCHY
   - (A) chaos
   - (B) competition
   - (C) danger
   - (D) rule
   - (E) secrecy

4. APATHY
   - (A) aptness
   - (B) indifference
   - (C) poverty
   - (D) sickness
   - (E) sorrow

5. ASSIDUOUS
   - (A) amenable
   - (B) enthusiastic
   - (C) neglectful
   - (D) persistent
   - (E) sarcastic

6. BELLIGERENT
   - (A) artistic
   - (B) furious
   - (C) hostile
   - (D) loud
   - (E) worldly

7. BIZARRE
   - (A) accurate
   - (B) ancient
   - (C) fantastic
   - (D) market
   - (E) solvent

8. BUOYANT
   - (A) cautious
   - (B) conceited
   - (C) resilient
   - (D) resistant
   - (E) youthful

9. CAPITULATE
   - (A) destroy
   - (B) finance
   - (C) repeat
   - (D) retreat
   - (E) surrender

10. CENSURE
    - (A) appraise
    - (B) blame
    - (C) count
    - (D) pause
    - (E) withhold

11. CHARLATAN
    - (A) guest
    - (B) official
    - (C) quack
    - (D) specialist
    - (E) stranger

12. COLLATE

(A) assemble
(B) copy
(C) mix
(D) prepare
(E) separate

13. COMPETENT

(A) capable
(B) caring
(C) courteous
(D) inept
(E) informed

14. CONSTRUE

(A) build
(B) contradict
(C) interpret
(D) misrepresent
(E) question

15. CREDIBLE

(A) believable
(B) correct
(C) gullible
(D) intelligent
(E) obvious

16. CONTRITION

(A) abrasion
(B) controversy
(C) insistence
(D) intolerance
(E) repentance

17. DELETE

(A) complete
(B) damage
(C) delay
(D) exclude
(E) retain

18. DERISION

(A) anger
(B) disguise
(C) fear
(D) heredity
(E) ridicule

19. DETERRENT

(A) cleansing
(B) concluding
(C) deciding
(D) defending
(E) restraining

20. DISSEMINATE

(A) disagree
(B) slander
(C) spread
(D) strip
(E) unite

21. DIVERGENCE

(A) annoyance
(B) difference
(C) distraction
(D) entertainment
(E) revenge

22. ENERVATE

(A) approximate
(B) energize
(C) exact
(D) invite
(E) weaken

23. EXCESS

(A) exit
(B) failure
(C) inflation
(D) luxury
(E) surplus

24. EXTANT

(A) destroyed
(B) out-of-date
(C) profound
(D) still existing
(E) widespread

25. FALLACIOUS

(A) logical
(B) misleading
(C) obscene
(D) reasonable
(E) solemn

26. FUNDAMENTAL
    (A) accessible
    (B) difficult
    (C) essential
    (D) financial
    (E) serious

27. GHASTLY
    (A) breathless
    (B) frightening
    (C) furious
    (D) hasty
    (E) spiritual

28. ILLICIT
    (A) insignificant
    (B) overpowering
    (C) secret
    (D) unlawful
    (E) unreadable

29. INDIGENT
    (A) angry
    (B) crowded
    (C) foreign
    (D) natural
    (E) poor

30. INNATE
    (A) acquired
    (B) eternal
    (C) internal
    (D) native
    (E) prospective

31. INTREPID
    (A) complicated
    (B) cowardly
    (C) fanciful
    (D) fearless
    (E) willing

32. LIAISON
    (A) laziness
    (B) permission
    (C) satisfaction
    (D) scarf
    (E) tie

33. LUDICROUS
    (A) excessive
    (B) ridiculous
    (C) profitable
    (D) shallow
    (E) superior

34. MANDATORY
    (A) evident
    (B) insane
    (C) obligatory
    (D) strategic
    (E) undesirable

35. MOBILE
    (A) assembled
    (B) mechanical
    (C) movable
    (D) scornful
    (E) stationary

36. NEGOTIATE
    (A) bargain
    (B) exhaust
    (C) speak
    (D) suffer
    (E) think

37. NOXIOUS
    (A) gaseous
    (B) harmful
    (C) immoral
    (D) oily
    (E) repulsive

38. OFFICIOUS
    (A) arbitrary
    (B) brutal
    (C) meddlesome
    (D) unreasonable
    (E) vulgar

39. PLIGHT
    (A) conspiracy
    (B) departure
    (C) predicament
    (D) stamp
    (E) weight

40. PROFICIENCY
    (A) aptitude
    (B) expertness
    (C) sincerity
    (D) tolerance
    (E) wisdom

41. RECALCITRANT
    (A) defendant
    (B) obedient
    (C) obstinate
    (D) powder
    (E) unconcerned

42. REDUNDANT
    (A) concise
    (B) informed
    (C) reappearing
    (D) superfluous
    (E) unclear

43. REGALE
    (A) adjust
    (B) annoy
    (C) beat
    (D) delight
    (E) return

44. RELINQUISH
    (A) abandon
    (B) pursue
    (C) regret
    (D) secure
    (E) unite

45. SCRUPULOUS
    (A) careful
    (B) intricate
    (C) neurotic
    (D) persistent
    (E) unprincipled

46. SUBTERFUGE
    (A) confirmation
    (B) deception
    (C) excuse
    (D) flight
    (E) substitute

47. SURREPTITIOUS
    (A) complicated
    (B) magnificent
    (C) repetitive
    (D) stealthy
    (E) unbelievable

48. TURBID
    (A) clear
    (B) cloudy
    (C) flowing
    (D) swollen
    (E) twisted

49. VACILLATE
    (A) humiliate
    (B) inoculate
    (C) relinquish
    (D) waver
    (E) withdraw

50. VINDICTIVE
    (A) aggressive
    (B) boastful
    (C) impolite
    (D) revengeful
    (E) unconcerned

Questions 51–100 are four-option items. For each question, select the option that means the same or most nearly the same as the underlined word.

51. We were told to abandon the ship.
    (A) encompass
    (B) infiltrate
    (C) quarantine
    (D) relinquish

52. Acquired most nearly means
    (A) desired
    (B) obtained
    (C) plowed
    (D) sold

53. The door was left <u>ajar</u>.

    (A) blocked
    (B) locked
    (C) open
    (D) unlocked

54. <u>Alias</u> most nearly means

    (A) enemy
    (B) hero
    (C) other name
    (D) sidekick

55. <u>Approximate</u> most nearly means

    (A) mathematically correct
    (B) nearly exact
    (C) remarkable
    (D) worthless

56. <u>Assemble</u> most nearly means

    (A) bring together
    (B) examine carefully
    (C) fill
    (D) locate

57. The <u>captive</u> was treated kindly.

    (A) jailer
    (B) prisoner
    (C) savage
    (D) spy

58. Did the storm <u>cease</u> during the night?

    (A) change
    (B) continue
    (C) start
    (D) stop

59. <u>Commended</u> most nearly means

    (A) blamed
    (B) praised
    (C) promoted
    (D) reprimanded

60. <u>Concisely</u> most nearly means

    (A) accurately
    (B) briefly
    (C) fully
    (D) officially

61. The police officer <u>consoled</u> the weeping child.

    (A) carried home
    (B) comforted
    (C) found
    (D) scolded

62. The reply will be <u>conveyed</u> by messenger.

    (A) carried
    (B) damaged
    (C) guarded
    (D) refused

63. <u>Customary</u> most nearly means

    (A) common
    (B) curious
    (C) difficult
    (D) necessary

64. The foreman <u>defended</u> the striking workers.

    (A) delayed
    (B) informed on
    (C) protected
    (D) shot at

65. <u>Deportment</u> most nearly means

    (A) attendance
    (B) behavior
    (C) intelligence
    (D) neatness

66. The town will <u>erect</u> the bridge.

    (A) construct
    (B) design
    (C) destroy
    (D) paint

67. <u>Fictitious</u> most nearly means

    (A) easy to remember
    (B) imaginary
    (C) odd
    (D) well known

68. <u>Flexible</u> most nearly means

    (A) athletic
    (B) pliable
    (C) rigid
    (D) weak

69. <u>Forthcoming</u> events are published daily.

    (A) approaching
    (B) interesting
    (C) social
    (D) weekly

70. <u>Frugal</u> most nearly means

    (A) economical
    (B) expendable
    (C) musical
    (D) profitable

71. <u>Grimy</u> most nearly means

    (A) dirty
    (B) ill-fitted
    (C) poorly made
    (D) ragged

72. <u>Hollow</u> most nearly means

    (A) brittle
    (B) empty
    (C) rough
    (D) smooth

73. The judge ruled it to be <u>immaterial</u>.

    (A) not debatable
    (B) unclear
    (C) unimportant
    (D) unpredictable

74. <u>Impose</u> most nearly means

    (A) disguise
    (B) escape
    (C) prescribe
    (D) purchase

75. <u>Increment</u> most nearly means

    (A) an account
    (B) an improvision
    (C) an increase
    (D) a specification

76. <u>Insignificant</u> most nearly means

    (A) secret
    (B) thrilling
    (C) unimportant
    (D) unpleasant

77. The fog horn sounded <u>intermittently</u>.

    (A) annually
    (B) at irregular intervals
    (C) constantly
    (D) continuously

78. <u>Itinerant</u> most nearly means

    (A) aggressive
    (B) ignorant
    (C) shrewd
    (D) traveling

79. <u>Juvenile</u> most nearly means

    (A) delinquent
    (B) humorous
    (C) lovesick
    (D) youthful

80. The machine has <u>manual</u> controls.

    (A) handmade
    (B) hand-operated
    (C) self-acting
    (D) simple

81. We <u>misconstrued</u> what she had said.

    (A) followed directions
    (B) ignored
    (C) interpreted erroneously
    (D) strongly disagreed

82. <u>Pedestrian</u> most nearly means

    (A) passenger
    (B) street-crosser
    (C) traffic light
    (D) walker

83. The <u>preface</u> of the book was very interesting.

    (A) appendix
    (B) introduction
    (C) table of contents
    (D) title page

84. <u>Prior</u> most nearly means

    (A) earlier
    (B) more attractive
    (C) more urgent
    (D) personal

85. <u>Punctual</u> most nearly means

(A) polite
(B) prompt
(C) proper
(D) thoughtful

86. <u>Resolve</u> most nearly means

(A) decide
(B) forget
(C) recall
(D) understand

87. <u>Revenue</u> most nearly means

(A) expenses
(B) income
(C) produce
(D) taxes

88. <u>Rudiments</u> most nearly means

(A) basic procedures
(B) minute details
(C) rough manners
(D) ship's rudders

89. <u>Self-sufficient</u> most nearly means

(A) clever
(B) conceited
(C) independent
(D) stubborn

90. <u>Solidity</u> most nearly means

(A) color
(B) firmness
(C) smoothness
(D) unevenness

91. The classroom has <u>stationary</u> desks.

(A) carved
(B) heavy
(C) not movable
(D) written-upon

92. <u>Stench</u> most nearly means

(A) dead animal
(B) foul odor
(C) pile of debris
(D) puddle of slimy water

93. <u>Sullen</u> most nearly means

(A) angrily silent
(B) grayish yellow
(C) soaking wet
(D) very dirty

94. His answer was a <u>superficial</u> one.

(A) cursory
(B) excellent
(C) official
(D) profound

95. All service was <u>suspended</u> during the emergency.

(A) checked carefully
(B) regulated strictly
(C) stopped temporarily
(D) turned back

96. <u>Terse</u> most nearly means

(A) concise
(B) lengthy
(C) oral
(D) trivial

97. The cyclist pedaled at a <u>uniform</u> rate.

(A) increasing
(B) unchanging
(C) unusual
(D) very slow

98. <u>Urgent</u> most nearly means

(A) exciting
(B) pressing
(C) startling
(D) sudden

99. <u>Verdict</u> most nearly means

(A) approval
(B) arrival
(C) decision
(D) sentence

100. <u>Villainous</u> most nearly means

(A) dignified
(B) homely
(C) untidy
(D) wicked

PRACTICE EXERCISE 2: VERBAL ANALOGIES

Questions 1–20 consist of a pair of capitalized words and a third capitalized word that is related to one of the five options in the same way that the first capitalized word is related to the second capitalized word. Choose the option that, when paired with the third capitalized word, shows a relationship similar to the one shown by the first and second capitalized words. Answers are on page 221.

1. ARTIST is to EASEL as WEAVER is to
   (A) cloth
   (B) garment
   (C) loom
   (D) pattern
   (E) yarn

2. AUTOMOBILE is to HIGHWAY as TRAIN is to
   (A) axles
   (B) cars
   (C) rails
   (D) schedule
   (E) wheels

3. BIOGRAPHY is to FACT as NOVEL is to
   (A) art
   (B) book
   (C) fiction
   (D) history
   (E) library

4. CROWD is to PERSONS as FLEET is to
   (A) convoy
   (B) firepower
   (C) guns
   (D) navy
   (E) ships

5. DARKNESS is to LIGHT as STILLNESS is to
   (A) health
   (B) illness
   (C) quietness
   (D) serenity
   (E) sound

6. EFFICIENCY is to REWARD as CARELESSNESS is to
   (A) error
   (B) experience
   (C) inefficiency
   (D) reprimand
   (E) training

7. FALL is to FALLEN as FLY is to
   (A) fled
   (B) flew
   (C) flied
   (D) flown
   (E) flying

8. PORK is to HOG as MUTTON is to
   (A) cattle
   (B) deer
   (C) fowl
   (D) rabbit
   (E) sheep

9. SANDAL is to FOOT as SHAWL is to
   (A) knees
   (B) shoulders
   (C) thighs
   (D) waist
   (E) wrist

10. THEATER is to RECREATION as SCHOOL is to

    (A) education
    (B) examination
    (C) experimentation
    (D) exposition
    (E) orientation

11. III is to XIV as 3 is to

    (A) 13
    (B) 14
    (C) 15
    (D) 16
    (E) 19

12. WHEN is to TIME as HOW is to

    (A) degree
    (B) gender
    (C) manner
    (D) number
    (E) person

13. CLOCK is to TIME as THERMOMETER is to

    (A) climate
    (B) degrees
    (C) hour
    (D) temperature
    (E) weather

14. GAVEL is to JUDGE as BATON is to

    (A) carpenter
    (B) conductor
    (C) dancer
    (D) lawyer
    (E) writer

15. 1 is to 1000 as GRAM is to

    (A) centigram
    (B) hectogram
    (C) kilogram
    (D) megagram
    (E) milligram

16. SENTENCE is to PARAGRAPH as CHAPTER is to

    (A) book
    (B) magazine
    (C) novel
    (D) poem
    (E) verse

17. SEPARATE is to DIVIDE as THAW is to

    (A) dissolve
    (B) freeze
    (C) melt
    (D) rain
    (E) solidify

18. SPARROW is to BIRD as WASP is to

    (A) fish
    (B) insect
    (C) mammal
    (D) reptile
    (E) worm

19. SUBMARINE is to FISH as KITE is to

    (A) bird
    (B) boy
    (C) limousine
    (D) park
    (E) train

20. WINTER is to SUMMER as COLD is to

    (A) breezy
    (B) hot
    (C) humid
    (D) mild
    (E) warm

Questions 21–50 consist of a pair of capitalized words followed by five pairs of words. Choose the option that shows a relationship similar to the one shown by the original pair of capitalized words.

21. AFFIRM is to HINT as

    (A) accused is to dismissed
    (B) assert is to convince
    (C) charge is to insinuate
    (D) confirm is to reject
    (E) say is to deny

22. CAUTIOUS is to PRUDENT as

    (A) brave is to watchful
    (B) carefree is to ruthless
    (C) full is to summarized
    (D) greedy is to cruel
    (E) rash is to reckless

23. GLOVE is to BALL as

    (A) game is to pennant
    (B) hook is to fish
    (C) skates is to ice
    (D) stadium is to seats
    (E) winter is to weather

24. INTIMIDATE is to FEAR as

    (A) astonish is to wonder
    (B) awaken is to tiredness
    (C) feed is to hunger
    (D) maintain is to satisfaction
    (E) mirth is to sorrow

25. KICK is to FOOTBALL as

    (A) break is to pieces
    (B) kill is to bomb
    (C) message is to envelope
    (D) question is to team
    (E) smoke is to pipe

26. MIAMI is to FLORIDA as

    (A) Albany is to New York
    (B) Chicago is to the United States
    (C) Los Angeles is to San Francisco
    (D) Minneapolis is to St. Paul
    (E) Trenton is to Princeton

27. RACE is to FATIGUE as

    (A) ant is to bug
    (B) fast is to hunger
    (C) laughter is to tears
    (D) track is to athlete
    (E) walking is to running

28. STOVE is to KITCHEN as

    (A) pot is to pan
    (B) sink is to bathroom
    (C) sofa is to dinette
    (D) television is to living room
    (E) trunk is to attic

29. THROW is to BALL as

    (A) hit is to run
    (B) kill is to bullet
    (C) question is to answer
    (D) show is to tell
    (E) shoot is to gun

30. TRIANGLE is to PYRAMID as

    (A) cone is to circle
    (B) corner is to angle
    (C) pentagon is to hexagon
    (D) square is to cube
    (E) tube is to cylinder

31. WARM is to HOT as

    (A) bright is to genius
    (B) climate is to weather
    (C) enormous is to huge
    (D) glue is to paste
    (E) snow is to cold

32. WOODSMAN is to AX as

    (A) carpenter is to saw
    (B) draftsman is to ruler
    (C) mechanic is to wrench
    (D) soldier is to rifle
    (E) tailor is to needle

33. ASTUTE is to STUPID as

    (A) afraid is to ignorant
    (B) agile is to clumsy
    (C) cruel is to feeble
    (D) dislike is to despise
    (E) intelligent is to clever

34.   BRICKLAYER is to CARPENTER as
      (A)   dust is to sawdust
      (B)   house is to apartment
      (C)   mortar is to glue
      (D)   saw is to lathe
      (E)   trowel is to scalpel

35.   BOAT is to DOCK as
      (A)   airplane is to land
      (B)   bicycle is to path
      (C)   bus is to highway
      (D)   ship is to sea
      (E)   train is to depot

36.   CENTURY is to DECADE as
      (A)   day is to hour
      (B)   decade is to year
      (C)   month is to week
      (D)   week is to day
      (E)   year is to month

37.   DECIBEL is to SOUND as
      (A)   area is to distance
      (B)   calorie is to weight
      (C)   color is to light
      (D)   temperature is to weather
      (E)   volt is to electricity

38.   DEFER is to PROCRASTINATE as
      (A)   advance is to retreat
      (B)   delay is to postpone
      (C)   draft is to exempt
      (D)   hesitate is to stutter
      (E)   natural is to artificial

39.   EYE is to HURRICANE as
      (A)   hub is to spoke
      (B)   hub is to wheel
      (C)   rim is to spoke
      (D)   spoke is to wheel
      (E)   wheel is to rim

40.   FISSION is to FUSION as
      (A)   conservative is to liberal
      (B)   hydrogen is to uranium
      (C)   melt is to split
      (D)   miscellaneous is to homogeneous
      (E)   segregation is to integration

41.   GOOD is to ANGELIC as
      (A)   bad is to poor
      (B)   correct is to incorrect
      (C)   glad is to joyous
      (D)   mean is to unkind
      (E)   sweet is to sour

42.   HARE is to HOUND as
      (A)   cattle is to cow
      (B)   duckling is to duck
      (C)   lion is to lamb
      (D)   mare is to horse
      (E)   mouse is to cat

43.   HERD is to CATTLE as
      (A)   cage is to birds
      (B)   den is to thieves
      (C)   flock is to geese
      (D)   pair is to lions
      (E)   trap is to lobsters

44.   INCARCERATE is to EMANCIPATE as
      (A)   conserve is to liberate
      (B)   free is to jail
      (C)   indict is to exonerate
      (D)   investigate is to convict
      (E)   restrain is to release

45.   KEEL is to SHIP as
      (A)   engine is to car
      (B)   head is to tail
      (C)   sole is to shoe
      (D)   soul is to body
      (E)   starboard is to port

46.   LION is to CARNIVOROUS as
      (A)   bird is to aquatic
      (B)   dog is to canine
      (C)   frog is to amphibious
      (D)   horse is to herbivorous
      (E)   tiger is to ferocious

47. MARGARINE is to BUTTER as
    (A) cream is to milk
    (B) egg is to chicken
    (C) lace is to cotton
    (D) nylon is to silk
    (E) oak is to acorn

48. MILLIGRAM is to DECILITER as
    (A) mass is to distance
    (B) mass is to time
    (C) pint is to quart
    (D) weight is to pressure
    (E) weight is to volume

49. NEGLIGENT is to REQUIREMENT as
    (A) careful is to position
    (B) cautious is to injury
    (C) cogent is to task
    (D) easy is to difficult
    (E) remiss is to duty

50. ORANGE is to MARMALADE as
    (A) cake is to picnic
    (B) jelly is to jam
    (C) potato is to vegetable
    (D) sandwich is to cheese
    (E) tomato is to ketchup

PRACTICE EXERCISE 3: READING COMPREHENSION

Questions 1–25 are five-option items. For each question, select the option that best completes the statement or answers the question. Answers are on page 225.

1. The mental attitude of the employee toward safety is exceedingly important in preventing accidents. All efforts designed to keep safety on the employee's mind and to keep accident prevention a live subject in the office will help substantially in a safety program. Although it might seem strange, it is common for people to be careless. Therefore, safety education is a continuous process.

   The reason given in the above passage for maintaining ongoing safety education is that

   (A) employees must be told to stay alert at all times.
   (B) office tasks are often dangerous.
   (C) people are often careless.
   (D) safety rules change frequently.
   (E) safety rules change infrequently.

2. One goal of law enforcement is the reduction of stress between one population group and another. When no stress exists between population groups, law enforcement can deal with other tensions or simply perform traditional police functions. However, when stress between population groups does exist, law enforcement, in its efforts to prevent disruptive behavior, becomes committed to reduce that stress.

   According to the above passage, during times of stress between population groups in the community, it is necessary for law enforcement to attempt to

   (A) continue traditional police functions.
   (B) eliminate tension resulting from social change.
   (C) punish disruptive behavior.
   (D) reduce intergroup stress.
   (E) warn disruptive individuals.

Questions 3–5 are based on the information contained in the following passage.

Microwave ovens use a principle of heating different from that employed by ordinary ovens.

The key part of a microwave oven is its magnetron, which generates the microwaves that then go into the oven. Some of these energy waves hit the food directly, while others bounce around the oven until they find their way into the food. Sometimes the microwaves intersect, strengthening their effect. Sometimes they cancel each other out. Parts of the food might be heavily saturated with energy, while other parts might receive very little. In conventional cooking, you select the oven temperature. In microwave cooking, you select the power level. The walls of the microwave oven are made of metal, which helps the microwaves bounce off them. However, this turns to a disadvantage for the cook who uses metal cookware.

3. Based on the information contained in this passage, it is easy to see some advantages and disadvantages of microwave ovens. The greatest disadvantage would probably be

   (A) overcooked food.
   (B) radioactive food.
   (C) unevenly cooked food.
   (D) the high cost of preparing food.
   (E) cold food.

4. In a conventional oven, the temperature selection would be based upon degrees. In a microwave oven, the power selection would probably be based upon

(A) wattage.
(B) voltage.
(C) lumens.
(D) solar units.
(E) ohms.

5. The source of the microwaves in the oven is

(A) reflected energy.
(B) convection currents.
(C) the magnetron.
(D) short waves and bursts of energy.
(E) the food itself.

Questions 6 and 7 are based on the information contained in the following passage.

For the past six or seven years, a group of scientists has been attempting to make fortunes by breeding "bugs"—microorganisms that will manufacture valuable chemicals and drugs. This budding industry is called genetic engineering, and out of this young program, at least one company has induced a lowly bacterium to manufacture human interferon, a rare and costly substance that fights virus infections by "splicing" human genes into their natural hereditary material. But there are dangers in this activity, including the accidental development of a mutant bacterium that might change the whole life pattern on earth. There are also legal questions about whether a living organism can be patented and what new products can be marketed from living matter. The congressional agency that oversees these new developments says that it will be about seven years before any new product developed by genetic engineering will be allowed to be placed on the market.

6. One of the potential problems of genetic engineering is the possibility of

(A) an oversupply of bacteria.
(B) dangerous mutations.
(C) overpopulation.
(D) excess food.
(E) too many engineers.

7. Human interferon can be used to fight viral infections. This means that it may be a tool in curing

(A) the common cold.
(B) diseases caused by drugs and alcohol.
(C) diseases that cause deformities.
(D) diseases that are genetic in origin.
(E) problems related to psychological stress.

Questions 8–10 are based on the information contained in the following passage.

Progress in human achievement is never straightforward. Sometimes, a simple attempt to build a road can do incredible damage to the environment. The Brazilian government, which has been attempting to link highways in that enormous country, has had to build roads through the Amazon River basin. In the process, this road-building program has inadvertently destroyed much valuable timberland. The basin, which originally occupied nearly two million square miles, has fallen victim in the past five years to destruction that has wiped out more than a quarter-million square miles of the world's largest forest surrounding the world's longest river. The Trans-Amazonian Highway caused the felling of millions of trees and drastically changed the forest ecology. Attempts were made to establish farms along its route where rice, other grains, and cattle would be raised. But the soil of the Amazon, which gave rise to this magnificent timber, is unsuitable to agriculture. Many of the farmers who attempted to work the forestland went bankrupt. As a result, the Brazilian government has diminished its interest in the network of auxiliary and connecting roads that would have joined with the Trans-Amazonian Highway, only part of which has yet been completed.

8. Although there has been a great deal of timberland destruction in the Amazon River basin, most of it still remains intact. The Brazilian government deliberately set out to build a highway through the basin in order to

   (A) establish new farming areas.
   (B) harvest crops of timber.
   (C) create new cities in the basin.
   (D) link remote parts of Brazil.
   (E) conquer the Amazon River.

9. A good title for this paragraph might be

   (A) "Progress Isn't Always Easy."
   (B) "Changes in Brazil's Ecology."
   (C) "Don't Fool with Mother Nature."
   (D) "Governments Are Bunglers."
   (E) "The Amazon—A Great River."

10. In this paragraph, the word "inadvertently" (sentence 4) means

   (A) specifically.
   (B) accidentally.
   (C) cleverly.
   (D) knowingly.
   (E) aimlessly.

Questions 11–14 are based on the information contained in the following passage.

Modern cartography was born in royal France during the latter part of the seventeenth century when King Louis XIV offered a handsome prize for anyone who could devise a method for accurately determining longitude. For two thousand years, sailors had been trying to find an exact way to locate different places on earth. The circumference of the earth had been calculated by the Greek Eratosthenes four hundred years before the birth of Christ, but as late as 1650 it was still difficult to exactly locate any single position on a map, and particularly difficult to determine

longitude on land or sea. Longitude is used to determine the distance of a place east or west of a point of reference. By the end of the seventeenth century, two instruments had been invented which would provide greater accuracy in calculating longitude. The two new instruments were the telescope and the accurate clock. One final instrument remained to be devised. It was perfected by John Harrison in the latter part of the eighteenth century. It was called a chronometer.

11. The benefit of modern cartography was

   (A) more accurate clocks.
   (B) the determination of the exact location of the North Pole.
   (C) newer and better maps.
   (D) the introduction of excellent telescopes.
   (E) the invention of the chronometer.

12. It can be inferred from this paragraph that

   (A) John Harrison was a Frenchman.
   (B) the French government was interested in accurate maps.
   (C) the clock was invented in the seventeenth century.
   (D) the Greeks had calculated the size of the earth.
   (E) None of the above is true.

13. One direct consequence of modern cartography was the adoption, in succeeding years, of

   (A) radar as a time measurement.
   (B) plutonium temperature-recording devices.
   (C) pollution control devices.
   (D) armaments by France.
   (E) universally accepted time zones.

14. A famous cartographer who helped determine the location of the New World but who is not mentioned in this paragraph is

   (A) Amerigo Vespucci.
   (B) Thomas Jefferson.
   (C) Christopher Columbus.
   (D) George Washington.
   (E) Robert Perry.

Questions 15–17 are based on the information contained in the following passage.

Many educators have asserted that one of the major problems of business today is the excess of specialists and the paucity of generalists. They decry the lack of broadly educated men and women in the ranks of business. According to this narrow view of reality, most business leaders demand, first, a specific vocational skill of job applicants and then, as an afterthought, accept persons with broad general knowledge. This alleged fixation of a trade school mentality reflects an important gap in information on the part of the people making the charges.

Today, most business officials believe that management is deeply involved in the art of communication because success and profit depend upon it. The ability to communicate generally reflects a wide range of education, not a narrow one. Most business officials believe that without the ability to read intelligently and to communicate coherently, the young man or woman starting out in the business world faces a difficult, perhaps impossible, task in climbing the ladder of financial success.

15. The preceding paragraphs are divided into two separate and distinct ideas. The first idea conveys the belief that business is looking for people

    (A) with the proper image.
    (B) with narrow vocational skills.
    (C) who will be loyal to the company.
    (D) who have years of experience.
    (E) who can bring in profit.

16. The author of this passage, however, does not agree with the concepts stated in the first paragraph. Two key words that show the author's disagreement with those ideas are

    (A) "narrow" and "alleged."
    (B) "difficult" and "impossible."
    (C) "specialist" and "generalist."
    (D) "excess" and "paucity."
    (E) "success" and "profit."

17. The author's point of view is that young people wishing to get ahead in business today should

    (A) have a specialty.
    (B) be related to management.
    (C) be able to read intelligently and write coherently.
    (D) graduate from a trade school.
    (E) understand the intricacies of business.

Questions 18–20 are based on the information contained in the following passage.

Men who live in democratic communities not only seldom indulge in meditation, but they naturally entertain very little esteem for it. A democratic state of society and democratic institutions keep the greater part of men in constant activity; and the habits of mind that are suited to an active life are not always suited to a contemplative one. The man of action is frequently obliged to content himself with the best he can get because he would never accomplish his purpose if he chose to carry out every detail to perfection. He has occasion to perpetually rely on ideas that he has not had leisure to search to the bottom; for he is much more frequently aided by the reasonableness of an idea than by its strict accuracy; and in the long run he risks less in making use of some false principles than in spending his time in establishing all his principles on the basis of truth.

—from Alexis de Tocqueville
Democracy in America

18. The author of this passage, a French aristocrat who toured the United States in the early nineteenth century, believed that the Americans he encountered during his travels were NOT

    (A) intellectual.
    (B) shrewd.
    (C) hardworking.
    (D) active.
    (E) pragmatic.

19. If what de Tocqueville says is acceptable as a description of modern America, then it would be reasonable to assume that Americans are most affected by
    (A) political authorities.
    (B) college professors.
    (C) science fiction.
    (D) rumors.
    (E) fads and advertising.

20. De Tocqueville believes that Americans are much more likely to make significant personal achievements because they are
    (A) introspective.
    (B) action-oriented.
    (C) passive.
    (D) sedentary.
    (E) phlegmatic.

Questions 21–23 are based on the information contained in the following passage.

Can the interpretation of an inkblot reveal personality traits? The Rorschach Test, which uses the inkblot, is still not fully accepted as a valuable diagnostic tool by professionals in the field of psychology. If properly interpreted, a Rorschach Test, in one hour, could provide personality data that would take weeks or months of ordinary interviews to reveal. The test consists of ten cards, each of which contains an inkblot intended to elicit a response from the subject. Test result analysis is a complex computation of many variables, including what colors, designs, and images are reported by the subject. Normal subjects usually respond to the whole design, while disturbed subjects are more likely to focus on individual details. Highly excitable subjects often show intense response to color, while depressed subjects may not mention color at all. Lack of reliability is the major reason for the limited use of the Rorschach Test.

21. The Rorschach Test is a
    (A) universally accepted method of diagnosing a state of mind.
    (B) psychological test with limited reliability.
    (C) set of fifteen inkblots that subjects are asked to describe.
    (D) quick and easy new test that is used to diagnose behavior.
    (E) series of puzzles.

22. The major value of the Rorschach Test is
    (A) its ability to distinguish between sane people and lunatics.
    (B) the ease with which the results can be analyzed.
    (C) the speed that the test can be given.
    (D) the total acceptance of the test as a useful form of diagnosis.
    (E) Both choices (A) and (D) are correct.

23. A highly emotional and excited person, according to Rorschach standards, is most likely to
    (A) respond to color.
    (B) respond to card size.
    (C) not respond at all.
    (D) see whole designs in the inkblots.
    (E) focus on details rather than designs.

Questions 24 and 25 are based on the information contained in the following passage.

Proteins in all forms of plant and animal life are constructed of the same basic set of twenty amino acids. Proteins are assembled within living organisms by a second set of building blocks called nucleotides. Nucleotides are substances joined together within every cell to form very long chains called nucleic acids. The most important of these nucleic acids is called deoxyribonucleic acid, or DNA. DNA is the largest molecule known, containing, in animals and man alike, as many as ten billion separate atoms. It is also the most important molecule in every living organism, even more important than protein, because it determines how proteins will be assembled. In other words, the DNA molecule contains the master plan that shapes the organism. It is believed that the very first living organisms on earth contained DNA.

24. From this paragraph, one can infer that DNA
    (A) is a protein.
    (B) is an organ.
    (C) is an organism.
    (D) is found in every living plant or animal.
    (E) was the first living creature.

25. Although all molecules contain a great many atoms, DNA is seen as
    (A) the largest molecule in man.
    (B) a structure that contains no carbon or hydrogen.
    (C) a protein that contains many acids.
    (D) a nucleotide that forms large chains.
    (E) a result of the cooling of the earth.

Questions 26–50 are four-option items. Read the paragraph(s) and select one of the lettered choices that best completes the statement or answers the question.

26. Few drivers realize that steel is used to keep the road surface flat in spite of the weight of buses and trucks. Steel bars, deeply embedded in the concrete, are sinews to take the stresses so that the stresses cannot crack the slab or make it wavy.

    The passage best supports the statement that a concrete road
    (A) is expensive to build.
    (B) usually cracks under heavy weights.
    (C) looks like any other road.
    (D) is reinforced with other material.

27. Blood pressure, the force that the blood exerts against the walls of the vessels through which it flows, is commonly meant to be the pressure in the arteries. The pressure in the arteries varies with contraction (work period) and the relaxation (rest period) of the heart. When the heart contracts, the blood in the arteries is at its greatest, or systolic, pressure. When the heart relaxes, the blood in the arteries is at its lowest, or diastolic, pressure. The difference between the two pressures is called the pulse pressure.

    According to the passage, which one of the following statements is most accurate?
    (A) The blood in the arteries is at its greatest pressure during contraction.
    (B) Systolic pressure measures the blood in the arteries when the heart is relaxed.
    (C) The difference between systolic and diastolic pressure determines the blood pressure.
    (D) Pulse pressure is the same as blood pressure.

28. More patents have been issued for inventions relating to transportation than for those in any other line of human activity. These inventions have resulted in a great financial savings to the people and have made possible a civilization that could not have existed without them.

    The one of the following that is best supported by the passage is that transportation
    (A) would be impossible without inventions.
    (B) is an important factor in our civilization.
    (C) is still to be much improved.
    (D) is more important than any other activity.

29. The Supreme Court was established by Article 3 of the Constitution. Since 1869 it has been made up of nine members—the chief justice and eight associate justices—who are appointed for life. Supreme Court justices are named by the president and must be confirmed by the Senate.

The Supreme Court

(A) was established in 1869.
(B) consists of nine justices.
(C) consists of justices who are appointed by the Senate.
(D) changes with each presidential election.

30. With the exception of Earth, all the planets in our solar system are named for gods and goddesses in Greek or Roman legends. This is because the other planets were thought to be in heaven like the gods and our planet lay beneath, like the earth.

All the planets except Earth

(A) were part of Greek and Roman legends.
(B) were thought to be in heaven.
(C) are part of the same solar system.
(D) were worshipped as gods.

31. Both the high school and the college should take the responsibility for preparing the student to get a job. Since the ability to write a good application letter is one of the first steps toward this goal, every teacher should be willing to do what he can to help the student learn to write such letters.

The paragraph best supports the statement that

(A) inability to write a good letter often reduces one's job prospects.
(B) the major responsibility of the school is to obtain jobs for its students.
(C) success is largely a matter of the kind of work the student applies for first.
(D) every teacher should teach a course in the writing of application letters.

32. Many people think that only older men who have a great deal of experience should hold public office. These people lose sight of an important fact. Many of the founding fathers of our country were comparatively young men. Today more than ever, our country needs young, idealistic politicians.

The best interpretation of what this author believes is that

(A) only experienced men should hold public office.
(B) only idealistic men should hold public office.
(C) younger men can and should take part in politics.
(D) young people don't like politics.

33. The X-ray has gone into business. Developed primarily to aid in diagnosing human ills, the machine now works in packing plants, foundries, service stations, and in a dozen ways contributes to precision and accuracy in industry.

The X-ray

(A) was first developed to aid business.
(B) is being used to improve the functioning of industry.
(C) is more accurate in packing plants than in foundries.
(D) increases the output of such industries as service stations.

34. In large organizations some standardized, simple, inexpensive method of giving employees information about company policies and rules, as well as specific instructions regarding their duties, is practically essential. This is the purpose of all office manuals of whatever type.

The paragraph best supports the statement that office manuals

(A) are all about the same.
(B) should be simple enough for the average employee to understand.
(C) are necessary to large organizations.
(D) act as constant reminders to the employee of his or her duties.

35. In the relationship of humankind to nature, the procuring of food and shelter is fundamental. With the migration of humans to various climates, ever new adjustments to the food supply and to the climate became necessary.

According to the passage, the means by which humans supply their material needs are

(A) accidental.
(B) inadequate.
(C) limited.
(D) varied.

Questions 36 and 37 are based on the following passage.

Many experiments on the effects of alcoholic beverages show that alcohol decreases alertness and efficiency. It decreases self-consciousness and at the same time increases confidence and feelings of ease and relaxation. It impairs attention and judgment. It destroys fear of consequences. Usual cautions are thrown to the winds. Drivers who use alcohol tend to disregard their usual safety practices. Their reaction time slows down; normally quick reactions are not possible for them. They cannot judge the speed of their car or any other car. They become highway menaces.

36. The above passage states that the drinking of alcohol makes drivers

(A) more alert.
(B) less confident.
(C) more efficient.
(D) less attentive.

37. It is reasonable to assume that drivers may overcome the bad effects of drinking by

(A) relying on their good driving habits to a greater extent than normally.
(B) waiting for the alcohol to wear off before driving.
(C) watching the road more carefully.
(D) being more cautious.

Questions 38–40 are based on the passage shown below.

Arsonists are persons who set fires deliberately. They don't look like criminals, but they cost the nation millions of dollars in property loss and sometimes loss of life. Arsonists set fires for many different reasons. Sometimes a shopkeeper sees no way out of losing his business and sets fire to it to collect the insurance. Another type of arsonist is one who wants revenge and sets fire to the home or shop of someone he feels has treated him unfairly. Some arsonists just like the excitement of seeing the fire burn and watching the firefighters at work; arsonists of this type have been known to help fight the fire.

38. According to the passage above, an arsonist is a person who

(A) intentionally sets a fire.
(B) enjoys watching fires.
(C) wants revenge.
(D) needs money.

39. Arsonists have been known to help fight fires because they

(A) felt guilty.
(B) enjoyed the excitement.
(C) wanted to earn money.
(D) didn't want anyone hurt.

40. According to the passage above, we may conclude that arsonists

(A) would make good firefighters.
(B) are not criminals.
(C) are mentally ill.
(D) are not all alike.

41. The lead-acid storage battery is used for storing energy in its chemical form. The battery does not actually store electricity but converts an electrical charge into chemical energy that is stored until the battery terminals are connected to a closed external circuit. When the circuit is closed, the battery's chemical energy is transformed back into electrical energy, and as a result, current flows through the circuit.

According to this passage, a lead-acid battery stores

(A) current.
(B) electricity.
(C) electric energy.
(D) chemical energy.

42. A good or service has value only because people want it. Value is an extrinsic quality wholly created in the minds of people and is not intrinsic in the property itself.

According to this passage, it is correct to say that an object will be valuable if it is

(A) beautiful.
(B) not plentiful.
(C) sought after.
(D) useful.

43. You can tell a frog from a toad by its skin. In general, a frog's skin is moist, smooth, and shiny, while a toad's skin is dry, dull, and rough or covered with warts. Frogs are also better at jumping than toads are.

You can recognize a toad by its

(A) great jumping ability.
(B) smooth, shiny skin.
(C) lack of warts.
(D) dry, rough skin.

44. The speed of a boat is measured in knots. One knot is equal to a speed of one nautical mile an hour. A nautical mile is equal to 6,080 feet, while an ordinary mile is 5,280 feet.

According to the passage, which of the following statements is true?

(A) A nautical mile is longer than an ordinary mile.
(B) A speed of 2 knots is the same as 2 miles per hour.
(C) A knot is the same as a mile.
(D) The distance a boat travels is measured in knots.

45. There are only two grooves on a record—one on each side. The groove is cut in a spiral on the surface of the record. For stereophonic sound, a different sound is recorded in each wall of the groove. The pickup produces two signals, one of which goes to the left-hand speaker and one to the right-hand speaker.

Stereophonic sound is produced by

(A) cutting extra grooves in a record.
(B) recording different sounds in each wall of the groove.
(C) sending the sound to two speakers.
(D) having left- and right-hand speakers.

46. It is a common assumption that city directories are prepared and published by the cities concerned. However, the directory business is as much a private business as is the publishing of dictionaries and encyclopedias. The companies financing the publication make their profits through the sales of the directories themselves and through the advertising in them.

The paragraph best supports the statement that

(A) the publication of a city directory is a commercial enterprise.
(B) the size of a city directory limits the space devoted to advertising.
(C) many city directories are published by dictionary and encyclopedia concerns.
(D) city directories are sold at cost to local residents and businessmen.

47. Although rural crime reporting is spottier and less efficient than city and town reporting, sufficient data has been collected to support the statement that rural crime rates are lower than those in urban communities.

The paragraph best supports the statement that

(A) better reporting of crime occurs in rural areas than in cities.
(B) there appears to be a lower proportion of crime in rural areas than in cities.
(C) cities have more crime than towns.
(D) no conclusions can be drawn regarding crime in rural areas because of inadequate reporting.

48. Iron is used in making our bridges and skyscrapers, subways and steamships, railroads and automobiles, and nearly all kinds of machinery—besides millions of small articles, from the farmer's scythe to the tailor's needle.

The paragraph best supports the statement that iron

(A) is the most abundant of the metals.
(B) has many different uses.
(C) is the strongest of all metals.
(D) is the only material used in building skyscrapers and bridges.

49. Most solids, like most liquids, expand when heated and contract when cooled. To allow for this, roads, sidewalks, and railroad tracks are constructed with spacings between sections so that they can expand during the hot weather.

If roads, sidewalks, and railroad tracks were not constructed with spacings between sections,

(A) nothing would happen to them when the weather changed.
(B) they could not be constructed as easily as they are now.
(C) they would crack or break when the weather changed.
(D) they would not appear to be even.

50. Twenty-five percent of all household burglaries can be attributed to unlocked windows or doors. Crime is the result of opportunity plus desire. To prevent crime, it is each individual's responsibility to

(A) provide the desire.
(B) provide the opportunity.
(C) prevent the desire.
(D) prevent the opportunity.

Questions 51–75 are four-option items. Each of questions 51–59 consists of a sentence in which one word is omitted. Select the lettered option that best completes the thought expressed in each sentence.

51. The explanation by the teacher was so _____ that the students solved the problem with ease.

(A) complicated
(B) explicit
(C) protracted
(D) vague

52. A(n) _____ listener can distinguish fact from fiction.

(A) astute
(B) ingenuous
(C) prejudiced
(D) reluctant

53. Your young nephew is going to ring the doorbells of the neighbors and say, "Trick or treat." You should send him a(n) _____ card.

(A) April Fool's
(B) Halloween
(C) Thanksgiving
(D) Valentine

54. We applauded the able cheerleader who _____ her baton so skillfully.

(A) twiddled
(B) twirled
(C) twisted
(D) twitched

55. His hatred for his brother Abel was so intense that Cain committed _____

    (A) fratricide
    (B) genocide
    (C) patricide
    (D) suicide

56. Because corn is _____ to the region, it is not expensive.

    (A) alien
    (B) exotic
    (C) indigenous
    (D) indigent

57. Our colleague was so _____ that we could not convince him that he was wrong.

    (A) capitulating
    (B) complaisant
    (C) light-hearted
    (D) obdurate

58. A lover of democracy has a(n) _____ toward totalitarianism.

    (A) antipathy
    (B) appreciation
    (C) empathy
    (D) proclivity

59. As the Declaration of Independence was signed in 1776, the United States held its _____ celebration in 1976.

    (A) biannual
    (B) bicentennial
    (C) biennial
    (D) centennial

Questions 60–64 consist of a sentence with two blank spaces, each blank indicating that a word or figure has been omitted. Select one of the lettered options that, when inserted in the sentence, best completes the thought expressed in the sentence as a whole.

60. Human behavior is far _____ variable, and therefore _____ predictable, than that of any other species.

    (A) less . . . as
    (B) less . . . not
    (C) more . . . not
    (D) more . . . less

61. The _____ limitation of this method is that the results are based _____ a narrow sample.

    (A) chief . . . with
    (B) chief . . . on
    (C) only . . . for
    (D) only . . . to

62. He is rather _____ and, therefore, easily _____.

    (A) caustic . . . hurt
    (B) dangerous . . . noticed
    (C) immature . . . deceived
    (D) worldly . . . misunderstood

63. _____ education was instituted for the purpose of preventing _____ of young children, and guaranteeing them a minimum of education.

    (A) Compulsory . . . exploitation
    (B) Free . . . abuse
    (C) Kindergarten . . . ignorance
    (D) Secondary . . . delinquency

64. Any person who is in _____ while awaiting trial is considered _____ until he or she has been declared guilty.

    (A) custody . . . innocent
    (B) jail . . . suspect
    (C) jeopardy . . . suspicious
    (D) prison . . . rehabilitated

Questions 65–72 consist of a quotation that contains one word that is incorrectly used, because it is not in keeping with the meaning that the quotation is intended to convey. Determine which word is incorrectly used. Then select from the lettered options the word that, when substituted for the incorrectly used word, would best help to convey the intended meaning of the quotation.

65. "Under a good personnel policy, the number of employee complaints and grievances will tend to be a number which is sufficiently great to keep the supervisory force on its toes and yet large enough to leave time for other phases of supervision."

    (A) complete
    (B) definite
    (C) limit
    (D) small

66. "One of the important assets of a democracy is an active, energetic local government, meeting local needs, and giving an immediate opportunity to legislators to participate in their own public affairs."

    (A) citizens
    (B) convenient
    (C) local
    (D) officials

67. "If the supervisor of a group of employees is to supply the necessary leadership to his or her subordinates, they will seek a leader outside the group for guidance and inspiration, because leadership must be supplied by someone whenever people work together for a common purpose."

    (A) fails
    (B) information
    (C) manager
    (D) plan

68. "The cost of wholesale food distribution in large urban centers is related to the cost of food to ultimate consumers, because they cannot pay for any added distribution costs."

    (A) eventually
    (B) sales
    (C) some
    (D) unrelated

69. "Why is it that in these times, when poetry brings in little prestige and more money, people are found who devote their lives to the unrewarding occupation of writing poetry?"

    (A) art
    (B) great
    (C) less
    (D) publicity

70. "In whatever form and at whatever intervals, the written report submitted by the operating unit can never adequately supplement personal, firsthand acquaintance with the work."

    (A) expect
    (B) experience
    (C) objective
    (D) replace

71. "Unless reasonable managerial control is exercised over office supplies, one can be certain that there will be extravagance, rejected items out of stock, excessive prices paid for some items, and obsolete material in the stockroom."

    (A) instituted
    (B) needed
    (C) overlooked
    (D) supervisory

72. "Consumer information and trade compliance cannot be emphasized in low income areas where language and education difficulties may exist."

    (A) do
    (B) must
    (C) not
    (D) whether

Questions 73–75 are based on different reading passages. Answer each question on the basis of the information contained in the passage.

73. "Although foreign ministries and their ministers exist for the purpose of explaining the viewpoints of one nation in terms understood by the ministries of another, honest people in one nation find it difficult to understand the viewpoints of honest people in another."

The passage best supports the statement that

(A) it is unusual for many people to share similar ideas.

(B) people of different nations may not consider matters in the same light.

(C) suspicion prevents understanding between nations.

(D) the people of one nation must sympathize with the viewpoints of the people of other nations.

74. "Personal appearance may be relevant if the job is one involving numerous contacts with the public or with other people, but in most positions it is a matter of distinctly secondary importance; other qualities that have no bearing on the job to be filled should also be discounted."

According to this quotation,

(A) in positions involving contact with the public, the personal appearance of the applicant is the most important factor to be considered.

(B) the personal appearance of a candidate should not be considered of primary importance when interviewing persons for most positions.

(C) the personal appearance of the candidate should never be considered during an interview.

(D) there are many factors that should be considered during an interview, even though they have no direct bearing on the job to be filled.

75. "No matter how carefully planned or how painstakingly executed a sales letter may be, it will be useless unless it is sent to people selected from a good mailing list consisting of the correct names and addresses of bona fide prospects or customers."

This quotation best supports the statement that

(A) a good mailing list is more important than the sales letter.

(B) a sales letter should not be sent to anyone who is not already a customer.

(C) carefully planned letters may be wasted on poor mailing lists.

(D) sales letters are more effective when sent to customers rather than bona fide prospects.

PRACTICE EXERCISE 4: ARITHMETIC REASONING

Questions 1–50 are five-option items. For each question, select the option that is most nearly correct. Answers are on page 231.

1. If a car uses $1\frac{1}{2}$ gallons of gas every 30 miles, how many miles can be driven with 6 gallons of gas?

   (A) 100
   (B) 110
   (C) 120
   (D) 130
   (E) 140

2. A car has a gasoline tank that holds 20 gallons. When the gauge reads $\frac{1}{4}$ full, how many gallons are needed to fill the tank?

   (A) 16
   (B) 15
   (C) 10
   (D) 5
   (E) 4

3. An airplane flying a distance of 875 miles used 70 gallons of gasoline. How many gallons will it need to travel 3000 miles?

   (A) 108
   (B) 120
   (C) 144
   (D) 240
   (E) 280

4. The *Mayflower* sailed from Plymouth, England, to Plymouth Rock, a distance of approximately 2800 miles, in 63 days. The average speed in miles per hour was closest to which one of the following?

   (A) $\frac{1}{2}$
   (B) 1
   (C) 2
   (D) 3
   (E) 4

5. A man drives 60 miles to his destination at an average speed of 40 miles per hour and makes the return trip at an average rate of 30 miles per hour. His average speed in miles per hour for the entire trip is most nearly

   (A) 34
   (B) 36
   (C) 38
   (D) 40
   (E) 42

6. A plane flies over Cleveland at 10:20 A.M. It passes over a community 120 miles away at 10:32 A.M. Find the plane's flight rate in miles per hour.

   (A) 600
   (B) 540
   (C) 480
   (D) 420
   (E) 360

7. Two trains start from the same station at 10:00 A.M., one traveling east at 60 mph and the other traveling west at 70 mph. At what time will these trains be 455 miles apart?

   (A) 12:30 P.M.
   (B) 1:00 P.M.
   (C) 1:30 P.M.
   (D) 2:00 P.M.
   (E) 2:30 P.M.

8. Two trains running on the same track travel at the rates of 25 and 30 mph, respectively. If the slower train starts out an hour earlier, how long will it take the faster train to catch up with it?

   (A) $3\frac{1}{2}$ hours

   (B) 4 hours

   (C) $4\frac{1}{2}$ hours

   (D) 5 hours

   (E) $5\frac{1}{2}$ hours

9. On a map, $\frac{1}{2}$ inch = 10 miles. How many miles apart are two towns that are $2\frac{1}{4}$ inches apart on the map?

   (A) 33
   (B) 36
   (C) 39
   (D) 42
   (E) 45

10. The total savings in purchasing 30 13-cent candies for a class party at a reduced rate of $1.38 per dozen is

    (A) $0.35
    (B) $0.40
    (C) $0.45
    (D) $0.50
    (E) $0.55

11. Mr. Jackson takes his wife and two children to the circus. If the price of a child's ticket is half the price of an adult ticket and Mr. Jackson pays a total of $12.60, the price of a child's ticket is

    (A) $2.10
    (B) $2.60
    (C) $3.10
    (D) $3.60
    (E) $4.10

12. What part of a day is 5 hours 15 minutes?

    (A) $\frac{7}{16}$

    (B) $\frac{9}{16}$

    (C) $\frac{7}{32}$

    (D) $\frac{9}{32}$

    (E) $\frac{11}{32}$

13. A team lost 10 games in a 35-game season. Find the ratio of games won to games lost.

    (A) 2 : 5
    (B) 5 : 2
    (C) 5 : 7
    (D) 7 : 2
    (E) 7 : 5

14. In a 3-hour examination of 350 questions, there are 50 mathematics problems. If twice as much time should be allowed for each mathematics problem as for each of the other questions, how many minutes should be spent on the mathematics problems?

    (A) 45 minutes
    (B) 52 minutes
    (C) 60 minutes
    (D) 72 minutes
    (E) 80 minutes

15. The parts department's profit is 12 percent on a new magneto. How much did the magneto cost if the selling price is $145.60?

    (A) $120.00
    (B) $125.60
    (C) $130.00
    (D) $133.60
    (E) $136.00

16. A typewriter was listed at $120.00 and was bought for $96.00. What was the rate of discount?

    (A) 16%
    (B) 20%
    (C) 24%
    (D) 28%
    (E) 32%

17. A class of 198 recruits consists of three racial and ethnic groups. If $\frac{1}{3}$ are black and $\frac{1}{4}$ of the remainder are Hispanic, how many of the recruits in the class are white?

    (A) 198
    (B) 165
    (C) 132
    (D) 99
    (E) 66

18. One third of the students at Central High are seniors. Three fourths of the seniors will go to college next year. What percentage of the students at Central High will go to college next year?

    (A) 25%
    (B) $33\frac{1}{3}$%
    (C) 45%
    (D) 50%
    (E) 75%

19. If 2.5 centimeters = 1 inch, and 36 inches = 1 yard, how many centimeters are in 1 yard?

    (A) 14
    (B) 25
    (C) 70
    (D) 80
    (E) 90

20. A rectangular fuel tank measures 60 inches in length, 30 inches in width, and 12 inches in depth. How many cubic feet are within the tank?

    (A) 12.5
    (B) 15.0
    (C) 18.5
    (D) 21.0
    (E) 24.5

21. How many gallons of fuel will be contained in a rectangular tank that measures 2 feet in width, 3 feet in length, and 1 foot 8 inches in depth (7.5 gallons = 1 cubic foot)?

    (A) 110
    (B) 75
    (C) 66.6
    (D) 55
    (E) 45

22. A rectangular bin 4 feet long, 3 feet wide, and 2 feet high is solidly packed with bricks whose dimensions are 8 inches by 4 inches by 2 inches. The number of bricks in the bin is

    (A) 54
    (B) 324
    (C) 648
    (D) 1072
    (E) 1296

23. A resolution was passed by a ratio of 5:4. If 90 people voted for the resolution, how many voted against it?

    (A) 40
    (B) 50
    (C) 60
    (D) 66
    (E) 72

24. If 2.5 centimeters = 1 inch, how many centimeters are in 1 foot?

    (A) 5
    (B) 10
    (C) 15
    (D) 30
    (E) 60

25. A gasoline tank is $\frac{1}{4}$ full. After adding 10 gallons of gasoline, the gauge indicates that the tank is $\frac{2}{3}$ full. What is the capacity of the tank in gallons?

    (A) 20
    (B) 24
    (C) 28
    (D) 32
    (E) 36

26. The water level of a swimming pool, 75 feet by 42 feet, is to be raised 4 inches. How many gallons of water are needed (7.5 gallons = 1 cubic foot)?

(A) 7875
(B) 15,750
(C) 23,625
(D) 31,500
(E) 63,000

27. If the outer diameter of a cylindrical oil tank is 54.28 inches and the inner diameter is 48.7 inches, the thickness of the wall of the tank, in inches, is

(A) 2.79
(B) 3.29
(C) 4.58
(D) 5.58
(E) 6.47

28. A person travels 30 miles at 6 mph, 20 miles at 10 mph, and 15 miles at 5 mph. What is the person's average rate for the complete distance?

(A) 6 mph
(B) $6\frac{1}{2}$ mph
(C) 7 mph
(D) $7\frac{1}{2}$ mph
(E) 8 mph

29. Sue and Joe are on opposite sides of a circular lake that is 1260 feet in circumference. They walk around it, starting at the same time and walking in the same direction. Sue walks at the rate of 50 yards a minute, and Joe walks at the rate of 60 yards a minute. In how many minutes will Joe overtake Sue?

(A) 14
(B) 21
(C) 28
(D) 35
(E) 42

30. Two ships are 1550 miles apart and sailing toward each other. One sails at the rate of 85 miles per day and the other at the rate of 65 miles per day. How far apart will they be at the end of 9 days?

(A) 100 miles
(B) 150 miles
(C) 175 miles
(D) 200 miles
(E) 225 miles

31. A family drove from New York to San Francisco, a distance of 3000 miles. They covered $\frac{1}{10}$ of the distance the first day and $\frac{2}{9}$ of the remaining distance on the second day. How many miles were left to be driven?

(A) 2000
(B) 2100
(C) 2300
(D) 2400
(E) 2500

32. Assuming that on a blueprint $\frac{1}{8}$ inch equals 12 inches of actual length, the actual length (in feet) of a steel bar represented on the blueprint by a line $3\frac{3}{4}$ inches long is

(A) 30
(B) 45
(C) 75
(D) 160
(E) 360

33. If pencils are bought at 36 cents per dozen and sold at 3 for 10 cents, the total profit on 5 dozen is

(A) 18¢
(B) 20¢
(C) 22¢
(D) 24¢
(E) 26¢

34. The tunnel toll is $1.25 for car and driver and $0.75 for each additional passenger. How many people were riding in a car for which the toll was $4.25?

(A) 3
(B) 4
(C) 5
(D) 6
(E) 7

35. Pren and Wright invested $8000 and $6000, respectively, in a hardware business. At the end of the year, the profits were $3800. Each partner received 6% on his investment and the remainder was shared equally. What was the total that Pren received?

(A) $1960
(B) $2040
(C) $2180
(D) $2300
(E) $2380

36. How much money is saved by buying a car priced at $12,000 with a single discount of 15% rather than buying the same car with discounts of 10% and 5%?

(A) $60
(B) $120
(C) $180
(D) $360
(E) $720

37. The price of an article has been reduced 25%. In order to restore the original price, the price must be increased by

(A) 15.5%
(B) 20%
(C) 25%
(D) $33\frac{1}{3}$%
(E) 40%

38. A stationer buys books at $0.75 per dozen and sells them at 25 cents apiece. The gross profit based on the cost is

(A) 50%
(B) 100%
(C) 150%
(D) 200%
(E) 300%

39. A, B, and C invested $8000, $7500, and $6500, respectively. Their profits were to be divided according to the ratio of their investment. If B uses his share of the firm's profit of $825 to pay a personal debt of $230, how much will he have left?

(A) $51.25
(B) $51.20
(C) $51.10
(D) $51.05
(E) $51.00

40. A merchant who has debts totaling $43,250 has gone bankrupt and can pay off only 15¢ on the dollar. How much will his creditors receive?

(A) $6287.00
(B) $6387.00
(C) $6387.50
(D) $6487.50
(E) $6587.00

41. If 15 cans of food are needed for 6 adults for 2 days, the number of cans needed for 4 adults for 5 days is

(A) 10
(B) 15
(C) 20
(D) 25
(E) 30

42. The school enrollment is 1700. Eighteen percent of the students study French, 25% study Spanish, 12% study Italian, 15% study German, and the rest study no foreign language. Assuming that each student may study only one foreign language, how many students do not study any foreign language?

    (A) 510
    (B) 520
    (C) 530
    (D) 540
    (E) 550

43. Four men working together can dig a ditch in 42 days. They begin the job, but one man works only half days. How long will it take to complete the job?

    (A) 46 days
    (B) 48 days
    (C) 50 days
    (D) 52 days
    (E) 54 days

44. What part of an hour elapses between 6:45 P.M. and 7:09 P.M.?

    (A) $\dfrac{2}{5}$

    (B) $\dfrac{5}{12}$

    (C) $\dfrac{1}{24}$

    (D) $\dfrac{6}{25}$

    (E) $\dfrac{10}{30}$

45. If a distance estimated at 150 feet is really 140 feet, the percent of error in this estimate is

    (A) $6\dfrac{2}{3}\%$
    (B) $7\dfrac{1}{7}\%$
    (C) 8%
    (D) 9%
    (E) 10%

46. Jack sells appliances and receives a salary of $150 per week plus 5% commission on all sales over $750. How much does he earn in a week in which his sales amount to $2400?

    (A) $222.50
    (B) $225
    (C) $227.50
    (D) $230
    (E) $232.50

47. If the average weight of girls of Jane's age and height is 105 pounds and if Jane weighs 110% of average, then Jane's weight in pounds is

    (A) 110
    (B) 112.5
    (C) 115.5
    (D) 118.5
    (E) 126

48. A man willed his property to his three children. To the youngest he gave $10,000; to the second, 2.5 times as much as to the youngest; and to the eldest, 1.5 times as much as to the second. What was the value of the estate?

    (A) $72,000
    (B) $72,500
    (C) $73,000
    (D) $73,500
    (E) $74,000

49. A person wishing to borrow a certain sum of money for 4 months goes to a bank offering an interest rate of 12%. If the interest is $720, how much does the person borrow?

    (A) $10,000
    (B) $12,000
    (C) $14,000
    (D) $16,000
    (E) $18,000

50. What is the ratio of 2 feet 3 inches to 1 yard?

    (A) 2:3
    (B) 3:4
    (C) 1:1
    (D) 4:3
    (E) 3:2

Questions 51–75 are four-option items. For each question, select the option that is most nearly correct.

51. A woman's weekly salary is increased from $350 to $380. The percent of increase is most nearly

(A) 6%

(B) $8\frac{1}{2}$%

(C) 10%

(D) $12\frac{1}{2}$%

52. A clerk divided his 35-hour work week as follows: $\frac{1}{5}$ of his time in sorting mail; $\frac{1}{2}$ of his time in filing letters; and $\frac{1}{7}$ of his time in reception work. The rest of his time was devoted to messenger work. The percentage of time spent on messenger work by the clerk during the week was most nearly

(A) 6%
(B) 10%
(C) 14%
(D) 16%

53. Many American cars feature speedometers that show kilometers per hour. If you are required to drive 500 miles, and you know that 1 kilometer is approximately $\frac{5}{8}$ of a mile, how many kilometers would you cover in that journey?

(A) 625
(B) 800
(C) 850
(D) 1000

54. A stock clerk had 600 pads on hand. He then issued $\frac{3}{8}$ of his supply of pads to Division X, $\frac{1}{4}$ to Division Y, and $\frac{1}{6}$ to Division Z. The number of pads remaining in stock is

(A) 48
(B) 125
(C) 240
(D) 475

55. Two sailors traveled by bus from one point to another. The trip took 15 hours, and they left their point of origin at 8 A.M. What time did they arrive at their destination?

(A) 11 A.M.
(B) 10 P.M.
(C) 11 P.M.
(D) 12 A.M.

56. A man deposited a check for $1000 to open an account. Shortly after that, he withdrew $400.00 and then $541.20. How much did he have left in his account?

(A) $56.72
(B) $58.80
(C) $59.09
(D) $60.60

57. After an employer figures out an employee's weekly salary of $190.57, he deducts $13.05 for Social Security and $5.68 for pension. What is the amount of the check after these deductions?

(A) $171.84
(B) $171.92
(C) $172.84
(D) $172.99

58. A pole 12 feet high has a shadow 4 feet long. A nearby pole is 24 feet high. How long is its shadow?

(A) 4 feet
(B) 8 feet
(C) 12 feet
(D) 16 feet

59. A skier started a fire in the fireplace. Each log she put on burned for a half-hour. If she started with a supply of 10 logs, for how many hours could the fire burn?

(A) 5 hours
(B) 7 hours
(C) $8\frac{1}{2}$ hours
(D) 10 hours

60. Mrs. Jones wishes to buy 72 ounces of canned beans for the least possible cost. Which of the following should she buy?

    (A) six 12-ounce cans at 39¢ per can
    (B) seven 10-ounce cans at 34¢ per can
    (C) three 24-ounce cans at 79¢ per can
    (D) two 25-ounce cans at 62¢ per can

61. A carpenter needs four boards, each 2 feet 9 inches long. If wood is sold only by the foot, how many feet must he buy?

    (A) 9
    (B) 10
    (C) 11
    (D) 12

62. It costs 31¢ a square foot to lay linoleum. To lay 20 square yards of linoleum it will cost

    (A) $16.20
    (B) $18.60
    (C) $55.80
    (D) $62.00

63. A piece of wood 35 feet, 6 inches long was used to make 4 shelves of equal length. The length of each shelf was most nearly

    (A) 9 feet, $1\frac{1}{2}$ inches

    (B) 8 feet, $10\frac{1}{2}$ inches

    (C) 7 feet, $10\frac{1}{2}$ inches

    (D) 7 feet, $1\frac{1}{2}$ inches

64. A change purse contained 3 half dollars, 8 quarters, 7 dimes, 6 nickels, and 9 pennies. Express in dollars and cents the total amount of money in the purse.

    (A) $3.78
    (B) $3.95
    (C) $4.32
    (D) $4.59

65. A champion runner ran the 100-yard dash in three track meets. The first time he ran it in 10.2 seconds; the second in 10.4 seconds; and the third in 10 seconds. What was his average time?

    (A) 10.1 seconds
    (B) 10.2 seconds
    (C) 10.3 seconds
    (D) 10.4 seconds

66. A crate containing a tool weighs 12 pounds. If the tool weighs 9 pounds, 9 ounces, how much does the crate weigh?

    (A) 2 pounds, 1 ounce
    (B) 2 pounds, 7 ounces
    (C) 3 pounds, 1 ounce
    (D) 3 pounds, 7 ounces

67. The daily almanac report for one day during the summer stated that the sun rose at 6:14 A.M. and set at 6:06 P.M. Find the number of hours and minutes in the time between the rising and setting of the sun on that day.

    (A) 11 hours, 2 minutes
    (B) 11 hours, 52 minutes
    (C) 12 hours, 8 minutes
    (D) 12 hours, 48 minutes

68. If $\frac{1}{2}$ cup of spinach contains 80 calories and the same amount of peas contains 300 calories, how many cups of spinach have the same caloric content as $\frac{2}{3}$ cup of peas?

    (A) $\frac{2}{5}$

    (B) $1\frac{1}{3}$

    (C) 2

    (D) $2\frac{1}{2}$

69. A night watchman must check a certain storage area every 45 minutes. If he first checks the area as he begins a 9-hour tour of duty, how many times will he have checked this storage area?

(A) 13
(B) 12
(C) 11
(D) 10

70. What is the fifth term in the series: $4\frac{1}{2}$; $8\frac{3}{4}$; 13; $17\frac{1}{4}$; _____?

(A) $21\frac{1}{2}$

(B) $21\frac{3}{4}$

(C) 22

(D) $22\frac{1}{4}$

71. Three workers assemble 360 switches per hour, but 5% of the switches are defective. How many good (nondefective) switches will these 3 workers assemble in an 8-hour shift?

(A) 2736
(B) 2880
(C) 2944
(D) 3000

72. The butcher made $22\frac{1}{2}$ pounds of beef into hamburger and wrapped it in $1\frac{1}{4}$-pound packages. How many packages did he make?

(A) 15
(B) 16
(C) 17
(D) 18

73. If a car-renting agency charges a fixed rate of $12 per day plus 17¢ per mile, what would the charge be for using a car for 6 days and traveling 421 miles?

(A) $143.57
(B) $153.57
(C) $163.57
(D) $173.57

74. If the area of the figure below, which consists of 5 equal squares, is 125, what is the perimeter of this figure?

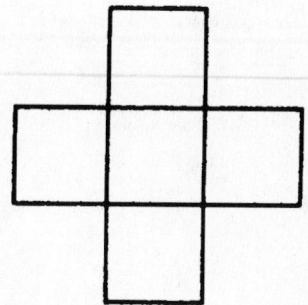

(A) 125
(B) 100
(C) 80
(D) 60

75. If the cost of digging a trench is $8.48 a cubic yard, what would be the cost of digging a trench 2 yards by 5 yards by 4 yards?

(A) $93.28
(B) $186.56
(C) $237.44
(D) $339.20

PRACTICE EXERCISE 5: MATH KNOWLEDGE

Questions 1–50 are five-option items. For each question, select the option that is most nearly correct. Answers are on page 239.

1. Which of the following fractions is the largest?

   (A) $\frac{1}{2}$

   (B) $\frac{3}{4}$

   (C) $\frac{5}{8}$

   (D) $\frac{11}{16}$

   (E) $\frac{23}{32}$

2. Arrange these fractions in order of size from largest to smallest: $\frac{1}{3}, \frac{2}{5}, \frac{4}{15}$.

   (A) $\frac{4}{15}, \frac{2}{5}, \frac{1}{3}$

   (B) $\frac{2}{5}, \frac{4}{15}, \frac{1}{3}$

   (C) $\frac{2}{5}, \frac{1}{3}, \frac{4}{15}$

   (D) $\frac{1}{3}, \frac{4}{15}, \frac{2}{5}$

   (E) $\frac{1}{3}, \frac{2}{5}, \frac{4}{15}$

3. Which of the following fractions is equal to $\frac{1}{4}\%$?

   (A) $\frac{1}{4}$

   (B) $\frac{1}{25}$

   (C) $\frac{4}{25}$

   (D) $\frac{1}{40}$

   (E) $\frac{1}{400}$

4. What percent of 90 is 120?

   (A) $133\frac{1}{3}$

   (B) 125

   (C) 120

   (D) 75

   (E) $1\frac{1}{3}$

5. What number added to 40% of itself is equal to 84?

   (A) 64.0

   (B) 60.0

   (C) 50.4

   (D) 40.6

   (E) 33.6

6. Find the square of 212.

   (A) 40,144

   (B) 44,944

   (C) 45,924

   (D) 46,944

   (E) 47,924

7. If $2^{n-3} = 32$, then n equals

   (A) 5

   (B) 6

   (C) 7

   (D) 8

   (E) 9

8. How many digits are there in the square root of a perfect square of 6 digits?

    (A) 12
    (B) 6
    (C) 4
    (D) 3
    (E) 2

9. If $a = 4$, then $\sqrt{a^2 + 9}$

    (A) 1
    (B) 5
    (C) $\sqrt{5}$
    (D) 25
    (E) -25

10. Solve the following: $5[4 - (+3 - 4) + 13] - 6 =$

    (A) −11
    (B) 16
    (C) 17
    (D) 21
    (E) 84

11. If x is less than 10, and y is less than 5, it follows that

    (A) $x > y$
    (B) $x - y = 5$
    (C) $x = 2y$
    (D) $x + y < 15$
    (E) $x + y = 15$

12. If the length and width of a rectangle are each multiplied by 2, then the

    (A) perimeter is multiplied by 4 and the area by 8.
    (B) area is multiplied by 2 and the perimeter by 4.
    (C) area is multiplied by 4 and the perimeter by 2.
    (D) area and perimeter are both multiplied by 2.
    (E) area and perimeter are both multiplied by 4.

13. The average of two numbers is A. If one of the numbers is x, the other number is

    (A) $\dfrac{A}{2} - x$
    (B) $\dfrac{A + x}{2}$
    (C) $A - x$
    (D) $x - A$
    (E) $2A - x$

14. If p pencils cost $2D$ dollars, how many pencils can be bought for c cents?

    (A) $\dfrac{pc}{2D}$
    (B) $\dfrac{pc}{200D}$
    (C) $\dfrac{2Dp}{c}$
    (D) $\dfrac{50pc}{D}$
    (E) $200\,pcD$

15. When −4 is subtracted from the sum of −3 and +5, the result is

    (A) +12
    (B) +6
    (C) −6
    (D) +2
    (E) −2

16. Find the product of $(-6)(+5)(-4)$.

    (A) +5
    (B) −5
    (C) −34
    (D) −120
    (E) +120

17. When the product of (-10) and $(+\frac{1}{2})$ is divided by the product of (-15) and $(-\frac{1}{3})$, the quotient is

    (A) +2
    (B) −2
    (C) +1
    (D) −1
    (E) 0

18. If $r = 25 - s$, then $4r + 4s =$
    (A) 100
    (B) −100
    (C) 25
    (D) −25
    (E) 0

19. Solve for x: $\dfrac{2x}{3} = \dfrac{x+5}{4}$
    (A) 2
    (B) 3
    (C) 4
    (D) 5
    (E) 6

20. If $a = 7, b = 8$, and $c = 5$, solve for x: $\dfrac{a-3}{x} = \dfrac{b+2}{4c}$
    (A) 4
    (B) 5
    (C) 6
    (D) 7
    (E) 8

21. The difference between $\sqrt{144}$ and $\sqrt{36}$ is
    (A) 180
    (B) 108
    (C) 18
    (D) 6
    (E) 2

22. $\sqrt{150}$ is between which of the following consecutive integers?
    (A) 10 and 11
    (B) 11 and 12
    (C) 12 and 13
    (D) 13 and 14
    (E) 14 and 15

23. Simplify the expression $2\sqrt{50}$.
    (A) $7\sqrt{2}$
    (B) $10\sqrt{2}$
    (C) 14
    (D) $25\sqrt{2}$
    (E) $50\sqrt{2}$

24. The sum of $4\sqrt{8}$, $3\sqrt{18}$, and $2\sqrt{50}$ is
    (A) $9\sqrt{76}$
    (B) $17\sqrt{2}$
    (C) $17\sqrt{6}$
    (D) $27\sqrt{2}$
    (E) $27\sqrt{6}$

25. If $\dfrac{1}{a} + \dfrac{1}{b} = \dfrac{1}{c}$, then $c =$
    (A) ab
    (B) $a + b$
    (C) $\dfrac{1}{2}ab$
    (D) $\dfrac{ab}{b+a}$
    (E) $\dfrac{a+b}{ab}$

26. If $a + b = 9$ and $a - b = 3$, then $a^2 - b^2 =$
    (A) 12
    (B) 27
    (C) 36
    (D) 72
    (E) 75

27. Solve for x: $x + y = a$
                       $x - y = b$
    (A) $a + b$
    (B) $a - b$
    (C) $\dfrac{1}{2}ab$
    (D) $\dfrac{1}{2}(a + b)$
    (E) $\dfrac{1}{2}(a - b)$

28. Solve for y: $7x - 2y = 2$
$$3x + 4y = 30$$
    (A) -4
    (B) 1
    (C) 2
    (D) 6
    (E) 11

29. Mr. Mason is 24 years older than his son Mark. In 8 years, Mr. Mason will be twice as old as Mark. How old is Mr. Mason now?
    (A) 24
    (B) 32
    (C) 40
    (D) 48
    (E) 56

30. Samantha is one half as old as her father. Twelve years ago, Samantha was one third as old as her father was then. What is Samantha's present age?
    (A) 24
    (B) 30
    (C) 36
    (D) 42
    (E) 48

31. How many ounces of a 75% acid solution must be mixed with 16 ounces of 30% acid solution to produce a 50% acid solution?
    (A) 12.8
    (B) 13.2
    (C) 13.6
    (D) 14.0
    (E) 14.4

32. $\dfrac{6!}{3!} =$
    (A) 2
    (B) 3
    (C) 63
    (D) 120
    (E) 200

33. Determine the pattern for the arrangement and then select the proper option to complete the following series of numbers: 2 4 8 10 20 22 —
    (A) 24
    (B) 28
    (C) 36
    (D) 44
    (E) 48

34. Determine the pattern for the arrangement and then select the proper option that gives the next two letters in the following series: C E H J M O __ __
    (A) Q T
    (B) Q S
    (C) Q R
    (D) R U
    (E) R T

35. The first term of an arithmetic progression is 3, and the sixth term is 23. The common difference is
    (A) 2
    (B) 4
    (C) 6
    (D) 8
    (E) 10

36. At 3:30 P.M., the angle between the hands of a clock is
    (A) 65°
    (B) 75°
    (C) 77.5°
    (D) 80°
    (E) 90°

37. In triangle *ABC*, *AB* = *BC* and *AC* is extended to *D*. If angle *BCD* contains 110°, find the number of degrees in angle *B*.

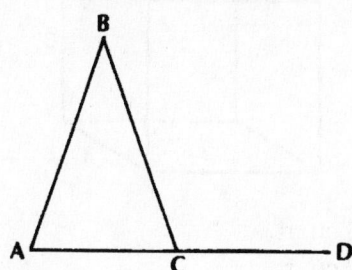

(A) 20°
(B) 40°
(C) 50°
(D) 60°
(E) 80°

38. If one acute angle of a right triangle is 5 times as large as the other, the number of degrees in the smallest angle of the triangle is

(A) 15°
(B) 30°
(C) 45°
(D) 60°
(E) 75°

39. If the angles of a triangle are in the ratio of 2 : 3 : 4, the triangle is

(A) equilateral.
(B) isosceles.
(C) right.
(D) obtuse.
(E) acute.

40. If a base angle of an isosceles triangle is represented by *x*°, the number of degrees in the vertex angle is represented by

(A) $180 - x$
(B) $180 - 2x$
(C) $90 - x$
(D) $x - 180$
(E) $2x - 180$

41. Find the area of the right triangle shown below.

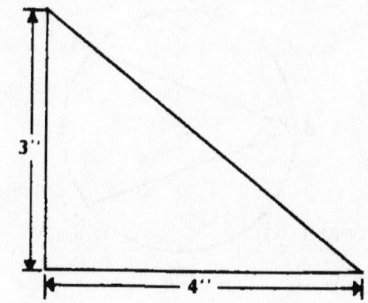

(A) 5 sq. in.
(B) 6 sq. in.
(C) 9 sq. in.
(D) 10 sq. in.
(E) 12 sq. in.

42. A square lot has a diagonal path cut through it. If the path is 40 yards long, what is the area of the lot?

(A) 400 square yards
(B) 600 square yards
(C) 800 square yards
(D) 1200 square yards
(E) 1600 square yards

43. If 140 feet of fencing is needed to enclose a rectangular field and the ratio of length to width in the field is 4 : 3, find the diagonal of the field.

(A) 10 feet
(B) 20 feet
(C) 30 feet
(D) 40 feet
(E) 50 feet

44. In the figure shown below, if arc $AC = 80°$, then angle ABC is equal to

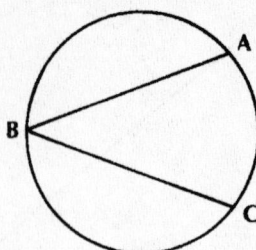

   (A) 20°
   (B) 40°
   (C) 60°
   (D) 80°
   (E) 100°

45. What is the area of a circle whose diameter is 6 inches?

   (A) 3π sq. in.
   (B) 6π sq. in.
   (C) 9π sq. in.
   (D) 12π sq. in.
   (E) 15π sq. in.

46. An automobile wheel has a diameter of 24 inches. How many revolutions will it make in covering one mile ($\pi = \frac{22}{7}$)?

   (A) 420
   (B) 630
   (C) 840
   (D) 1260
   (E) 1680

47. The area of circle O shown in the figure below is 16π. The perimeter of square $ABCD$ is

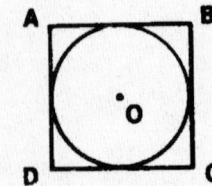

   (A) 4
   (B) 8
   (C) 16
   (D) 24
   (E) 32

48. The volume of the cube shown below is equal to

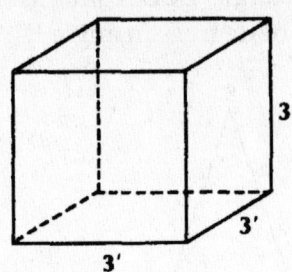

   (A) 3 cu. ft.
   (B) 9 cu. ft.
   (C) 18 cu. ft.
   (D) 27 cu. ft.
   (E) 54 cu. ft.

49. A cylindrical pail has a radius of 8 inches and a height of 10 inches. Approximately how many gallons will the pail hold? (There are 231 cubic inches to a gallon.)

   (A) 9
   (B) 11
   (C) 13
   (D) 15
   (E) 17

50. A circle graph shows that 30% of one year's immigrants were Hispanic, 28% were black, 20% were Asian, 17% were white, and the rest were classified as miscellaneous. How many degrees of the circle should be allocated to miscellaneous?

   (A) 5°
   (B) 9°
   (C) 10°
   (D) 14°
   (E) 18°

Questions 51–75 are four-option items. For each question, select the option that is most nearly correct.

51.

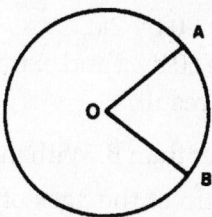

In the figure above, $\angle AOB = 60°$. If O is the center of the circle, then minor arc AB is what part of the circumference of the circle?

(A) $\dfrac{1}{2}$

(B) $\dfrac{1}{3}$

(C) $\dfrac{1}{6}$

(D) $\dfrac{1}{8}$

52. In a bag there are red, green, black, and white marbles. If there are 6 red, 8 green, 4 black, and 12 white, and one marble is to be selected at random, what is the probability it will be white?

(A) $\dfrac{1}{5}$

(B) $\dfrac{2}{5}$

(C) $\dfrac{4}{15}$

(D) $\dfrac{2}{15}$

53. 5 is what percent of 25?

(A) 5

(B) 20

(C) 80

(D) 125

54. If $a = 3$, then $a^a \cdot a =$

(A) 9

(B) 18

(C) 51

(D) 81

55. If $.04y = 1$, then $y =$

(A) .025

(B) 25

(C) .25

(D) 250

56. A certain highway intersection has had A accidents over a ten-year period, resulting in B deaths. What is the yearly average death rate for the intersection?

(A) $A + B - 10$

(B) $\dfrac{B}{10}$

(C) $10 - \dfrac{A}{B}$

(D) $\dfrac{A}{10}$

57. $2.2 \times .00001 =$

(A) .0022

(B) .00022

(C) .000022

(D) .0000022

58. If T tons of snow fall in 1 second, how many tons fall in M minutes?

(A) $60MT$

(B) $MT + 60$

(C) MT

(D) $\dfrac{60M}{T}$

59. If $A^2 + B^2 = A^2 + X^2$, then B equals

(A) $\pm X$

(B) $X^2 - 2A^2$

(C) A

(D) $A^2 + X^2$

60. If $6 + x + y = 20$, and $x + y = k$, then $20 - k =$

(A) 6
(B) 0
(C) 14
(D) 20

61. $\sqrt{960}$ is a number between

(A) 20 and 30
(B) 60 and 70
(C) 80 and 90
(D) 30 and 40

62. If $x = y$, find the value of $8 + 5(x - y)$.

(A) $8 + 5x - 5y$
(B) $8 + 5xy$
(C) $13x - 13y$
(D) 8

63.

Triangle R is 3 times triangle S.

Triangle S is 3 times triangle T.

If triangle $S = 1$, what is the sum of the three triangles?

(A) $2\dfrac{1}{3}$

(B) $3\dfrac{1}{3}$

(C) $4\dfrac{1}{3}$

(D) 6

64. A boy has 5 pairs of slacks and 3 sport jackets. How many different combinations can he wear?

(A) 3
(B) 5
(C) 8
(D) 15

65. To find the radius of a circle whose circumference is 60 inches,

(A) multiply 60 by π.
(B) divide 60 by 2π.
(C) divide 30 by 2π.
(D) divide 60 by π and extract the square root of the result.

66. A is younger than B. With the passage of time,

(A) the ratio of the ages of A and B remains unchanged.
(B) the ratio of the ages of A and B increases.
(C) the ratio of the ages of A and B decreases.
(D) the difference in their ages varies.

67. If you multiply $x + 3$ by $2x + 5$, how many x's will there be in the product?

(A) 3
(B) 6
(C) 9
(D) 11

68. The area of a triangle ABC can be determined by the formula

(A) $AC \div B$

(B) $\dfrac{1}{2}bh$

(C) $BC \div A$
(D) bh^2

69. If psychological studies of college students show K percent to be emotionally unstable, the number of college students not emotionally unstable per 100 college students is

(A) $100 - K$
(B) $1 - K$
(C) $K - 1$

(D) $\dfrac{100}{K}$

70. If the circumference of a circle has the same numbered value as its area, then the radius of the circle must be

(A) 1
(B) 5
(C) 2
(D) 0

71.

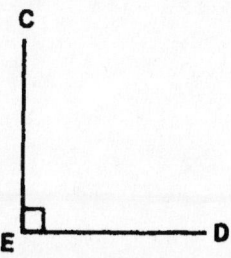

In the diagram above, $CE \perp ED$. If $CE = 7$ and $ED = 6$, what is the shortest distance from C to D?

(A) 6
(B) $4\sqrt{12}$
(C) 7
(D) $\sqrt{85}$

72. What is the correct time if the hour hand is exactly $\frac{2}{3}$ of the way between 5 and 6?

(A) 5:25
(B) 5:40
(C) 5:30
(D) 5:45

73. A square is changed into a rectangle by increasing its length 10% and decreasing its width 10%. Its area

(A) remains the same.
(B) decreases by 10%.
(C) increases by 1%.
(D) decreases by 1%.

74. If all P are S and no S are Q, it necessarily follows that

(A) all Q are S.
(B) all Q are P.
(C) no P are Q.
(D) no S are P.

75. The area of circle O is 64π. The perimeter of square $ABCD$ is

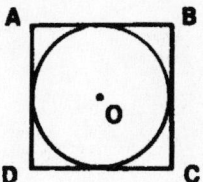

(A) 32
(B) 32π
(C) 64
(D) 16

PRACTICE EXERCISE 6: DATA INTERPRETATION

Questions 1–50 measure your ability to interpret data from tables and graphs. Each table and graph is followed by two, three, or four questions pertaining to that table or graph only. Answers are on page 245.

Questions 1–3 refer to the petty cash tabulation given below. Note that prior to July 1, the balance in the account was $0.00.

PETTY CASH

Date	Deposits	Withdrawals
July 1	$636.50	—
August 4	—	$115.00
September 5	$200.00	$15.00
October 6	$90.00	$150.00

1. On September 1, the amount of money in the account was
   - (A) $421.50
   - (B) $521.50
   - (C) $551.50
   - (D) $656.50
   - (E) $756.50

2. As a result of a transaction on August 4, the amount of money in the account was reduced by approximately
   - (A) 18%
   - (B) 19%
   - (C) 20%
   - (D) 21%
   - (E) 22%

3. The money in the account at the close of business on October 1 was
   - (A) $645.50
   - (B) $646.50
   - (C) $706.50
   - (D) $745.50
   - (E) $746.50

Questions 4–6 are based on the information given below.

RECORD OF EMPLOYEES

Name of Employee	Where Assigned	Number of Days Absent		Yearly Salary
		Vacation	Sick Leave	
Carty	Laundry	18	4	$ 9,300
Hart	Laboratory	24	8	7,860
Ingersoll	Buildings	20	17	8,580
King	Supply	12	10	7,860
Lopez	Laboratory	17	8	9,500
Martin	Buildings	13	12	7,500
Page	Administration	5	7	7,500
Quinn	Supply	19	0	7,380
Sage	Buildings	23	10	8,940
Vetter	Laundry	21	8	8,300

4. The employee who took 8 days of sick leave and 21 days of vacation was

(A) Hart.
(B) Kin.
(C) Lopez.
(D) Page.
(E) Vetter.

5. The employee with the highest salary is assigned to

(A) Administration.
(B) Buildings.
(C) Laboratory.
(D) Laundry.
(E) Supply.

6. Which one of the following was absent on vacation for more than 20 days?

(A) Carty
(B) Ingersoll
(C) Lopez
(D) Quinn
(E) None of the above

Questions 7–10 are based on the data contained in the Airport Information table shown below.*

AIRPORT INFORMATION

都市名 CITY	空港名 AIRPORT	市内との交通 料金・所要時間（分） TRANSPORTATION FARE & TIME (min.) TO AND FROM DOWNTOWN			空港税等 AIRPORT TAX ETC.	ポーターサービス 荷物1個につき PORTERAGE PER PIECE OF LUGGAGE
		リムジン LIMOUSINE	バス BUS	タクシー TAXI		
東京 TOKYO(TYO)	新東京国際空港（成田） NEW TOKYO INTERNATIONAL AIRPORT (NARITA)		2,500 YEN 70～90 min.	16,000 YEN 70・90 min.	2,000 YEN(12Yrs.~) 1,000 YEN(・12Yrs)	200 YEN
	東京国際空港（羽田） TOKYO INTERNATIONAL AIRPORT (HANEDA)	(MONORAIL) 270 YEN 15 min.		4,000 YEN 30 min.		
札幌 SAPPORO(SPK)	千歳空港 CHITOSE AIRPORT	(RAILWAY) 900 YEN 40　60 min.	700 YEN 60・90 min.	6,000 9,500 YEN 60 min.		
新潟 NIIGATA(KIJ)	新潟空港 NIIGATA AIRPORT		260 YEN 30 min.	1,600 YEN 20 min.		
名古屋 NAGOYA(NGO)	名古屋空港 NAGOYA AIRPORT		480 YEN 50 min.	3,000 YEN 30・40 min.		200 YEN
金沢 KANAZAWA(QKW)	小松空港 KOMATSU AIRPORT		830 YEN 50 min.	6,500 YEN (KOMATSU-KANA- ZAWA) 40 min.		
大阪 OSAKA(OSA)	大阪国際空港（伊丹） OSAKA INTERNATIONAL AIRPORT (ITAMI)		320 YEN 30 min.	3,000 YEN 25 min.		150 YEN 200 YEN(DOM・・INT)
福岡 FUKUOKA(PUK)	福岡空港 FUKUOKA AIRPORT		240 YEN 30 min.	1,200 YEN 20 min.		100 YEN 200 YEN(DOM・・INT)
長崎 NAGASAKI(NGS)	長崎空港 NAGASAKI AIRPORT		960 YEN 65 min.	7,000 YEN 60 min.		
熊本 KUMAMOTO(KMJ)	熊本空港 KUMAMOTO AIRPORT		550 YEN 45 min.	3,500 YEN 40 min.		
鹿児島 KAGOSHIMA(KOJ)	鹿児島空港 KAGOSHIMA AIRPORT		900 YEN 50 min.	7,000 YEN 40 min.		
沖縄（那覇） OKINAWA(NAHA)(OKA)	那覇空港 NAHA AIRPORT			700 YEN 15 min.		
北京 BEIJING(PEKING)(PEK)	北京首都空港 BEIJING (PEKING) CAPITAL AIRPORT			24 YUAN 40 min.	10 YUAN	
上海 SHANGHAI(SHA)	上海虹橋空港 SHANGHAI HONGQIAO (HONGCHIAO) AIRPORT			10 YUAN 30 min.	10 YUAN	
香港 HONGKONG(HKG)	香港国際空港（カイタク） HONGKONG INTERNATIONAL AIRPORT (KAI TAK)	31.50 DOLLARS (HONG KONG) 25 min.	2.30　4.00 DOLLARS 35 min.	35 DOLLARS 25 min.	100 DOLLARS (adult) 50 DOLLARS (child)	1 DOLLAR
台北 TAIPEI(TPE)	中正国際空港 CHIANG KAI SHEK INTERNATIONAL AIRPORT	65 NEW TAIWAN DOLLARS 40 min.	32 NTD 50 min.	800　900 NTD 40 min.	200 NTD	
高雄 KAOHSIUNG(KHH)	高雄国際空港 KAOHSIUNG INTERNATIONAL AIRPORT		10 NTD 25 min.	110　120 NTD 20 min.	200 NTD	10 NTD
ソウル SEOUL(SEL)	キンポ国際空港 KIMPO INTERNATIONAL AIRPORT	500 WON 40 min.		3,500 WON 30 min.	3,500 WON	500～1,000 WON for 1 cart
釜山 PUSAN(PUS)	キムへ国際空港 KIMHAE INTERNATIONAL AIRPORT		350 WON 80 min.	3,500 WON 50 min.	3,500 WON	500 WON
マニラ MANILA(MNL)	マニラ国際空港 MANILA INTERNATIONAL AIRPORT			50 PESOS (PHILIPPINE) 20 min.	50 PESOS	3 PESOS
バンコク BANGKOK(BKK)	バンコク国際空港 BANGKOK INTERNATIONAL AIRPORT		80 BAHT 40 min.	280 BAHT 40 min.	120 BAHT	5 BAHT
シンガポール SINGAPORE(SIN)	シンガポール国際空港 SINGAPORE CHANGI AIRPORT			10 DOLLARS 25 min.	12 DOLLARS	1 DOLLAR
クアラルンプール KUALA LUMPUR(KUL)	クアラルンプール国際空港（スバン） KUALA LUMPUR INTERNATIONAL AIRPORT (SUBANG)			14・18 DOLLARS (MALAYSIA) 40 min.	15 R.G.T. (INT) 5 R.G.T. (SIN BRUNEI) 3 R.G.T. (DOM)	
ジャカルタ JAKARTA(JKT)	ハリム国際空港 HALIM PERJDANAKUSUMA INTERNATIONAL AIRPORT			1,500　3,000 RUPIAH 30 min.	4,000 RUPIAH	200 RUPIAH
デリー DELHI(DEL)	デリー空港 DELHI AIRPORT		8.00 RUPEE (INDIA) 25 min.	30 RUPEE (Ambar 22゜・1)pm 5am)　20 min.	100 RUPEE	1 RUPEE
カラチ KARACHI(KHI)	カラチ国際空港 KARACHI INTERNATIONAL AIRPORT		10 RUPEE 30 min.	50 RUPEE (PAKISTAN) 50 min.	100 RUPEE	2～5 RUPEE
アブダビ ABU DHABI(AUH)	アブダビ国際空港 ABU DHABI INTERNATIONAL AIRPORT			50～100 DIRHAM 30 min.		
クウェート KUWAIT(KWI)	クウェート国際空港 KUWAIT INTERNATIONAL AIRPORT			3 DINAR (KUWAIT) 30 min.		0.25～0.50 DINAR
カイロ CAIRO(CAI)	カイロ国際空港 CAIRO INTERNATIONAL AIRPORT	2.5 POUNDS (EGYPT) 60 min.	20 PIASTRES 60 min.	4.5 POUNDS 60 min.	3 POUNDS	10 PIASTRES
ジェッダ JEDDAH(JED)	キング・アブドルアジーズ国際空港 KING ABDUL AZIZ INTERNATIONAL AIRPORT			SAUDI LMSN 35 RIYAL 20 min.		

* Courtesy of Japan Air Lines

7. Porterage per piece of luggage at Nagoya Airport is

(A) 100 yen
(B) 150 yen
(C) 200 yen
(D) 240 yen
(E) 260 yen

8. Transportation fare by bus from downtown Pusan to Kimhae International Airport is

(A) 80 won
(B) 350 won
(C) 500 won
(D) 1000 won
(E) 3500 won

9. Transportation time by taxi from downtown Nagasaki to Nagasaki Airport is

(A) 20 minutes
(B) 30 minutes
(C) 40 minutes
(D) 50 minutes
(E) 60 minutes

10. Transportation time by bus from downtown Taipei to Chiang Kai Shek International Airport is

(A) 35 minutes
(B) 40 minutes
(C) 45 minutes
(D) 50 minutes
(E) 55 minutes

Questions 11–14 are based on the information given in the following chart, which shows the toll rates charged for various types of vehicles using the bridges and tunnels in Grand City.

TOLL RATES FOR BRIDGES AND TUNNELS IN GRAND CITY

Vehicle Type	Main Street Bridge	Wilson Tunnel	Memorial Bridge	Fillmore Bridge	Jackson Avenue Tunnel
Two-axle vehicle weighing less than 8,000 pounds, including cars, trucks, and buses	$ .50	$ .75	$ .25	$ .60	$ .75
Passenger car with trailer	$ .75	$1.00	$ .50	$ .90	$1.00
Two-axle vehicle weighing more than 8,000 pounds	$1.00	$1.25	$ .80	$1.30	$1.40
Three-axle vehicle	$1.25	$1.50	$1.10	$1.75	$1.80
Four-axle vehicle	$1.75	$1.80	$1.40	$2.00	$2.30
Each additional axle	$ .50	$ .40	$ .40	$ .50	$ .50

11. According to the above chart, the highest toll charged for a three-axle vehicle using a bridge is

    (A) $1.40
    (B) $1.50
    (C) $1.75
    (D) $1.80
    (E) $2.30

12. Which of the following charges the lowest toll for a two-axle truck weighing 6,000 pounds?

    (A) Fillmore Bridge
    (B) Jackson Avenue Tunnel
    (C) Main Street Bridge
    (D) Memorial Bridge
    (E) Wilson Tunnel

13. The difference between the tolls charged for a three-axle vehicle using the Wilson Tunnel and a three-axle vehicle using the Jackson Avenue Tunnel is

    (A) 30 cents.
    (B) 40 cents.
    (C) 50 cents.
    (D) 60 cents.
    (E) 70 cents.

14. The toll charged for driving a five-axle vehicle through the Wilson Tunnel is

    (A) $2.15
    (B) $2.20
    (C) $2.25
    (D) $2.30
    (E) $2.35

Questions 15–18 are based on the weekly train schedule given below for the Dumont Line.

WEEKDAY TRAIN SCHEDULE—DUMONT LINE

| Train # | Eastbound | | | Magic Mall | | Westbound | | |
	Harvard Square Leave	Pleasure Plaza Leave	Harding Street Leave	Arrive	Leave	Harding Street Leave	Pleasure Plaza Leave	Harvard Square Arrive
69	7:48	7:51	7:56	8:00	8:06	8:10	8:15	8:18
70	7:54	7:57	8:02	8:06	8:12	8:16	8:21	8:24
71	8:00	8:03	8:08	8:12	8:18	8:22	8:27	8:30
72	8:04	8:07	8:13	8:17	8:22	8:26	8:31	8:34
73	8:08	8:11	8:17	8:21	8:26	8:30	8:35	8:38
74	8:12	8:15	8:20	8:24	8:30	8:34	8:39	8:42
75	8:16	8:19	8:24	8:28	8:34	8:38	8:43	8:46
69	8:20	8:23	8:28	8:32	8:38	8:42	8:47	8:50
70	8:26	8:29	8:34	8:38	8:44	8:48	8:53	8:56

15. As shown on this schedule, the number of trains arriving at Magic Mall and standing there for less than 6 minutes before leaving is

(A) 7
(B) 5
(C) 3
(D) 2
(E) none

16. The number of trains shown on the schedule having different train numbers is

(A) 10
(B) 9
(C) 8
(D) 7
(E) 6

17. The time it should take Train #74 to go from Harvard Square to Magic Mall is

(A) 10 minutes
(B) 12 minutes
(C) 14 minutes
(D) 16 minutes
(E) 18 minutes

18. Train #70 is scheduled to leave Pleasure Plaza on its second westbound trip to Harvard Square at

(A) 8:21
(B) 8:48
(C) 8:50
(D) 8:53
(E) 8:56

Questions 19–20 are based on the information given in the following table, which shows the amount of money counted by cashiers on each of five days in a certain week.

Name of Cashier	Monday	Tuesday	Wednesday	Thursday	Friday
Lanigan	$7,264	$8,461	$8,348	$9,600	$7,641
Peters	8,917	7,932	7,491	8,731	9,417
Harding	9,432	7,647	9,620	8,408	7,248
Williams	7,816	8,216	7,422	7,691	8,697
Considine	8,124	9,042	8,735	8,004	8,715

19. The total amount counted by Williams on Tuesday and Wednesday combined is

   (A) $15,113
   (B) $15,638
   (C) $16,524
   (D) $17,267
   (E) $17,777

20. The amount counted by Peters on Thursday exceeded the amount counted by Harding on Thursday by

   (A) $166
   (B) $224
   (C) $285
   (D) $323
   (E) $415

Questions 21–23 are based on the information given in the following graph, which shows the average monthly temperature of Resort City.

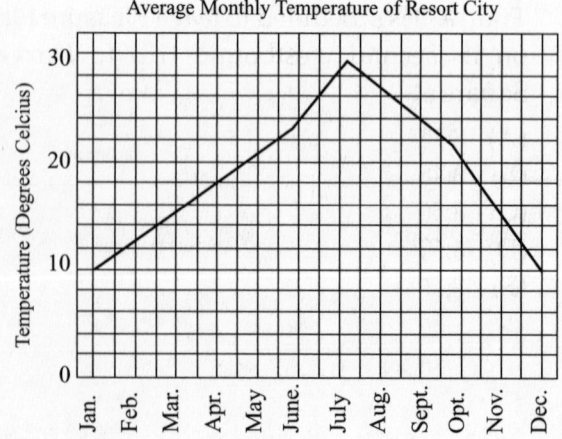

Average Monthly Temperature of Resort City

21. The average monthly temperature of Resort City is lowest during the months of

   (A) January and November.
   (B) January and December.
   (C) February and November.
   (D) February and December.
   (E) November and December.

22. The average monthly temperature in May is the same as in

   (A) June.
   (B) July.
   (C) August.
   (D) September.
   (E) October.

23. The average monthly temperature of Resort City in May exceeds the average monthly temperature in December by approximately

   (A) 11°C
   (B) 16°C
   (C) 21°C
   (D) 25°C
   (E) 29°C

Questions 24–26 are based on the following table and the accompanying notes.

Ration A	Ration B	Ration C	Ration D
5.8	6.1	9.3	6.8
7.0	4.4	6.8	6.6
5.4	5.4	8.2	7.5
6.9	4.8	6.8	5.2
5.9	2.9	4.5	7.7
4.3	6.7	8.1	4.7
8.2	5.6	7.0	6.3
5.6	3.8	6.0	6.1
4.1	7.5	5.3	8.7
3.2	5.2	7.1	4.0
56.4	52.4	69.1	63.6

Four groups of ten rabbits were fed a complete commercial ration from birth until 6 months of age. Each animal was weighed at birth and at 6 months. The weight of the animal at birth was subtracted from its weight at 6 months. These differences, in pounds, are shown above for each rabbit.

24. The average weight gain of the rabbits used in this experiment is most nearly

(A) 6.0 lbs.
(B) 6.2 lbs.
(C) 6.4 lbs.
(D) 6.6 lbs.
(E) 6.8 lbs.

25. The difference in weight gain between the rabbit fed Ration B who gained the most and the rabbit fed Ration B who gained the least is

(A) 2.9 lbs.
(B) 3.7 lbs.
(C) 3.8 lbs.
(D) 4.0 lbs.
(E) 4.6 lbs.

26. The individual rabbit showing the most gain was fed

(A) Ration A
(B) Ration B
(C) Ration C
(D) Ration D
(E) Ration E

Questions 27–29 are based on the information given in the following chart, which shows the area of the continents.

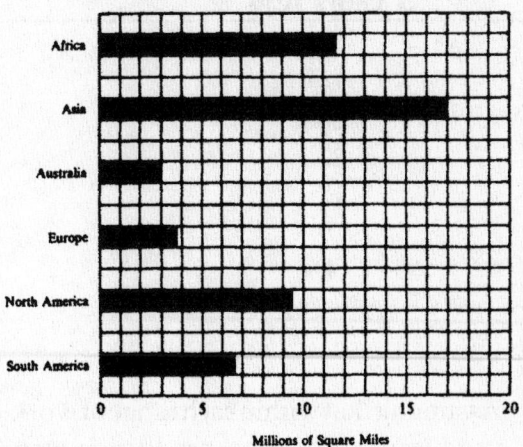

THE AREA OF THE CONTINENTS

27. The area of the largest continent is approximately

(A) 16 million square miles.
(B) 17 million square miles.
(C) 18 million square miles.
(D) 19 million square miles.
(E) 20 million square miles.

28. The area of the smallest continent is approximately

(A) 2 million square miles.

(B) $2\frac{1}{2}$ million square miles.

(C) 3 million square miles.

(D) $3\frac{1}{2}$ million square miles.

(E) 4 million square miles.

29. The continent with an area of approximately $9\frac{1}{2}$ million square miles is

(A) Africa.
(B) Asia.
(C) Europe.
(D) North America.
(E) South America.

Questions 30–32 are based on the information contained in the table below, which shows the differences between the rates of production of employees in the Works Department last year and 5 years ago.

Number of Employees Producing Work-Units within Range 5 Years Ago	Range of Work-Units Produced	Number of Employees Producing Work-Units within Range Last Year
7	501-1000	4
14	1001-1500	11
26	1501-2000	28
22	2001-2500	36
17	2501-3000	39
10	3001-3500	23
4	3501-4000	9

30. Assuming that within each range of work-units produced, the average production was at the midpoint of that range (*e.g.*, 501-1000 = 750), then the average number of work-units produced per employee 5 years ago fell into the range of

    (A) 1001-1500
    (B) 1501-2000
    (C) 2001-2500
    (D) 2501-3000
    (E) 3001-3500

31. The ratio of the number of employees producing more than 2000 work-units 5 years ago to the number of employees producing more than 2000 work-units last year is most nearly

    (A) 1 : 2
    (B) 2 : 3
    (C) 3 : 4
    (D) 4 : 5
    (E) 1 : 1

32. In Works Department, which of the following were greater last year than 5 years ago?

    I.   Total number of employees
    II.   Total number of work-units produced
    III. Number of employees producing 2000 or fewer work-units

    (A) I
    (B) I and II
    (C) I and III
    (D) II and III
    (E) I, II, and III

Questions 33–36 are based on the data contained in the graph below.

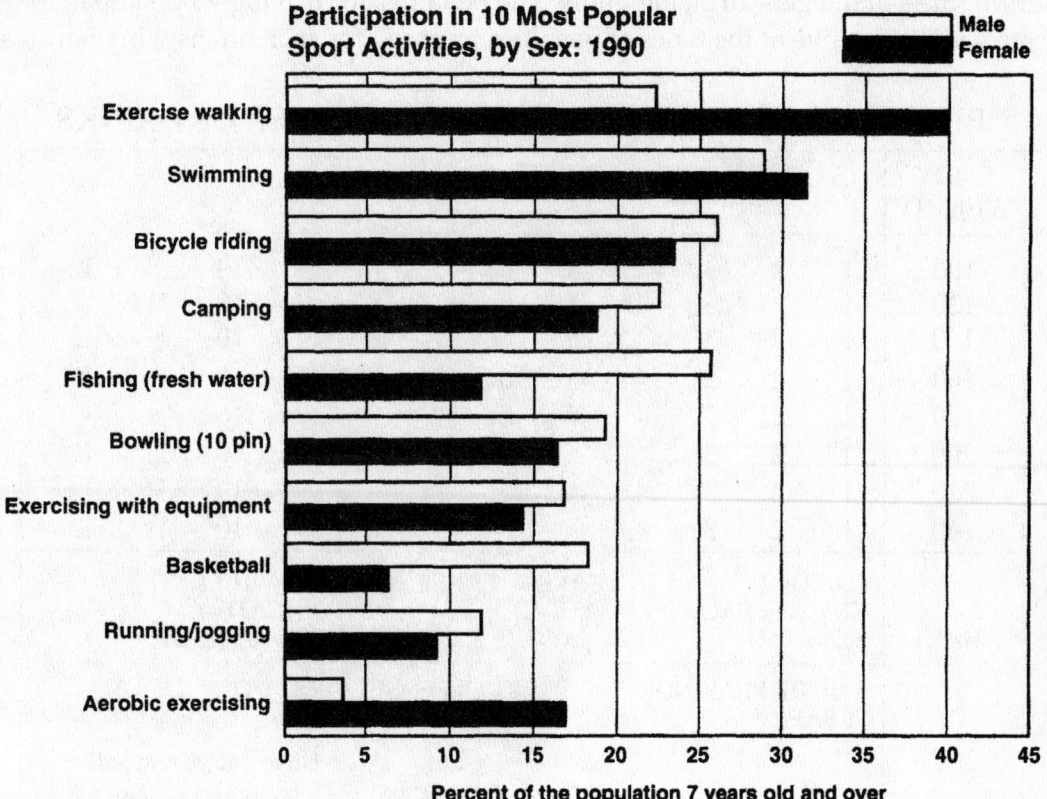

Participation in 10 Most Popular Sport Activities, by Sex: 1990

Male / Female

Exercise walking
Swimming
Bicycle riding
Camping
Fishing (fresh water)
Bowling (10 pin)
Exercising with equipment
Basketball
Running/jogging
Aerobic exercising

0 5 10 15 20 25 30 35 40 45

Percent of the population 7 years old and over

33. According to the graph, the percentage of males who participate in exercise walking is most nearly the same as the percentage of females who participate in

(A) bowling.
(B) swimming.
(C) fishing.
(D) bicycle riding.
(E) camping.

34. In which of the following activities is the percent of participation by males and females most nearly the same?

(A) Fishing
(B) Camping
(C) Bowling
(D) Aerobic exercising
(E) Basketball

35. In which of the following activities is the percent of participation by males twice the percent of participation by females?

(A) Exercise walking
(B) Aerobic exercising
(C) Bicycle riding
(D) Basketball
(E) Fishing

36. If the number of females over 7 years of age is 115 million, the number of females who participate in basketball is most nearly

(A) 5,500,000
(B) 8,000,000
(C) 10,000,000
(D) 11,500,000
(E) 12,000,000

Questions 37–40 are based on the information contained in the following table, which highlights the need to recognize safe—and legal—drinking limits. The penalties for driving while impaired or for driving while intoxicated are illustrative of the types of penalties imposed for such offenses in many states.

BLOOD ALCOHOL CONTENT (BAC) – NUMBER OF DRINKS

BODY WEIGHT	Drinks (2–Hour Period)											
100	1	2	3	4	5	6	7	8	9	10	11	12
120	1	2	3	4	5	6	7	8	9	10	11	12
140	1	2	3	4	5	6	7	8	9	10	11	12
160	1	2	3	4	5	6	7	8	9	10	11	12
180	1	2	3	4	5	6	7	8	9	10	11	12
200	1	2	3	4	5	6	7	8	9	10	11	12
220	1	2	3	4	5	6	7	8	9	10	11	12
240	1	2	3	4	5	6	7	8	9	10	11	12

BAC	CAUTION Keep your BAC below .05%	DRIVING WHILE IMPAIRED ABOVE .05%	DRIVING WHILE INTOXICATED (DWI) .10% & UP
	YOU'RE PLAYING IT SAFE	FIRST OFFENSE • $250 • Up to 15 days in jail • 90–day loss of license	FIRST CONVICTION • $350 – $500 fine • Up to one year in jail • Possible 3 year probation • Minimum 6 months loss of license

37. A 140-pound person would be deemed to be driving while impaired after consuming during a 2-hour period a minimum of

    (A) 2 drinks.
    (B) 3 drinks.
    (C) 4 drinks.
    (D) 5 drinks.
    (E) 6 drinks.

38. The maximum number of drinks a 100-pound person may consume during a 2-hour period without being deemed to be driving while impaired is

    (A) 1 drink.
    (B) 2 drinks.
    (C) 3 drinks.
    (D) 4 drinks.
    (E) 5 drinks.

39. A 180-pound person would be deemed to be driving while intoxicated after consuming during a 2-hour period a minimum of

    (A) 1 drink.
    (B) 2 drinks.
    (C) 4 drinks.
    (D) 6 drinks.
    (E) 8 drinks.

40. The maximum number of drinks a 200-pound person may consume during a 2-hour period without being deemed to be driving while impaired is

    (A) 3 drinks.
    (B) 4 drinks.
    (C) 5 drinks.
    (D) 6 drinks.
    (E) 7 drinks.

Questions 41–44 are based on the information contained in the graph shown below. Lines A and B represent the cumulative progress in the work of two quality control inspectors, each of whom was given 500 items to inspect over a 5-day period.

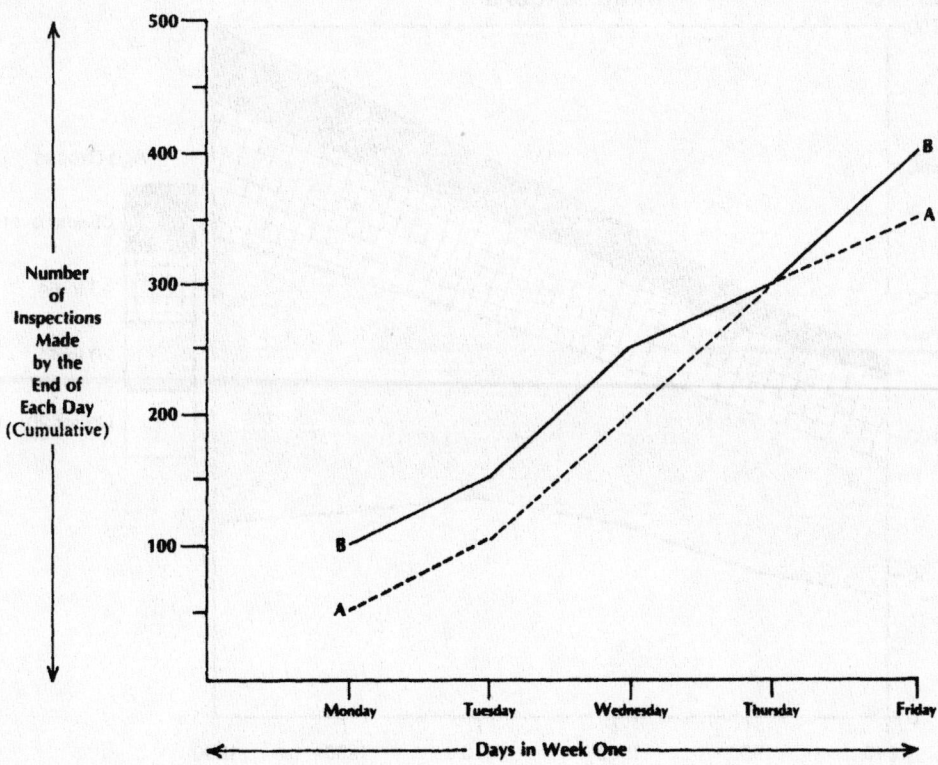

41. Inspector A was more productive than Inspector B on

    (A) Monday.
    (B) Tuesday.
    (C) Wednesday.
    (D) Thursday.
    (E) Friday.

42. On which day was the smallest number of inspections made by the two inspectors?

    (A) Monday
    (B) Tuesday
    (C) Wednesday
    (D) Thursday
    (E) Friday

43. At the end of the second day, the percentage of inspections still to be made was

    (A) 25%
    (B) 33%
    (C) 50%
    (D) 66%
    (E) 75%

44. The same number of inspections was made by both inspectors on

    (A) Monday and Tuesday.
    (B) Tuesday and Wednesday.
    (C) Wednesday and Thursday.
    (D) Wednesday and Friday.
    (E) Thursday and Friday.

Questions 45–48 are based on the data contained in the following chart that shows the population of the United States for the 1940–1990 period.

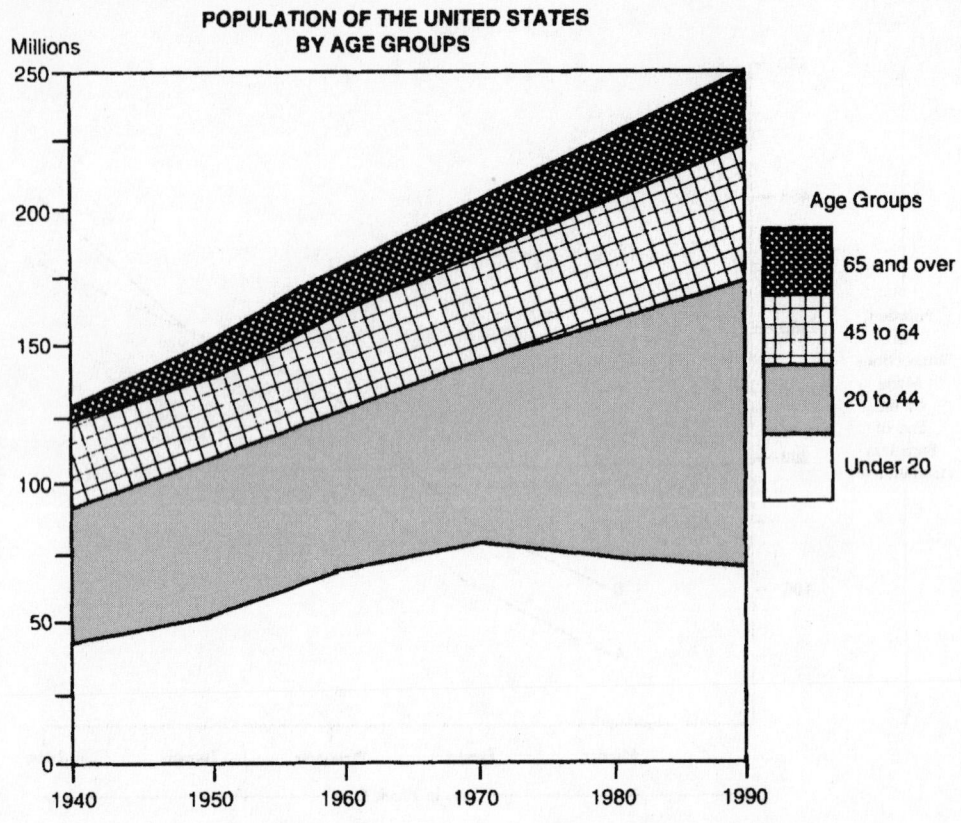

POPULATION OF THE UNITED STATES BY AGE GROUPS

45. In which year was the total population approximately 50% greater than in 1950?

(A) 1940
(B) 1960
(C) 1970
(D) 1980
(E) 1990

46. In 1970, the population in the "20 to 44" age group was most near

(A) 40 million.
(B) 65 million.
(C) 80 million.
(D) 110 million.
(E) 140 million.

47. Which one of the following age groups showed a numerical decrease for two decades during the 1940–1990 period?

(A) "Under 20"
(B) "20 to 44"
(C) "45 to 64"
(D) "65 and over"
(E) None

48. The percentage of the total population that was in the "45 to 64" age group in 1960 is most nearly

(A) 10%
(B) 20%
(C) 30%
(D) 40%
(E) 50%

Questions 49–50 are based on the facts and figures given in the graph below.

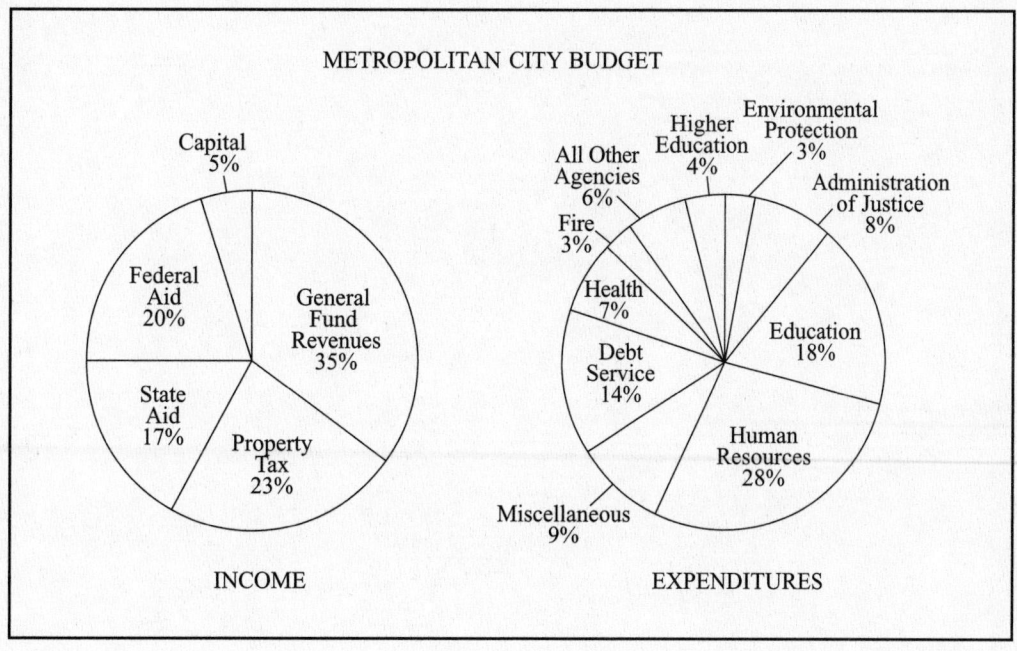

METROPOLITAN CITY BUDGET

INCOME

EXPENDITURES

49. Thirty-seven percent of the city income is derived from

(A) capital and general fund revenues.
(B) general fund revenues and federal aid.
(C) federal aid and state aid.
(D) state aid and property taxes.
(E) property taxes and capital.

50. The two areas on which an equal amount of the income is expended are

(A) higher education and environmental protection.
(B) environmental protection and fire.
(C) education and human resources.
(D) health and administration of justice.
(E) health and miscellaneous.

PRACTICE EXERCISE 7: GENERAL SCIENCE

Questions 1–50 are four-option items. For each question, select the option that best completes the statement or answers the question. Answers are on page 249.

1. Citrus fruits include
   (A) apples.
   (B) bananas.
   (C) oranges.
   (D) peaches.

2. What temperature is shown on a Fahrenheit thermometer when a centigrade thermometer reads 0°?
   (A) –40°
   (B) –32°
   (C) 0°
   (D) +32°

3. The major chemical constituent of a cell (by weight) is
   (A) protein.
   (B) ash.
   (C) water.
   (D) carbohydrates.

4. The Wassermann test may indicate the presence of
   (A) syphilis.
   (B) tuberculosis.
   (C) measles.
   (D) AIDS.

5. Alcoholic beverages contain
   (A) wood alcohol.
   (B) isopropyl alcohol.
   (C) glyceryl alcohol.
   (D) grain alcohol.

6. The air around us is composed mostly of
   (A) carbon.
   (B) nitrogen.
   (C) hydrogen.
   (D) oxygen.

7. The process that is responsible for the continuous removal of carbon dioxide from the atmosphere is
   (A) respiration.
   (B) oxidation.
   (C) metabolism.
   (D) photosynthesis.

8. Ringworm is caused by a(n)
   (A) alga.
   (B) fungus.
   (C) bacterium.
   (D) protozoan.

9. Light passes through the crystalline lens in the eye and focuses on the
   (A) cornea.
   (B) iris.
   (C) pupil.
   (D) retina.

10. Saliva contains an enzyme that acts on
    (A) carbohydrates.
    (B) proteins.
    (C) minerals.
    (D) vitamins.

11. The vitamin that helps coagulation of the blood is
    (A) C
    (B) E
    (C) D
    (D) K

12. Of the following, the part of a ship that gives it stability by lowering the center of gravity is the
    (A) bulkhead.
    (B) keel.
    (C) anchor.
    (D) prow.

13. To reduce soil acidity, a farmer should use
    (A) lime.
    (B) phosphate.
    (C) manure.
    (D) peat moss.

14. Which of the following minerals is restored to the soil by plants of the pea and bean family?
    (A) Sulfates
    (B) Carbonates
    (C) Nitrates
    (D) Phosphates

15. The greater the frequency of sound waves
    (A) the louder the sound.
    (B) the higher the pitch of the sound.
    (C) the softer the sound.
    (D) the lower the pitch of the sound.

16. Of the following, the food that contains the largest amount of vitamin C is
    (A) carrots.
    (B) sweet potatoes.
    (C) lima beans.
    (D) tomatoes.

17. The cyclotron is used to
    (A) measure radioactivity.
    (B) measure the speed of the earth's rotation.
    (C) split atoms.
    (D) store radioactive energy.

18. The earth completes one trip around the sun approximately every
    (A) 24 hours.
    (B) 52 weeks.
    (C) 7 days.
    (D) 30 days.

19. A person is more buoyant when swimming in salt water than in fresh water because
    (A) he keeps his head out of salt water.
    (B) salt coats his body with a floating membrane.
    (C) salt water has great tensile strength.
    (D) salt water weighs more than an equal volume of fresh water.

20. A volcanic eruption is caused by
    (A) sunspots.
    (B) pressure inside the earth.
    (C) nuclear fallout.
    (D) boiling lava.

21. The vitamin manufactured by the skin with the help of the sun is
    (A) A.
    (B) B_6.
    (C) B_{12}.
    (D) D.

22. A tumor is a
    (A) cancer.
    (B) growth.
    (C) sore spot.
    (D) kind of mushroom.

23. All types of steel contain
    (A) iron.
    (B) chromium.
    (C) nickel.
    (D) tungsten.

24. The *most important* provision for a hike in hot, dry countryside is
    (A) dried meat.
    (B) raisins.
    (C) fresh fruit.
    (D) water.

25. The moon is a
    (A) star.
    (B) satellite.
    (C) planetoid.
    (D) planet.

26. During a thunderstorm, we see a lightning bolt before we hear the sound of the accompanying thunder chiefly because
    (A) the eye is more sensitive than the ear.
    (B) the wind interferes with the sound of the thunder.
    (C) the storm may be very far away.
    (D) the speed of light is much greater than the speed of sound.

27. Of the following, a human blood disease that has been definitely shown to be due to a hereditary factor or factors is
    (A) pernicious anemia.
    (B) polyscythemia.
    (C) sickle cell anemia.
    (D) leukemia.

28. The number of degrees on the Fahrenheit thermometer between the freezing point and the boiling point of water is
    (A) 100 degrees.
    (B) 212 degrees.
    (C) 180 degrees.
    (D) 273 degrees.

29. An observer on Earth sees the phases of the moon because the
    (A) moon revolves around the sun.
    (B) moon revolves around the earth.
    (C) earth revolves around the sun.
    (D) moon rotates on its axis.

30. The temperature of the air falls at night because the earth loses heat by
    (A) radiation.
    (B) conduction.
    (C) convection.
    (D) rotation.

31. The normal height of a mercury barometer at sea level is
    (A) 15 inches.
    (B) 32 feet.
    (C) 30 inches.
    (D) 34 feet.

32. Nitrogen-fixing bacteria are found in nodules on the roots of the
    (A) beet.
    (B) potato.
    (C) carrot.
    (D) clover.

33. The vascular system of the body is concerned with
    (A) respiration.
    (B) sense of touch.
    (C) circulation of blood.
    (D) enzymes.

34. Of the following substances, the one that is nonmagnetic is
    (A) iron.
    (B) aluminum.
    (C) nickel.
    (D) cobalt.

35. If you wish to cut down on saturated fats and cholesterol in your diet, which of the following foods should you avoid?
    (A) Fish
    (B) Dry beans and peas
    (C) Cheese
    (D) Spaghetti

36. Which one of the following is NOT a fruit?
    (A) Potato
    (B) Tomato
    (C) Cucumber
    (D) Green pepper

37. The hammer, anvil, and stirrup bones lie in the
    (A) knee.
    (B) hip.
    (C) ear.
    (D) elbow.

38. Of the following, a condition NOT associated with heavy cigarette smoking is
    (A) shorter life span.
    (B) slowing of the heartbeat.
    (C) cancer of the lung.
    (D) heart disease.

39. You are most likely to develop hypothermia when

    (A) it is very hot and you have nothing to drink.
    (B) you are bitten by a rabid dog.
    (C) you fall asleep in the sun.
    (D) it is very cold and your clothes are wet.

40. Of the following, the gas that is needed for burning is

    (A) carbon dioxide.
    (B) nitrogen.
    (C) oxygen.
    (D) argon.

41. Of the following, the only safe blood transfusion would be

    (A) Group A blood into a Group O person.
    (B) Group B blood into a Group A person.
    (C) Group O blood into a Group AB person.
    (D) Group AB blood into a Group B person.

42. Of the following, the statement that best describes a "high" on a weather map is

    (A) the air extends farther up than normal.
    (B) the air pressure is greater than normal.
    (C) the air temperature is higher than normal.
    (D) the air moves faster than normal.

43. The smallest particle of gold that still retains the characteristics of gold is

    (A) a molecule.
    (B) a proton.
    (C) an electron.
    (D) an atom.

44. Narcotics may be dangerous if used without supervision, but they are useful in medicine because they

    (A) increase production of red blood cells.
    (B) kill bacteria.
    (C) relieve pain.
    (D) stimulate the heart.

45. The primary reason why fungi are often found growing in abundance deep in the forest is that there

    (A) it is cooler.
    (B) it is warmer.
    (C) they have little exposure to sunlight for photosynthesis.
    (D) they have a plentiful supply of organic matter.

46. The presence of coal deposits in Alaska shows that at one time Alaska

    (A) had a tropical climate.
    (B) was covered with ice.
    (C) was connected to Asia.
    (D) was formed by volcanic action.

47. If a person has been injured in an accident and damage to the back and neck is suspected, it is best to

    (A) roll the person over so that he does not lie on his back.
    (B) rush the person to the nearest hospital.
    (C) force the person to drink water to replace body fluids.
    (D) wait for professional help.

48. A 1,000-ton ship must displace a weight of water equal to

    (A) 500 tons.
    (B) 1,500 tons.
    (C) 1,000 tons.
    (D) 2,000 tons.

49. Vitamin C is also known as

    (A) citric acid.
    (B) ascorbic acid.
    (C) lactic acid.
    (D) glutamic acid.

50. If you are caught away from home during a thunderstorm, the safest place to be is

    (A) in a car.
    (B) under a tree.
    (C) in an open field.
    (D) at the top of a small hill.

PRACTICE EXERCISE 8: ELECTRONICS INFORMATION

Questions 1–50 are four-option items on electrical, radio, and electronics information. Select the correct response from the options given. Answers are on page 253.

1. In lights controlled by three-way switches, the switches should be treated and put in as
   (A) flush switches.
   (B) single-pole switches.
   (C) three double-pole switches.
   (D) three-pole switches.

2. When working on live 600-volt equipment where rubber gloves might be damaged, an electrician should
   (A) work without gloves.
   (B) carry a spare pair of rubber gloves.
   (C) reinforce the fingers of the rubber gloves with rubber tape.
   (D) wear leather gloves over the rubber gloves.

3. A "mil" measures
   (A) an eighth of an inch.
   (B) a millionth of an inch.
   (C) a thousandth of an inch.
   (D) a ten-thousandth of an inch.

4.

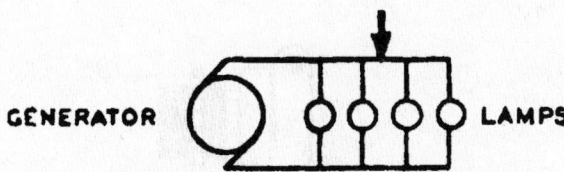

EACH LAMP TAKES 1 AMPERE
The current in the wire at the point indicated by the arrow is
   (A) 1 ampere.
   (B) 2 amperes.
   (C) 3 amperes.
   (D) 4 amperes.

5. If a fuse of higher than the required current rating is used in an electrical circuit,
   (A) better protection will be afforded.
   (B) the fuse will blow more often since it carries more current.
   (C) serious damage may result to the circuit from overload.
   (D) maintenance of the large fuse will be higher.

6. The electrical contacts in the tuner of a television set are usually plated with silver. Silver is used to
   (A) avoid tarnish.
   (B) improve conductivity.
   (C) improve appearance.
   (D) avoid arcing.

7. The following equipment is required for a "2-line return-can" electric bell circuit:
   (A) 2 bells, 2 metallic lines, 2 ordinary push buttons, and one set of batteries.
   (B) 2 bells, 2 metallic lines, 2 return-call push buttons, and 2 sets of batteries.
   (C) 2 bells, 2 metallic lines, 2 return-call push buttons, and one set of batteries.
   (D) 2 bells, 2 metallic lines, one ordinary push button, one return-call push button, and one set of batteries.

8.

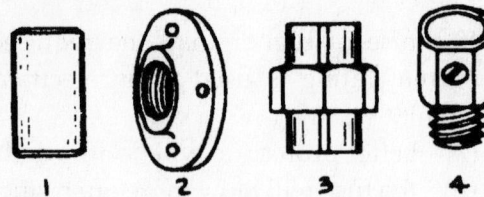

The standard coupling for rigid electrical conduit is

(A) 1.
(B) 2.
(C) 3.
(D) 4.

9. Metal cabinets used for lighting circuits are grounded to

(A) eliminate electrolysis.
(B) assure that the fuse in a defective circuit will blow.
(C) reduce shock hazard.
(D) simplify wiring.

10. Low Potential is a trade term that refers to

(A) 700 volts.
(B) 600 volts or less.
(C) 1,200 volts.
(D) 900 volts.

11. The purpose of having a rheostat in the field circuit of a DC shunt motor is to

(A) control the speed of the motor.
(B) minimize the starting current.
(C) limit the field current to a safe value.
(D) reduce sparking at the brushes.

12. A polarized plug generally has

(A) two parallel prongs of the same size.
(B) prongs at an angle with each other.
(C) magnetized prongs.
(D) prongs marked plus and minus.

13.

The reading of the kilowatt-hour meter is

(A) 7972
(B) 1786
(C) 2786
(D) 6872

14. Commutators are found on

(A) mercury rectifiers.
(B) DC motors.
(C) circuit breakers.
(D) alternators.

15. Neutral wire can be quickly recognized by the

(A) greenish color.
(B) bluish color.
(C) natural or whitish color.
(D) black color.

16. The term that is NOT applicable in describing the *construction* of a microphone is

(A) dynamic.
(B) carbon.
(C) crystal.
(D) feedback.

17.

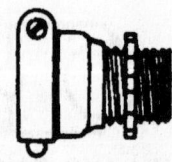

The fitting shown is used in electrical construction to

(A) clamp two adjacent junction boxes together.
(B) act as a ground clamp for the conduit system.
(C) attach a flexible metallic conduit to a junction box.
(D) protect exposed wires where they pass through a wall.

18. A good magnetic material is
   (A) copper.
   (B) iron.
   (C) tin.
   (D) brass.

19. Rosin is a material generally used
   (A) in batteries.
   (B) for high-voltage insulation.
   (C) as a dielectric.
   (D) as a soldering flux.

20. The letters RHW when applied to electrical wire indicate the wire
   (A) has a solid conductor.
   (B) has rubber insulation.
   (C) is insulated with paper.
   (D) has lead sheath.

21. Boxes and fittings intended for outdoor use should be of
   (A) weatherproof type.
   (B) stamped steel of not less than No. 16.
   (C) standard gauge.
   (D) stamped steel plated with cadmium.

22. A direct-current supply may be obtained from an alternating-current source by means of
   (A) a frequency changer set.
   (B) an inductance-capacitance filter.
   (C) a silicon diode rectifier.
   (D) none of the devices mentioned above.

23. Fuses protecting motor circuits have to be selected to permit a momentary surge of
   (A) voltage when the motor starts.
   (B) voltage when the motor stops.
   (C) current when the motor starts.
   (D) current when the motor stops.

24. When working near lead acid storage batteries, extreme care should be taken to guard against sparks, essentially to avoid
   (A) overheating the electrolyte.
   (B) an electric shock.
   (C) a short circuit.
   (D) an explosion.

25. The voltage that will cause a current of 5 amperes to flow through a 20-Ohm resistance is
   (A) $\frac{1}{4}$ volt.
   (B) 4 volts.
   (C) 20 volts.
   (D) 100 volts.

26. Receptacles in a house-lighting system are regularly connected in
   (A) parallel.
   (B) series.
   (C) diagonal.
   (D) perpendicular.

27. The electronic symbol shown below usually represents a(n)

   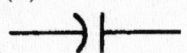

   (A) resistor.
   (B) inductor.
   (C) capacitor.
   (D) transformer.

28. If a live conductor is contacted accidentally, the severity of the electrical shock is determined primarily by
   (A) the size of the conductor.
   (B) the current of the conductor.
   (C) whether the current is AC or DC.
   (D) the contact resistance.

29. Locknuts are frequently used in making electrical connections on terminal boards. The purpose of the locknuts is to
   (A) eliminate the use of flat washers.
   (B) prevent unauthorized personnel from tampering with the connections.
   (C) keep the connections from loosening through vibration.
   (D) increase the contact area at the connection point.

30. If a condenser is connected across the make-and-break contact of an ordinary electric bell, the effect will be to

(A) speed up the action of the clapper.
(B) reduce the amount of arcing at the contact.
(C) slow down the action of the clapper.
(D) reduce the load on the bell transformer or battery.

31. A material NOT used in the makeup of lighting wires or cables is

(A) rubber.
(B) paper.
(C) lead.
(D) cotton.

32.

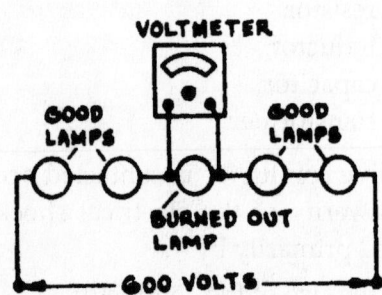

The reading of the voltmeter should be

(A) 600
(B) 300
(C) 120
(D) 0

33. Silver is a better conductor of electricity than copper; however, copper is generally used for electrical conductors. The main reason for using copper instead of silver is its

(A) cost.
(B) weight.
(C) strength.
(D) melting point.

34. Direct-current arcs are "hotter" and harder to extinguish than alternating-current arcs, so electrical appliances that include a thermostat are frequently marked for use on "AC only." One appliance that might be so marked because it includes a thermostat is a

(A) soldering iron.
(B) floor waxer.
(C) vacuum cleaner.
(D) household iron.

35. An alternator is

(A) an AC generator.
(B) a frequency meter.
(C) a ground detector device.
(D) a choke coil.

36. Operating an incandescent electric lightbulb at less than its rated voltage will result in

(A) shorter life and brighter light.
(B) brighter light and longer life.
(C) longer life and dimmer light.
(D) dimmer light and shorter life.

37.

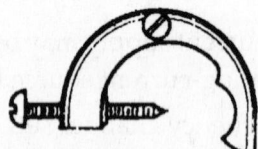

The device shown above is a

(A) C-clamp.
(B) test clip.
(C) battery connector.
(D) ground clamp.

38. When the electric refrigerator in a certain household kitchen starts up, the kitchen light at first dims considerably and then it increases somewhat in brightness while the refrigerator motor is running; the light finally returns to full brightness when the refrigerator shuts off. This behavior of the light shows that most likely the

(A) circuit wires are too small.
(B) refrigerator motor is defective.
(C) circuit fuse is too small.
(D) kitchen lamp is too large.

39. A circular mil is a measure of electrical conductor

    (A) length.
    (B) area.
    (C) volume.
    (D) weight.

40. The instrument by which electric power may be measured is a

    (A) rectifier.
    (B) scanner drum.
    (C) ammeter.
    (D) watt-meter.

41. The most likely cause of a burned-out fuse in the primary circuit of a transformer in a rectifier is

    (A) grounding of the electrostatic shield.
    (B) an open circuit in a bleeder resistor.
    (C) an open circuit in the secondary winding.
    (D) a short-circuit filter capacitor.

42. The primary coil of a power transformer has 100 turns, and the secondary coil has 50 turns. The voltage across the secondary will be

    (A) four times that of the primary.
    (B) twice that of the primary.
    (C) half that of the primary.
    (D) one fourth that of the primary.

43. The best electrical connection between two wires is obtained when

    (A) the insulations are melted together.
    (B) all insulation is removed and the wires bound together with friction tape.
    (C) both are wound on a common binding post.
    (D) they are soldered together.

44. Excessive resistance in the primary circuit will lessen the output of the ignition coil and cause the

    (A) battery to short out and the generator to run down.
    (B) battery to short out and the plugs to wear out prematurely.
    (C) generator to run down and the timing mechanism to slow down.
    (D) engine to perform poorly and be hard to start.

45. During a "short circuit," the

    (A) current flow becomes very large.
    (B) resistance becomes very large.
    (C) voltage applied becomes very small.
    (D) power input becomes very small.

46. The main reason for making wire stranded is

    (A) to make it easier to insulate.
    (B) so that the insulation will not come off.
    (C) to decrease its weight.
    (D) to make it more flexible.

47. The oscilloscope image shown above represents

    (A) steady DC.
    (B) resistance in a resistor.
    (C) AC.
    (D) pulsating DC.

48. Voltage drop in a circuit is usually due to

    (A) inductance.
    (B) capacitance.
    (C) resistance.
    (D) conductance.

49. Which of the following sizes of electric heaters is the largest one that can be used in a 120-volt circuit protected by a 15-ampere circuit breaker?

    (A) 1000 watts
    (B) 1300 watts
    (C) 2000 watts
    (D) 2600 watts

50. The one of the following devices that will store an electric charge is the

    (A) capacitor.
    (B) inductor.
    (C) thyristor.
    (D) resistor.

PRACTICE EXERCISE 9: MECHANICAL COMPREHENSION

Study each diagram carefully and select the choice that best answers the question or completes the statement. Answers are on page 259.

1.

Shown above is a second-class lever. A common example of a second-class lever is

(A) a crowbar.
(B) a nutcracker.
(C) pliers.

2.

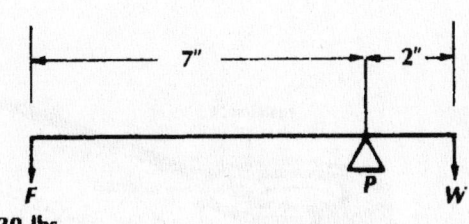

The weight on the lever being balanced by the force of 30 pounds, shown in the diagram above, is most nearly

(A) 42 lbs.
(B) 84 lbs.
(C) 105 lbs.

3.

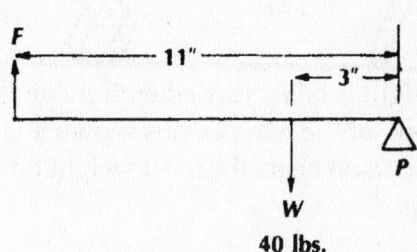

The force F required to balance the weight of 40 pounds on the lever shown in the diagram above is most nearly

(A) 8 lbs.
(B) 10 lbs.
(C) 11 lbs.

4.

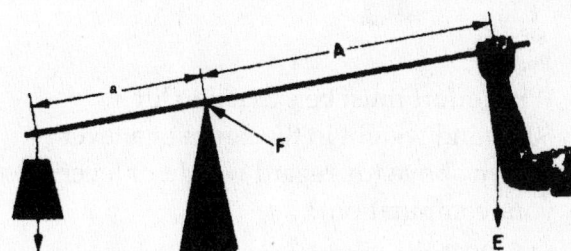

The mechanical advantage of the lever shown above is

(A) $\dfrac{a}{A}$

(B) $\dfrac{A}{a}$

(C) $a \times A$

5.

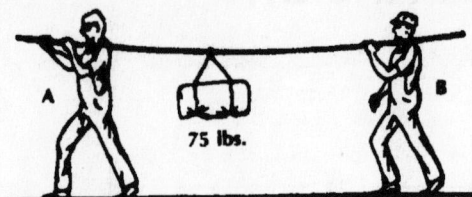

The weight is being carried entirely on the shoulders of the two persons shown above. Which person bears the most weight on the shoulder?

(A) A
(B) B
(C) Both are carrying the same weight.

6.

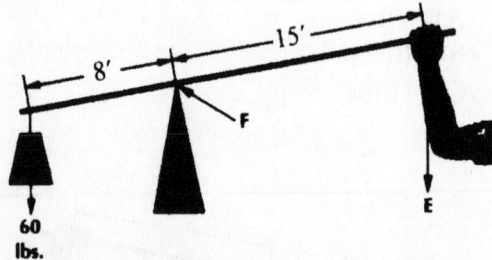

What effort must be exerted to lift a 60-pound weight in the figure of a lever shown above (disregard weight of lever in your computation)?

(A) 30 lbs.
(B) 32 lbs.
(C) 34 lbs.

7.

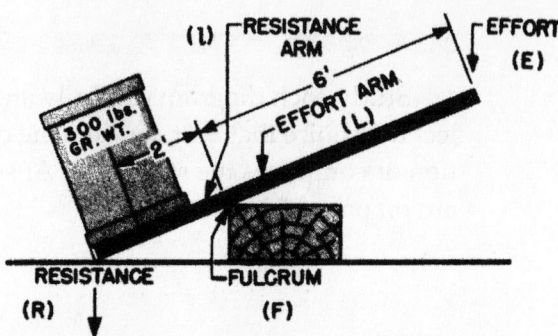

In the figure shown above, what effort must be exerted on the iron bar to raise a 300-pound crate off the floor (disregard weight of bar in your computation)?

(A) 50 lbs.
(B) 100 lbs.
(C) 150 lbs.

8.

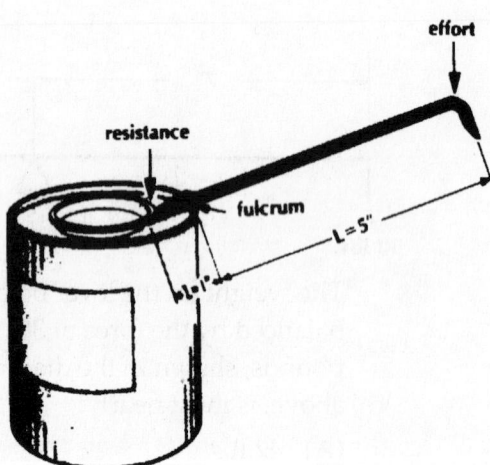

In the figure shown above, what force must be applied to the 6-inch file scraper to pry up the lid of the paint can? Assume that the average force holding the lid is 50 pounds (disregard weight of the scraper).

(A) 10 lbs.
(B) 20 lbs.
(C) 30 lbs.

9.

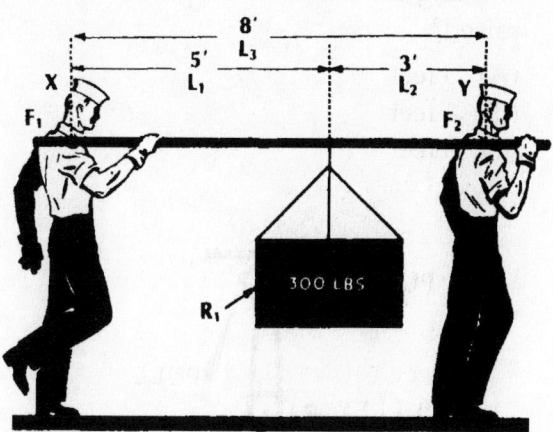

In the figure above, two sailors are carrying a 300-pound crate slung on a 10-foot pole. On the basis of the data shown in the figure,

(A) each sailor is carrying 150 pounds.
(B) sailor X is carrying approximately 188 pounds.
(C) sailor Y is carrying approximately 188 pounds.

10.

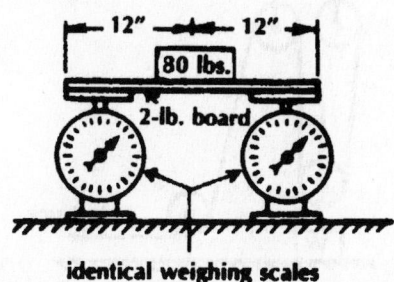

identical weighing scales

In the figure shown above, the weight held by the board and placed on the two identical scales will cause *each* scale to read

(A) 40 lbs.
(B) 41 lbs.
(C) 42 lbs.

11.

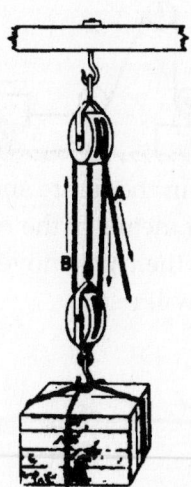

The crate shown in the figure above weighs 300 pounds. Neglecting block friction, the weight of the movable block, and the weight of the line, what pull is necessary to raise the crate?

(A) 50 pounds
(B) 100 pounds
(C) 150 pounds

12.

400 lbs.

The theoretical mechanical advantage of the pulley system shown above is

(A) 3
(B) 4
(C) 5

13.

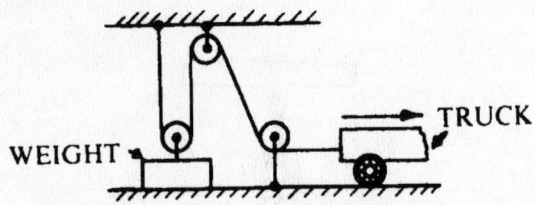

WEIGHT

TRUCK

The weight in the figure shown above is to be raised by means of the rope attached to the truck. If the truck moves forward 10 feet, the weight will rise

(A) $2\frac{1}{2}$ feet.
(B) 5 feet.
(C) 10 feet.

Answer questions 14 and 15 on the basis of the pulley system shown below.

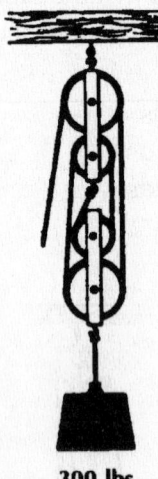

300 lbs.

14. Neglecting friction and the weight of the pulley system, what effort is needed to lift the 300-pound weight?

(A) 75 pounds
(B) 100 pounds
(C) 150 pounds

15. If 12 feet of rope was pulled by the person exerting the effort, how high was the weight raised?

(A) 3 feet
(B) 4 feet
(C) 5 feet

16.

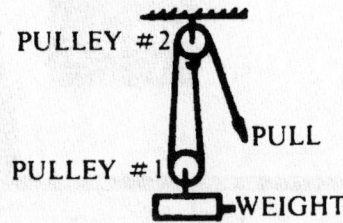

PULLEY #2

PULLEY #1

PULL

WEIGHT

The block and tackle shown has two pulleys of equal diameter. While the weight is being raised, pulley #1 will rotate at

(A) twice the speed of pulley #2.
(B) the same speed as pulley #2.
(C) one half the speed of pulley #2.

17.

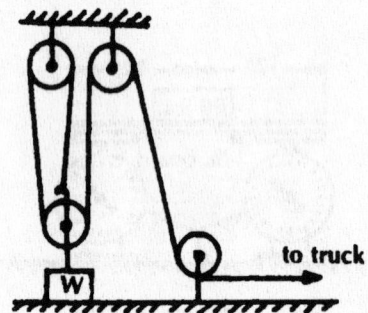

to truck

W

The tank "W" is to be raised as shown by attaching the pull rope to a truck. If the tank is to be raised six feet, the truck will have to move

(A) 12 feet.
(B) 15 feet.
(C) 18 feet.

18.

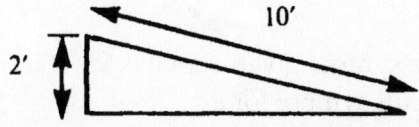

What is the ideal mechanical advantage of the incline shown in the above diagram?

(A) 5
(B) 4
(C) 3

19.

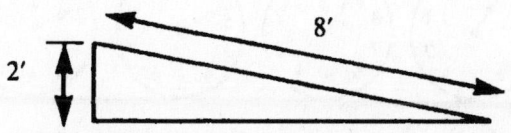

Neglecting friction, what effort is needed to roll a barrel weighing 400 pounds up the incline shown in the above diagram?

(A) 200 pounds
(B) 100 pounds
(C) 50 pounds

20.

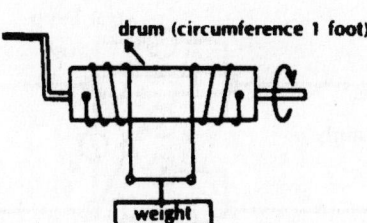

In the figure shown above, one complete revolution of the windlass drum will move the weight up

(A) 12 inches.
(B) 18 inches.
(C) 24 inches.

21.

A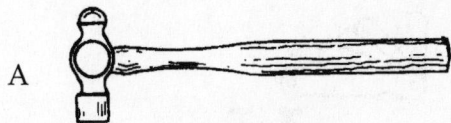

B

C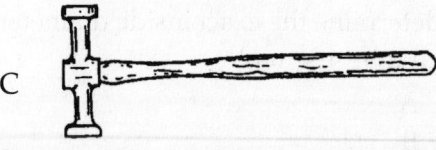

To smooth out a dent in a piece of formed sheet metal, use tool

(A) A
(B) B
(C) C

22.

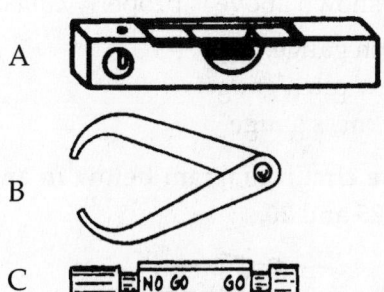

To lay out a horizontal line in the center of the wall, use tool

(A) A
(B) B
(C) C

23.

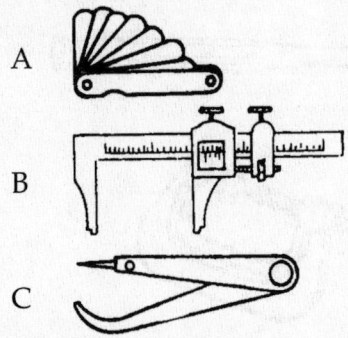

To determine the exact inside diameter of a metal tube, use tool

(A) A
(B) B
(C) C

24.

The tool shown above is properly called a

(A) depth gauge.
(B) screw pitch gauge.
(C) thickness gauge.

Refer to the circuit diagram below in answering questions 25 and 26.

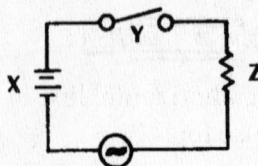

25. X is a

(A) battery.
(B) capacitor.
(C) motor.

26. Y is a

(A) fuse.
(B) rheostat.
(C) switch.

27.

The symbol given above is the standard circuit symbol for a

(A) capacitor.
(B) fixed resistor.
(C) variable resistor.

28.

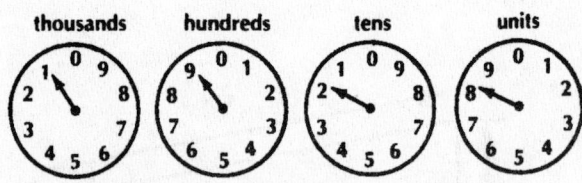

In the figure above, the reading of the kilowatt-hour meter, as shown by the dials, is

(A) 0918
(B) 1928
(C) 8190

29.

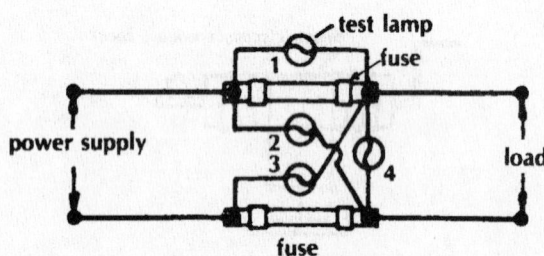

In the diagram shown above, if the upper fuse is good and the lower fuse is burned out, the test lamp that will be lighted is

(A) 1
(B) 2
(C) 3

Questions 30 and 31 are based on the following diagram of circuits numbered 1, 2, and 3.

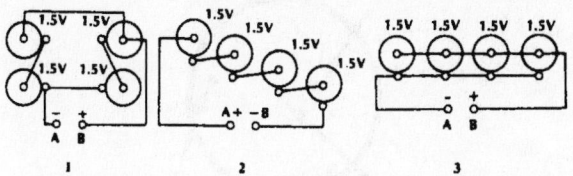

30. Which one of the circuits shown is a parallel circuit?

(A) 1
(B) 2
(C) 3

31. Which one of the circuits shown is a series-parallel circuit?

(A) 1
(B) 2
(C) 3

32.

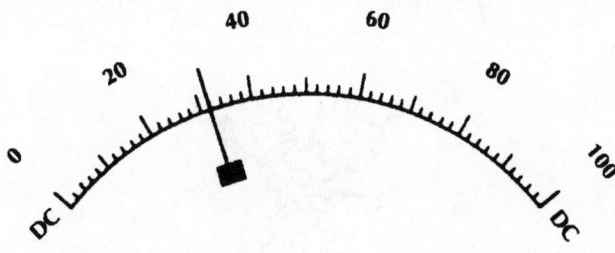

The correct reading on the voltmeter shown above is

(A) 26 volts.
(B) 32 volts.
(C) 36 volts.

Questions 33 and 34 are based on the ohmmeter scale shown below. Note that zero is at the right end of the scale.

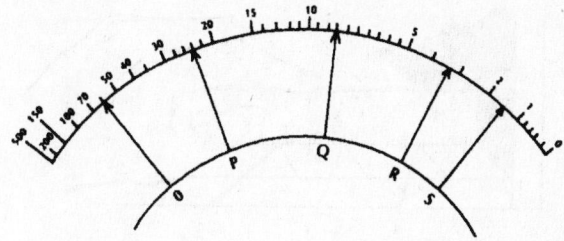

33. Point O has a value of

(A) 57
(B) 60
(C) 63

34. Point S lies midway between 1 and 2. 1.5 lies

(A) to the left of point S.
(B) at point S.
(C) to the right of point S.

Question 35 is based on the sketch of a portion of a multimeter (V-O-M) scale shown below. The selector switch on the meter can be set to several different resistance ranges, as well as a number of different DC voltage and milliampere ranges.

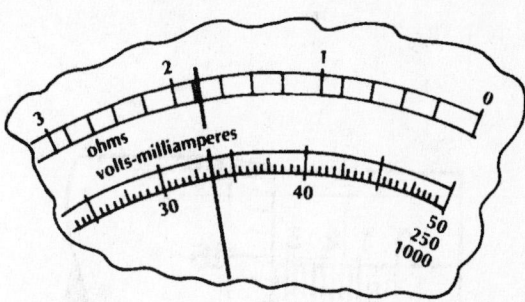

35. If the selector switch is set on the ohms × 100 range, the resistance value indicated is

(A) 175 ohms.
(B) 17.5 ohms.
(C) 1.75 ohms.

Questions 36 and 37 are based on the diagram given below pertaining to the measuring with and reading of a common rule.

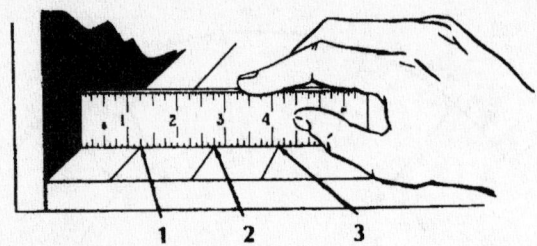

36. The reading at point 1 is

(A) $1\frac{1}{8}''$

(B) $1\frac{1}{4}''$

(C) $1\frac{3}{8}''$

37. The distance between point 2 and point 3 is

(A) $1\frac{3}{8}''$

(B) $1\frac{1}{2}''$

(C) $1\frac{5}{8}''$

38.

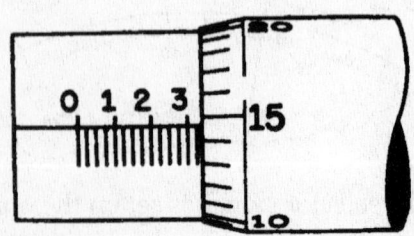

In the figure shown above, the micrometer reading to three decimal places is

(A) .338
(B) .339
(C) .340

39.

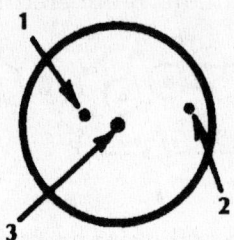

The figure above represents a revolving wheel. The numbers 1 and 2 indicate two fixed points on the wheel. The number 3 indicates the center of the wheel. Of the following, the most accurate statement is that

(A) point 1 traverses a greater linear distance than point 2.
(B) point 2 traverses a greater linear distance than point 1.
(C) all three points traverse the same linear distance.

40.

Four gears are shown in the figure above. If gear 1 turns as shown, then the gear turning in a counterclockwise direction is gear

(A) 2
(B) 3
(C) 4

41.

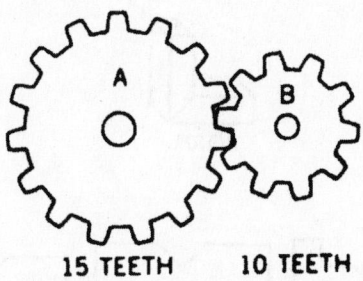

15 TEETH   10 TEETH

If the larger gear is revolving at 200 revolutions per minute, at how many revolutions per minute is the smaller gear revolving?

(A) 100
(B) 250
(C) 300

42.

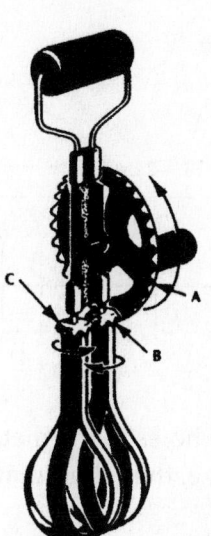

In the figure above, a simple gear arrangement is shown. If there are 32 teeth on the large vertical wheel A, 8 teeth on horizontal wheel B, and 8 teeth on horizontal wheel C, one complete revolution of wheel A results in

(A) two complete revolutions of gear C.
(B) three complete revolutions of gear C.
(C) four complete revolutions of gear C.

43.

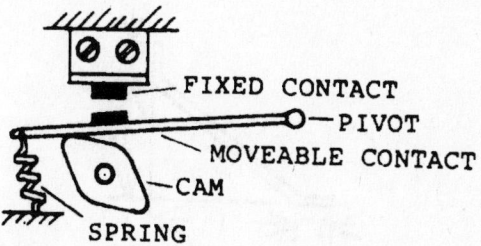

If the contacts come together twice every second, the cam is rotating at

(A) 30 RPM.
(B) 60 RPM.
(C) 120 RPM.

44.

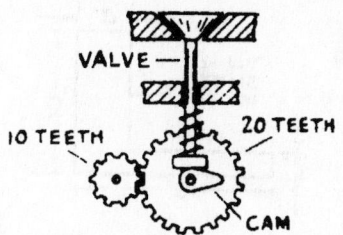

The figure above shows a cam that actuates a valve. If the 10-tooth gear makes six revolutions, the valve will open

(A) 6 times.
(B) 4 times.
(C) 3 times.

45.

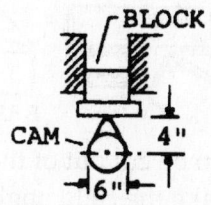

In the figure above, rotation of the cam will permit the block to drop a maximum of

(A) 1"
(B) 2"
(C) 4"

46.

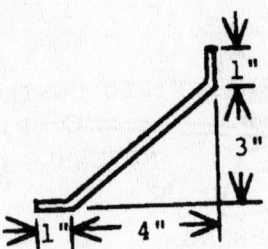

The length of the sheet metal strap before bending was most nearly

(A) 7 inches.
(B) 8 inches.
(C) 9 inches.

47.

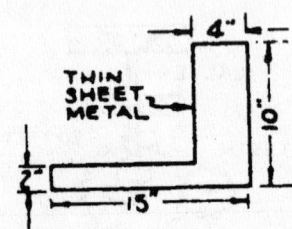

The maximum number of rectangular pieces, each two inches by eight inches, that can be cut from the thin metal sheet shown above is

(A) two.
(B) three.
(C) four.

48.

A piece is to be cut out of the angle iron in order to make the right angle bracket. Angle X should be

(A) 45 degrees.
(B) 60 degrees.
(C) 90 degrees.

49.

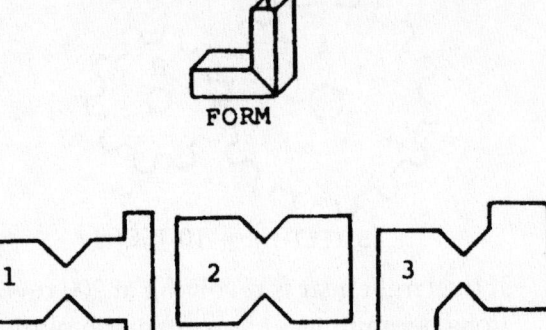

The form shown above, which is open at both ends, can be shaped from sheet metal number

(A) 1
(B) 2
(C) 3

50.

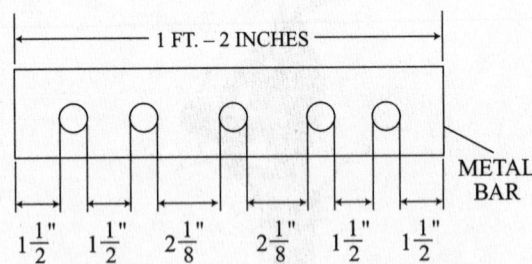

If all of the holes in the metal bar are to be equal in size, then their diameters should be

(A) $\frac{1}{2}$ inch.

(B) $\frac{3}{4}$ inch.

(C) 1 inch.

PART VIII

Key Answers and Rationale for Practice Exercises

KEY ANSWERS AND RATIONALE FOR PRACTICE EXERCISE 1: SYNONYMS

Items 1–50 (5 options)

1. The correct answer is (E).
2. The correct answer is (C).
3. The correct answer is (A).
4. The correct answer is (B).
5. The correct answer is (D).
6. The correct answer is (C).
7. The correct answer is (C).
8. The correct answer is (C).
9. The correct answer is (E).
10. The correct answer is (B).
11. The correct answer is (C).
12. The correct answer is (A).
13. The correct answer is (A).
14. The correct answer is (C).
15. The correct answer is (A).
16. The correct answer is (E).
17. The correct answer is (D).
18. The correct answer is (E).
19. The correct answer is (E).
20. The correct answer is (C).
21. The correct answer is (B).
22. The correct answer is (E).
23. The correct answer is (E).
24. The correct answer is (D).
25. The correct answer is (B).
26. The correct answer is (C).
27. The correct answer is (B).
28. The correct answer is (D).
29. The correct answer is (E).
30. The correct answer is (D).
31. The correct answer is (D).
32. The correct answer is (E).
33. The correct answer is (B).
34. The correct answer is (C).
35. The correct answer is (C).
36. The correct answer is (A).
37. The correct answer is (B).
38. The correct answer is (C).
39. The correct answer is (C).
40. The correct answer is (B).
41. The correct answer is (C).
42. The correct answer is (D).
43. The correct answer is (D).
44. The correct answer is (A).
45. The correct answer is (A).
46. The correct answer is (B).
47. The correct answer is (D).
48. The correct answer is (B).
49. The correct answer is (D).
50. The correct answer is (D).

Items 51-100 (4 options)

51. The correct answer is (D).
52. The correct answer is (B).
53. The correct answer is (C).
54. The correct answer is (C).
55. The correct answer is (B).
56. The correct answer is (A).
57. The correct answer is (B).
58. The correct answer is (D).
59. The correct answer is (B).
60. The correct answer is (B).
61. The correct answer is (B).
62. The correct answer is (A).
63. The correct answer is (A).
64. The correct answer is (C).
65. The correct answer is (B).
66. The correct answer is (A).
67. The correct answer is (B).
68. The correct answer is (B).
69. The correct answer is (A).
70. The correct answer is (A).
71. The correct answer is (A).
72. The correct answer is (B).
73. The correct answer is (C).
74. The correct answer is (C).
75. The correct answer is (C).

76. The correct answer is (C).
77. The correct answer is (B).
78. The correct answer is (D).
79. The correct answer is (D).
80. The correct answer is (B).
81. The correct answer is (C).
82. The correct answer is (D).
83. The correct answer is (B).
84. The correct answer is (A).
85. The correct answer is (B).
86. The correct answer is (A).
87. The correct answer is (B).
88. The correct answer is (A).
89. The correct answer is (C).
90. The correct answer is (B).
91. The correct answer is (C).
92. The correct answer is (B).
93. The correct answer is (A).
94. The correct answer is (A).
95. The correct answer is (C).
96. The correct answer is (A).
97. The correct answer is (B).
98. The correct answer is (B).
99. The correct answer is (C).
100. The correct answer is (D).

Items Answered Incorrectly: __; __; __; __; __; __; __; __.
Items Unsure Of: __; __; __; __; __; __; __; __.

**TOTAL NUMBER
ANSWERED CORRECTLY: _____**

Rationale

Review those questions you did not answer correctly and those you did answer correctly but are unsure of. Refer to any good unabridged dictionary for the meaning of those words that are giving you trouble.

Developing your own list of such words and their meanings will enable you to review these troublesome words periodically. Such practices will aid materially in increasing your vocabulary and raising your vocabulary scores.

Add to your vocabulary list whenever you come across a word whose meaning is unclear to you.

KEY ANSWERS AND RATIONALE FOR PRACTICE EXERCISE 2: VERBAL ANALOGIES

Key Answers

1. The correct answer is (C).
2. The correct answer is (C).
3. The correct answer is (C).
4. The correct answer is (E).
5. The correct answer is (E).
6. The correct answer is (D).
7. The correct answer is (D).
8. The correct answer is (E).
9. The correct answer is (B).
10. The correct answer is (A).
11. The correct answer is (B).
12. The correct answer is (C).
13. The correct answer is (D).
14. The correct answer is (B).
15. The correct answer is (C).
16. The correct answer is (A).
17. The correct answer is (C).
18. The correct answer is (B).
19. The correct answer is (A).
20. The correct answer is (B).
21. The correct answer is (C).
22. The correct answer is (E).
23. The correct answer is (B).
24. The correct answer is (A).
25. The correct answer is (E).
26. The correct answer is (A).
27. The correct answer is (B).
28. The correct answer is (B).
29. The correct answer is (E).
30. The correct answer is (D).
31. The correct answer is (A).
32. The correct answer is (A).
33. The correct answer is (B).
34. The correct answer is (C).
35. The correct answer is (E).
36. The correct answer is (B).
37. The correct answer is (E).
38. The correct answer is (B).
39. The correct answer is (B).
40. The correct answer is (E).
41. The correct answer is (C).
42. The correct answer is (E).
43. The correct answer is (C).
44. The correct answer is (E).
45. The correct answer is (C).
46. The correct answer is (D).
47. The correct answer is (D).
48. The correct answer is (E).
49. The correct answer is (E).
50. The correct answer is (E).

Items Answered Incorrectly: __; __; __; __; __; __; __; __.
Items Unsure Of: __; __; __; __; __; __; __; __.

TOTAL NUMBER ANSWERED CORRECTLY: _____

Rationale

1. The correct answer is (C). An *easel* is used by *an artist* to support the canvas; a *loom* is used by a *weaver* to hold the yarn that makes up the fabric.

2. The correct answer is (C). An *automobile* travels on a *highway*; a *train* moves on the *rails*.

3. The correct answer is (C). A *biography* deals with the *facts* of a person's life; a *novel* deals with imaginative narration or *fiction*.

4. The correct answer is (E). A *crowd* consists of a large number of *persons*; a *fleet* consists of a large number of *ships*.

5. The correct answer is (E). *Darkness* and *light* are antonyms; *stillness* and *sound* are antonyms.

6. The correct answer is (D). *Efficiency* generally leads to a *reward; carelessness* generally leads to a severe reproof or *reprimand*.

7. The correct answer is (D). *Fallen* is the past participle of the infinitive *to fall; flown* is the past participle of the infinitive to *fly*.

8. The correct answer is (E). *Pork* is obtained from the *hog; mutton* is obtained from *sheep*.

9. The correct answer is (B). A *sandal* is worn on the *foot*; a *shawl* is worn around the *shoulders*.

10. The correct answer is (A). A *theater* is a building expressly designed for special forms of *recreation*; a *school* is a building expressly designed for the *education* of students.

11. The correct answer is (B). *III* is the Roman numeral for *3; XIV* is the Roman numeral for *14*.

12. The correct answer is (C). *When* refers to *time; how* refers to *manner*.

13. The correct answer is (D). A *clock* is used to determine the *time*; a *thermometer* is used to determine the *temperature*.

14. The correct answer is (B). A *gavel* is used by a *judge* to signal for attention or order; a *baton* is used by a *conductor* for the same purpose.

15. The correct answer is (C). A *kilogram* consists of 1000 *grams*. Therefore, *1* is to *1000* as *gram* is to *kilogram*.

16. The correct answer is (A). A *sentence* is a major subdivision of a *paragraph*; a *chapter* is a major subdivision of a *book*.

17. The correct answer is (C). The first pair of words are synonyms. *Melt* and *thaw* are synonymous also.

18. The correct answer is (B). A *sparrow* is a type of *bird*; a *wasp* is a type of *insect*.

19. The correct answer is (A). *Submarines* and *fish* are generally found in water. *Kites* and *birds* are generally seen in the air.

20. The correct answer is (B). The first pair of words are antonyms. The antonym for *cold* is *hot*.

21. The correct answer is (C). *Affirm* is direct; *hint* is indirect or suggestive. *Charge* is direct; *insinuate* is indirect or suggestive.

22. The correct answer is (E). The first pair of words are synonyms; *rash* and *reckless* are synonymous also.

23. The correct answer is (B). This is a purpose relationship. The *glove* is used to catch a *ball*; the *hook* is used to catch *fish*.

24. The correct answer is (A). To *intimidate* is to inspire *fear*; to *astonish* is to inspire *wonder*.

25. The correct answer is (E). This is an action-to-object relationship. You *kick* a *football* and *smoke* a *pipe*.

26. The correct answer is (A). This is a city/state relationship. *Miami* is a city in *Florida; Albany* is a city in *New York*.

27. The correct answer is (B). This is a cause-and-effect relationship. *Fatigue* results from *racing; hunger* results from *fasting*.

28. The correct answer is (B). A *stove* is an essential piece of equipment for a *kitchen;* a *sink* is essential for a *bathroom*.

29. The correct answer is (E). This is an action-to-object relationship. You *throw* a *ball* and *shoot* a *gun*.

30. The correct answer is (D). A *triangle*, a three-sided plane figure, is the side of a *pyramid;* a *square*, a four-sided plane figure, is the side of a *cube*.

31. The correct answer is (A). The relationship is that of degree. *Hot* is excessively *warm;* a *genius* is very *bright*.

32. The correct answer is (A). A *woodsman* cuts lumber with an *ax;* a *carpenter* cuts lumber with a *saw*.

33. The correct answer is (B). *Astute* and *stupid* are antonyms. Of the options given, only choice (B) contains antonyms.

34. The correct answer is (C). A *bricklayer* uses *mortar* as an adhesive for bricks; a *carpenter* uses *glue* as an adhesive for wood.

35. The correct answer is (E). *Boats* are laid up in a *dock; trains* are laid up in a *depot*.

36. The correct answer is (B). There are ten *decades* in a *century* and ten *years* in a *decade*.

37. The correct answer is (E). *Decibel* is a measure of *sound;* a *volt* is a measure of *electricity*.

38. The correct answer is (B). The relationship is that of synonyms. *Delay* and *postpone* are synonyms.

39. The correct answer is (B). The *eye* of a *hurricane* is the circular region surrounding the center of the storm's rotation. The *hub* of a *wheel* surrounds the axle, which is the center of the wheel's rotation.

40. The correct answer is (E). The relationship of *fission* and *fusion* is that of splitting and merging. The only parallel relationship is found in choice (E).

41. The correct answer is (C). An extremely *good* person would be *angelic*. An extremely *glad* person would be *joyous*.

42. The correct answer is (E). The relationship of the capitalized words is that of an animal that is normally pursued by another animal. The only parallel relationship is found in choice (E).

43. The correct answer is (C). The relationship of the two capitalized words is that of the term used with a number of animals of one kind kept or living together and the individuals making up this number. The only parallel relationship is found in choice (C).

44. The correct answer is (E). *Incarcerate* means to *restrain; emancipate* means to *release*.

45. The correct answer is (C). *Keel* is the bottom of a *ship; sole* is the bottom of a *shoe*.

46. The correct answer is (D). *Lions* are meat-eaters *(carnivorous); horses* are plant-eaters *(herbivorous)*.

47. The correct answer is (D). *Margarine* is a manufactured substitute for *butter; nylon* is a manufactured substitute for *silk*.

48. The correct answer is (E). The relationship of the two capitalized words is that of a unit of *weight* and a unit of *volume*.

49. The correct answer is (E). One is generally *negligent* in meeting a *requirement* or *remiss* in performing a *duty*.

50. The correct answer is (E). *Marmalade* is made from *oranges; ketchup* is made from *tomatoes*.

KEY ANSWERS AND RATIONALE FOR PRACTICE EXERCISE 3: READING COMPREHENSION

Items 1-25 (5 options)

1. The correct answer is (C).
2. The correct answer is (D).
3. The correct answer is (C).
4. The correct answer is (A).
5. The correct answer is (C).
6. The correct answer is (B).
7. The correct answer is (A).
8. The correct answer is (D).
9. The correct answer is (A).
10. The correct answer is (B).
11. The correct answer is (C).
12. The correct answer is (B).
13. The correct answer is (E).
14. The correct answer is (A).
15. The correct answer is (B).
16. The correct answer is (A).
17. The correct answer is (C).
18. The correct answer is (A).
19. The correct answer is (E).
20. The correct answer is (B).
21. The correct answer is (B).
22. The correct answer is (C).
23. The correct answer is (A).
24. The correct answer is (D).
25. The correct answer is (A).

Items 26-50 (4 options)

26. The correct answer is (D).
27. The correct answer is (A).
28. The correct answer is (B).
29. The correct answer is (B).
30. The correct answer is (B).
31. The correct answer is (A).
32. The correct answer is (C).
33. The correct answer is (B).
34. The correct answer is (C).
35. The correct answer is (D).
36. The correct answer is (D).
37. The correct answer is (B).
38. The correct answer is (A).
39. The correct answer is (B).
40. The correct answer is (D).
41. The correct answer is (D).
42. The correct answer is (C).
43. The correct answer is (D).
44. The correct answer is (A).
45. The correct answer is (B).
46. The correct answer is (A).
47. The correct answer is (B).
48. The correct answer is (B).
49. The correct answer is (C).
50. The correct answer is (D).

Items 51-75 (4 options)

51. The correct answer is (B).

52. The correct answer is (A).

53. The correct answer is (B).

54. The correct answer is (B).

55. The correct answer is (A).

56. The correct answer is (C).

57. The correct answer is (D).

58. The correct answer is (A).

59. The correct answer is (B).

60. The correct answer is (D).

61. The correct answer is (B).

62. The correct answer is (C).

63. The correct answer is (A).

64. The correct answer is (A).

65. The correct answer is (D).

66. The correct answer is (A).

67. The correct answer is (A).

68. The correct answer is (A).

69. The correct answer is (C).

70. The correct answer is (D).

71. The correct answer is (B).

72. The correct answer is (B).

73. The correct answer is (B).

74. The correct answer is (B).

75. The correct answer is (C).

Items Answered Incorrectly: __; __; __; __; __; __; __; __.
Items Unsure Of: __; __; __; __; __; __; __; __.

TOTAL NUMBER
ANSWERED CORRECTLY: _____

Rationale

1. The correct answer is (C). Safety education must be a continuous process because it is common for people to be careless.

2. The correct answer is (D). During times of stress, law enforcement becomes committed to reducing that stress between population groups.

3. The correct answer is (C). The uneven saturation of energy would result in unevenly cooked food.

4. The correct answer is (A). The watt is a measure of electrical energy. Electrical power in the home is measured in watts or kilowatts.

5. The correct answer is (C). The magnetron within the microwave oven generates the energy.

6. The correct answer is (B). A danger is the possible development of a mutant bacteria that may change the life pattern on Earth.

7. The correct answer is (A). The common cold is considered to be a viral infection. Interferon may be used to cure the infection.

8. The correct answer is (D). The purpose of the highway was to link various parts of Brazil. This included parts that were relatively inaccessible.

9. The correct answer is (A). The intent of the Brazilian government was to do good rather than harm. Plans to achieve human progress are not always realized.

10. The correct answer is (B). *Inadvertently* is synonymous with *accidentally* or *unintentionally*.

11. The correct answer is (C). Cartography is the science of mapmaking. Improved cartography means better maps.

12. The correct answer is (B). Offering a prize for better maps indicates the French government's concern with the development of better maps.

13. The correct answer is (E). The only direct consequence of improved mapmaking was that it enabled nations to agree on clearly defined time zones.

14. The correct answer is (A). Amerigo Vespucci is the only one of those listed who was a famous cartographer and who gave his name to the New World in the early part of the sixteenth century.

15. The correct answer is (B). Educators believe that business is looking for people who have specific vocational skills.

16. The correct answer is (A). The two key words that show the author does not agree with the educators' arguments are *narrow* and *alleged*.

17. The correct answer is (C). The author believes that most business leaders are looking for well-educated personnel who are able to communicate.

18. The correct answer is (A). The first sentence in the passage states that they neither indulge in nor esteem meditation.

19. The correct answer is (E). " . . . he is much more frequently aided by the reasonableness of an idea than by its strict accuracy."

20. The correct answer is (B). "A democratic state of society and democratic institutions keep the greater part of men in constant activity."

21. The correct answer is (B). Lack of reliability is the major reason for the limited use of the Rorschach test.

22. The correct answer is (C). The major value of the test is the speed with which it can be administered (one hour).

23. The correct answer is (A). "Highly excitable subjects often show intense response to color. . . ."

24. The correct answer is (D). DNA is the most important molecule in every living organism.

25. The correct answer is (A). DNA is the largest known molecule in all animals, including man.

26. The correct answer is (D). The first three choices are not supported by the passage. The second sentence in the passage states that steel bars, deeply embedded in the concrete, are sinews to take the stresses.

27. The correct answer is (A). The third sentence in the passage states that when the heart contracts, the blood in the arteries is at its greatest pressure.

28. The correct answer is (B). The second sentence states that inventions relating to transportation have made possible a civilization that could not have existed without them. This supports the correct answer—transportation is an important factor in our civilization.

29. The correct answer is (B). One chief justice plus eight associate justices equals nine justices.

30. The correct answer is (B). The second sentence states that the other planets were thought to be in heaven.

31. The correct answer is (A). Step one in the job application process is often the application letter. If the letter is not effective, the applicant will not move on to the next step, and job prospects will be greatly lessened.

32. The correct answer is (C). The last sentence states that the country needs young, idealistic politicians.

33. The correct answer is (B). The passage states that the X-ray machine "contributes to precision and accuracy in industry."

34. The correct answer is (C). The passage states that office manuals are a necessity in large organizations.

35. The correct answer is (D). The first three choices are not supported by the passage. The correct answer is supported by the second sentence, which states, "With the migration of humans to various climates, ever new adjustments to the food supply and to the climate became necessary."

36. The correct answer is (D). The first three choices are not supported by the passage. The third sentence in the passage states that the drinking of alcohol impairs attention, that is, it makes the driver less attentive.

37. The correct answer is (B). Drinking alcohol causes harmful effects on the driver. The implication is that these effects do not last forever but wear off in time.

38. The correct answer is (A). The first sentence in the passage states that arsonists set fires deliberately or intentionally.

39. The correct answer is (B). The last sentence in the passage states that some arsonists just like the excitement of seeing the fire burn and watching the firefighters at work, and even helping fight the fire.

40. The correct answer is (D). The first three choices are not supported by the passage. Different types of arsonists given in the passage lead to the conclusion that arsonists are not all alike.

41. The correct answer is (D). The second sentence in the passage states that the battery converts an electrical charge into chemical energy that is stored until the battery terminals are connected to a closed external circuit.

42. The correct answer is (C). The first sentence states that a good or service has value only because people want it.

43. The correct answer is (D). The second sentence states that a toad's skin is both dry and rough.

44. The correct answer is (A). The last sentence states that a nautical mile is equal to 6,080 feet, while a land mile is 5,280 feet. Accordingly, a nautical mile is longer than a land mile.

45. The correct answer is (B). The third sentence states that for stereophonic sound, a different sound is recorded in each wall of the groove.

46. The correct answer is (A). The business of publishing city directories is a private business operated for profit. As such, it is a commercial enterprise.

47. The correct answer is (B). The passage says that enough data have been collected to draw the conclusion that the rural crime rates are lower than those in urban communities.

48. The correct answer is (B). The passage lists many different uses for iron.

49. The correct answer is (C). The spaces allow roads, sidewalks, and railroad tracks to expand in the summer and contract in winter without cracking or breaking.

50. The correct answer is (D). The second sentence states that crime is the result of opportunity plus desire. Accordingly, to prevent crime, it is each individual's responsibility to prevent the opportunity.

51. The correct answer is (B). For the students to solve the problem with ease, the teacher's explanation must have been clearly expressed or explicit.

52. The correct answer is (A). To differentiate between fact and fiction requires that the listeners have keen discernment or be shrewd.

53. The correct answer is (B). On Halloween, the eve of All Saints' Day, it is customary for children to engage in "trick or treat" visitations.

54. The correct answer is (B). A baton can be rotated rapidly, whirled, or twirled by a trained and skilled cheerleader.

55. The correct answer is (A). Fratricide is the act of killing one's brother.

56. The correct answer is (C). If corn is native or indigenous to the region, it is readily available and is generally inexpensive as transportation costs are reduced or eliminated.

57. The correct answer is (D). It is difficult to change the mind of a stubborn or obdurate individual even when he is in error.

58. The correct answer is (A). A lover of democracy has a dislike or antipathy for totalitarianism.

59. The correct answer is (B). As the event occurred 200 years before the time of celebration, it would be the bicentennial celebration.

60. The correct answer is (D). A general characteristic of human behavior is that it is highly variable and somewhat unpredictable. The behavior of other species tends to be less variable and more predictable.

61. The correct answer is (B). Using a narrow sample reduces the validity of a statistical analysis. In general, there are several or many limitations to different methods. Choice (A) is incorrect because *with* is not grammatically acceptable.

62. The correct answer is (C). Of the choices given, the only one that gives the sentence meaning states that one who is immature can readily be deceived or deluded.

63. The correct answer is (A). Of the choices given, the only one that gives the sentence meaning states that compulsory education was established to prevent exploitation of young children and to give them a minimum of education.

64. The correct answer is (A). The only choice that provides a meaningful sentence states that a person in custody awaiting trial is considered innocent until found to be guilty.

65. The correct answer is (D). The word *large* appears to be inconsistent. Substituting *small* for *large* restores the intended meaning of the quotation.

66. The correct answer is (A). The word *legislators* appears to be inconsistent. Substituting *citizens* for *legislators* helps convey the meaning intended.

67. The correct answer is (A). The troublesome word appears to be *is* as it is inconsistent with the main clause of the sentence. Substituting *fails* for *is* furnishes the meaning intended.

68. The correct answer is (A). The word *cannot* appears to be the cause of confusion. By substituting *eventually* for *cannot*, the intended meaning of the sentence is restored.

69. The correct answer is (C). The words *little prestige* and *more money* are inconsistent, especially with *unrewarding occupation*. Substituting *less* for *more* restores the intended meaning of the sentence.

70. The correct answer is (D). The word *supplement* appears to be inconsistent. Substituting *replace* restores the intended meaning of the sentence.

71. The correct answer is (B). The word *rejected* appears to be inconsistent. Substituting *needed* for *rejected* makes the sentence meaningful.

72. The correct answer is (B). The word *cannot* appears to be the troublesome word. Substituting *must* for *cannot* restores the intended meaning of the sentence.

73. The correct answer is (B). There is no support for choices (A), (C), or (D) in the passage. Choice (B) is the only correct answer and is supported by the main clause of the sentence.

74. The correct answer is (B). If personal appearance is a matter of distinctly secondary importance in most positions, it should not be considered of primary importance when interviewing persons for most positions.

75. The correct answer is (C). Both carefully planned sales letters and a good mailing list are essential. Carefully planned letters would be wasted on poor mailing lists.

KEY ANSWERS AND RATIONALE FOR PRACTICE EXERCISE 4: ARITHMETIC REASONING

Items 1-50 (5 options)

1. The correct answer is (C).
2. The correct answer is (B).
3. The correct answer is (D).
4. The correct answer is (C).
5. The correct answer is (A).
6. The correct answer is (A).
7. The correct answer is (C).
8. The correct answer is (D).
9. The correct answer is (E).
10. The correct answer is (C).
11. The correct answer is (A).
12. The correct answer is (C).
13. The correct answer is (B).
14. The correct answer is (A).
15. The correct answer is (C).
16. The correct answer is (B).
17. The correct answer is (D).
18. The correct answer is (A).
19. The correct answer is (E).
20. The correct answer is (A).
21. The correct answer is (B).
22. The correct answer is (C).
23. The correct answer is (E).
24. The correct answer is (D).
25. The correct answer is (B).
26. The correct answer is (A).
27. The correct answer is (A).
28. The correct answer is (B).
29. The correct answer is (B).
30. The correct answer is (D).
31. The correct answer is (B).
32. The correct answer is (A).
33. The correct answer is (B).
34. The correct answer is (C).
35. The correct answer is (A).
36. The correct answer is (A).
37. The correct answer is (D).
38. The correct answer is (E).
39. The correct answer is (A).
40. The correct answer is (D).
41. The correct answer is (D).
42. The correct answer is (A).
43. The correct answer is (B).
44. The correct answer is (A).
45. The correct answer is (B).
46. The correct answer is (E).
47. The correct answer is (C).
48. The correct answer is (B).
49. The correct answer is (E).
50. The correct answer is (B).

Items 51–75 (4 options)

51. The correct answer is (B).

52. The correct answer is (D).

53. The correct answer is (B).

54. The correct answer is (B).

55. The correct answer is (C).

56. The correct answer is (B).

57. The correct answer is (A).

58. The correct answer is (B).

59. The correct answer is (A).

60. The correct answer is (A).

61. The correct answer is (C).

62. The correct answer is (C).

63. The correct answer is (B).

64. The correct answer is (D).

65. The correct answer is (B).

66. The correct answer is (B).

67. The correct answer is (B).

68. The correct answer is (D).

69. The correct answer is (A).

70. The correct answer is (A).

71. The correct answer is (A).

72. The correct answer is (D).

73. The correct answer is (A).

74. The correct answer is (D).

75. The correct answer is (D).

Items Answered Incorrectly: __; __; __; __; __; __; __; __.
Items Unsure Of: __; __; __; __; __; __; __; __.

**TOTAL NUMBER
ANSWERED CORRECTLY:** _____

Rationale

1. The correct answer is (C).

$1\frac{1}{2} : 30 = 6 : x; \frac{3}{2} \times x = 180; x = \frac{2}{3} \times 180 = 120$ miles.

2. The correct answer is (B). $\frac{1}{4}$ of 20 = 5 gallons in tank; 20 − 5 = 15 gallons needed to fill tank

3. The correct answer is (D).

$\frac{875}{70} = \frac{3000}{x}; 875x = 210,000; x = 240$ gallons

4. The correct answer is (C).

$\frac{2800}{63 \times 24} = \frac{2800}{1512} = 1.85$, closest to 2 mph

5. The correct answer is (A).

60 miles at 40 mph = $1\frac{1}{2}$ hours driving time

60 miles at 20 mph = 2 hours driving time

Total time = $3\frac{1}{2}$ hours

Total distance =   120 miles

Average speed = $\frac{120}{3\frac{1}{2}} = 120 \times \frac{2}{7} = \frac{240}{7}$

$34\frac{2}{7}$ miles per hour

6. The correct answer is (A). $\frac{120}{12} = 10$ miles per minute; $10 \times 60 = 600$ mph

7. The correct answer is (C). $60x$ traveling east; $70x$ traveling west; $60x + 70x = 455; 130x = 455; x = \frac{455}{130} = 3\frac{1}{2}$ hours; 10:00 A.M. + $3\frac{1}{2}$ hours = 1:30 P.M.

8. The correct answer is (D). Train is 25 miles ahead in 1 hour. Difference in rate is 5 mph $\frac{25}{5} = 5$ hours

9. The correct answer is (E).

$\frac{1}{2} : 10 = \frac{9}{4} : x; \frac{x}{2} = \frac{90}{4}; 4x = 180; x = 45.$

10. The correct answer is (C). $.13 \times 30 = \$3.90$, cost at regular rate. $1.38 \times 2.5 = \$3.45$, cost at reduced rate. $\$3.90 − \$3.45 = \$.45$

11. The correct answer is (A). Two children's tickets cost the same as one adult ticket. $\frac{12.60}{3} = \$4.20$ for each adult ticket. $\frac{1}{2}$ of $\$4.20 = \$2.10.$

12. The correct answer is (C). 5 hours 15 minutes = 21 quarter-hours; 24 hours = 96 quarter-hours; $\frac{21}{96} = \frac{7}{32}.$

13. The correct answer is (B). 35 − 10 = 25 games won; 10 games lost; 25 : 10 = 5 : 2

14. The correct answer is (A). 50 math problems; 300 other problems; let x = minutes spent for each math problem.

$x \times 50 + \frac{x}{2} \times 300 = 180; 50x + 150x = 180;$

$200x = 180; x = \frac{180}{200}; 50x = 50 \times \frac{180}{200} = 45$ minutes

15. The correct answer is (C). $x + .12x = 145.60; 1.12x = 145.60; x = \frac{145.60}{1.12} = \$130.00.$

16. The correct answer is (B). $\$120 − \$96 = \$24$ discount; $\frac{24}{120} = 20\%.$

17. The correct answer is (D). $\frac{1}{3}$ of 198 = 66; 198 − 66 = 132; $\frac{1}{4}$ of 132 = 33; 132 − 33 = 99.

18. The correct answer is (A). $\frac{1}{3} \times \frac{3}{4} = \frac{3}{12} = \frac{1}{4}$ or 25%.

19. The correct answer is (E). $2.5 \times 36 = 90$

20. The correct answer is (A). 60 in. = 5 ft.; 30 in. = 2.5 ft.; 12 in. = 1 ft.; $5 \times 2.5 \times 1 = 12.5$ cubic feet

21. The correct answer is (B). $2 \times 3 \times \frac{5}{3} = 10$ cubic feet; $10 \times 7.5 = 75$ gallons

22. The correct answer is (C).

$\frac{48 \times 36 \times 24}{8 \times 4 \times 2} = 24 \times 27 = 648$.

23. The correct answer is (E).

$5 : 4 = 90 : x$; $360 = 5x$; $x = 72$.

24. The correct answer is (D).

$2.5 : 1 = x : 12$; $x = 2.5 \times 12 = 30$

25. The correct answer is (B).

$\frac{2}{3}x - \frac{1}{4}x = 10$; $\frac{8}{12}x - \frac{3}{12}x = 10$; $\frac{5}{12}x = 10$; $x = \frac{120}{5} = 24$.

26. The correct answer is (A).

$75 \times 42 \times \frac{1}{3} = 1050$ cu. ft.; $7.5 : 1 = x : 1050$;

$x = 1050 \times 7.5 = 7875$.

27. The correct answer is (A). $54.28 - 48.7 = 5.58$ for two thickness. $\frac{5.58}{2} = 2.79$-inch wall thickness.

28. The correct answer is (B).

5 hrs. at 6 mph	=	30 miles
2 hrs. at 10 mph	=	20 miles
3 hrs. at 5 mph	=	150 miles
10 hrs.	=	65 miles

$$\frac{65}{10} = 6.5 \text{ mph}$$

29. The correct answer is (B). Joe must make up $\frac{1260}{2}$ feet, or $\frac{420}{2}$ yards, or 210 yards to meet. There is a 10-yard difference per minute in rate of travel. $\frac{210}{10} = 21$ minutes.

30. The correct answer is (D). Initially, the ships are 1550 miles apart. $85 \times 9 = 765$; $65 \times 9 = 585$; $1550 - (765 + 585) = 1550 - 1350 = 200$ miles.

31. The correct answer is (B). $\frac{1}{10}$ of $3000 = 300$; $3000 - 300 = 2700$; $\frac{2}{9}$ of $2700 = 600$; $2700 - 600 = 2100$ miles still to be driven.

32. The correct answer is (A). Let x = length of bar in inches. $\frac{1}{8} : 12 = \frac{15}{4} : x$; $\frac{1}{8}x = 12 \times \frac{15}{4}$; $x = 12 \times \frac{15}{4} \times 8$ = 360 inches. $\frac{360}{12} = 30$ feet.

33. The correct answer is (B). 36¢ $\times 5 = \$1.80$ for cost of 60 pencils; $3 : .10 = 60 : x$; $3x = 6.00$; $x = \$2.00$ obtained from selling 60 pencils; $\$2.00 - \$1.80 = \$0.20$.

34. The correct answer is (C). $\$4.25 - \$1.25 = \$3.00$; $\frac{3.00}{.75} = 4$ additional passengers; driver + 4 additional passengers = 5 people.

35. The correct answer is (A). $\$8000 \times .06 = \$480 = 6\%$ of Pren's investment; $\$6000 \times .06 = \$360 = 6\%$ of Wright's investment; $\$480 + \$360 = \$840$; $\$3800 - \$840 = \$2960$; $\frac{1}{2}$ of $\$2960 = \$1480$; Pren's total = $\$480 + \$1480 = \$1960$.

36. The correct answer is (A). $\$12,000 \times .15 = \$1800$; $\$12,000 \times \$1800 = \$10,200$ = Cost of car at 15% discount.

$\$12,000 \times .10 = \$1200$; $\$12,000 - \$1200 = \$10,800$

$\$10,800 \times .05 = \$540$; $\$10,800 - \$540 = \$10,260$ = Cost of car at successive discounts.

$\$10,260 - \$10,200 = \$60$.

37. The correct answer is (D). $100 - 25 = 75$; $75 + 25 = 100$; $\frac{25}{75} = 33\frac{1}{3}\%$.

38. The correct answer is (E). Cost = $.75 per dozen; selling price is $0.25 each or $3.00 per dozen. $\$3.00 - .75 = \$2.25$ gross profit per dozen. $\frac{2.25}{.75} \times 100 = 300\%$.

39. The correct answer is (A). Total investment = $8000 + $7500 + $6500 = $22,000; B's share in profit = $\frac{7500}{22000} \times 825 = \$281.25.$ $281.25 - \$230.00 = \$51.25.$

40. The correct answer is (D). $\frac{15}{100} = .15$; $43,250 \times .15 = \$6487.50.$

41. The correct answer is (D). $15 : 12 = x : 20; 12x = 300; x = \frac{300}{12} = 25.$

42. The correct answer is (A). $18\% + 25\% + 12\% + 15\% = 70\%$; 30% study no foreign language; $1700 \times .30 = 510.$

43. The correct answer is (B). Let x = time required to complete ditch with $3\frac{1}{2}$ men.

$4 \times 42 = 3\frac{1}{2} \times x; 4 \times 42 = \frac{7}{2} x; x = 4 \times 42 \times \frac{2}{7} = 48$ days.

44. The correct answer is (A). $15 + 9 = 24$ minutes; $\frac{24}{60} = \frac{2}{5}.$

45. The correct answer is (B). $150 - 140 = 10; \frac{10}{140} = .0714$ or $7\frac{1}{7}\%.$

46. The correct answer is (E). $2400 - \$750 = \$1650;$ $1650 \times .05 = \$82.50; \$150 + \$82.50 = \$232.50.$

47. The correct answer is (C). $\frac{110}{100}$ of $105 = 115.5$ pounds.

48. The correct answer is (B).

Youngest	$10,000
Second	25,000
Eldest	37,500
	$72,500

49. The correct answer is (E).

Let x = amount borrowed.

$12x \times \frac{1}{3} = 720; .04x = 720; x = \frac{720}{.04} = \$18,000.$

50. The correct answer is (B). $27'' : 36'' = 3 : 4$

51. The correct answer is (B). To find percent of increase, subtract the original figure from the new figure. Then divide the amount of change by the original figure. $380 - \$350 = \$30; \$30 \div \$350 = .0857$ (which is approximately $8\frac{1}{2}\%$)

52. The correct answer is (D). The number of hours in the clerk's work week is irrelevant. Figure the percent of his time that he spent at the enumerated tasks. The difference between that percent and his full week (100%) is the percent of his time spent on messenger work.

$$\frac{1}{5} = \frac{14}{70}$$

$$\frac{1}{2} = \frac{35}{70}$$

$$\frac{1}{7} = \frac{10}{70}$$

$$\frac{59}{70} = .84 = 84\%$$

100% – 84% = 16% on messenger work

53. The correct answer is (B). Convert the miles to kilometers by dividing them by $\frac{5}{8}$.

$$500 \text{ miles} \div \frac{5}{8} = \frac{\overset{100}{\cancel{500}}}{1} \times \frac{8}{\underset{1}{\cancel{5}}} = 800 \text{ kilometers.}$$

54. The correct answer is (B).

$$\frac{3}{8} = \frac{9}{24}$$

$$\frac{1}{4} = \frac{6}{24}$$

$$\frac{1}{6} = \frac{4}{24}$$

$$\frac{19}{24} = \text{of the pads were issued;}$$

$\frac{5}{24}$ remained; $\frac{5}{_1 \cancel{24}} \times \frac{\cancel{600}^{25}}{1} = 125$ pads remained

55. The correct answer is (C). 8 A.M. + 15 hours = 23 o'clock = 11 P.M.

56. The correct answer is (B). $1,000.00 − $941.20 = $58.80

57. The correct answer is (A). $190.57 − $13.05 − $5.68 = $171.84

58. The correct answer is (B). Let x = length of shadow of nearby pole. 12 : 4 = 24 : x; 12x = 96; x = 8 feet.

59. The correct answer is (A). $10 \times \frac{1}{2}$ hour = 5 hours.

60. The correct answer is (A). Only choices (A) and (C) represent 72 ounces. 6 × $.39 = $2.34, which is less than 3 × $.79 = $2.37

61. The correct answer is (C). 2 ft 9 in. × 4 = 8 ft. 36 in. = 11 ft.

62. The correct answer is (C). It costs 31¢ per sq. ft., so it costs 31¢ × 9 = $2.79 per sq. yd. $2.79 × 20 sq. yds. = $55.80

63. The correct answer is (B). First convert the feet to inches. 35 ft. 6 in. = 420 in. + 6 in. = 426 in. 426 ÷ 4 = 106.5 in. per shelf = 8 ft. $10\frac{1}{2}$ in. per shelf

64. The correct answer is (D).

$.50 × 3	=	$1.50
.25 × 8	=	$2.00
.10 × 7	=	$0.70
.05 × 6	=	$0.30
.01 × 9	=	$0.09
		$4.59

65. The correct answer is (B). 10.2 + 10.4 + 10 = 30.6 ÷ 3 = 10.2 seconds

66. The correct answer is (B). 11 lb., 16 oz. − 9 lb., 9 oz. = 2 lb., 7 oz.

67. The correct answer is (B). If you look at the entire problem, you will see that the time between sunrise and sunset was just 8 minutes short of 12 hours (14 − 6 = 8).

   11 hrs 60 min.

−   8 min.

   11 hrs 52 min.

68. The correct answer is (D).

$\frac{1}{2}$ c spinach = 80 calories

$\frac{1}{2}$ c peas   = 300 calories

1 c peas   = 600 calories

$\frac{2}{3}$ c peas   = 400 calories

400 ÷ 80   = 5 cups of spinach

              = $2\frac{1}{2}$ cups of spinach

69. The correct answer is (A). 9 hrs = 540 mins.; 540 ÷ 45 = 12

The night watchman stops at the storage area 12 times during his tour plus once at the beginning of his tour of duty for a total of 13 times.

70. The correct answer is (A). The interval between each member of the series is $4\frac{1}{4}$. $17\frac{1}{4} + 4\frac{1}{4} = 21\frac{1}{2}$.

71. The correct answer is (A).

$360 \times 8 = 2880$ switches in 8 hours

$2880 \times .05 = 144$ defective switches

$2880 - 144 = 2736$ good switches

72. The correct answer is (D).

$$22\frac{1}{2} + 1\frac{1}{4} = \frac{45}{2} \div \frac{5}{4} = \frac{\overset{9}{\cancel{45}}}{\underset{1}{\cancel{2}}} \times \frac{\overset{2}{\cancel{4}}}{\underset{1}{\cancel{5}}} = 18 \text{ packages}$$

73. The correct answer is (A). $\$12 \times 6 = \$72.00$ for daily use

$421 \times .17 = \$71.57$ for mileage charge

$\$72.00 + \$71.57 + \$143.57$

74. The correct answer is (D). Area of each square is 25; each side = 5; perimeter consists of 12 sides; $12 \times 5 = 60$

75. The correct answer is (D). 2 yards $\times$ 5 yards $\times$ 4 yards = 40 cubic yards. $\$8.48 \times 40 = \$339.20$.

KEY ANSWERS AND RATIONALE FOR PRACTICE EXERCISE 5: MATH KNOWLEDGE

Items 1-50 (5 options)

1. The correct answer is (B).
2. The correct answer is (C).
3. The correct answer is (E).
4. The correct answer is (A).
5. The correct answer is (B).
6. The correct answer is (B).
7. The correct answer is (D).
8. The correct answer is (D).
9. The correct answer is (B).
10. The correct answer is (E).
11. The correct answer is (D).
12. The correct answer is (C).
13. The correct answer is (E).
14. The correct answer is (B).
15. The correct answer is (B).
16. The correct answer is (E).
17. The correct answer is (D).
18. The correct answer is (A).
19. The correct answer is (B).
20. The correct answer is (E).
21. The correct answer is (D).
22. The correct answer is (C).
23. The correct answer is (B).
24. The correct answer is (D).
25. The correct answer is (D).
26. The correct answer is (B).
27. The correct answer is (D).
28. The correct answer is (D).
29. The correct answer is (C).
30. The correct answer is (A).
31. The correct answer is (A).
32. The correct answer is (D).
33. The correct answer is (D).
34. The correct answer is (E).
35. The correct answer is (B).
36. The correct answer is (B).
37. The correct answer is (B).
38. The correct answer is (A).
39. The correct answer is (E).
40. The correct answer is (B).
41. The correct answer is (B).
42. The correct answer is (C).
43. The correct answer is (E).
44. The correct answer is (B).
45. The correct answer is (C).
46. The correct answer is (C).
47. The correct answer is (E).
48. The correct answer is (D).
49. The correct answer is (A).
50. The correct answer is (E).

Items 51-75 (4 options)

51. The correct answer is (C).

52. The correct answer is (B).

53. The correct answer is (B).

54. The correct answer is (D).

55. The correct answer is (B).

56. The correct answer is (B).

57. The correct answer is (C).

58. The correct answer is (A).

59. The correct answer is (A).

60. The correct answer is (A).

61. The correct answer is (D).

62. The correct answer is (D).

63. The correct answer is (C).

64. The correct answer is (D).

65. The correct answer is (B).

66. The correct answer is (B).

67. The correct answer is (D).

68. The correct answer is (B).

69. The correct answer is (A).

70. The correct answer is (C).

71. The correct answer is (D).

72. The correct answer is (B).

73. The correct answer is (D).

74. The correct answer is (C).

75. The correct answer is (C).

Items Answered Incorrectly: __; __; __; __; __; __; __; __.

Items Unsure Of: __; __; __; __; __; __; __; __.

**TOTAL NUMBER
ANSWERED CORRECTLY:** _____

Rationale

1. The correct answer is (B).

$$\frac{1}{2} = \frac{16}{32}; \frac{3}{4} = \frac{24}{32}; \frac{5}{8} = \frac{20}{32}; \frac{11}{16} = \frac{22}{32}; \frac{23}{32} = \frac{23}{32}$$

2. The correct answer is (C). $\frac{1}{3} = \frac{5}{15}; \frac{2}{5} = \frac{6}{15}; \frac{4}{15} = \frac{4}{15}.$

3. The correct answer is (E). $\frac{1}{4}\% = \frac{1}{4} \times \frac{1}{100} = \frac{1}{400}.$

4. The correct answer is (A). $\frac{120}{90} = \frac{4}{3}; \frac{4}{3} \times 100 = 133\frac{1}{3}\%.$

5. The correct answer is (B). $x + .40x = 84; 1.40x = 84;$
$x = \frac{84}{1.40} = 60.$

6. The correct answer is (B). $212 \times 212 = 44,944.$

7. The correct answer is (D). $2^5 = 32; n - 3 = 5; n = 8.$

8. The correct answer is (D). There is one digit in the square root for every pair of digits in the whole number.

9. The correct answer is (B). $\sqrt{4^2 + 9} = \sqrt{25} = 5.$

10. The correct answer is (E). $5[4 - (-1) + 13] - 6 = 5[5 + 13] - 6 = 5 \times 18 - 6 = 90 - 6 = 84$

11. The correct answer is (D). If x is less than 10 and y is less than 5, $x + y$ is less than 15.

12. The correct answer is (C). The area is multiplied by 2^2, or 4; the perimeter is doubled or multiplied by 2.

13. The correct answer is (E). Let $x =$ one of the numbers and $y =$ the other number; $\frac{x+y}{2} = A; x + y = 2A; y = 2A - x.$

14. The correct answer is (B).

$p : 200D = x : c; x \times 200D = pc; x = \frac{pc}{200D}.$

15. The correct answer is (B).

$(-3) + (+5) = +2$
$(+2) - (-4) = +6$

16. The correct answer is (E). An even number of negative signs when multiplying gives a positive product: $(-6) (+5) (-4) = + 120.$

17. The correct answer is (D).

$(-10)(+\frac{1}{2}) = -5; (-15)(-\frac{1}{3}) = +5; -5$ divided by $+5 = -1.$

18. The correct answer is (A). $r + s = 25; 4(r + s) = 100.$

19. The correct answer is (B). $8x = 3x + 15; 5x = 15;$
$x = 3.$

20. The correct answer is (E).

$\frac{7-3}{x} = \frac{8+2}{4 \times 5}; \frac{4}{x} = \frac{10}{20}; 10x = 80; x = 8.$

21. The correct answer is (D).

$\sqrt{144} = 12; \sqrt{36} = 6; 12 - 6 = 6.$

22. The correct answer is (C). $12 \times 12 = 144; 13 \times 13 = 169;$ thus, the square root of 150 is between 12 and 13.

23. The correct answer is (B).
$2\sqrt{50} = 2\sqrt{25 \times 2} = 2 \times 5\sqrt{2} = 10\sqrt{2}.$

24. The correct answer is (D).
$4\sqrt{4 \times 2} + 3\sqrt{9 \times 2} + 2\sqrt{25 \times 2} = 8\sqrt{2} + 9\sqrt{2} + 10\sqrt{2} = 27\sqrt{2}.$

25. The correct answer is (D). Multiply by abc;
$bc + ac = ab; c(b + a) = ab; c = \frac{ab}{b + a}$

26. The correct answer is (B).
$a^2 - b^2 = (a + b)(a - b) = 9 \times 3 = 27.$

27. The correct answer is (D). Adding both equations: $2x = a + b$; $x = \frac{a+b}{2} = \frac{1}{2}(a + b)$.

28. The correct answer is (D).

Multiply the first equation by 3 and the second equation by 7. $21x - 6y = 6$; $21x + 28y = 210$; subtracting, $34y = 204$; $y = \frac{204}{34} = 6$.

29. The correct answer is (C).

Person	Ages Now	Ages Then
Mr. Mason	x	$x + 8$
Mark	$x - 24$	$x - 24 + 8$

Let x = Mr. Mason's present age.

$x + 8 = 2(x - 16)$; $x + 8 = 2x - 32$; $x = 40$

30. The correct answer is (A).

Person	Ages Now	Ages Then
Samantha	x	$x - 12$
Father	$2x$	$2x - 12$

Let x = Samantha's age.

$x - 12 = \frac{1}{3}(2x - 12)$; $x - 12 = \frac{2}{3}x - 4$; $\frac{1}{3}x = 8$; $x = 8 \times 3 = 24$.

31. The correct answer is (A).

	No. of Ounces	Concentration	Ounces of Pure Substance
75% Solution	x	.75	$.75x$
30% Solution	16	.30	4.80
50% Solution	$16 + x$	.50	$.50(16 + x)$

$.75x + 4.80 = 8.00 + .50x$; $.25x = 3.20$; $x = \frac{3.20}{.25} = 12.8$.

32. The correct answer is (D).

$6! = 6 \times 5 \times 4 \times 3 \times 2 \times 1 = 720$;

$3! = 3 \times 2 \times 1 = 6$; $\frac{720}{6} = 120$.

33. The correct answer is (D). Add 2, multiply by 2; add 2, multiply by 2; etc.

34. The correct answer is (E).

C   E   H   J   M   O   R   T
 D   FG   I   KL   N   PQ   S
   (Skip 1, skip 2; repeat.)

35. The correct answer is (B). There is a difference of 20 between the last term and the first term. There are 5 terms following the initial term. $\frac{20}{5} = 4$, the common difference (3, 7, 11, 15, 19, 23).

36. The correct answer is (B). At 3:30 P.M., the minute hand is at the 6 and the hour hand is midway between the 3 and the 4. $\frac{360°}{12} = 30°$ between numbers. $2\frac{1}{2} \times 30° = 75°$.

37. The correct answer is (B). If angle $BCD = 110°$, angle $BCA = 70°$, and angle $BAC = 70°$. Angle $ABC = 180° - 140°$ or $40°$.

38. The correct answer is (A). $x + 5x = 90°$; $6x = 90°$; $x = 15°$.

39. The correct answer is (E). $2x + 3x + 4x = 9x$; $9x = 180°$; $x = 20°$; the angles are $40°$, $60°$, and $80°$—all acute angles.

40. The correct answer is (B). The sum of the two base angles is $2x$. Therefore, the number of degrees in the vertex angle = $180 - 2x$.

41. The correct answer is (B).
Area = $\frac{1}{2}$ × base × altitude; Area = $\frac{1}{2}(4 \times 3) = \frac{1}{2}(12) = 6$ sq. in.

42. The correct answer is (C).
Area of square = $\frac{1}{2}$ of product of the diagonals.
$\frac{1}{2}(40 \times 40) = \frac{1}{2}(1600) = 800$.

43. The correct answer is (E). Let $4x$ = length and $3x$ = width.
$4x + 3x + 4x + 3x = 140; 14x = 140; x = 10$.
Length = 40 feet; width = 30 feet. If two sides of a right triangle are 40 and 30 feet, the hypotenuse or diagonal = 50 feet.

44. The correct answer is (B). An inscribed angle is equal in degrees to one half its intercepted arc. Angle ABC, an inscribed angle, is equal to one half of 80°. Angle $ABC = 40°$.

45. The correct answer is (C). Area = πr^2. If diameter = 6 inches, radius = 3 inches; area = $\pi \times 3^2$; area = 9π.

46. The correct answer is (C). 24 inches = 2 feet; circumference = $2\pi = \frac{44}{7}$; 5280 feet = 1 mile; 5280 divided by $\frac{44}{7}$ = 5280 times $\frac{7}{44}$ = 840.

47. The correct answer is (E). Area = πr^2; $r^2 = 16$; $r = 4$; diameter = 8; $4 \times 8 = 32$.

48. The correct answer is (D). The length, width, and height of a cube are all equal. The volume of a cube is equal to the cube of an edge. Each edge = 3 feet. Volume = $3' \times 3' \times 3' = 27$ cubic feet.

49. The correct answer is (A). $\pi r^2 \times$ height = volume; $\pi \times 8^2 \times 10$ = volume; volume = $\frac{22 \times 64 \times 10}{7} = 2011.4$; 2011.4 cubic inches divided by 231 cubic inches = 8.7 gallons.

50. The correct answer is (E). $30 + 28 + 20 + 17 = 95$; $100 - 95 = 5$. The miscellaneous classification comprised 5% of the immigrants for that year. $360° \times .05 = 18°$.

51. The correct answer is (C). A circle is 360°; 60° is $\frac{1}{6}$ of 360°.

52. The correct answer is (B). There are $6 + 8 + 4 + 12 = 30$ marbles. $12 + 30 = .40 = \frac{2}{5}$.

53. The correct answer is (B). $\frac{\cancel{5}^1}{\cancel{25}_5} = .2 = 20\%$.

54. The correct answer is (D). $3^3 \times 3 = 27 \times 3 = 81$

55. The correct answer is (B). $0.04y = 1; y = 1 \div 0.04 = 25$.

56. The correct answer is (B). The number of accidents is irrelevant to the question, so A has no place in the equation. B(total deaths) $\div$ 10 years = $\frac{B}{10}$ average deaths per year.

57. The correct answer is (C). To place the decimal point in the product, add together the number of digits to the right of the decimal points in all of the multipliers. In this case, the answer requires 6 decimal places.

58. The correct answer is (A). To find how many tons fall in a given number of minutes, multiply the number of tons that fall in one minute by the number of minutes. There are 60 seconds in 1 minute, and T tons fall in 1 second. In M minutes, the amount of snow that falls is $60MT$.

59. The correct answer is (A). Subtract A^2 from both sides of the equation: $B^2 = X^2$, therefore $B = X$ or $-X$.

60. The correct answer is (A).
$6 + x + y = 20$
$x + y = 14 = k$; now substitute
$20 - 14 = 6$

61. The correct answer is (D). The first step in finding a square root is grouping the digits into pairs, starting at the decimal point. If necessary, place a 0 to the left of the first digit to create a pair. Each pair represents one digit in the square root. The square root of 960 is a two-digit number in the 30s because the square root of 09 is 3.

62. The correct answer is (D). $8 + 5(x - y) = 8 + 5x - 5y$

Since $x = y$, $5x = 5y$ and $5x - 5y = 0$

Substituting: $8 + 0 = 8$

63. The correct answer is (C).

$$\frac{S = 1 \\ R = 3 \times 1 \\ T = \frac{1}{3}}{4\frac{1}{3}}$$

64. The correct answer is (D). Each sport jacket can be worn with 5 pairs of slacks. $3 \times 5 = 15$

65. The correct answer is (B).

$C = 2\pi r$

$60 = 2\pi r$ (Divide both sides by 2π)

$r = 60 \div 2\pi$

66. The correct answer is (B). Pick a pair of ages and try for yourself. A is 2; B is 4; the ratio of their ages is 2 to 4 or 1 to 2. In two years, A is 4 and B is 6. The ratio of their ages is 4 to 6 or 2 to 3.

67. The correct answer is (D).

$$\begin{array}{r} x + 3 \\ \times\, 2x + 5 \\ \hline 2x^2 + 6x \\ 5x + 15 \\ \hline 2x^2 + 11x + 15 \end{array}$$

68. The correct answer is (B). The formula for the area of a triangle is $\frac{1}{2}$ the base times the height.

69. The correct answer is (A). "Percent" means out of 100. If K percent are emotionally unstable, then K out of 100 are emotionally unstable. The remainder, $100 - K$, is not unstable.

70. The correct answer is (C). The formula to find the circumference of a circle is $2\pi r$. The formula to find the area of a circle is πr^2. The only number that has the same value when multiplied by 2 or squared is 2.

71. The correct answer is (D). CD is a hypotenuse, so use the Pythagorean theorem:

$$CD = \sqrt{CE^2 + ED^2}$$
$$CD = \sqrt{7^2 + 6^2} = \sqrt{49 + 36} = \sqrt{85}$$

72. The correct answer is (B). $\frac{2}{3}$ of 60 min. = 40 min. 5:00 + 40 min. = 5:40

73. The correct answer is (D). Assign arbitrary values to solve this problem:

A square 10 ft. × 10 ft. = 100 sq. ft.

A rectangle 9 ft. × 11 ft. = 99 sq. ft.

$100 - 99 = 1$; $\frac{1}{100} = 1\%$.

74. The correct answer is (C). Diagram this problem:

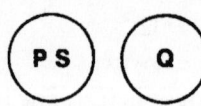

75. The correct answer is (C). The formula for the area of a circle is πr^2. In this problem, $r^2 = 64$, so $r = 8$. The circle is tangent with the square on all four sides; the radius is exactly $\frac{1}{2}$ the length of a side of the square. Each side then, is 16 units long. The formula for the perimeter of a square is $P = 4s$, so $4 \times 16 = 64$.

KEY ANSWERS AND RATIONALE FOR PRACTICE EXERCISE 6: DATA INTERPRETATION

Key Answers

1. The correct answer is (B).
2. The correct answer is (A).
3. The correct answer is (C).
4. The correct answer is (E).
5. The correct answer is (C).
6. The correct answer is (E).
7. The correct answer is (C).
8. The correct answer is (B).
9. The correct answer is (E).
10. The correct answer is (D).
11. The correct answer is (C).
12. The correct answer is (D).
13. The correct answer is (A).
14. The correct answer is (B).
15. The correct answer is (D).
16. The correct answer is (D).
17. The correct answer is (B).
18. The correct answer is (D).
19. The correct answer is (B).
20. The correct answer is (D).
21. The correct answer is (B).
22. The correct answer is (E).
23. The correct answer is (A).
24. The correct answer is (A).
25. The correct answer is (E).
26. The correct answer is (C).
27. The correct answer is (B).
28. The correct answer is (C).
29. The correct answer is (D).
30. The correct answer is (C).
31. The correct answer is (A).
32. The correct answer is (B).
33. The correct answer is (D).
34. The correct answer is (C).
35. The correct answer is (E).
36. The correct answer is (B).
37. The correct answer is (B).
38. The correct answer is (B).
39. The correct answer is (D).
40. The correct answer is (A).
41. The correct answer is (D).
42. The correct answer is (B).
43. The correct answer is (E).
44. The correct answer is (B).
45. The correct answer is (D).
46. The correct answer is (B).
47. The correct answer is (A).
48. The correct answer is (B).
49. The correct answer is (C).
50. The correct answer is (B).

Items Answered Incorrectly: __; __; __; __; __; __; __; __.
Items Unsure Of: __; __; __; __; __; __; __; __.

**TOTAL NUMBER
ANSWERED CORRECTLY:** _____

Rationale

1. The correct answer is (B). $636.50 - $115.00 = $521.50

2. The correct answer is (A). $\frac{115.00}{636.50} \times 100 = 18\%$

3. The correct answer is (C).

$$
\begin{array}{rl}
636.50 & \\
+\ 200.00 & \text{(deposit)} \\
\hline
836.50 & \\
-\ 130.00 & \text{(withdrawals)} \\
\hline
706.50 &
\end{array}
$$

4. The correct answer is (E). As shown in the "Sick Leave" and "Vacation" columns, the only employee who was absent because of sick leave for 8 days and took 21 days of vacation was Vetter.

5. The correct answer is (C). The highest yearly salary listed is $9500, which is received by Lopez, who is assigned to Laboratory.

6. The correct answer is (E). Although the records show that three employees were absent on vacation for more than 20 days, none of them is listed in choices (A) through (D).

7. The correct answer is (C). Enter at left of table at *Nagoya* and move to right to column with heading, *Porterage per Piece of Luggage*.

8. The correct answer is (B). Enter at left of table at *Pusan* and move right to column with heading of *Transportation Fare & Time* and subheading of *Bus*.

9. The correct answer is (E). Enter at left of table at *Nagasaki* and move right to column with heading of *Transportation Fare & Time* and subheading of *Taxi*.

10. The correct answer is (D). Enter at left of table at *Taipei* and move right to column with heading of *Transportation Fare & Time* and subheading of *Bus*.

11. The correct answer is (C). The highest toll charge for a three-axle vehicle using a bridge is on the Fillmore Bridge ($1.75).

12. The correct answer is (D). The smallest toll charge for a two-axle truck weighing less than 8,000 pounds is on the Memorial Bridge ($.25).

13. The correct answer is (A).

Jackson Avenue Tunnel toll	$1.80
Wilson Tunnel toll	$-$1.50
	$0.30

14. The correct answer is (B). $1.80 + $.40 = $2.20

15. The correct answer is (D). The train arriving at 8:17 and the one arriving at 8:21 stand at Magic Mall for less than 6 minutes before leaving.

16. The correct answer is (D). The trains axe numbered from 69 to 75, a total of 7 trains.

17. The correct answer is (B). Train #74 leaves Harvard Square at 8:12 and arrives at Magic Mall at 8:24, exactly 12 minutes.

18. The correct answer is (D). Train #70 leaves Pleasure Plaza on its second westbound trip at 8:53 and arrives at Harvard Square at 8:56.

19. The correct answer is (B). $8216 + $7422 = $15,638.

20. The correct answer is (D). $8731 - $8408 = $323.

21. The correct answer is (B). The average monthly temperature of Resort City is lowest during the months of January and December (10°C).

22. The correct answer is (E). The average monthly temperature of Resort City in May is the same as in October, 21°C.

23. The correct answer is (A).

May   21°C
December   10°C

21°C – 10°C = 11°C

24. The correct answer is (A).

$56.4 + 52.4 + 69.1 + 63.6 = 241.5$; $\dfrac{241.50}{40} = 6.04$

25. The correct answer is (E). For Ration B, the greatest weight gain was 7.5 lbs.; the lowest weight gain was 2.9 lbs. 7.5 – 2.9 = 4.6

26. The correct answer is (C). 9.3 lbs. was the greatest weight gain. The rabbit was fed on Ration C.

27. The correct answer is (B). The area of Asia, the largest continent, is 17 million square miles.

28. The correct answer is (C). The area of Australia, the smallest continent, is 3 million square miles.

29. The correct answer is (D). The continent of North America has an area of approximately $9\frac{1}{2}$ million square miles.

30. The correct answer is (C). Multiply the midpoint of each range by the number of employees who produced work-units within that range five years ago, then add the products and divide by 100 (the number of employees who worked five years ago) to obtain the average number of work-units produced per employee:

$$
\begin{aligned}
750 \times 7 &= 5250 \\
1250 \times 14 &= 17500 \\
1750 \times 26 &= 45500 \\
2250 \times 22 &= 49500 \\
2750 \times 17 &= 46750 \\
3250 \times 10 &= 32500 \\
3750 \times 4 &= 15000 \\
212000 \div 100 &= 2120
\end{aligned}
$$

2120 falls within the 2001 – 2500 range.

31. The correct answer is (A). Add the bottom four numbers in the left-hand column of the table to obtain the number of employees producing more than 2000 work-units five years ago (22 + 17 + 10 + 4 = 53). Add the bottom four numbers in the right-hand column of the table to obtain the number of employees producing more than 2000 work-units last year (36 + 39 + 23 + 9 = 107). The ratio of 53 to 107 is most nearly equivalent to 1:2.

32. The correct answer is (B). The following calculations must be made:

	Last Year	Five Years Ago
Total number of employees	150	100
Total number of work-units produced	362500	212000
Employees producing 2000 or less	43	47

From these calculations, it is evident that only I and II were greater last year than five years ago.

33. The correct answer is (D). Approximately 23% of males over age 7 participate in exercise walking and 24% of females over age 7 participate in bicycle riding.

34. The correct answer is (C). Of the activities mentioned, the one with the smallest difference in percent of participation by males and females is bowling (19% of males and 17% of females participate).

35. The correct answer is (E). About $12\frac{1}{2}$% of females participate in fishing and double that number, or 25%, of males.

36. The correct answer is (B). The percentage of females participating in basketball is about 7 percent. Seven percent of 115,000,000 is 8,050,000—which is closest to answer choice (B).

37. The correct answer is (B). Enter table at 140 pounds and move right to the "DRIVING WHILE IMPAIRED" range. Note that the minimum is 3 drinks.

38. The correct answer is (B). Enter table at 100 pounds and move right to the highest figure in the "CAUTION" range. Note that 2 drinks is the highest figure in the "CAUTION" range.

39. The correct answer is (D). Enter table at 180 pounds and move right to the "DRIVING WHILE INTOXICATED" range. Note that 6 drinks is the minimum amount.

40. The correct answer is (A). Enter table at 200 pounds and move right to the top figure in the "CAUTION" range. Note that 3 drinks is the maximum.

41. The correct answer is (D). Daily inspections:

	A	B
Monday	50	100
Tuesday	50	50
Wednesday	100	100
Thursday	100	50
Friday	50	100
	350	400

Inspector A inspected twice as much as Inspector B on Thursday.

42. The correct answer is (B). On Tuesday, each inspector completed 50 inspections, for a total of 100 inspections for the day, the lowest daily number for that week.

43. The correct answer is (E). At the end of the second day, 250 (25%) had been made. 750 inspections (75%) still had to be made.

44. The correct answer is (B). The inspectors completed 50 each on Tuesday and 100 each on Wednesday.

45. The correct answer is (D). Enter the chart at 1950 and move up until it intersects with the top of the "65 and over" age group. Note that the point is 150 million—the total population in 1950. 150 + (.50 × 150) = 150 + 75 = 225. The only year in which the total population was approximately 225 million was 1980.

46. The correct answer is (B). Enter the chart at 1970 and move up until it intersects with the top of the "20 to 44" age group. Note that the point is 143 million and includes both the "20 to 44" and the "Under 20" age groups. Similarly, the top of the "Under 20" age group point of intersection is 78 million. 143 − 78 = 65 million.

47. The correct answer is (A). All groups except the "Under 20" age group showed numerical increases during this 50-year period. The "Under 20" age group showed increases from 1940 to 1970 and then showed decreases for 1980 and 1990.

48. The correct answer is (B). Enter the chart at 1960 and move up until it intersects with the top of the "45 to 64" age group. Note that the point is 162.5 and includes the population of all age groups except the "65 and over" age group. Similarly, the top of the "20 to 44" age group point of intersection is 127.5 million. 162.5 − 127.5 = 35 million—the population of the "20 to 44" age group. As the total population in 1960 was 177.5 million, $\frac{35}{177.5}$ = 0.197, or most nearly 20%.

49. The correct answer is (C). The only two components of income that add up to 37% are federal aid (20%) and state aid (17%).

50. The correct answer is (B). The only two components of expenditure that have the same percentage are environmental protection (3%) and fire (3%).

KEY ANSWERS AND RATIONALE FOR PRACTICE EXERCISE 7: GENERAL SCIENCE

Key Answers

1. The correct answer is (C).
2. The correct answer is (D).
3. The correct answer is (C).
4. The correct answer is (A).
5. The correct answer is (D).
6. The correct answer is (B).
7. The correct answer is (D).
8. The correct answer is (B).
9. The correct answer is (D).
10. The correct answer is (A).
11. The correct answer is (D).
12. The correct answer is (B).
13. The correct answer is (A).
14. The correct answer is (C).
15. The correct answer is (B).
16. The correct answer is (D).
17. The correct answer is (C).
18. The correct answer is (B).
19. The correct answer is (D).
20. The correct answer is (B).
21. The correct answer is (D).
22. The correct answer is (B).
23. The correct answer is (A).
24. The correct answer is (D).
25. The correct answer is (B).
26. The correct answer is (D).
27. The correct answer is (C).
28. The correct answer is (C).
29. The correct answer is (B).
30. The correct answer is (A).
31. The correct answer is (C).
32. The correct answer is (D).
33. The correct answer is (C).
34. The correct answer is (B).
35. The correct answer is (C).
36. The correct answer is (A).
37. The correct answer is (C).
38. The correct answer is (B).
39. The correct answer is (D).
40. The correct answer is (C).
41. The correct answer is (C).
42. The correct answer is (B).
43. The correct answer is (D).
44. The correct answer is (C).
45. The correct answer is (D).
46. The correct answer is (A).
47. The correct answer is (D).
48. The correct answer is (C).
49. The correct answer is (B).
50. The correct answer is (A).

Items Answered Incorrectly: __; __; __; __; __; __; __; __.
Items Unsure Of: __; __; __; __; __; __; __; __.

**TOTAL NUMBER
ANSWERED CORRECTLY:** _____

Rationale

1. The correct answer is (C). Citrus fruits include lemons, limes, oranges, and grapefruit.

2. The correct answer is (D). Water freezes at 0° on a centigrade or Celsius thermometer. Water freezes at 32° Fahrenheit.

3. The correct answer is (C). The major chemical constituent of a cell by importance is protein, but by weight it is water.

4. The correct answer is (A). The Wassermann test, developed by a German bacteriologist in 1906, is a blood test for syphilis.

5. The correct answer is (D). Wood alcohol is methyl alcohol, which is extremely toxic; drinking it may cause blindness. Isopropyl alcohol is rubbing alcohol. Glyceryl alcohol is an industrial solvent.

6. The correct answer is (B). Nitrogen constitutes about four fifths of the earth's atmosphere, by volume.

7. The correct answer is (D). By the process of photosynthesis, green plants remove carbon dioxide from the atmosphere and replace it with oxygen.

8. The correct answer is (B). Ringworm is a skin disease caused by a fungus.

9. The correct answer is (D). Light enters the eye through the pupil (the opening in the center of the iris), travels through the transparent crystalline lens, then travels through the vitreous humor (eyeball), and finally is focused on the retina.

10. The correct answer is (A). The salivary glands secrete the enzyme ptyalin, which acts on carbohydrates.

11. The correct answer is (D). Vitamin K is useful in the coagulation of blood. Vitamin C prevents scurvy; vitamin E maintains muscle tone and aids in fertility; vitamin D prevents rickets.

12. The correct answer is (B). A bulkhead is a wall; the anchor keeps the ship from moving; and the prow is the front of the ship.

13. The correct answer is (A). Lime is highly alkaline.

14. The correct answer is (C). Bacteria on the roots of legumes, plants that include peas and beans, serve to fixate free nitrogen and return it to the soil as nitrates.

15. The correct answer is (B). Frequency is directly related to pitch. The higher pitched a sound is, the greater its frequency is. Low-pitched sounds have low frequencies.

16. The correct answer is (D). Most vegetables contain some vitamin C, and yellow vegetables contain more vitamin C than green ones. Tomatoes, however, are actually fruits and contain far more vitamin C than any vegetables.

17. The correct answer is (C). The cyclotron is an accelerating device that splits atoms.

18. The correct answer is (B). It takes the earth 1 year to complete an orbit of the sun. A year contains 365 days, or 52 weeks.

19. The correct answer is (D). The weight of the salt water displaced by a human body is greater than the weight of fresh water displaced by that same body. Since the water displaced is heavier, the body is proportionally lighter and is more buoyant.

20. The correct answer is (B). Boiling lava erupts from a volcano. The force that causes the eruption is pressure inside the earth.

21. The correct answer is (D). Vitamin D can be found in fish-liver oils and egg yolks. It can also be manufactured within skin that is exposed to sunlight.

22. The correct answer is (B). A tumor is a growth. A malignant tumor or growth is a cancer.

23. The correct answer is (A). Steel is a compound of iron and carbon.

24. The correct answer is (D). The greatest danger during exercise under hot, dry conditions is dehydration. A person can survive for a relatively long period of time without food, but for only a short time without water. Hot, dry conditions make the need for water more urgent.

25. The correct answer is (B). The moon is a satellite of the earth.

26. The correct answer is (D). The speed of light is about a million times that of sound.

27. The correct answer is (C). While the hereditary components of most diseases are still under study, the hereditary nature of sickle cell anemia is documented and well understood. Sickle cell anemia is most common among black people.

28. The correct answer is (C). Water boils at 212°F and freezes at 32°F. 212° – 32° = 180°.

29. The correct answer is (B). As viewed from space, one half of the moon is always illuminated by the sun. However, as the moon changes its position in its orbit around the earth, different amounts of the illuminated side are visible from the earth.

30. The correct answer is (A). Radiation is the process by which energy is transferred in space.

31. The correct answer is (C). Barometric pressure is expressed in inches. The range is generally from 28 to 31 inches.

32. The correct answer is (D). Clover serves to return nitrates to the soil through the action of nitrogen-fixing bacteria in nodules on its roots.

33. The correct answer is (C). The vascular system is the system of vessels for the circulation of blood. The respiratory system is concerned with respiration (breathing) and the endocrine system with enzymes.

34. The correct answer is (B). Aluminum is not magnetic. Cobalt and nickel are somewhat magnetic, while iron is highly magnetic.

35. The correct answer is (C). Milk and milk products such as cheese and butter are high in saturated fat and cholesterol.

36. The correct answer is (A). Fruits have seeds. Tomatoes, cucumbers, and green peppers have seeds. A potato is a tuber.

37. The correct answer is (C). The hammer, anvil, and stirrup are the three tiny bones that connect the eardrum with the inner ear.

38. The correct answer is (B). Cigarette smoking can speed up the heartbeat.

39. The correct answer is (D). The prefix *hypo* means *below* or *abnormally deficient*. *Hypo*thermia is a condition in which the body's temperature falls well below the normal 98.6°F. If it is very hot and you have nothing to drink, you may become dehydrated and might develop *hyper*thermia, overheating. Another name for rabies is hydrophobia.

40. The correct answer is (C). Combustion cannot occur in the absence of oxygen.

41. The correct answer is (C). Antigens and antibodies are hostile to one another. If antigens of a factor are introduced into a person who has antibodies toward that factor, a severe reaction and even possible death will result. Group A blood contains A antigens and B antibodies. Group B blood contains B antigens and A antibodies. Group AB blood contains A and B antigens but no antibodies. Group AB persons can receive any group blood; they are called "universal recipients." Group O blood contains no antigens but A and B antibodies. Group O persons are called "universal donors."

42. The correct answer is (B). The "highs" on a weather map are based on barometric pressure. The greater the air pressure, the higher the mercury in the barometer.

43. The correct answer is (D). An atom is the smallest part of an element that retains all the properties of the element.

44. The correct answer is (C). The action of narcotics is to deaden pain.

45. The correct answer is (D). Fungi do not contain chlorophyll so they cannot produce their own food through photosynthesis. Since fungi must rely for their food upon decaying organic matter, the forest is a hospitable home.

46. The correct answer is (A). Coal is formed by the partial decomposition of vegetable matter under the influence of moisture, pressure, and temperature, and in the absence of air. If there is coal in Alaska, there must once have been abundant vegetation in Alaska.

47. The correct answer is (D). Damage to the neck and back is especially dangerous because the spinal cord is so vulnerable. Once the spinal cord is severed, paralysis is inevitable and irreversible, so if there is any question of back or neck injury, the person should be moved only by a skilled professional.

48. The correct answer is (C). Like displaces like.

49. The correct answer is (B). Vitamin C, contained in citrus fruits, tomatoes, and green vegetables, is also known as ascorbic acid.

50. The correct answer is (A). Lightning is most likely to strike the highest object in an area. If you are standing in an open field or at the top of a small hill, you are likely to be the highest object and a good target. If you stand under a tree, lightning might hit the tree and cause it to fall on you. A car is grounded. If you are inside a car that is hit by lightning, the lightning will be transmitted into the ground by the car.

KEY ANSWERS AND RATIONALE FOR PRACTICE EXERCISE 8: ELECTRONICS INFORMATION

Key Answers

1. The correct answer is (B).
2. The correct answer is (D).
3. The correct answer is (C).
4. The correct answer is (B).
5. The correct answer is (C).
6. The correct answer is (B).
7. The correct answer is (B).
8. The correct answer is (A).
9. The correct answer is (C).
10. The correct answer is (B).
11. The correct answer is (A).
12. The correct answer is (B).
13. The correct answer is (D).
14. The correct answer is (B).
15. The correct answer is (C).
16. The correct answer is (D).
17. The correct answer is (C).
18. The correct answer is (B).
19. The correct answer is (D).
20. The correct answer is (B).
21. The correct answer is (A).
22. The correct answer is (C).
23. The correct answer is (C).
24. The correct answer is (D).
25. The correct answer is (D).
26. The correct answer is (A).
27. The correct answer is (C).
28. The correct answer is (D).
29. The correct answer is (C).
30. The correct answer is (B).
31. The correct answer is (B).
32. The correct answer is (A).
33. The correct answer is (A).
34. The correct answer is (D).
35. The correct answer is (A).
36. The correct answer is (C).
37. The correct answer is (D).
38. The correct answer is (A).
39. The correct answer is (B).
40. The correct answer is (D).
41. The correct answer is (D).
42. The correct answer is (C).
43. The correct answer is (D).
44. The correct answer is (D).
45. The correct answer is (A).
46. The correct answer is (D).
47. The correct answer is (D).
48. The correct answer is (C).
49. The correct answer is (B).
50. The correct answer is (A).

Items Answered Incorrectly: __; __; __; __; __; __; __; __.
Items Unsure Of: __; __; __; __; __; __; __; __.

TOTAL NUMBER
ANSWERED CORRECTLY: _____

Rationale

1. The correct answer is (B). A three-way switch is a single-pole double-throw switch or two single-pole switches.

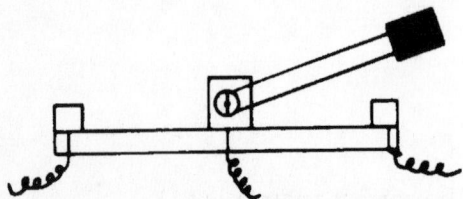

2. The correct answer is (D). Leather gloves offer the best protection over the rubber gloves. The leather can withstand severe conditions before it will tear. The rubber acts as insulation.

3. The correct answer is (C). A "mil" is short for milli or $\frac{1}{1,000}$ of an inch.

4. The correct answer is (B). The formula for determining the current in a parallel circuit is: $I_t = I_1 + I_2 + I_3 + \ldots I_n$. The current going through the lamps is 1 amp + 1 amp = 2 amps.

5. The correct answer is (C). Never use a fuse having a higher rating than that specifically called for in the circuit. A fuse is a safety device used to protect a circuit from serious damage caused by too high a current.

6. The correct answer is (B). Silver is a much better conductor of electricity than copper. However, gold is also used for tuner contacts because it will not tarnish. Silver can tarnish.

7. The correct answer is (B). A "2-line return-call" electric bell circuit would have 2 bells, 2 metallic lines, 2 return-call push buttons, and 2 sets of batteries. It might look like this:

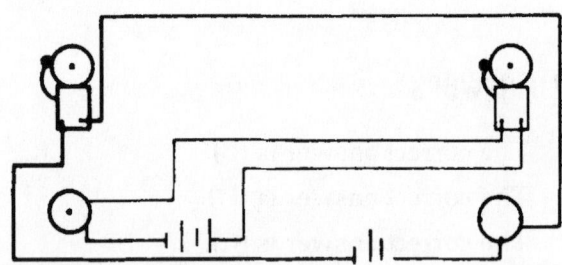

8. The correct answer is (A). Figure 1, a connector, is used to join two sections of aluminum pipe conduit.

9. The correct answer is (C). Grounding a fixture is a safety precaution used to lessen the chance of shock.

10. The correct answer is (B). In electrical terms, potential or E.M.F. is the voltage. Electricians consider any voltage of 600 volts or less to be Low Potential.

11. The correct answer is (A). A rheostat regulates the amount of voltage to the motor. The more voltage to a motor, the faster it will turn.

12. The correct answer is (B). A polarized plug is used so that the plug can go into the receptacle in only one way. The prongs are at an angle to each other.

13. The correct answer is (D). When reading an electric meter, you read the lower number just before the pointer. This meter would show 6872 kilowatt hours.

14. The correct answer is (B). In a DC motor, the commutators are the metal contact points that the brushes come into contact with.

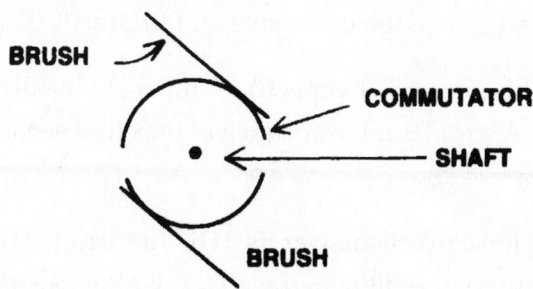

15. The correct answer is (C). The neutral wire is whitish in color; the hot lead is black; and the ground wire is green.

16. The correct answer is (D). Carbon, crystal, and dynamic are all types of microphones. Feedback is a condition caused when sound coming from a speaker is fed back into a microphone, causing noise.

17. The correct answer is (C). This type of connector will join a flexible metallic conduit to a junction box. The wire is secured by tightening the compression screw. The locknut is tightened to secure the connector to the junction box.

18. The correct answer is (B). Good magnetic metals are iron, steel, nickel, and cobalt. Iron is the only one mentioned here.

19. The correct answer is (D). Rosin is used to remove copper oxide from wires so that the solder can join the copper wires.

20. The correct answer is (B). In the letters RHW, R stands for rubber insulation, H stands for heat resistant, and W stands for waterproof.

21. The correct answer is (A). Outdoor boxes and fittings must be weatherproof to withstand any problems caused by moisture.

22. The correct answer is (C). A rectifier is a device that converts AC current into DC current by allowing the current to flow in only one direction while blocking the flow of electricity in the reverse direction.

23. The correct answer is (C). The starting current of a motor is normally six times greater than its running current.

24. The correct answer is (D). Lead acid batteries give off highly explosive hydrogen gas. This is a normal product of the acid reacting with the lead plates when electricity is made. A single spark can explode the gas.

25. The correct answer is (D). According to Ohm's law:

$V = IR$; $V = 5 \times 20$; $V = 100$ volts.

26. The correct answer is (A). Receptacles in a house are connected in parallel. In parallel circuits, the current increases as more appliances are added but the voltage remains the same. $E_t = E_1 = E_2 \ldots E_n$ $I_t = I_1 + I_2 + \ldots I_n$

27. The correct answer is (C). The symbol is a standard one and shows the two conducting surfaces of a capacitor.

28. The correct answer is (D). An electric shock is determined by the contact resistance. If a person is standing in water while being shocked, the shock will be very severe because water reduces the amount of resistance and the electricity will flow freely through his body.

29. The correct answer is (C). Locknuts are bent so that their metal edges will bite into the terminal board and will require the use of a wrench to loosen them.

30. The correct answer is (B). A condenser or capacitor is an electrical device that will store and discharge an electrical charge. When the bell is off, the condenser will store electricity. When the circuit is on, the condenser will discharge. This will eliminate arcing.

31. The correct answer is (B). Paper is not used in the makeup of a lighting wire because a small electrical charge could set it on fire.

32. The correct answer is (A). No electricity flows through a burned out bulb. However, the voltmeter acts as a bypass around the burned out bulb and is therefore connected in series. It measures all of the voltage in the circuit. The voltage is 600 volts.

33. The correct answer is (A). Silver is a much better conductor than copper. It is not used in wires because it is very expensive.

34. The correct answer is (D). A household iron is the only device that depends on a thermostat to control its use. An overheated iron will damage the clothing that it is supposed to press.

35. The correct answer is (A). An alternator is a device found in automobiles. It is used to produce AC in a car; the electronic circuitry changes AC to DC.

36. The correct answer is (C). An incandescent electric light bulb is a typical light bulb found in the home. When the incandescent bulb, which is rated for 110 volts, is run at 90 volts, it will not burn as brightly. Since the 110-volt capacity is not being used, it will last longer.

37. The correct answer is (D). This object is a ground clamp. It will be tightened around a cold water pipe. A grounding wire will be attached to the screw and thus stray electricity will be grounded.

38. The correct answer is (A). When a refrigerator motor starts up, it draws considerable current. This takes current away from the bulb. Thicker wires would allow more electricity to pass through, but they would be too expensive and impractical.

39. The correct answer is (B). A mil is [1/1,000] of an inch. A circular mil is the area of the cross-section of a wire.

40. The correct answer is (D). Electric power is measured in units called watts. A watt is calculated by multiplying voltage by amperage. Watts are measured by a watt-meter.

41. The correct answer is (D). Consider the following filtered rectifier circuit with a short circuit across capacitor A:

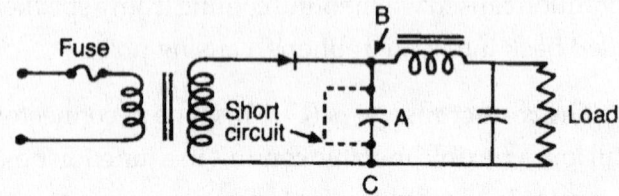

The current at point ⑧, which would ordinarily flow through the load resistor, will now flow through the short circuit to ⓒ and back through the transformer. The short circuit has virtually no resistance, causing large currents to flow in both the primary and secondary windings of the transformer. These large currents cause the fuse to burn out.

42. The correct answer is (C). Voltages are transformed directly as the ratio of the secondary to the primary turns:

$$\frac{\text{VOLTAGE}_{\text{Secondary}}}{\text{VOLTAGE}_{\text{Primary}}} = \frac{\text{TURNS}_{\text{Secondary}}}{\text{TURNS}_{\text{Primary}}}$$

$$\frac{V_S}{V_P} = \frac{T_S}{T_P}; V_S = \frac{T_S}{T_P} \times V_P; V_S = \frac{50}{100} V_P = \frac{1}{2} V_P$$

43. The correct answer is (D). A good electrical connection has as low a resistance as possible. Soldering provides a low resistance path through the connection. It is also a mechanically secure connection.

44. The correct answer is (D). Resistance in the primary will reduce the current flow and reduce the voltage and current available at the spark plug. A "hot" spark with as high a voltage and current as possible is necessary for easy starting and smooth performance.

45. The correct answer is (A). The resistance of a short circuit usually consists of little more than the resistance of the circuit's copper wires since the load has been "shorted" or bypassed. This very low resistance results in very high current flow.

46. The correct answer is (D). Wires larger than No. 10 AWG are usually stranded because a solid wire of that diameter is too stiff to make good connections or to "fish" readily through raceways.

47. The correct answer is (D). The image shows the current rising and falling from some minimum value indicated by the straight-line portions of the image. The current, therefore, pulses without changing direction. AC involves a reversal of direction.

48. The correct answer is (C). Ohm's law; V = IR gives the voltage drop across a resistor. Inductance and capacitance do not produce a voltage drop. Conductance is the reciprocal of resistance. A high resistance has a low conductance.

49. The correct answer is (B). Maximum wattage that will cause a 15-ampere breaker to trip is (15 amps) (120 volts) = 1800 watts. Accordingly, 1300 watts is the largest heater that will operate without causing the circuit breaker to trip.

50. The correct answer is (A). A capacitor contains two conducting surfaces separated by an insulator and can, therefore, store static electrical charges. Caution should be exercised before touching capacitors. They should have their terminals "shorted" before being handled.

KEY ANSWERS AND RATIONALE FOR PRACTICE EXERCISE 9: MECHANICAL COMPREHENSION

Key Answers

1. The correct answer is (B).
2. The correct answer is (C).
3. The correct answer is (C).
4. The correct answer is (B).
5. The correct answer is (A).
6. The correct answer is (B).
7. The correct answer is (B).
8. The correct answer is (A).
9. The correct answer is (C).
10. The correct answer is (B).
11. The correct answer is (B).
12. The correct answer is (C).
13. The correct answer is (B).
14. The correct answer is (A).
15. The correct answer is (A).
16. The correct answer is (C).
17. The correct answer is (C).
18. The correct answer is (A).
19. The correct answer is (B).
20. The correct answer is (A).
21. The correct answer is (C).
22. The correct answer is (A).
23. The correct answer is (B).
24. The correct answer is (B).
25. The correct answer is (A).
26. The correct answer is (C).
27. The correct answer is (C).
28. The correct answer is (A).
29. The correct answer is (C).
30. The correct answer is (C).
31. The correct answer is (A).
32. The correct answer is (B).
33. The correct answer is (B).
34. The correct answer is (A).
35. The correct answer is (A).
36. The correct answer is (B).
37. The correct answer is (A).
38. The correct answer is (C).
39. The correct answer is (B).
40. The correct answer is (A).
41. The correct answer is (C).
42. The correct answer is (C).
43. The correct answer is (B).
44. The correct answer is (C).
45. The correct answer is (A).
46. The correct answer is (A).
47. The correct answer is (B).
48. The correct answer is (C).
49. The correct answer is (C).
50. The correct answer is (B).

Items Answered Incorrectly: __; __; __; __; __; __; __; __.
Items Unsure Of: __; __; __; __; __; __; __; __.

TOTAL NUMBER
ANSWERED CORRECTLY: _____

Rationale

1. The correct answer is (B). The second-class lever has the fulcrum at one end; the effort is applied at the other end. The resistance is somewhere between these points. A nutcracker is a good example of a second-class lever.

2. The correct answer is (C). $30 \times 7 = 2 \times W$; $2W = 210$; $W = 105$ lbs.

3. The correct answer is (C). $40 \times 3 = 11 \times F$; $11F = 120$; $F = \frac{120}{11}$; $F = 10\frac{10}{11}$.

4. The correct answer is (B).

$$\text{Mechanical Advantage} = \frac{\text{Effort Arm}}{\text{Resistance Arm}}; \text{M.A.} = \frac{A}{a}.$$

5. The correct answer is (A). B has a greater effort arm; therefore, A would bear the most weight on the shoulder.

6. The correct answer is (B). $60 \times 8 = 15 \times E$; $15E = 480$; $E = \frac{480}{15} = 32$ lbs.

7. The correct answer is (B). $300 \times 2 = 6 \times E$; $6E = 600$; $E = \frac{600}{6}$; $E = 100$ lbs.

8. The correct answer is (A). $E \times 5 = 1 \times 50$; $5E = 50$; $E = \frac{50}{5}$; $E = 10$ lbs.

9. The correct answer is (C). As the weight is closer to sailor Y, sailor Y has the shorter effort arm and is therefore carrying the greater weight.

10. The correct answer is (B). The weight is equally distributed. $80 + 2 = 82$ lbs. $\frac{82}{2} = 41$ lbs.

11. The correct answer is (B). The number of the parts of rope going to and from the movable block determines the mechanical advantage. With a mechanical advantage of 3, a 100-pound pull is necessary to lift a 300-pound weight.

12. The correct answer is (C). There are five parts of rope going to and from the movable blocks. The MA is 5.

13. The correct answer is (B). The TMA of the pulley system is 2.

$$\text{TMA} = \frac{d_E}{d_R}; 2 = \frac{10}{d_R}; 2 \times d_R = 10; d_R = \frac{10}{2} = 5 \text{ feet.}$$

14. The correct answer is (A). There are four parts of rope going to and from the movable blocks.

TMA = 4. $\frac{300}{4} = 75$ lbs.

15. The correct answer is (A).

$$\text{TMA} = \frac{d_E}{d_R}; 4 = \frac{12}{d_R}; 4d_R = 12; d_R = \frac{12}{4} = 3 \text{ feet.}$$

16. The correct answer is (C). Pulley #2 is a fixed pulley; pulley #1 is a movable one. Both are of equal diameter. If the rope is pulled a distance equal to the circumference of pulley #2 (one full turn), pulley #1 would move up only half that distance making only a half turn.

17. The correct answer is (C). The theoretical mechanical advantage is 3.

$$\frac{d_E}{d_R} = 3; \frac{d_E}{6} = 3; d_E = 3 \times 6 = 18 \text{ feet.}$$

18. The correct answer is (A).

$$\text{Theoretical Mechanical Advantage} = \frac{\text{Length of Slope}}{\text{Height}};$$

$$\text{TMA} = \frac{10}{2} = 5.$$

19. The correct answer is (B).

$$\text{TMA} = \frac{8}{2} = 4; 4 = \frac{W}{E}; 4 = \frac{400}{E}; 4E = 400;$$

$E = 100$ pounds.

20. The correct answer is (A). As the circumference of the drum is one foot, or 12 inches, one complete revolution of the windlass will pull each strand up one foot and will pull the weight up 12 inches.

21. The correct answer is (C). Tool C is a hammer that is generally used to smooth out dents in formed sheet metal.

22. The correct answer is (A). Tool A is a level used to ascertain whether a plane is true horizontal or true vertical.

23. The correct answer is (B). Tool B is a slide caliper used for measuring both inside and outside dimensions.

24. The correct answer is (B). The tool is a screw pitch gauge used to determine the pitch and number of threads per inch of threaded fasteners.

25. The correct answer is (A). The standard symbol for a battery is ⊢⊣⊢⊢

26. The correct answer is (C). The standard symbol for a switch is ⌐◦⌐

27. The correct answer is (C). The standard symbol for a variable resistor is ⌐◦◦⌐

28. The correct answer is (A). 0 thousands + 9 hundreds + 1 ten + 8 units = 0918.

29. The correct answer is (C). Although the lower fuse is burned out, lamp 3 will be lighted as it is in a complete circuit.

30. The correct answer is (C). Note that there are two paths for the flow of electrons in circuit 3 and that the resistors are connected in parallel.

31. The correct answer is (A). Note that circuit 1 contains resistors in parallel and in series.

32. The correct answer is (B). Note that the pointer is on the first mark above the 30 mark. As each mark is a 2-volt increment, the proper reading is 32 volts.

33. The correct answer is (B). Point O is directly on the mark having a value of 60 on this nonlinear scale.

34. The correct answer is (A). This is a nonlinear scale increasing in value from right to left. The midpoint has a value less than 1.5; therefore, 1.5 lies to the left of point S.

35. The correct answer is (A). The value on the basic scale is 1.75. On the ohms × 100 range, the resistance value would be $1.75 \times 100 = 175$ ohms.

36. The correct answer is (B). The point 1 reading is exactly $1\frac{1}{4}''$.

37. The correct answer is (A). Point 3 reading is $4\frac{1}{8}''$; point 2 reading is $2\frac{3}{4}''$. $4\frac{1}{8}'' - 2\frac{3}{4}'' = 3\frac{9}{8}'' - 2\frac{6}{8}'' = 1\frac{3}{8}''$.

38. The correct answer is (C). $.300 + .025 + .015 = .340$

39. The correct answer is (B). Point 2 is a greater distance away from the center of the wheel than is point 1. Accordingly, point 2 will traverse a greater linear distance than would point 1.

40. The correct answer is (A). If gear 1 turns clockwise, gear 2 will turn counterclockwise. Gears 3 and 4 will turn clockwise.

41. The correct answer is (C). Let x = revolutions per minute of smaller gear

$15 \times 200 = 10x; 10x = 3000; x = \frac{3000}{10} = 300$ revolutions per minute.

42. The correct answer is (C). One complete revolution of wheel A with 32 teeth will result in 4 complete revolutions of wheel B with 8 teeth; wheel C will also make 4 complete revolutions.

43. The correct answer is (B). Every complete revolution results in two contacts. Two contacts every second results from one complete revolution per second or 60 revolutions per minute.

44. The correct answer is (C). If the 10-tooth gear makes 6 revolutions, the 20-tooth gear will make 3 revolutions, causing the cam to activate the valve 3 times.

45. The correct answer is (A). The radius of the 6″ wheel is 3″. Therefore, the cam extends 1″ beyond the wheel's circumference. This permits the block to drop a maximum of 1″.

46. The correct answer is (A). According to the Pythagorean theorem, the hypotenuse of the right triangle is 5″. 1″ + 5″ + 1″ = 7″.

47. The correct answer is (B). Two 2″ × 8″ rectangular pieces can be cut from the vertical section. One 2″ × 8″ rectangular piece can be cut from the horizontal section. 2 + 1 = 3.

48. The correct answer is (C). To make the right angle bracket, the angle iron must be bent 90°. The two sides of a 90° angle X would then meet to form the bracket shown.

49. The correct answer is (C). Careful analysis will show that only sheet metal number 3 can be shaped to make the form that is open at both ends.

50. The correct answer is (B).

$$1\frac{1}{2}″+1\frac{1}{2}″+2\frac{1}{8}″+2\frac{1}{8}″+1\frac{1}{2}″+1\frac{1}{2}″=10\frac{1}{4}″;$$

$$14″-10\frac{1}{4}″=3\frac{3}{4}″;$$

$$\frac{3\frac{3}{4}}{5}=\frac{15}{4\times5}=\frac{3}{4}″$$

PART IX

United States Air Force Officer Qualifying Test

(Academic Aptitude Composite)

Specimen Subtests

Part 1: Verbal Analogies
Part 2: Arithmetic Reasoning
Part 3: Reading Comprehension
Part 4: Data Interpretation
Part 5: Word Knowledge
Part 6: Math Knowledge

This part contains a specimen answer sheet for use in answering the questions on the first six subtests of the Air Force Officer Qualifying Test, specimen subtests, key answers for determining your scores on these subtests, and the rationale or explanation for each key answer.

Remove (cut out) the specimen answer sheet on the following page for use in recording your answers to the subtest questions. These specimen subtests are similar in format and content to the subtests given in the actual Air Force Officer Qualifying Test. Take these subtests under "real" test conditions. Time each subtest carefully.

Use the key answers to obtain your subtest scores and to evaluate your performance on each subtest. Record the number of items you answered correctly, as well as the number of each item you answered incorrectly or wish to review, in the space provided below the key answers for each subtest.

Be certain to review carefully and understand the explanations for the answers to all questions you answered incorrectly and for each of the questions you answered correctly but are unsure of. This is absolutely essential in order to acquire the knowledge and expertise necessary to obtain the maximum scores possible on the subtests of the real Air Force Officer Qualifying Test.

SCHEMATIC SAMPLE

PART 1 VERBAL ANALOGIES

1 A B C D E   5 A B C D E   9 A B C D E   13 A B C D E   17 A B C D E   21 A B C D E   25 A B C D E

2 A B C D E   6 A B C D E   10 A B C D E   14 A B C D E   18 A B C D E   22 A B C D E

3 A B C D E   7 A B C D E   11 A B C D E   15 A B C D E   19 A B C D E   23 A B C D E

4 A B C D E   8 A B C D E   12 A B C D E   16 A B C D E   20 A B C D E   24 A B C D E

PART 2 ARITHMETIC REASONING

1 A B C D E   5 A B C D E   9 A B C D E   13 A B C D E   17 A B C D E   21 A B C D E   25 A B C D E

2 A B C D E   6 A B C D E   10 A B C D E   14 A B C D E   18 A B C D E   22 A B C D E

3 A B C D E   7 A B C D E   11 A B C D E   15 A B C D E   19 A B C D E   23 A B C D E

4 A B C D E   8 A B C D E   12 A B C D E   16 A B C D E   20 A B C D E   24 A B C D E

PART 3 READING COMPREHENSION

1 A B C D E   5 A B C D E   9 A B C D E   13 A B C D E   17 A B C D E   21 A B C D E   25 A B C D E

2 A B C D E   6 A B C D E   10 A B C D E   14 A B C D E   18 A B C D E   22 A B C D E

3 A B C D E   7 A B C D E   11 A B C D E   15 A B C D E   19 A B C D E   23 A B C D E

4 A B C D E   8 A B C D E   12 A B C D E   16 A B C D E   20 A B C D E   24 A B C D E

PART 4 DATA INTERPRETATION

1 A B C D E   5 A B C D E   9 A B C D E   13 A B C D E   17 A B C D E   21 A B C D E   25 A B C D E

2 A B C D E   6 A B C D E   10 A B C D E   14 A B C D E   18 A B C D E   22 A B C D E

3 A B C D E   7 A B C D E   11 A B C D E   15 A B C D E   19 A B C D E   23 A B C D E

4 A B C D E   8 A B C D E   12 A B C D E   16 A B C D E   20 A B C D E   24 A B C D E

PART 5 WORD KNOWLEDGE

1 A B C D E   5 A B C D E   9 A B C D E   13 A B C D E   17 A B C D E   21 A B C D E   25 A B C D E

2 A B C D E   6 A B C D E   10 A B C D E   14 A B C D E   18 A B C D E   22 A B C D E

3 A B C D E   7 A B C D E   11 A B C D E   15 A B C D E   19 A B C D E   23 A B C D E

4 A B C D E   8 A B C D E   12 A B C D E   16 A B C D E   20 A B C D E   24 A B C D E

PART 6 MATH KNOWLEDGE

1 A B C D E   5 A B C D E   9 A B C D E   13 A B C D E   17 A B C D E   21 A B C D E   25 A B C D E

2 A B C D E   6 A B C D E   10 A B C D E   14 A B C D E   18 A B C D E   22 A B C D E

3 A B C D E   7 A B C D E   11 A B C D E   15 A B C D E   19 A B C D E   23 A B C D E

4 A B C D E   8 A B C D E   12 A B C D E   16 A B C D E   20 A B C D E   24 A B C D E

PART 1: VERBAL ANALOGIES

Directions: This part of the test has 25 questions designed to measure your ability to reason and see relationships between words. Each question begins with a pair of capitalized words. You are to choose the option that best completes the analogy developed at the beginning of each question. That is, select the option that shows a relationship similar to the one shown by the original pair of capitalized words. Then mark the space on your answer form that has the same number and letter as your choice.

Now look at the two sample questions below.

S1.   FINGER is to HAND as TOOTH is to

    (A) tongue
    (B) lips
    (C) nose
    (D) mouth
    (E) molar

A *finger* is part of the *hand*; a *tooth* is part of the *mouth*. Choice (D) is the correct answer.

S2.   RACQUET is to COURT as

    (A) tractor is to field
    (B) blossom is to bloom
    (C) stalk is to prey
    (D) plan is to strategy
    (E) moon is to planet

A *racquet* is used by a tennis player on the *court*; a *tractor* is used by a farmer on the *field*. Choice (A) is the correct answer.

Your score on this test will be based on the number of questions you answer correctly. You should try to answer every question. You will not lose points or be penalized for guessing. Do not spend too much time on any one question.

When you begin, be sure to start with question No. 1 of Part 1 of your test booklet and number 1 of Part 1 on your answer form.

DO NOT TURN PAGE UNTIL TOLD TO DO SO.

PART I: VERBAL ANALOGIES

TIME: 8 Minutes—25 Questions

Choose the answer that best completes the analogy developed at the beginning of each question.

1. PROSPECTOR is to GOLD as

   (A) carpenter is to wood
   (B) detective is to clue
   (C) doctor is to medicine
   (D) machinist is to lathe
   (E) preacher is to prayer

2. QUARRY is to MARBLE as

   (A) game is to preserve
   (B) igneous is to metamorphic
   (C) iron is to ore
   (D) mine is to coal
   (E) timber is to forest

3. RAM is to LAMB as

   (A) buck is to doe
   (B) bull is to calf
   (C) cat is to kitten
   (D) chicken is to hen
   (E) ewe is to sheep

4. GENERAL is to ADMIRAL as

   (A) squadron is to platoon
   (B) commander is to follower
   (C) soldier is to sailor
   (D) captain is to officer
   (E) leader is to manager

5. ROBIN is to SPARROW as

   (A) dog is to terrier
   (B) bluejay is to finch
   (C) mosquito is to insect
   (D) rodent is to rat
   (E) tree is to flower

6. SCRAWNY is to LEAN as BRAWNY is to

   (A) fat
   (B) slim
   (C) strong
   (D) tall
   (E) thin

7. SHY is to BASHFUL as INQUIRE is to

   (A) ask
   (B) conceal
   (C) frighten
   (D) suggest
   (E) tell

8. STALLION is to GELDING as BULL is to

   (A) boar
   (B) buck
   (C) mare
   (D) rooster
   (E) steer

9. TOIL is to STRIFE as WORK is to

   (A) arbitrate
   (B) labor
   (C) maneuver
   (D) struggle
   (E) suffer

10. VALID is to FALLACIOUS as VERACIOUS is to

    (A) delinquent
    (B) illegal
    (C) reliable
    (D) unsupportive
    (E) untrue

11. SHOOT is to SHOT as

    (A) bend is to bent
    (B) bleed is to bled
    (C) build is to built
    (D) feel is to felt
    (E) keep is to kept

12. AD LIB is to REHEARSAL as
    (A) random is to foresight
    (B) accidental is to preparation
    (C) unnecessary is to intention
    (D) improvised is to logic
    (E) aleatory is to plan

13. PAINT is to DAUB as
    (A) sculpt is to carve
    (B) pluck is to strum
    (C) sing is to caterwaul
    (D) versify is to compose
    (E) dance is to perform

14. 36 is to 4 as
    (A) 3 is to 2
    (B) 3 is to 24
    (C) 9 is to 1
    (D) 9 is to 4
    (E) 9 is to 6

15. TRUMPET is to INSTRUMENT as
    (A) barrel is to pistol
    (B) compass is to protractor
    (C) pliers is to tool
    (D) scissors is to shears
    (E) weapon is to bomb

16. DRIFT is to SNOW as DUNE is to
    (A) hail
    (B) hill
    (C) desert
    (D) rain
    (E) sand

17. MOON is to EARTH as EARTH is to
    (A) galaxy
    (B) ground
    (C) Mars
    (D) sky
    (E) sun

18. NECKLACE is to ADORNMENT as MEDAL is to
    (A) bravery
    (B) bronze
    (C) jewel
    (D) metal
    (E) decoration

19. PULP is to PAPER as HEMP is to
    (A) baskets
    (B) cotton
    (C) rope
    (D) sweaters
    (E) yarn

20. REGRESSIVE is to REGRESS as STERILE is to
    (A) sterilely
    (B) sterility
    (C) sterilization
    (D) sterilize
    (E) sterilizer

21. WAVE is to CREST as
    (A) breaker is to swimming
    (B) island is to archipelago
    (C) levee is to dike
    (D) mountain is to peak
    (E) sea is to ocean

22. WITCH is to WIZARD as
    (A) duck is to drake
    (B) filly is to foal
    (C) gander is to goose
    (D) mare is to horse
    (E) ram is to sheep

23. ENIGMA is to MYSTIFIED as
    (A) problem is to apathetic
    (B) deception is to misinterpreted
    (C) mistake is to worried
    (D) dilemma is to undecided
    (E) threat is to irritated

GO ON TO THE NEXT PAGE

24. WRING is to WRUNG as
   (A) bring is to brang
   (B) go is to went
   (C) lay is to laid
   (D) rang is to rung
   (E) think is to thank

25. ZINC is to SULFURIC ACID as
   (A) atom is to molecule
   (B) copper is to brass
   (C) element is to compound
   (D) metal is to salt
   (E) molecule is to mixture

STOP! DO NOT TURN THIS PAGE UNTIL TOLD TO DO SO. IF YOU FINISH BEFORE THE TIME IS UP, YOU MAY CHECK OVER YOUR WORK ON THIS PART ONLY.

PART 2: ARITHMETIC REASONING

Directions: This part of the test measures arithmetic reasoning or your ability to arrive at solutions to mathematical problems. Each problem is followed by five possible answers. Decide which one of the five options is most nearly correct. Then mark the space on your answer form that has the same number and letter as your choice. Use the scratch paper that has been given to you to do any figuring that you wish.

Now look at the two sample problems below.

S1. A field with an area of 420 square yards is twice as large in area as a second field. If the second field is 15 yards long, how wide is it?

    (A) 7 yards
    (B) 14 yards
    (C) 28 yards
    (D) 56 yards
    (E) 90 yards

The second field has an area of 210 square yards. If one side is 15 yards, the other side must be 14 yards ($15 \times 14 = 210$). Choice (B) is the correct answer.

S2. A typist took three typing tests. The average typing speed on these three tests was 48 words per minute. If the typist's speed on two of these tests was 52 words per minute, what was the typist's speed on the third test?

    (A) 46 words per minute
    (B) 44 words per minute
    (C) 42 words per minute
    (D) 40 words per minute
    (E) 38 words per minute

The total time for the three tests is 144 minutes (48×3). The time for two tests is 104 minutes. Therefore, the time on the third test is 40 minutes ($144 - 104 = 40$). Choice (D) is the correct answer.

Your score on this test will be based on the number of questions you answer correctly. You should try to answer every question. You will not lose points or be penalized for guessing. Do not spend too much time on any one question.

When you begin, be sure to start with question No. 1 of Part 2 of your test booklet and No. 1 of Part 2 on your answer sheet.

DO NOT TURN PAGE UNTIL TOLD TO DO SO.

PART 2: ARITHMETIC REASONING

TIME: 29 Minutes—25 Questions

1. Assume that a musical instrument depreciates by 20% of its value each year. What would be the value of a piano purchased new for $2400 after 2 years?

   (A) $1350
   (B) $1536
   (C) $1692
   (D) $1824
   (E) $2304

2. A room 27 feet by 32 feet is to be carpeted wall to wall. The width of the carpet is 27 inches. The length, in yards, of the carpet needed for this room is

   (A) 128
   (B) 256
   (C) 384
   (D) 648
   (E) 1188

3. The cost of 4 rolls, 6 muffins, and 3 loaves of bread is $9.10. The cost of 2 rolls, 3 muffins, and a loaf of bread is $3.90. What is the cost of a loaf of bread?

   (A) $1.05
   (B) $1.10
   (C) $1.20
   (D) $1.25
   (E) $1.30

4. Maximum engine life is 900 hours. Recently, 27 engines were removed with an average life of 635.30 hours. What percent of the maximum engine life has been achieved?

   (A) 71%
   (B) 72%
   (C) 73%
   (D) 74%
   (E) 75%

5. Nicholas receives a basic weekly salary of $180 plus a 5% commission. In a week in which his sales amounted to $1800, the ratio of his basic salary to his commission was

   (A) 3 : 1
   (B) 2 : 1
   (C) 3 : 2
   (D) 1 : 1
   (E) 1 : 2

6. Mrs. Norton spent $\frac{2}{3}$ of the family income one year and divided the remainder among 4 different savings accounts. If she put $2000 into each account, what was the amount of her family income that year?

   (A) $8000
   (B) $16,000
   (C) $24,000
   (D) $32,000
   (E) $40,000

7. What is the tax rate per $1000 if a base of $338,555 would yield $616.07?

   (A) $1.82
   (B) $1.86
   (C) $1.90
   (D) $1.95
   (E) $2.00

8. The ratio of Democrats to Republicans in a certain state legislature is 5 : 7. If the legislature has 156 members, all of whom are either Democrats or Republicans (but not both), what is the difference between the number of Republicans and the number of Democrats?

   (A) 14
   (B) 26
   (C) 35
   (D) 37
   (E) 46

9. What part of a dime is a quarter?

(A) $\frac{5}{2}$

(B) $\frac{3}{2}$

(C) $\frac{2}{5}$

(D) $\frac{2}{3}$

(E) $\frac{3}{4}$

10. A pole 24 feet high has a shadow 8 feet long. A nearby pole is 72 feet high. How long is its shadow?

(A) 16 feet
(B) 24 feet
(C) 32 feet
(D) 40 feet
(E) 56 feet

11. If 15 cans of food are needed for 7 adults for 2 days, the number of cans needed for 4 adults for 7 days is

(A) 15
(B) 20
(C) 25
(D) 30
(E) 35

12. The school enrollment is 1400. Twenty percent of the students study French, 25% study Spanish, 15% study Italian, 10% study German, and the rest study no foreign language. Assuming that each student may study only one foreign language, how many students do not study any foreign language?

(A) 42
(B) 280
(C) 420
(D) 480
(E) 565

13. How many liters of 50% antifreeze must be mixed with 80 liters of 20% antifreeze to get a mixture that is 40% antifreeze?

(A) 160
(B) 140
(C) 120
(D) 100
(E) 80

14. Eight hundred persons are employed by the Metropolitan Transit Authority. One quarter of the employees are college graduates; $\frac{5}{6}$ of the remainder are high school graduates. What part of the total number of employees never graduated from high school?

(A) $\frac{1}{8}$

(B) $\frac{1}{6}$

(C) $\frac{1}{4}$

(D) $\frac{5}{6}$

(E) $\frac{7}{8}$

15. Two children weighing 60 pounds and 80 pounds, respectively, balance a seesaw. How many feet from the fulcrum must the heavier child sit if the lighter child is 8 feet from the fulcrum?

(A) $4\frac{1}{2}$

(B) 6

(C) $7\frac{1}{2}$

(D) 9

(E) $10\frac{1}{2}$

GO ON TO THE NEXT PAGE

16. A pole 63 feet long was broken into two un-equal parts so that $\frac{3}{5}$ of the longer piece equaled $\frac{3}{5}$ of the shorter piece. Find the length of the longer piece.

(A) 33 feet

(B) $33\frac{1}{2}$ feet

(C) 34 feet

(D) $34\frac{1}{2}$ feet

(E) 35 feet

17. A rectangular flower bed whose dimensions are 16 yards by 12 yards is surrounded by a walk 3 yards wide. The area of the walk is

(A) 93 square yards.

(B) 96 square yards.

(C) 144 square yards.

(D) 204 square yards.

(E) 244 square yards.

18. The temperatures reported at hourly intervals on a winter evening were +6°, +3°, 0°, –4°, and –10°. What was the average temperature for this period of time?

(A) +5°

(B) –5°

(C) 0°

(D) +1°

(E) –1°

19. A purse contains $2.20 in dimes and quarters. If the number of dimes is $\frac{1}{4}$ the number of quarters, how many dimes are there?

(A) 2

(B) 4

(C) 6

(D) 8

(E) 10

20. Two trains are 630 miles apart. At 9:00 a.m., they start traveling toward each other at aver-age rates of 50 and 55 mph, respectively. At what time will they pass each other?

(A) 1:00 p.m.

(B) 1:30 p.m.

(C) 2:00 p.m.

(D) 2:30 p.m.

(E) 3:00 p.m.

21. At 12:00 noon, two vessels started sailing to-ward each other from ports that are 450 miles apart. They traveled at average rates of 22 and 28 mph respectively. How many miles apart will the vessels be at 8 p.m.?

(A) 125

(B) 100

(C) 75

(D) 50

(E) 25

22. Two planes left at the same time from two airports that are 6000 miles apart and flew toward each other. They passed each other in five hours. The rate of the fast plane was twice the rate of the slow plane. What was the speed of the fast plane?

(A) 400 mph

(B) 500 mph

(C) 600 mph

(D) 700 mph

(E) 800 mph

23. Harvey paid $400 for a used car that travels 28 miles per gallon on the highway and 20 miles per gallon in the city. If he drove twice as many highway miles as city miles last month while using 34 gallons of gasoline, how many miles did he drive altogether?

(A) 1,000

(B) 840

(C) 400

(D) 340

(E) 280

24. How much water must be evaporated from 120 pounds of a 3% saline solution to make it an 8% saline solution?

   (A) 36 pounds
   (B) 45 pounds
   (C) 75 pounds
   (D) 105 pounds
   (E) 120 pounds

25. One printing press can do a job in 8 hours. Another printing press can do the same job in 12 hours. How long would it take both presses, working together, to do the job?

   (A) 4 hours 12 minutes
   (B) 4 hours 24 minutes
   (C) 4 hours 36 minutes
   (D) 4 hours 48 minutes
   (E) 5 hours

STOP! DO NOT TURN THIS PAGE UNTIL TOLD TO DO SO. IF YOU FINISH BEFORE THE TIME IS UP, YOU MAY CHECK OVER YOUR WORK ON THIS PART ONLY.

PART 3: READING COMPREHENSION

Directions: This part of the test has 25 questions designed to measure your ability to read and understand paragraphs. For each question, you are to select the answer that best completes the statement or answers the question based on the information contained in the passage. Then mark the space on your answer form that has the same number and letter as your choice.

Here are two sample questions.

S1. Because of our short life span of seventy-odd years, it is easy for human beings to think of Earth as a planet which never changes. Yet we live on a dynamic planet with many factors contributing to change. We know that wind and rain erode and shape our planet. Many other forces are also at work, such as volcanic activity, temperature fluctuations, and even extraterrestrial interaction such as meteors and gravitational forces. The earth, in actuality, is a large rock

    (A) in a state of inertia.
    (B) that is quickly eroding.
    (C) that is evolving.
    (D) that is subject to temperature fluctuations caused by interplanetary interaction.
    (E) that is subject to winds caused by meteor activity.

Of the choices given, only choice (C) can be implied from the passage. Accordingly, choice (C) is the correct answer.

S2. One theory that explains the similarities between Mayan art and ancient Chinese art is called "diffusion." This theory evolves from the belief that invention is so unique that it happens only once, then is "diffused" to other cultures through travel, trade, and war. This theory might explain why

    (A) the airplane and birds both have wings.
    (B) certain artifacts in Central America resemble those found in Southeast Asia.
    (C) most great art comes from Europe, where there is much travel between countries.
    (D) rivers in South America and Africa have some similar features.
    (E) England, being so remote in the Middle Ages, is the only country to have castles.

Of the choices given, choice (B) is the only one that the theory might explain. Accordingly, choice (B) is the correct answer.

Your score on this test will be based on the number of questions you answer correctly. You should try to answer every question. You will not lose points or be penalized for guessing. Do not spend too much time on any one question.

When you begin, be sure to start with question No. 1 of Part 3 of your test booklet and No. 1 of Part 3 on your answer form.

DO NOT TURN PAGE UNTIL TOLD TO DO SO.

PART 3: READING COMPREHENSION

TIME: 18 Minutes—25 Questions

1. Statutes to prevent and penalize adulteration of foods, and to provide for sanitary food preparation, are enforced in every state. Such legislation has been upheld as proper under the police power of the state, since this legislation is obviously designed to promote the health and general welfare of the people.

   The paragraph best supports the statement that

   (A) the state provides for drastic measures to deal with violations of the pure food laws.
   (B) to make laws for the purpose of promoting the general health and general welfare of the people is a proper function of the state.
   (C) adulterated food is an outstanding menace to public health.
   (D) every state has adequately provided for the prevention of adulteration of foods by enforcement of suitable legislation.
   (E) the right of the state to penalize adulteration of foods has never been questioned.

2. Whenever two groups of people whose interests conflict meet to discuss a solution to that conflict, there is laid a basis for an interchange of facts and ideas that increases the total range of knowledge of both parties and tends to break down the barrier that their restricted field of information has helped to create.

   The paragraph best supports the statement that conflicts between two parties may be brought closer to a settlement through

   (A) frank acknowledgment of error.
   (B) the exchange of accusations.
   (C) gaining a wider knowledge of facts.
   (D) submitting the dispute to an impartial judge.
   (E) limiting discussion to plans acceptable to both groups.

3. Unfortunately, specialization in industry creates workers who lack versatility. When a laborer is trained to perform only one task, he is almost entirely dependent for employment upon the demand for that particular skill. If anything happens to interrupt that demand he is unemployed.

   The paragraph best supports the statement that

   (A) the unemployment problem is a direct result of specialization in industry.
   (B) the demand for labor of a particular type is constantly changing.
   (C) the average laborer is not capable of learning more than one task at a time.
   (D) some cases of unemployment are due to laborers' lack of versatility.
   (E) too much specialization is as dangerous as too little.

   Questions 4 and 5 are based on the information contained in the following passage.

   The American Revolution is the only one in modern history that, rather than devouring the intellectuals who prepared it, carried them to power. Most of the signatories of the Declaration of Independence were intellectuals. This tradition is ingrained in America, whose greatest statesmen have been intellectuals—Jefferson and Lincoln, for example. These statesmen performed their political function, but at the same time they felt a more universal responsibility, and they actively defined this responsibility. Thanks to them there is in America a living school of political science. In fact, it is at the moment the only one perfectly adapted to the emergencies of the contemporary world, and one which can be victoriously opposed to communism. A European who follows American politics will be struck by the constant reference in the press and from the platform to this political philosophy, to the historical events through which it was best expressed, to the great statesmen who were its best representatives.

4. The title below that best expresses the ideas of this passage is

(A) "Fathers of the American Revolution."
(B) "Jefferson and Lincoln—Ideal Statesmen."
(C) "Democracy Versus Communism."
(D) "The Basis of American Political Philosophy."
(E) "The Responsibility of Statesmen."

5. According to this passage, intellectuals who pave the way for revolutions are usually

(A) misunderstood.
(B) honored.
(C) forgotten.
(D) elected to office.
(E) destroyed.

Questions 6–8 are based on the information contained in the following passage.

The Greek language is a member of the Aryan or Indo-European family, and its various dialects constitute the Hellenic group. It was probably spoken in Europe and Asia at least 1,500 years before the Christian Era by Greeks with classical learning. Later it was a universal language among the cultured classes, just as Latin afterward became the medium of international communication. During the Dark Ages, Greek was little known to Western Europe, except in monasteries, although it remained the language of the Byzantine Empire. The emigration of the Greeks to Italy after the fall of Constantinople, and during the century preceding, gave a new impetus to the study of the Greek language, and the revival of learning gave it the place it has ever since occupied.

6. The title below that best expresses the ideas of this passage is

(A) "An Interesting Language."
(B) "Greece, Past and Present."
(C) "Greek, the Universal Language."
(D) "Importance of the Greek Dialects."
(E) "The Greek Language."

7. A result of Greece's being the center of classical learning was that

(A) Greek displaced Latin.
(B) Greek was not important during the Dark Ages.
(C) Greek was the universal language among the cultured classes.
(D) it built great schools.
(E) its citizens were all cultured.

8. The Greek language

(A) became dominant in Italy.
(B) had more dialects than Latin.
(C) was introduced into Europe by way of Constantinople.
(D) was probably spoken in Europe as early as 1500 B.C.
(E) was responsible for the revival of learning.

GO ON TO THE NEXT PAGE

Questions 9 and 10 are based on the information contained in the following passage.

Since 1760, about the beginning of the Age of Steam, the earth's population has more than tripled. This increase has not been an evolutionary phenomenon with biological causes. Yet there was an evolution—it took place in the world's economic organization. Thus, 1,800,000,000 more human beings can now remain alive on the earth's surface, can support themselves by working for others who in turn work for them. This extraordinary tripling of human population in seven short generations is explained by the speeded-up economic unification which took place during the same period. Thus, most of us are now kept alive by this vast cooperative unified world society. Goods are the great travelers over the earth's surface, far more than human beings. Endlessly, streams of goods crisscross, as on Martian canals, with hardly an inhabited spot on the globe unvisited.

9. The basic change that led to the greatly increased population concerns
   (A) a revolution.
   (B) economic factors.
   (C) biological factors.
   (D) an increase in travel.
   (E) the growth of world government.

10. This passage was probably written during which of the following time spans?
    (A) 1905–1910
    (B) 1925–1930
    (C) 1945–1950
    (D) 1965–1970
    (E) 1985–1990

11. In the metric system, the unit of weight is the gram. There are 454 grams to a pound. One kilogram (1000 grams) is equal to 2.2 pounds. If a man weighs 90 kilograms, his equivalent weight would be
    (A) 190 pounds.
    (B) 198 pounds.
    (C) 206 pounds.
    (D) 214 pounds.
    (E) 220 pounds.

12. A heavy snowfall may cause delays in the movement of trains and buses. Both pedestrians and cars have accidents because of snow and ice. Pedestrians slip and fall. Cars skid and collide.

    According to the above passage, snow and ice may cause automobiles to
    (A) injure pedestrians.
    (B) overheat.
    (C) slow down.
    (D) stall.
    (E) skid.

13. As a rule, police officers arriving at the scene of an automobile accident should first care for victims who need immediate medical treatment. If necessary, the police officers should ask bystanders to help warn approaching cars and keep traffic moving.

    The *first* thing that police officers should do when they get to the scene of an accident is to
    (A) ask for the help of bystanders.
    (B) protect evidence that shows how the accident happened.
    (C) take care of any injured persons who need immediate help.
    (D) warn oncoming cars and keep traffic moving.
    (E) write up an accident report.

Questions 14–16 are based on the information contained in the following passage.

Self-contained diving suits have made it possible for a diver to explore the depths without the local authorities knowing very much about it. Should the diver be lucky enough to discover a wreck, he can recover the less cumbersome fragments, bronzes, marble, or bits of statuary without attracting official attention.

Today one can indulge in a secret treasure hunt right down to the sea bed with the added advantage that it is far harder to keep a watch on sunken treasure than it is to protect excavations on shore. So the modern despoiler is as great a pest to the serious archaeologist at sea as on land. In Egypt and Syria he has deprived us of invaluable data. He nearly always ransacks his objective to take away some portable trophy that he thinks valuable. He keeps his treasure house a secret, and we must blame him for the appearance of various objects impossible to date or catalogue.

14. The title below that best expresses the ideas found in this passage is
   (A) "Recovering Ships."
   (B) "Modem Diving Suits."
   (C) "The Irresponsible Explorer."
   (D) "Cataloging Long-Lost Objects."
   (E) "Concealing the Truth in the Near East."

15. The passage suggests that the author is
   (A) opposed to excavations on shore.
   (B) sympathetic to the officials.
   (C) sympathetic to the divers.
   (D) opposed to investigations in Syria and Egypt.
   (E) opposed to the despoilers cataloging their finds.

16. It is to the amateur archaeologist's advantage that local authorities
   (A) protect his findings on land.
   (B) allow him to keep portable treasures.
   (C) provide catalogues of underwater treasures.
   (D) are sometimes unaware of his diving activities.
   (E) are ignorant of the true value of sunken treasures.

Questions 17 and 18 are based on the information contained in the following passage.

Hail is at once the cruelest weapon in nature's armory, and the most incalculable. It can destroy one farmer's prospects of a harvest in a matter of seconds; it can leave his neighbor's unimpaired. It can slay a flock of sheep (it has killed children too) in one field, while the sun continues to shine in the next. To the harassed meteorologist, its behavior is even more Machiavellian than that of an ice storm. Difficult as it undoubtedly is for him to forecast the onset of an ice storm, he knows pretty well what its course and duration will be once it has started; just about all he can do with a hailstorm is to measure the size of the stones—and they have a habit of melting as soon as he gets his hands on them. He is not even too sure any more about the way in which hail forms—and until he knows this, of course, he isn't likely to stumble upon any very satisfactory prognostic rules.

17. The title below that best expresses the ideas found in this passage is
   (A) "Forecasting Ice Storms."
   (B) "The Way That Hail Forms."
   (C) "The Harassed Meteorologist."
   (D) "The Unpredictability of Hailstorms."
   (E) "Hail—the Killer."

GO ON TO THE NEXT PAGE

18. As used in the passage, the word "prognostic" (last sentence) most nearly means

    (A) restraining.
    (B) breakable.
    (C) day by day.
    (D) foretelling.
    (E) regular.

Questions 19–21 are based on the information contained in the following passage.

It has been more than fifty years since Clyde W. Tombaugh discovered the planet Pluto. He was a young man from a Kansas farm with only a high school education when he got a job as an astronomer's assistant at the Lowell Observatory in Flagstaff, Arizona, in 1929. There had been a suspicion since the turn of the century that a huge planet, nicknamed Planet X, with a mass seven times greater than Earth existed beyond Uranus and Neptune. The gravitational pull of such a planet, it was believed, would account for observed irregularities in the orbit of Uranus. Using a series of photographs taken of an area of the constellation Gemini, Tombaugh made an unusual observation, which was later determined to be a planet in our own solar system. Other astronomers calculated that Pluto is a mean distance of 3.67 billion miles from the sun, and it takes 248 Earth years to make a complete orbit of the sun. In 1976, it was finally determined that Pluto was small in both diameter and mass, smaller in fact than the earth's moon. It might be as small as 1750 miles. Astronomers now believe that no Planet X exists anywhere in our solar system.

19. Based on the information given in the passage, one can conclude that

    (A) Planet X does exist but has not yet been found.
    (B) the calculations, which predicted Planet X, were incorrect.
    (C) Pluto is a huge planet that affects the orbit of Uranus.
    (D) Pluto is in the constellation Gemini.
    (E) the planet Pluto must be Planet X.

20. It is known from the information given in the passage that

    (A) Pluto is closer to the sun than the earth.
    (B) Mars is farther from the sun than Pluto.
    (C) it is impossible to predict the existence of previously unseen planets.
    (D) since its discovery, Pluto has not yet made an orbit of the sun.
    (E) None of the above

21. The diameter of Pluto is

    (A) equal to that of Planet X.
    (B) as large as that of Earth.
    (C) the cause of the irregularities in the orbit of Uranus.
    (D) less than that of Earth's moon.
    (E) close to the area of the constellation Gemini.

Questions 22–25 are based on the information contained in the following paragraph.

In August 1972, a brilliant object streaked across the western sky, apparently trailing smoke. It was seen from Utah north to Alberta. In some places, startled observers also heard sonic booms and called police to report an aircraft in trouble. Among the observers were several amateur astronomers who realized that they were witnessing one of nature's rarest phenomena—a daylight fireball. Only later did one expert witness realize that he had seen an event unique in recorded history: a meteoroid that had flown by the earth as close as 36 miles but had neither crashed into the ground nor broken up in the atmosphere. What had happened is that the meteoroid had actually escaped back into space. Subsequent calculations established that the meteoroid will make another pass in 1997, with only a slight chance of hitting our planet the second time around. Meteoroids are chunks of rock and iron that move through space in orbits around the sun.

22. Based on this paragraph, it is correct to assume that
   (A) the fireball aspect was caused by friction with the earth's atmosphere.
   (B) the object seen was man-made.
   (C) the sonic boom was caused by a nearby airplane.
   (D) the meteoroid will probably collide with other interplanetary objects.
   (E) the meteoroid will probably smash into the earth in 1997.

23. If the calculations of the astronomers are correct, the earth's gravitational pull, in relation to the meteoroid, was
   (A) greater than that of the sun.
   (B) less than that of the sun.
   (C) the cause of most meteorite collisions.
   (D) able to change the shape of the meteor.
   (E) able to change its chemical balance.

24. The subject of this paragraph is unique in recorded history because it
   (A) burned up in space.
   (B) is a moon fragment.
   (C) could be seen by the naked eye.
   (D) escaped back into space.
   (E) was seen by thousands of people.

25. An accurate title for this selection would be
   (A) "A Star Is Born."
   (B) "A Near Miss."
   (C) "Distress Call from Outer Space."
   (D) "A Comet Turns Tail."
   (E) "Worlds in Collision."

STOP! DO NOT TURN THIS PAGE UNTIL TOLD TO DO SO. IF YOU FINISH BEFORE THE TIME IS UP, YOU MAY CHECK OVER YOUR WORK ON THIS PART ONLY.

PART 4: DATA INTERPRETATION

Directions: This part of the test has 25 questions designed to measure your ability to interpret data from tables and graphs. Each question is followed by four or five possible answers. Decide which answer is correct, then mark the space on your answer form that has the same number and letter as your choice.

Sample questions to illustrate some of the questions in this part follow.

Number of days absent per employee (sickness)	1	2	3	4	5	6	7	8 or over
Number of employees	76	23	6	3	1	0	1	0

Total Number of Employees: 400
Period Covered: January 1, 2002–December 31, 2002

S1.   Based on the data shown above, the total number of days lost due to sickness in 1989 was
   (A) 110
   (B) 137
   (C) 144
   (D) 158
   (E) 164

By multiplying the number of employees by the number of days absent per employee (sickness) and then adding the products, we arrive at: 76 + 46 + 18 + 12 + 5 + 0 + 7 + 0 = 164.

Choice (E) is the correct answer.

S2.   Based on the information given in the graph at the right, the average monthly temperature in November is the same as in
   (A) January.
   (B) February.
   (C) March.
   (D) April.

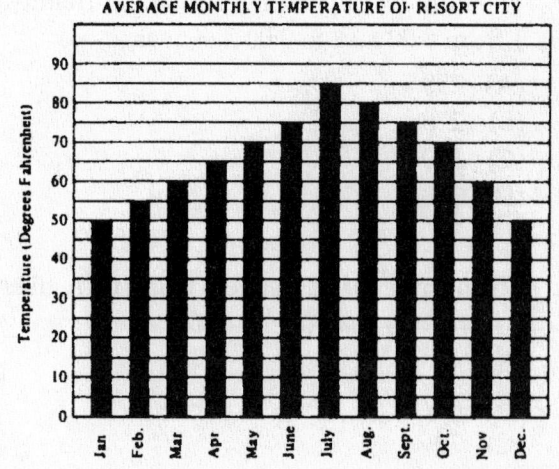

The average temperature in November is 60°F. The only other month in which the average temperature is 60°F is March. Choice (C) is the correct answer.

Your score on this test will be based on the number of questions you answer correctly. You should try to answer every question. You will not lose points or be penalized for guessing. Do not spend too much time on any one question.

When you begin, be sure to start with question No. 1 on Part 4 of your test booklet and No. 1 of Part 4 on your answer form.

DO NOT TURN PAGE UNTIL TOLD TO DO SO.

PART 4: DATA INTERPRETATION

TIME: 24 Minutes—25 Questions

Questions 1–4 are to be answered on the basis of the following tabulation of turnstile readings. The number of passengers passing through the turnstiles is registered and may be determined by taking turnstile readings at specified time intervals.

TABULATION OF TURNSTILE READINGS

Turnstile Number	Turnstile Readings At					
	5:30am	6:00am	7:00am	8:00am	9:00am	9:30am
1	79078	79090	79225	79590	79860	79914
2	24915	24930	25010	25441	25996	26055
3	39509	39530	39736	40533	41448	41515
4	58270	58291	58396	58958	59729	59807
5	43371	43378	43516	43888	44151	44217

1. The number of passengers using turnstile No. 1 from 8:00 A.M. to 9:00 A.M. was

    (A) 250
    (B) 270
    (C) 310
    (D) 350
    (E) 370

2. The number of passengers using turnstile No. 2 from 9:00 A.M. to 9:30 A.M. was

    (A) 59
    (B) 67
    (C) 79
    (D) 270
    (E) 314

3. The turnstile used by the least number of passengers from 6:00 A.M. to 7:00 A.M. was

    (A) No. 1
    (B) No. 2
    (C) No. 3
    (D) No. 4
    (E) No. 5

4. The peak load on turnstile No. 5 was between

    (A) 5:30 A.M. and 6:00 A.M.
    (B) 6:00 A.M. and 7:00 A.M.
    (C) 7:00 A.M. and 8:00 A.M.
    (D) 8:00 A.M. and 9:00 A.M.
    (E) 9:00 A.M. and 9:30 A.M.

Questions 5–8 are based on the data contained in the following circle graph, or pie chart.

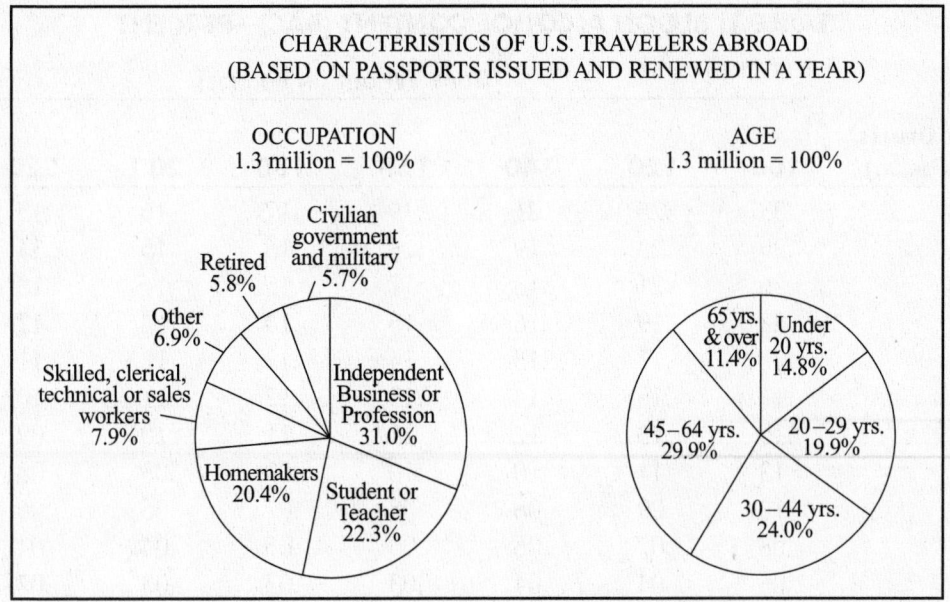

5. How many individuals in the classification of civilian government and military traveled abroad during the year?

    (A) 74,100
    (B) 75,400
    (C) 87,100
    (D) 89,700
    (E) 102,700

6. Approximately how many persons aged 29 or younger traveled abroad during the year?

    (A) 175,000
    (B) 245,000
    (C) 310,000
    (D) 385,000
    (E) 450,000

7. The number of homemakers who traveled abroad during the year is most nearly the same as those who are

    (A) under 20 years of age.
    (B) 20 to 29 years of age.
    (C) 30 to 44 years of age.
    (D) 45 to 64 years of age.
    (E) 65 years of age and over.

8. The number of those classified as retired is most nearly $\frac{1}{3.5}$ of those classified as

    (A) homemakers.
    (B) independent business or profession.
    (C) skilled, clerical, technical, or sales workers.
    (D) student or teacher.
    (E) civilian government and military.

GO ON TO THE NEXT PAGE

Questions 9–12 sare based on the information contained in the following table, which shows the blood alcohol content in relation to body weight and the number of drinks consumed during a two-hour period.

TABLE 1: BLOOD ALCOHOL CONTENT (BAC)—PERCENT

NUMBER OF DRINKS* (2-HOUR PERIOD)	BODY WEIGHT (IN POUNDS)							
	100	120	140	160	180	200	220	240
12	.33	.25	.21	.19	.17	.16	.15	.14
11	.29	.23	.19	.18	.16	.15	.14	.14
10	.26	.21	.18	.17	.15	.14	.13	.13
9	.23	.19	.16	.15	.14	.13	.12	.12
8	.20	.17	.15	.14	.13	.12	.11	.11
7	.17	.15	.14	.13	.12	.11	.10	.10
6	.15	.13	.12	.11	.11	.10	.09	.08
5	.13	.11	.10	.10	.09	.08	.08	.07
4	.10	.09	.08	.08	.07	.06	.06	.06
3	.08	.07	.06	.05	.05	.04	.04	.04
2	.05	.04	.04	.03	.03	.03	.02	.02
1	.03	.02	.02	.02	.01	.01	.01	.01

* One drink is equivalent to $1\frac{1}{2}$ oz. 85-proof liquor, 6 oz. wine, or 12 oz. beer.

9. A 180-pound person who consumes three drinks during a two-hour period would have an estimated blood alcohol content of

(A) .02%
(B) .03%
(C) .04%
(D) .05%
(E) .06%

10. A 100-pound person would have an estimated blood alcohol content of .10% after consuming during a two-hour period

(A) 2 drinks
(B) 3 drinks
(C) 4 drinks
(D) 5 drinks
(E) 6 drinks

11. A 200-pound person who consumes 6 ounces of 85-proof liquor during a two-hour period would have a blood alcohol content of

(A) .06%
(B) .07%
(C) .08%
(D) .09%
(E) .10%

12. A 140-pound person who consumes five 12-ounce cans of beer during a two-hour period would have an estimated blood alcohol content of

(A) .08%
(B) .10%
(C) .12%
(D) .14%
(E) .16%

Questions 13–16 are based on the information given in the following graph.

PERCENTAGE DISTRIBUTION OF TOTAL GOVERNMENT EXPENDITURES
FOR VARIOUS PURPOSES FOR NATIONS

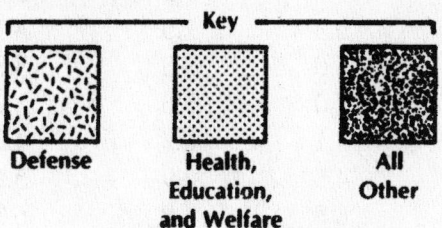

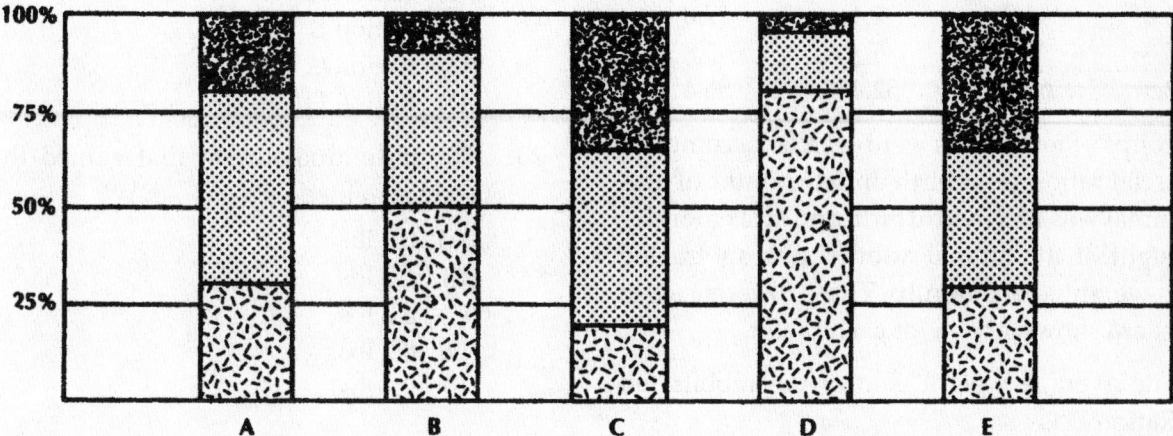

13. Which nation spends the most money for defense?

   (A) Nation A
   (B) Nation B
   (C) Nation C
   (D) Nation D
   (E) It cannot be determined from the data furnished.

14. If total government expenditures for Nation A are $4.2 billion, how much does it spend for defense?

   (A) $1.3 billion
   (B) $1.7 billion
   (C) $2.1 billion
   (D) $2.5 billion
   (E) $2.9 billion

15. Which nation spends half of its total expenditures on health, education, and welfare?

   (A) Nation A
   (B) Nation B
   (C) Nation C
   (D) Nation D
   (E) Nation E

16. The ratio of expenditures for health, education, and welfare to expenditures for defense for Nation A is most nearly

   (A) 5 : 3
   (B) 5 : 2
   (C) 2 : 1
   (D) 1 : 2
   (E) 3 : 5

GO ON TO THE NEXT PAGE

Questions 17–20 are based on the following table and the accompanying notes.

Ration A	Ration B	Ration C	Ration D
4.0	7.1	5.2	3.2
8.7	5.3	7.5	4.1
6.1	6.0	3.8	5.8
6.3	7.0	5.6	8.2
4.7	8.1	6.7	4.3
7.7	4.5	2.9	5.9
5.2	6.8	4.8	6.9
7.5	8.2	5.4	5.4
6.6	6.8	4.4	7.0
6.8	9.3	6.1	5.8
63.6	69.1	52.4	56.4

Four groups of ten rabbits were each fed a complete commercial ration from birth until 6 months of age. Each animal was weighed at birth and at six months. The weight of the animal at birth was subtracted from its weight at six months. These differences, in pounds, are shown above for each rabbit.

17. The average weight gain of the rabbits fed Ration D is

    (A) 5.23 lbs.
    (B) 5.64 lbs.
    (C) 6.39 lbs.
    (D) 6.26 lbs.
    (E) 6.90 lbs.

18. The average difference in weight gain between the group of rabbits who gained the most and the group who gained the least was

    (A) 0.40 lbs.
    (B) 0.52 lbs.
    (C) 0.54 lbs.
    (D) 1.27 lbs.
    (E) 1.67 lbs.

19. The individual rabbit showing the least gain was fed

    (A) Ration A
    (B) Ration B
    (C) Ration C
    (D) Ration D

20. The individual rabbit that gained the most weight gained

    (A) 6.9 lbs.
    (B) 7.5 lbs.
    (C) 8.2 lbs.
    (D) 8.7 lbs.
    (E) 9.3 lbs.

Questions 21–23 are based on the information contained in the picture graph shown below.

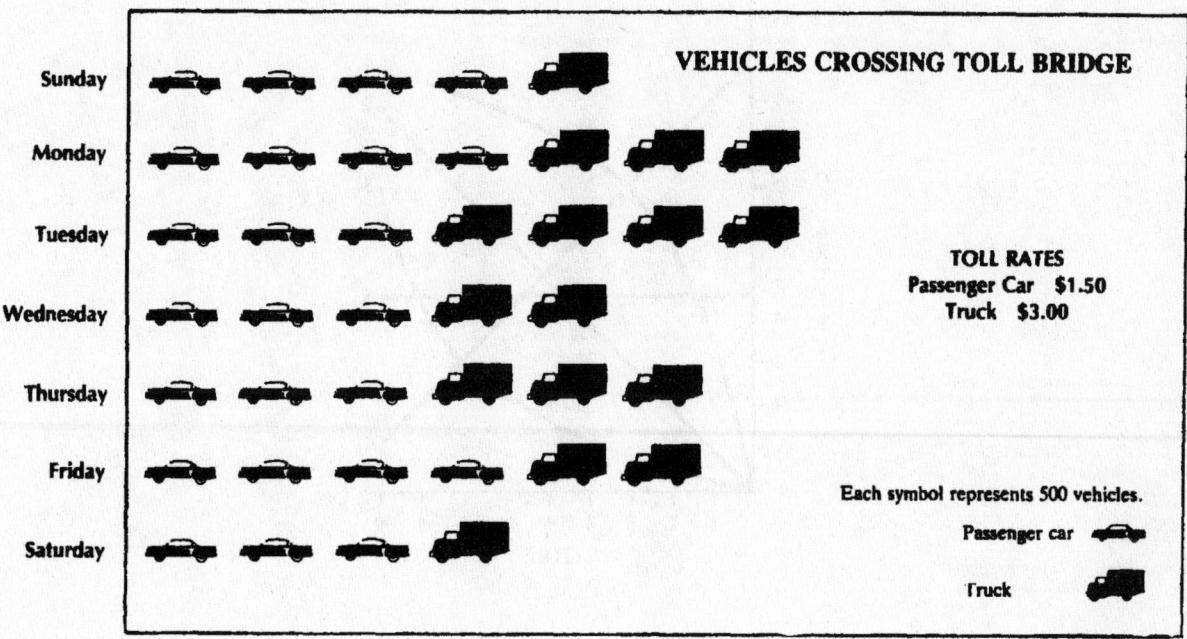

21. What percent of the total number of vehicles on Wednesday were passenger cars?

    (A) 30%
    (B) 40%
    (C) 50%
    (D) 60%
    (E) 70%

22. How many more trucks crossed the bridge on Monday than on Saturday?

    (A) 500
    (B) 1000
    (C) 1500
    (D) 2000
    (E) 2500

23. How much money was collected in tolls on Sunday?

    (A) $3000
    (B) $3750
    (C) $4500
    (D) $5250
    (E) $6000

GO ON TO THE NEXT PAGE

Questions 24–25 are based on the following graph.

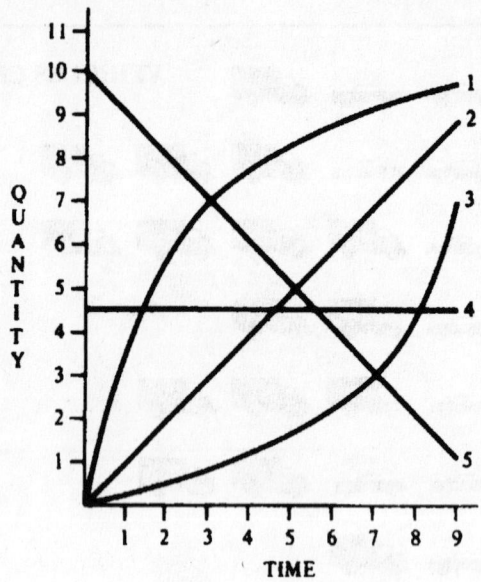

24. The line that shows a decreasing rate of increase for quantity is labeled

    (A) 1
    (B) 2
    (C) 3
    (D) 4
    (E) 5

25. A graph for the formula $Q = 2T$ would resemble most nearly the line labeled

    (A) 1
    (B) 2
    (C) 3
    (D) 4
    (E) 5

STOP! DO NOT TURN THIS PAGE UNTIL TOLD TO DO SO. IF YOU FINISH BEFORE THE TIME IS UP, YOU MAY CHECK OVER YOUR WORK ON THIS PART ONLY.

PART 5: WORD KNOWLEDGE

Directions: This part of the test is designed to measure verbal comprehension involving your ability to understand written language. For each question, you are to select the option that means the same or most nearly the same as the capitalized word. Then mark the space on your answer form that has the same number and letter as your choice.

Here are two sample questions.

S1. CRIMSON

    (A) bluish
    (B) colorful
    (C) crisp
    (D) lively
    (E) reddish

Crimson means "a deep purple red." Choice (E) has almost the same meaning. None of the other choices has the same or a similar meaning. Choice (E) is the only correct answer of the choices given.

S2. CEASE

    (A) continue
    (B) fold
    (C) start
    (D) stop
    (E) transform

Cease means "to stop." Choice (D) is the only choice with the same meaning and is, therefore, the correct answer.

Your score on this test will be based on the number of questions you answer correctly. You should try to answer every question. You will not lose points or be penalized for guessing. Do not spend too much time on any one question.

When you begin, be sure to start with question No. 1 of Part 5 of your test booklet and No. 1 of Part 5 on your answer form.

DO NOT TURN PAGE UNTIL TOLD TO DO SO.

PART 5: WORD KNOWLEDGE

TIME: 5 Minutes—25 Questions

For each question, select the choice that means the same or most nearly the same as the capitalized word.

1. ACCENTUATE

   (A) emphasize
   (B) hasten
   (C) modify
   (D) pronounce
   (E) sustain

2. ANCILLARY

   (A) genuine
   (B) lawful
   (C) obligatory
   (D) primary
   (E) subsidiary

3. CALUMNY

   (A) anxiety
   (B) calmness
   (C) chemical
   (D) journalism
   (E) slander

4. COHERENT

   (A) brief
   (B) detailed
   (C) impressive
   (D) logical
   (E) obvious

5. CONTRAVENE

   (A) appease
   (B) disassemble
   (C) oppose
   (D) postpone
   (E) proceed

6. CORROBORATION

   (A) compilation
   (B) confirmation
   (C) consternation
   (D) cooperation
   (E) coordination

7. CREDENCE

   (A) belief
   (B) claim
   (C) payment
   (D) surprise
   (E) understanding

8. DIFFIDENCE

   (A) awareness
   (B) confidence
   (C) dissimilarity
   (D) emotion
   (E) shyness

9. FLAUNT

   (A) display
   (B) insult
   (C) notify
   (D) praise
   (E) punish

10. FOMENT

    (A) spoil
    (B) torture
    (C) terrify
    (D) incite
    (E) release

11. GERMANE

    (A) budding
    (B) contemporary
    (C) essential
    (D) relevant
    (E) trivial

12. IMPLICATE

    (A) authorize
    (B) detain
    (C) dismiss
    (D) involve
    (E) mediate

13. INSIDIOUS

    (A) insincere
    (B) knowledgeable
    (C) rampant
    (D) treacherous
    (E) unimportant

14. IRRESOLUTE

   (A) impudent
   (B) insolvable
   (C) insubordinate
   (D) unobservant
   (E) vacillating

15. MALINGER

   (A) curse
   (B) deteriorate
   (C) loiter
   (D) shirk
   (E) slander

16. OBSTREPEROUS

   (A) childlike
   (B) delightful
   (C) hazardous
   (D) unruly
   (E) unyielding

17. PALTRY

   (A) adequate
   (B) dismal
   (C) fowl
   (D) petty
   (E) weakened

18. PERVERSE

   (A) contrary
   (B) persistent
   (C) secret
   (D) unconcerned
   (E) unfortunate

19. PRECISE

   (A) exact
   (B) expensive
   (C) long
   (D) short
   (E) trivial

20. PRISTINE

   (A) brilliant
   (B) captive
   (C) inexpensive
   (D) unspoiled
   (E) valuable

21. REPRISAL

   (A) denial
   (B) reevaluation
   (C) retaliation
   (D) upheaval
   (E) warning

22. STRIDENT

   (A) angry
   (B) domineering
   (C) harsh
   (D) swaggering
   (E) vigorous

23. UNSCRUPULOUS

   (A) careless
   (B) disagreeable
   (C) disorganized
   (D) inefficient
   (E) unprincipled

24. VESTIGE

   (A) blessing
   (B) design
   (C) garment
   (D) strap
   (E) trace

25. VICARIOUS

   (A) courageous
   (B) injurious
   (C) sparkling
   (D) substituted
   (E) ugly

STOP! DO NOT TURN THIS PAGE UNTIL TOLD TO DO SO. IF YOU FINISH BEFORE THE TIME IS UP, YOU MAY CHECK OVER YOUR WORK ON THIS PART ONLY.

PART 6: MATH KNOWLEDGE

Directions: This part of the test has 25 questions designed to measure your ability to use learned mathematical relationships. Each problem is followed by five possible answers. Decide which one of the five options is most nearly correct. Then mark the space on your answer form that has the same number and letter as your choice. Use scratch paper to do any figuring that you wish.

Here are three sample questions.

S1.   The reciprocal of 5 is

    (A) 0.1
    (B) 0.2
    (C) 0.5
    (D) 1.0
    (E) 2.0

The reciprocal of 5 is $\frac{1}{5}$, or 0.2. Choice (B) is the correct answer.

S2.   The expression "3 factorial" equals

    (A) $\frac{1}{9}$

    (B) $\frac{1}{6}$

    (C) 6
    (D) 9
    (E) 27

"3 factorial" or 3! equals $3 \times 2 \times 1 = 6$. Choice (C) is the correct answer.

S3.   The logarithm to the base 10 of 1,000 is

    (A) 1
    (B) 1.6
    (C) 2
    (D) 2.7
    (E) 3

$10 \times 10 \times 10 = 1,000$. The logarithm of 1,000 is the exponent 3 to which the base 10 must be raised. Choice (E) is the correct answer.

Your score on this test will be based on the number of questions you answer correctly. You should try to answer every question. You will not lose points or be penalized for guessing. Do not spend too much time on any one question.

When you begin, be sure to start with question No. 1 of Part 6 of your test booklet and No. 1 of Part 6 on your answer form.

DO NOT TURN PAGE UNTIL TOLD TO DO SO.

PART 6: MATH KNOWLEDGE

TIME: 22 Minutes—25 Questions

1. The square root of 250 is between

    (A) 15 and 16
    (B) 14 and 15
    (C) 13 and 14
    (D) 12 and 13
    (E) 11 and 12

2. $5\sqrt{12} - 2\sqrt{27} =$

    (A) $3\sqrt{4}$
    (B) $3\sqrt{5}$
    (C) $4\sqrt{3}$
    (D) $5\sqrt{2}$
    (E) $5\sqrt{3}$

3. The numerical value of $\dfrac{5!}{3!}$ is

    (A) 1.67
    (B) 2
    (C) 15
    (D) 20
    (E) None of the above

4. The logarithm to the base 10 of 10,000 is

    (A) 2
    (B) 3
    (C) 4
    (D) 5
    (E) None of the above

5. $10^3 \times 10^5 =$

    (A) 10^2
    (B) 10^8
    (C) 10^{15}
    (D) 10^{35}
    (E) None of the above

6. The relationship between .01% and .1% is

    (A) 1 to 1
    (B) 1 to 10
    (C) 1 to 100
    (D) 1 to 1000
    (E) 1 to 10,000

7. Which of the following is equal to 16,300?

    (A) 1.63×10^2
    (B) 1.63×10^3
    (C) 1.63×10^4
    (D) 1.63×10^5
    (E) 1.63×10^6

8. 3.47×10^{-2} is equal to

    (A) 347
    (B) 34.7
    (C) 3.47
    (D) .347
    (E) .0347

9. If a is greater than 2, which of the following is the smallest?

    (A) $\dfrac{2}{a}$

    (B) $\dfrac{a}{2}$

    (C) $\dfrac{2}{a-1}$

    (D) $\dfrac{a+1}{2}$

    (E) $\dfrac{2}{a+1}$

10. Which of the following has the greatest value?

    (A) $\dfrac{3}{5}$

    (B) $\left(\dfrac{2}{3}\right)\left(\dfrac{3}{4}\right)$

    (C) $\sqrt{25}$

    (D) $(.9)^2$

    (E) $\dfrac{2}{.3}$

11. If r varies directly as s and if $r = 3$ when $s = 8$, find r when $s = 12$.
    (A) 4
    (B) $4\frac{1}{2}$
    (C) 5
    (D) $5\frac{1}{2}$
    (E) 6

12. The Spencers took t dollars in traveler's checks with them on a trip. During the first week, they spent $\frac{1}{5}$ of their money. During the second week, they spent $\frac{1}{3}$ of the remainder. How much did they have left at the end of the second week?

    (A) $\frac{t}{15}$

    (B) $\frac{4t}{15}$

    (C) $\frac{7t}{15}$

    (D) $\frac{8t}{15}$

    (E) $\frac{11t}{15}$

13. If r planes carry p passengers, how many planes are needed to carry m passengers?

    (A) $\frac{m}{rp}$

    (B) $\frac{p}{rm}$

    (C) $\frac{rm}{p}$

    (D) $\frac{rp}{m}$

    (E) $\frac{pm}{r}$

14. If $a = b$ and $\frac{1}{c} = b$, then $c =$
    (A) $\frac{1}{a}$
    (B) a
    (C) $-a$
    (D) b
    (E) $-b$

15. If $x^2 - y^2 = 100$ and $x - y = 20$, then $x + y =$
    (A) 4
    (B) 5
    (C) 25
    (D) 50
    (E) 80

16. Find the average of four consecutive odd integers whose sum is 104.
    (A) 24
    (B) 25
    (C) 26
    (D) 27
    (E) 28

17. If x is less than 0 and y is less than 0, then
    (A) xy is less than 0
    (B) $x = y$
    (C) x is greater than y
    (D) $x + y$ is greater than 0
    (E) xy is greater than 0

18. When the fractions $\frac{2}{3}$, $\frac{5}{7}$, $\frac{8}{11}$, and $\frac{9}{13}$ are arranged in ascending order of size, the result is

    (A) $\frac{2}{3}, \frac{9}{13}, \frac{5}{7}, \frac{8}{11}$

    (B) $\frac{2}{3}, \frac{8}{11}, \frac{5}{7}, \frac{9}{13}$

    (C) $\frac{5}{7}, \frac{8}{11}, \frac{2}{3}, \frac{9}{13}$

    (D) $\frac{5}{7}, \frac{9}{13}, \frac{2}{3}, \frac{8}{11}$

    (E) $\frac{8}{11}, \frac{2}{3}, \frac{9}{13}, \frac{5}{7}$

GO ON TO THE NEXT PAGE

19. Points P, Q, and R are placed on line segment XY so that $XP = PQ = QR = RY$. What percent of PR is PY?

    (A) $66\frac{2}{3}\%$
    (B) 75%
    (C) 125%
    (D) 150%
    (E) 200%

20. If five triangles are constructed with sides of the lengths given below, which triangle will be a right triangle?

    (A) 2, 3, 4
    (B) 3, 4, 5
    (C) 5, 12, 15
    (D) 8, 9, 17
    (E) 12, 15, 18

21. At 6:00 A.M., the angle between the hands of a clock is

    (A) 45°
    (B) 90°
    (C) 120°
    (D) 180°
    (E) 360°

22. Find the number of degrees in the sum of the interior angles of a hexagon.

    (A) 360
    (B) 540
    (C) 720
    (D) 900
    (E) 1080

23. The radius of a wheel is 2 feet. What is the number of feet covered by this wheel in 10 revolutions?

    (A) 10
    (B) 10π
    (C) 20
    (D) 40
    (E) 40π

24. What is the appropriate number that should be inserted in the following series of numbers arranged in a logical order? 6 5 10 8 __ 9 12 8 10

    (A) 10
    (B) 11
    (C) 12
    (D) 13
    (E) 14

25. A round trip in a helicopter lasted 4 hours. If the helicopter flew away from the airport at 90 mph and returned at the rate of 45 mph, what was its greatest distance from the airport?

    (A) 100 miles
    (B) 105 miles
    (C) 110 miles
    (D) 115 miles
    (E) 120 miles

IF YOU FINISH BEFORE THE TIME IS UP, YOU MAY CHECK OVER YOUR WORK ON THIS PART ONLY.
END OF FIRST SIX SUBTESTS

KEY ANSWERS AND RATIONALE
FOR SUBTESTS 1 THROUGH 6

Use these key answers to determine the number of questions you answered correctly on each subtest and to list those questions that you answered incorrectly or that you are unsure of how to arrive at the correct answer.

Be certain to review carefully and understand the rationale for arriving at the correct answer for all items you answered incorrectly, as well as those you answered correctly but are unsure of. This is essential in order to acquire the knowledge and expertise necessary to obtain the maximum score possible on the subtests of the Air Force Officer Qualifying Test.

PART 1: VERBAL ANALOGIES

Key Answers

1. The correct answer is (B).
2. The correct answer is (D).
3. The correct answer is (B).
4. The correct answer is (C).
5. The correct answer is (B).
6. The correct answer is (C).
7. The correct answer is (A).
8. The correct answer is (E).
9. The correct answer is (D).
10. The correct answer is (E).
11. The correct answer is (B).
12. The correct answer is (E).
13. The correct answer is (C).
14. The correct answer is (C).
15. The correct answer is (C).
16. The correct answer is (E).
17. The correct answer is (E).
18. The correct answer is (E).
19. The correct answer is (C).
20. The correct answer is (D).
21. The correct answer is (D).
22. The correct answer is (A).
23. The correct answer is (D).
24. The correct answer is (C).
25. The correct answer is (C).

Items Answered Incorrectly: __; __; __; __; __; __; __; __.   **TOTAL NUMBER**
Items Unsure Of: __; __; __; __; __; __; __; __.   **ANSWERED CORRECTLY:** _____

Rationale

1. The correct answer is (B). A *prospector* searches for *gold*; a *detective* searches for a *clue*.

2. The correct answer is (D). *Marble* is obtained from a *quarry*; *coal* is obtained from a *mine*.

3. The correct answer is (B). A *ram* is an adult male sheep; a *lamb* is a young sheep. A *bull* is an adult male bovine animal; a *calf* is the young of a cow.

4. The correct answer is (C). Whereas a *general* is a military leader of soldiers who operate mainly on land, an *admiral* is a military leader whose troops operate mainly on the sea. Similarly, a *soldier* is based mainly on land, while a *sailor* is based mainly on the sea.

5. The correct answer is (B). Both capitalized words are names of birds. The only parallel relationship is found in choice (B).

6. The correct answer is (C). *Scrawny* and *lean* are synonyms. The only other set of synonyms is *brawny* and *strong*.

7. The correct answer is (A). The first two capitalized words are synonymous. *Ask* is a synonym for *inquire*.

8. The correct answer is (E). A *stallion* is a male horse; a *gelding* is a castrated horse. A *steer* is a castrated *bull*.

9. The correct answer is (D). There is no apparent relationship between the first two capitalized words. However, *toil* is synonymous with *work* and *strife* is synonymous with *struggle*.

10. The correct answer is (E). *Valid* and *fallacious* are adjectives with opposite meanings. The only antonym for *veracious* is *untrue*.

11. The correct answer is (B). The past tense of *shoot* is formed by deleting a vowel from the present infinitive form. The past tense of *bleed* is also formed by deleting a vowel from the present infinitive form.

12. The correct answer is (E). Something that is *ad lib* is done without *rehearsal*—it's improvised. Something that is *aleatory* (meaning driven by chance, like the toss of a pair of dice) is done without a *plan*.

13. The correct answer is (C). To *daub* is to *paint* in a haphazard way, showing little care or talent for the art of painting. Similarly, to *caterwaul* is to *sing* without care or talent, the way a cat in a back alley howls at the moon.

14. The correct answer is (C). This question pertains to a mathematical proportion: *36* is to *4* as *9* is to *1*.

15. The correct answer is (C). *Trumpet* is a type of *instrument*; *pliers* are a type of *tool*.

16. The correct answer is (E). *Drift* is a *snow* hill or ridge formed by the wind; *dune* is a *sand* hill or ridge formed by the wind.

17. The correct answer is (E). The *moon* revolves around the *earth*; the *earth* revolves around the *sun*.

18. The correct answer is (E). A *necklace* is an ornament or an *adornment*. A *medal* is a *decoration* for bravery or merit.

19. The correct answer is (C). *Paper* is made from *pulp*; *rope* is made from *hemp*.

20. The correct answer is (D). *Regressive* is the adjective form for *regress*; *sterile* is the adjective form for *sterilize*.

21. The correct answer is (D). The *crest* is the top of a *wave*; the *peak* is the top of a *mountain*.

22. The correct answer is (A). The relationship of the two capitalized words is that of the female and male. The only other parallel relationship is *duck* (female) and *drake* (male).

23. The correct answer is (D). An *enigma* (a difficult puzzle) is likely to leave you feeling *mystified*; a *dilemma* (a difficult choice) is likely to leave you feeling *undecided*.

24. The correct answer is (C). The past participle of *wring* is *wrung*; that of *lay* is *laid*.

25. The correct answer is (C). There is no apparent relationship between *zinc* and *sulfuric acid*. However, *zinc* is an *element* and *sulfuric acid* is a compound.

PART 2: ARITHMETIC REASONING

Key Answers

1. The correct answer is (B).
2. The correct answer is (A).
3. The correct answer is (E).
4. The correct answer is (A).
5. The correct answer is (B).
6. The correct answer is (C).
7. The correct answer is (A).
8. The correct answer is (B).
9. The correct answer is (A).
10. The correct answer is (B).
11. The correct answer is (D).
12. The correct answer is (C).
13. The correct answer is (A).

14. The correct answer is (A).
15. The correct answer is (B).
16. The correct answer is (E).
17. The correct answer is (D).
18. The correct answer is (E).
19. The correct answer is (A).
20. The correct answer is (E).
21. The correct answer is (D).
22. The correct answer is (E).
23. The correct answer is (B).
24. The correct answer is (C).
25. The correct answer is (D).

Items Answered Incorrectly: __; __; __; __; __; __; __; __.
Items Unsure Of: __; __; __; __; __; __; __; __.

**TOTAL NUMBER
ANSWERED CORRECTLY:** _____

Rationale

1. The correct answer is (B). 20% of $2400 = 480; 2400 − 480 = $1920; 20% of $1920 = 384; 1920 − 384 = $1536

2. The correct answer is (A). $27 \times 32 = 864$ square feet to be carpeted. Let x = number of linear feet of carpeting needed.

27 inches = $\frac{9}{4}$ feet; $\frac{9}{4} \times x = 864$;

$x = 864 \times \frac{4}{9} = 384$ feet; $\frac{384}{3} = 128$ yards

3. The correct answer is (E). Let r, m, and b be the prices in cents of rolls, muffins, and bread respectively. This yields two equations:

$4r + 6m + 3b = 910$
$2r + 3m + b = 390$

If we multiply the second equation by −2 and add the two together, we have: $b = 130$. Hence, the price of a loaf of bread is $1.30, which is choice (E).

4. The correct answer is (A). $\frac{635.30}{900} = .7058 = 71\%$.

5. The correct answer is (B).

$1800 \times .05 = \$90.00$; $\frac{180}{90} = \frac{2}{1}$.

6. The correct answer is (C). $\frac{1}{3}$ of family income, or $8000, was saved; $\frac{1}{3}$ of $x = 8000$; $x = \$24,000$

7. The correct answer is (A). Let x = tax rate. $338,555 \times x = 616.07$; $x = \frac{616.07}{338500} = .00182$;

$.00182 \times 1000 = \$1.82$

8. The correct answer is (B). Let the number of Democrats be $5m$ and the number of Republicans be $7m$, so that D : R :: $5m : 7m = 5 : 7$. The total is $5m + 7m = 12m$, which must be 156. Therefore, $12m = 156$, and $m = 13$. Of course, the difference is $7m − 5m = 2m = 2(13) = 26$. Hence the answer is choice (B).

9. The correct answer is (A).

$\frac{25}{10} = \frac{5}{2}$

10. The correct answer is (B).

$24 : 8 = 72 : x$; $3 : 1 = 72 : x$; $x = \frac{72}{3} = 24$ feet

11. The correct answer is (D).

$15 : 14 = x : 28$; $x = \frac{28 \times 15}{14} = 30$

12. The correct answer is (C). $20\% + 25\% + 15\% + 10\% = 70\%$; $100\% − 70\% = 30\%$ that do not study any foreign language; $1400 \times .30 = 420$.

13. The correct answer is (A). Let x be the unknown number of liters of 50% antifreeze. Now, the final mixture will have $(x + 80)$ liters, and the amount of antifreeze will be:

$$0.50x + 0.20(80) = 0.40(x + 80)$$
$$0.50x + 16 = 0.4x + 32$$
$$0.1x = 16$$
$$x = 160$$

14. The correct answer is (A).

$\frac{1}{4} \times 800 = 200$; $800 − 200 = 600$;

$\frac{5}{6} \times 600 = 500$; $600 − 500 = 100$

There are 100 non-high school graduates employed; $\frac{100}{800} = \frac{1}{8}$.

15. The correct answer is (B).

$60 \times 8 = 80 \times x$; $80x = 480$; $x = \frac{480}{80} = 6$

16. The correct answer is (E). Let x = length of longer piece; $63 − x$ = length of shorter piece.

$\frac{3}{5x} = \frac{3}{4}(63 − x)$; $\frac{3}{5x} = \frac{189}{4} − \frac{3}{4}x$; $\frac{3}{5x} + \frac{3}{4}x = \frac{189}{4}$;

$\frac{12}{20}x + \frac{15}{20}x = \frac{189}{4}$; $\frac{17}{20}x = \frac{189}{4}$; $x = \frac{189}{4} \times \frac{20}{27} = 35$ feet.

17. The correct answer is (D). Area of flower bed = 16 yards by 12 yards = 192 sq. yds.; area of bed and walk = (16 + 3 + 3) (12 + 3 + 3) = 22 × 18 = 396 sq. yds.; 396 − 192 = 204 sq. yds.

18. The correct answer is (E).

$$\frac{(+6) + (+3) + 0 + (-4) + (-10)}{5} = \frac{-5}{5} = -1$$

19. The correct answer is (A). Let x = number of dimes.

$.10x + .25(4x) = 2.20$; $.10x + x = 2.20$; $1.10x = 2.20$; $x = \frac{2.20}{1.10} = 2$.

20. The correct answer is (E). Let x = time.

$50x + 55x = 630$; $105x = 630$; $x = \frac{630}{105} = 6$ hours. Trains left at 9:00 A.M. Six hours later, it would be 3:00 P.M.

21. The correct answer is (D). Noon to 8 P.M. = 8 hours

Distance covered = $(22 \times 8) + (28 \times 8) = 176 + 224 = 400$ miles

Total distance = 450 miles; 450 − 400 = 50 miles apart

22. The correct answer is (E). Let x = rate of slower plane; $2x$ = rate of the faster plane.

$5x + 10x = 6000$; $15x = 6000$; $x = 400$; $2x = 800$.

23. The correct answer is (B). Let x be the number of city miles Harvey drove, and let $2x$ be the number of highway miles. Miles divided by miles per gallon should give the number of gallons of gas used. Thus:

$$\frac{x}{20} = \frac{2x}{28} = 34$$

$$\frac{x}{20} = \frac{x}{14} = 34$$

Multiply the equation by the LCD 140 to get:
$7x + 10x = 4760$
$17x = 4760$; $x = 280$
Since Harvey drove a total of $3x$ miles, the correct answer is $3(280) = 840$.

24. The correct answer is (C). 3% of 120 pounds of saline = 3.6 pounds of pure salt; $\frac{3.6}{x} = .08$; $.08x = 3.6$; $x = \frac{3.6}{.08}$; $x = 45$ pounds of saline solution that is needed for an 8% solution; 120 pounds of solution must be reduced to 45 pounds. Therefore, 120 − 45 or 75 pounds of water must be evaporated.

25. The correct answer is (D).

	First Press	Second Press	
$\dfrac{\text{Time actually needed}}{\text{Time needed to do job alone}}$	$\dfrac{x}{8}$ +	$\dfrac{x}{12}$	=1

Multiply by 24 to clear fractions.

$3x + 2x = 24$; $5x = 24$; $x = \frac{24}{5} = 4\frac{4}{5}$ hours or 4 hours 48 minutes.

PART 3: READING COMPREHENSION
Key Answers

1. The correct answer is (B).
2. The correct answer is (C).
3. The correct answer is (D).
4. The correct answer is (D).
5. The correct answer is (E).
6. The correct answer is (E).
7. The correct answer is (C).
8. The correct answer is (D).
9. The correct answer is (B).
10. The correct answer is (D).
11. The correct answer is (B).
12. The correct answer is (E).
13. The correct answer is (C).

14. The correct answer is (C).
15. The correct answer is (B).
16. The correct answer is (D).
17. The correct answer is (D).
18. The correct answer is (D).
19. The correct answer is (B).
20. The correct answer is (D).
21. The correct answer is (D).
22. The correct answer is (A).
23. The correct answer is (B).
24. The correct answer is (D).
25. The correct answer is (B).

Items Answered Incorrectly: __; __; __; __; __; __; __; __.

Items Unsure Of: __; __; __; __; __; __; __; __.

**TOTAL NUMBER
ANSWERED CORRECTLY:** _____

Rationale

1. The correct answer is (B). This is a restatement of the paragraph. Choice (D) is not the answer because the paragraph makes no judgment as to the adequacy of each state's legislation or enforcement.

2. The correct answer is (C). The passage states that frank interchange of ideas increases the total range of information and allows for a better chance of solving conflict.

3. The correct answer is (D). The passage describes the plight of the laborer who has been trained to do only one specialized task. Choice (A) is incorrect because it is too dogmatic. The paragraph speaks of specialization as one cause of unemployment, but does not rule out other causes.

4. The correct answer is (D). The theme of this passage relates to the development of political responsibility and political science in America.

5. The correct answer is (E). As indicated in the first sentence of the passage, revolutions usually devoured the intellectuals who paved the way for such upheavals.

6. The correct answer is (E). The central theme of this passage is the Greek language. None of the other options expresses this central theme.

7. The correct answer is (C). The second and third sentences of the passage state that Greek was spoken in Europe and Asia by Greeks with classical learning, and later was a universal language among the cultured classes.

8. The correct answer is (D). The second sentence of the passage states that Greek was probably spoken in Europe and Asia at least 1500 years before the Christian Era, or as early as 1500 B.C.

9. The correct answer is (B). The passage indicates that the greatly increased population was an evolutionary phenomenon that took place in the world's economic organization and can be explained by the speeded-up economic unification that took place during this period of time.

10. The correct answer is (D). Seven generations is 210 years ($7 \times 30 = 210$). $1760 + 210 = 1970$.

11. The correct answer is (B). His equivalent weight is 90 times 2.2, or 198 pounds.

12. The correct answer is (E). The last sentence in the passage states that cars skid and collide.

13. The correct answer is (C). The first sentence in the passage states that police officers should first care for victims who need immediate medical treatment.

14. The correct answer is (C). The passage indicates that some underwater explorers, in their eagerness to amass wealth, do engage in objectionable and irresponsible practices.

15. The correct answer is (B). The passage appears to have been written by an archaeologist who is highly critical of "irresponsible" explorers. The author appears to be most sympathetic and supportive of any official effort to prevent "irresponsible" explorations.

16. The correct answer is (D). Since they cannot be easily traced or found, amateur archaeologists who explore underwater have the advantage over the local authorities.

17. The correct answer is (D). The major idea of the passage, expressed several times, is that hailstorms are unpredictable.

18. The correct answer is (D). *Prognostic* means foretelling or indicating something in the future.

19. The correct answer is (B). The last sentence in the paragraph implies that the calculations that predicted Planet X were incorrect.

20. The correct answer is (D). Since it takes 248 Earth years for Pluto to orbit the sun, and since the planet was discovered just a little more than fifty years ago, Pluto could not have completed an orbit of the sun since its discovery.

21. The correct answer is (D). The diameter of Pluto is 1750 miles; the earth's moon is larger in both diameter and mass.

22. The correct answer is (A). The fireball aspect was caused by the meteoroid's entering the earth's atmosphere and being subjected to atmospheric friction.

23. The correct answer is (B). It can be assumed that the gravitational pull of the earth was less than that of the sun as the meteoroid did escape from the earth's atmosphere.

24. The correct answer is (D). It is the only recorded instance of an object escaping back into space after entering the earth's atmosphere.

25. The correct answer is (B). The meteoroid just missed hitting the earth.

PART 4: DATA INTERPRETATION

Key Answers

1. The correct answer is (B).
2. The correct answer is (A).
3. The correct answer is (B).
4. The correct answer is (C).
5. The correct answer is (A).
6. The correct answer is (E).
7. The correct answer is (B).
8. The correct answer is (A).
9. The correct answer is (D).
10. The correct answer is (C).
11. The correct answer is (A).
12. The correct answer is (B).
13. The correct answer is (E).
14. The correct answer is (A).
15. The correct answer is (A).
16. The correct answer is (A).
17. The correct answer is (B).
18. The correct answer is (E).
19. The correct answer is (C).
20. The correct answer is (E).
21. The correct answer is (D).
22. The correct answer is (B).
23. The correct answer is (C).
24. The correct answer is (A).
25. The correct answer is (B).

Items Answered Incorrectly: __; __; __; __; __; __; __; __.
Items Unsure Of: __; __; __; __; __; __; __; __.

**TOTAL NUMBER
ANSWERED CORRECTLY:** _____

Rationale

1. The correct answer is (B). 79860 – 79590 = 270.

2. The correct answer is (A). 26055 – 25966 = 59.

3. The correct answer is (B).

No. 1	No. 2	No. 3	No. 4	No. 5
79225	25010	39736	58396	43516
– 79090	– 24930	– 39530	–58291	– 43378
135	80	206	105	138

4. The correct answer is (C).

5:30-6:00	6:00-7:00	7:00-8:00	8:00-9:00	9:00-9:30
43378	43516	43888	44151	44217
– 43371	– 43378	– 43516	–43888	– 44151
7	138	372	263	66

5. The correct answer is (A). $1,300,000 \times .057 = 74,100$

6. The correct answer is (E). 14.8% (under 20) + 19.9% (20–29) = 34.7%; $1,300,000 \times .347 = 451,100$

7. The correct answer is (B). Homemakers, 20.4%; 20–29 years of age, 19.9%

8. The correct answer is (A). Retired, 5.8%; $5.8 : x = 1 : 3.5; x = 20.3$. 20.3% is closest to Homemakers (20.4%).

9. The correct answer is (D). Enter top table at 3 drinks and move right to column under 180 pounds. The answer is .05%.

10. The correct answer is (C). Enter top table at 100 pounds, move down to .10, and move left to 4 drinks, the correct answer.

11. The correct answer is (A). One drink = $1\frac{1}{2}$ oz. liquor. Therefore, the amount of liquor consumed is equivalent to 4 drinks. Enter top table at 4 drinks and move right to column under 200 pounds. The correct answer is .06%.

12. The correct answer is (B). Enter top table at 5 drinks (12 oz. beer is equivalent to 1 drink) and move right to column under 140 pounds. The answer is .10%.

13. The correct answer is (E). The graph shows percentage distribution and not dollar amounts. From the data given, no determination can be made as to which nation spends the most money for defense.

14. The correct answer is (A). 30% of 4.2 billion = 1.26 billion.

15. The correct answer is (A). Nation A, 50%; nation B, 40%; nation C, 45%; nation D, 15%; nation E, 35%.

16. The correct answer is (A). 50% : 30% = 5 : 3

17. The correct answer is (B). $\frac{56.4}{10}$ = 5.64 lbs.

18. The correct answer is (E). 69.1 – 52.4 = 16.7; $\frac{16.7}{10}$ = 1.67

19. The correct answer is (C). The least gain was 2.9 pounds by rabbit fed on Ration C.

20. The correct answer is (E). The most gain was 9.3 pounds by rabbit fed on Ration B.

21. The correct answer is (D). $\frac{3}{5}$ = 60%.

22. The correct answer is (B). Monday, 1500; Saturday, 500; 1500 – 500 = 1000.

23. The correct answer is (C). 2000 × $1.50 = $3000; 500 × $3.00 = $1500; $3000 + $1500 = $4500.

24. The correct answer is (A). Lines 1, 2, and 3 portray rates of increase. Line 1 shows a decreasing rate of increase; line 2 shows a constant rate of increase; line 3 shows an increasing rate of increase.

25. The correct answer is (B). This is a constant linear increase shown by line 2.

PART 5: WORD KNOWLEDGE

Key Answers

1. The correct answer is (A).
2. The correct answer is (E).
3. The correct answer is (E).
4. The correct answer is (D).
5. The correct answer is (C).
6. The correct answer is (B).
7. The correct answer is (A).
8. The correct answer is (E).
9. The correct answer is (A).
10. The correct answer is (D).
11. The correct answer is (D).
12. The correct answer is (D).
13. The correct answer is (D).
14. The correct answer is (E).
15. The correct answer is (D).
16. The correct answer is (D).
17. The correct answer is (D).
18. The correct answer is (A).
19. The correct answer is (A).
20. The correct answer is (D).
21. The correct answer is (C).
22. The correct answer is (C).
23. The correct answer is (E).
24. The correct answer is (E).
25. The correct answer is (D).

Items Answered Incorrectly: __; __; __; __; __; __; __; __.
Items Unsure Of: __; __; __; __; __; __; __; __.

**TOTAL NUMBER
ANSWERED CORRECTLY:** _____

Rationale

1. The correct answer is (A). *Accentuate* means to *emphasize*.

2. The correct answer is (E). *Ancillary* means *auxiliary* or *subsidiary*.

3. The correct answer is (E). *Calumny* means *false accusation* or *slander*.

4. The correct answer is (D). *Coherent* means *consistent* or *logical*.

5. The correct answer is (C). *Contravene* means to *oppose* or *infringe*.

6. The correct answer is (B). *Corroboration* and *confirmation* are synonymous.

7. The correct answer is (A). *Credence* and *belief* have similar meanings.

8. The correct answer is (E). *Diffidence, timidity,* and *shyness* have similar meanings.

9. The correct answer is (A). *Flaunt* means to *display*.

10. The correct answer is (D). *Foment* means to *stir up* or *incite*.

11. The correct answer is (D). *Germane* means *pertinent* or *relevant*.

12. The correct answer is (D). *Implicate* means to *involve*.

13. The correct answer is (D). *Insidious* and *treacherous* are synonymous.

14. The correct answer is (E). *Irresolute, uncertain,* and *vacillating* have similar meanings.

15. The correct answer is (D). *Malinger* and *shirk* have similar meanings.

16. The correct answer is (D). *Obstreperous* is synonymous with *unruly* and *boisterous*.

17. The correct answer is (D). *Paltry* is synonymous with *trifling* and *petty*.

18. The correct answer is (A). *Perverse* is synonymous with *stubborn* and *contrary*.

19. The correct answer is (A). *Precise* and *exact* have similar meanings.

20. The correct answer is (D). *Pristine, pure,* and *unspoiled* have similar meanings.

21. The correct answer is (C). *Reprisal, retaliation,* and *revenge* have similar meanings.

22. The correct answer is (C). *Strident, grating,* and *harsh* have similar meanings.

23. The correct answer is (E). *Unscrupulous* and *unprincipled* are synonymous.

24. The correct answer is (E). *Vestige* and *trace* are synonymous.

25. The correct answer is (D). *Vicarious* is a synonym for *substituted*.

PART 6: MATH KNOWLEDGE
Key Answers

1. The correct answer is (A).
2. The correct answer is (C).
3. The correct answer is (D).
4. The correct answer is (C).
5. The correct answer is (B).
6. The correct answer is (B).
7. The correct answer is (C).
8. The correct answer is (E).
9. The correct answer is (E).
10. The correct answer is (E).
11. The correct answer is (B).
12. The correct answer is (D).
13. The correct answer is (C).
14. The correct answer is (A).
15. The correct answer is (B).
16. The correct answer is (C).
17. The correct answer is (E).
18. The correct answer is (A).
19. The correct answer is (D).
20. The correct answer is (B).
21. The correct answer is (D).
22. The correct answer is (C).
23. The correct answer is (E).
24. The correct answer is (C).
25. The correct answer is (E).

Items Answered Incorrectly: __; __; __; __; __; __; __; __.

Items Unsure Of: __; __; __; __; __; __; __; __.

**TOTAL NUMBER
ANSWERED CORRECTLY:** _____

Rationale

1. The correct answer is (A). $15^2 = 225$; $16^2 = 266$. 250 is between 225 and 266.

2. The correct answer is (C).

$5\sqrt{12} = 5\sqrt{4 \times 3} = 5 \times 2\sqrt{3} = 10\sqrt{3}$;

$2\sqrt{27} = 2\sqrt{9 \times 3} = 2 \times 3\sqrt{3} = 6\sqrt{3}$;

$10\sqrt{3} - 6\sqrt{3} = 4\sqrt{3}$

3. The correct answer is (D). The factorial of a natural number is the product of that number and all the natural numbers less than it.

$5! = 5 \times 4 \times 3 \times 2 \times 1 = 120$;

$3! = 3 \times 2 \times 1 = 6$;

$\dfrac{120}{6} = 20$.

4. The correct answer is (C). The logarithm of a number is the exponent to which a base must be raised to produce the number. $10^2 = 100$; $10^3 = 1000$; $10^4 = 10{,}000$; $10^5 = 100{,}000$.

5. The correct answer is (B). When multiplying logarithms with the same base, add the exponents. $10^3 \times 10^5 = 10^8$.

6. The correct answer is (B).

$.01\% = \dfrac{.01}{100} = .0001$;

$.1\% = \dfrac{.1}{100} = .001$;

$\dfrac{.0001}{.001} = \dfrac{1}{10}$.

7. The correct answer is (C). $16{,}300 = 1.63 \times 10{,}000 = 1.63 \times 10^4$.

8. The correct answer is (E). $10^{-2} = .01$; $3.47 \times .01 = .0347$

9. The correct answer is (E). Choices (B) and (D) are greater than 1; other choices have the same numerator; however, choice (E) has the greatest denominator and, therefore, the smallest value, a value of less than 1.

10. The correct answer is (E). $A = .60$; $B = .50$; $C = .5$; $D = .81$; $E = 6.67$.

11. The correct answer is (B). $3 : 8 = x : 12$; $8x = 36$; $x = 4\frac{1}{2}$.

12. The correct answer is (D). $\frac{1}{5}t$ spent the first week; $t - \frac{t}{5}$ is left; $\frac{1}{3}(t - \frac{t}{5}) = \frac{1}{3}(\frac{5t}{5} - \frac{t}{5}) = \frac{1}{3} \times \frac{4}{5}t = \frac{4}{15}t$ spent the second week; $\frac{3}{15}t + \frac{4}{15}t = \frac{7}{15}t$ spent the first two weeks; $\frac{8}{15}t$ is left.

13. The correct answer is (C). Let x = number of planes needed to carry m passengers.

$r : p = x : m$; $px = rm$; $x = \dfrac{rm}{p}$.

14. The correct answer is (A).

$\dfrac{1}{c} = b = a$; $c = \dfrac{1}{a}$.

15. The correct answer is (B).

$x^2 - y^2 = (x + y)(x - y)$; $100 = (x + y) \times 20$;

$(x + y) = \dfrac{100}{20} = 5$.

16. The correct answer is (C). To find the average of any four numbers, divide the sum of the numbers by 4; $\frac{104}{4} = 26$.

17. The correct answer is (E). When two negative numbers are multiplied, the product is positive.

18. The correct answer is (A).

$$\frac{2}{3} = .67; \quad \frac{5}{7} = .71; \quad \frac{8}{11} = .73; \quad \frac{9}{13} = .69$$

19. The correct answer is (D).

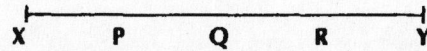

PR = 2 equal segments; PY = 3 equal segments; $\frac{3}{2}$ = 150%.

20. The correct answer is (B). In a right triangle, the square of the hypotenuse = the sum of the squares of the other two sides. $3^2 + 4^2 = 5^2$; 9 + 16 = 25.

21. The correct answer is (D). At 6:00 A.M., one hand is at the 6 and the other is at the 12, forming a straight angle, or 180°.

22. The correct answer is (C). A hexagon is a six-sided polygon. $180° (6 - 2) = x$; $180° \times 4 = x$; $x = 720°$.

23. The correct answer is (E). Radius = 2 feet; diameter = 4 feet; circumference = $\pi d = 4\pi$; $4\pi \times 10 = 40\pi$.

24. The correct answer is (C). Subtract 1, add 5; subtract 2, add 4; subtract 3, add 3; subtract 4, add 2.

25. The correct answer is (E). Let x = time flying out and $4 - x$ = time flying in.

$$90x = 45(4 - x); \quad 90x = 180 - 45x; \quad 135x = 180$$

$$x = \frac{180}{135} = \frac{4}{3}; \quad \frac{4}{3} \times 90 = 120 \text{ miles.}$$

PART X

Armed Services Vocational Aptitude Battery (ASVAB)

Specimen Test Items

Part 1: General Science
Part 2: Arithmetic Reasoning
Part 3: Word Knowledge
Part 4: Paragraph Comprehension
Part 5: Mathematics Knowledge
Part 6: Electronics Information

A specimen answer sheet for the Army commissioning program appears on page 323 and should be used for answering the following:

ASVAB, Part 2: Arithmetic Reasoning
ASVAB, Part 3: Word Knowledge
ASVAB, Part 4: Paragraph Comprehension

A specimen answer sheet for the Marine Corps commissioning program appears on page 324 and should be used for answering the following:

ASVAB, Part 1: General Science
ASVAB, Part 2: Arithmetic Reasoning
ASVAB, Part 5: Mathematics Knowledge
ASVAB, Part 6: Electronics Information

In addition to the pertinent subtests required for both the Army and the Marine Corps commissioning programs, this section also contains key answers for determining your scores on these subtests and the rationale or explanation for each key answer.

When you take this test, try to simulate the test conditions you will encounter when taking the real test. That is, try to eliminate all possible distractions (like the radio or TV) and have each subtest carefully timed. Cut out the appropriate answer sheet and record your answers to the test questions.

After you finish, use the key answers to obtain your subtest scores and to evaluate your performance on each subtest. Place the number of items you answered correctly, as well as the number of each item you answered incorrectly or wish to review, in the space provided below the key answers for each subtest.

Be certain to review carefully and understand the rationale for the key answers for all questions you answered incorrectly and for each of the questions that you answered correctly but are unsure of. This is absolutely essential in order to acquire the knowledge and expertise necessary to obtain the maximum scores possible on the test.

**For
ARMY
Commissioning
Program**

**ANSWER SHEET
ARMED SERVICES VOCATIONAL
APTITUDE BATTERY**

Part 2   Arithmetic Reasoning

PART 2—AR

1 A B C D	5 A B C D	9 A B C D	13 A B C D	17 A B C D	21 A B C D	25 A B C D	29 A B C D
2 A B C D	6 A B C D	10 A B C D	14 A B C D	18 A B C D	22 A B C D	26 A B C D	30 A B C D
3 A B C D	7 A B C D	11 A B C D	15 A B C D	19 A B C D	23 A B C D	27 A B C D	
4 A B C D	8 A B C D	12 A B C D	16 A B C D	20 A B C D	24 A B C D	28 A B C D	

Part 3   Word Knowledge

PART 3—WK

1 A B C D	6 A B C D	11 A B C D	16 A B C D	21 A B C D	26 A B C D	31 A B C D
2 A B C D	7 A B C D	12 A B C D	17 A B C D	22 A B C D	27 A B C D	32 A B C D
3 A B C D	8 A B C D	13 A B C D	18 A B C D	23 A B C D	28 A B C D	33 A B C D
4 A B C D	9 A B C D	14 A B C D	19 A B C D	24 A B C D	29 A B C D	34 A B C D
5 A B C D	10 A B C D	15 A B C D	20 A B C D	25 A B C D	30 A B C D	35 A B C D

Part 4   Paragraph Comprehension

PART 4—PC

| 1 A B C D | 3 A B C D | 5 A B C D | 7 A B C D | 9 A B C D | 11 A B C D | 13 A B C D | 15 A B C D |
| 2 A B C D | 4 A B C D | 6 A B C D | 8 A B C D | 10 A B C D | 12 A B C D | 14 A B C D | |

MI

FIRST

LAST

For
MARINE CORPS
Commissioning
Program

**ANSWER SHEET
ARMED SERVICES VOCATIONAL
APTITUDE BATTERY**

Part 1 General Science

	PRACTICE	1 A B C D	5 A B C D	9 A B C D	13 A B C D	17 A B C D	21 A B C D	25 A B C D
PART 1—GS	S1 A B ■ D	2 A B C D	6 A B C D	10 A B C D	14 A B C D	18 A B C D	22 A B C D	
	S2 A B C D	3 A B C D	7 A B C D	11 A B C D	15 A B C D	19 A B C D	23 A B C D	
	S3 A B C D	4 A B C D	8 A B C D	12 A B C D	16 A B C D	20 A B C D	24 A B C D	

Part 2 Arithmetic Reasoning

	1 A B C D	5 A B C D	9 A B C D	13 A B C D	17 A B C D	21 A B C D	25 A B C D	29 A B C D
PART 2—AR	2 A B C D	6 A B C D	10 A B C D	14 A B C D	18 A B C D	22 A B C D	26 A B C D	30 A B C D
	3 A B C D	7 A B C D	11 A B C D	15 A B C D	19 A B C D	23 A B C D	27 A B C D	
	4 A B C D	8 A B C D	12 A B C D	16 A B C D	20 A B C D	24 A B C D	28 A B C D	

Part 5 Mathematics Knowledge

	1 A B C D	5 A B C D	9 A B C D	13 A B C D	17 A B C D	21 A B C D	25 A B C D
PART 5—MK	2 A B C D	6 A B C D	10 A B C D	14 A B C D	18 A B C D	22 A B C D	
	3 A B C D	7 A B C D	11 A B C D	15 A B C D	19 A B C D	23 A B C D	
	4 A B C D	8 A B C D	12 A B C D	16 A B C D	20 A B C D	24 A B C D	

Part 6 Electronics Information

	1 A B C D	4 A B C D	7 A B C D	10 A B C D	13 A B C D	16 A B C D	19 A B C D
PART 10—EI	2 A B C D	5 A B C D	8 A B C D	11 A B C D	14 A B C D	17 A B C D	20 A B C D
	3 A B C D	6 A B C D	9 A B C D	12 A B C D	15 A B C D	18 A B C D	

PART 1: GENERAL SCIENCE

Directions: This is a test of 25 questions to find out how much you know about general science as usually covered in high school courses. Pick the best answer for each question, then blacken the space on your answer form that has the same number and letter as your choice.

Here are three sample questions.

S1.　Water is an example of a

　　(A)　solid.
　　(B)　gas.
　　(C)　liquid.
　　(D)　crystal.

Now look at the section of your answer sheet labeled Part I, "Practice." Notice that answer space (C) has been marked for question 1. Now do practice questions 2 and 3 by yourself. Find the correct answer to the question, then mark the space on your answer form that has the same letter as the answer you picked. Do this now.

S2.　Lack of iodine is often related to which of the following diseases?

　　(A)　Beriberi
　　(B)　Scurvy
　　(C)　Rickets
　　(D)　Goiter

S3.　An eclipse of the sun throws the shadow of the

　　(A)　earth on the moon.
　　(B)　moon on the earth.
　　(C)　moon on the sun.
　　(D)　earth on the sun.

You should have marked (D) for question 2 and (B) for question 3. If you made any mistakes, erase your mark carefully and blacken the correct answer space. Do this now.

Your score on this test will be based on the number of questions you answer correctly. You should try to answer every question. Do not spend too much time on any one question.

When you begin, be sure to start with question number 1 of Part 1 of your test booklet, and number 1 in Part 1 on your answer form.

DO NOT TURN PAGE UNTIL TOLD TO DO SO.

PART I: GENERAL SCIENCE

TIME: 11 Minutes—25 Questions

1. Under natural conditions, large quantities of organic matter decay after each year's plant growth has been completed. As a result of such conditions,
   (A) many animals are deprived of adequate food supplies.
   (B) soil erosion is accelerated.
   (C) soils maintain their fertility.
   (D) earthworms are added to the soil.

2. The thin, clear layer that forms the outer coat of the eyeball is called the
   (A) pupil.
   (B) iris.
   (C) lens.
   (D) cornea.

3. The most likely reason why dinosaurs became extinct was that they
   (A) were killed by erupting volcanoes.
   (B) were eaten as adults by the advancing mammalian groups.
   (C) failed to adapt to a changing environment.
   (D) killed each other in combat.

4. Which of the following is a chemical change?
   (A) Magnetizing a rod of iron
   (B) Burning one pound of coal
   (C) Mixing flake graphite with oil
   (D) Vaporizing one gram of mercury in a vacuum

5. A person with high blood pressure should
   (A) take frequent naps.
   (B) avoid salt.
   (C) eat only iodized salt.
   (D) exercise vigorously.

6. One-celled animals belong to the group of living things known as
   (A) protozoa.
   (B) annelida.
   (C) porifera.
   (D) arthropoda.

7. Spiders can be distinguished from insects by the fact that spiders have
   (A) hard outer coverings.
   (B) large abdomens.
   (C) four pairs of legs.
   (D) biting mouth parts.

8. An important ore of uranium is called
   (A) hermatite.
   (B) chalcopyrite.
   (C) bauxite.
   (D) pitchblende.

9. Of the following, the lightest element known on Earth is
   (A) hydrogen.
   (B) oxygen.
   (C) helium.
   (D) air.

10. Of the following gases in the air, the most plentiful is
    (A) argon.
    (B) oxygen.
    (C) nitrogen.
    (D) carbon dioxide.

11. The time it takes for light from the sun to reach the earth is approximately
    (A) four years.
    (B) eight minutes.
    (C) four months.
    (D) sixteen years.

12. Of the following types of clouds, the ones that occur at the greatest altitude are called
    (A) cirrus.
    (B) nimbus.
    (C) cumulus.
    (D) stratus.

13. A new drug for treatment of tuberculosis was being tested in a hospital. Patients in Group A actually received doses of the new drug; those in Group B were given only sugar pills. Group B represents

   (A) a scientific experiment.
   (B) a scientific method.
   (C) an experimental error.
   (D) an experimental control.

14. The statement that carrots help one to see in the dark is

   (A) ridiculous.
   (B) reasonable because orange is a reflective color.
   (C) reasonable because carrots are high in vitamin A.
   (D) reasonable because rabbits see very well at night.

15. Radium is stored in lead containers because

   (A) the lead absorbs the harmful radiation.
   (B) radium is a heavy substance.
   (C) lead prevents the disintegration of the radium.
   (D) lead is cheap.

16. The type of joint that attaches the arm to the shoulder blade is known as a

   (A) hinge.
   (B) pivot.
   (C) immovable.
   (D) ball and socket.

17. Limes were eaten by British sailors in order to

   (A) justify their nickname, "limeys."
   (B) pucker their mouths to resist the wind.
   (C) satisfy their craving for something acid.
   (D) prevent scurvy.

18. The time that it takes for the earth to rotate 45° is

   (A) 1 hour.
   (B) 4 hours.
   (C) 3 hours.
   (D) 10 hours.

19. Of the following glands, the one that regulates the metabolic rate is the

   (A) adrenal.
   (B) thyroid.
   (C) salivary.
   (D) thymus.

20. All of the following are amphibia EXCEPT the

   (A) salamander.
   (B) frog.
   (C) lizard.
   (D) toad.

21. Of the following planets, the one that has the shortest revolutionary period around the sun is

   (A) Earth.
   (B) Jupiter.
   (C) Mercury.
   (D) Venus.

22. The term *ft./sec.* is a unit of

   (A) mass.
   (B) speed.
   (C) length.
   (D) density.

23. A circuit breaker is used in many homes instead of a

   (A) switch.
   (B) fire extinguisher.
   (C) fuse.
   (D) meter box.

GO ON TO THE NEXT PAGE

24. What is the name of the negative particle that circles the nucleus of the atom?

   (A) Neutron
   (B) Meson
   (C) Proton
   (D) Electron

25. Which of the following rocks can be dissolved with a weak acid?

   (A) Sandstone
   (B) Gneiss
   (C) Granite
   (D) Limestone

STOP! DO NOT TURN THIS PAGE UNTIL TOLD TO DO SO. IF YOU FINISH BEFORE THE TIME IS UP, YOU MAY CHECK OVER YOUR WORK ON THIS PART ONLY.

PART 2: ARITHMETIC REASONING

Directions: This test has 30 questions on arithmetic reasoning. Each question is followed by four possible answers. Decide which answer is correct, then blacken the space on your answer form that has the same number and letter as your choice. Use your scratch paper for any figuring you wish to do.

Here are two sample questions.

S1.　A person buys a sandwich for $2.90, soda for 75¢, and pie for 90¢. What is the total cost?

　　(A)　$3.85
　　(B)　$4.45
　　(C)　$4.55
　　(D)　$4.65

The total cost is $4.55; therefore, choice (C) is the right answer.

S2.　If 8 workers are needed to run 4 machines, how many workers are needed to run 20 machines?

　　(A)　16
　　(B)　32
　　(C)　36
　　(D)　40

The number needed is 40; therefore, choice (D) is the correct answer.

Your score on this test will be based on the number of questions you answer correctly. You should try to answer every question. Do not spend too much time on any one question.

Notice that Part 2 begins with question number 1. When you begin, be sure to start with question No. 1 in Part 2 of your test booklet and No. 1 in Part 2 on your answer form.

DO NOT TURN PAGE UNTIL TOLD TO DO SO.

PART 2: ARITHMETIC REASONING

TIME: 36 Minutes—30 Questions

1. A man owned 75 shares of stock worth $50 each. The corporation declared a dividend of 8%, payable in stock. How many shares did he then own?

   (A) 81 shares
   (B) 90 shares
   (C) 80 shares
   (D) 85 shares

2. A certain type of siding for a house costs $10.50 per square yard. What does it cost for the siding for a wall 4 yards wide and 60 feet long?

   (A) $800
   (B) $840
   (C) $2,520
   (D) $3,240

3. A gallon contains 4 quarts. A cartoning machine can fill 120 one-quart cartons a minute. How long will it take to put 600 gallons of orange juice into cartons?

   (A) 1 minute and 15 seconds
   (B) 5 minutes
   (C) 10 minutes
   (D) 20 minutes

4. A typist uses lengthwise a sheet of paper 9 inches by 12 inches. She leaves a 1-inch margin on each side and a $1\frac{1}{2}$-inch margin on top and bottom. What fractional part of the page is used for typing?

   (A) $\frac{21}{22}$

   (B) $\frac{7}{12}$

   (C) $\frac{5}{9}$

   (D) $\frac{3}{4}$

5. A student deposited in her savings account the money she had saved during the week. Find the amount of her deposit if she had 10 one-dollar bills, 9 half dollars, 8 quarters, 16 dimes, and 25 nickels.

   (A) $16.20
   (B) $17.42
   (C) $18.60
   (D) $19.35

6. How many minutes are there in 1 day?

   (A) 60
   (B) 1,440
   (C) 24
   (D) $1,440 \times 60$

7. One year, the postage rate for sending 1 ounce of mail first class was increased from 25 cents to 29 cents. The percent of increase in the postage rate was most nearly

   (A) 12%
   (B) 14%
   (C) 16%
   (D) 18%

8. On a scale drawing, a line $\frac{1}{4}$ inch long represents a length of 1 foot. On the same drawing, what length represents 4 feet?

   (A) 1 inch
   (B) 2 inches
   (C) 3 inches
   (D) 4 inches

9. What is the greatest number of half-pint bottles that can be filled from a 10-gallon can of milk?

   (A) 160
   (B) 170
   (C) 16
   (D) 17

10. If 6 people can paint a fence in 2 days, how many people, working at the same uniform rate, can finish it in 1 day?

    (A) 2
    (B) 3
    (C) 12
    (D) 14

11. A team won 2 games and lost 10. The fraction of its games won is correctly expressed as

 (A) $\frac{1}{6}$

 (B) $\frac{1}{5}$

 (C) $\frac{4}{5}$

 (D) $\frac{5}{6}$

12. How much time is there between 8:30 A.M. today and 3:15 A.M. tomorrow?

 (A) $17\frac{3}{4}$ hrs.

 (B) $18\frac{2}{3}$ hrs.

 (C) $18\frac{1}{2}$ hrs.

 (D) $18\frac{3}{4}$ hrs.

13. A clerk is asked to file 800 cards. If he can file cards at the rate of 80 cards an hour, the number of cards remaining to be filed after 7 hours of work is

 (A) 140
 (B) 240
 (C) 250
 (D) 260

14. A telephone pole 60 feet high casts a shadow 80 feet long at the same time that a nearby tree casts a shadow 120 feet. What is the height of the tree?

 (A) 80 feet
 (B) 90 feet
 (C) 120 feet
 (D) 150 feet

15. A plane left New York at 3:30 P.M. EST and arrived in Los Angeles at 4:15 P.M. PST. How long did the flight take?

 (A) 7 hours 15 minutes
 (B) 6 hours 45 minutes
 (C) 3 hours 45 minutes
 (D) 3 hours 15 minutes

16. If a barrel has a capacity of 120 gallons, it will contain how many gallons when it is two-fifths full?

 (A) 36 gal.
 (B) 48 gal.
 (C) 60 gal.
 (D) 72 gal.

17. If a salary of $20,000 is subject to a 20 percent deduction, the net salary is

 (A) $14,000
 (B) $15,500
 (C) $16,000
 (D) $16,500

18. If $2,500 is the cost of repairing 100 square yards of pavement, the cost of repairing five square yards is

 (A) $125
 (B) $130
 (C) $135
 (D) $140

19. A car can travel 24 miles on a gallon of gasoline. How many gallons will be used on a 192 mile trip?

 (A) 8 gal.
 (B) 9 gal.
 (C) 10 gal.
 (D) 11 gal.

20. If an annual salary of $21,600 is increased by a bonus of $720 and by a service increment of $1,200, the total pay rate is

 (A) $22,320
 (B) $22,800
 (C) $23,320
 (D) $23,520

21. A man takes out a $5,000 life insurance policy at a yearly rate of $29.62 per $1,000. What is the yearly premium?

 (A) $ 90.10
 (B) $100.10
 (C) $126.10
 (D) $148.10

GO ON TO THE NEXT PAGE

22. On her maiden voyage, the *S.S. United States* made the trip from New York to England in 3 days, 10 hours and 40 minutes, beating the record set by the *R.M.S. Queen Mary* in 1938 by 10 hours and 2 minutes. How long did it take the *Queen Mary* to make the trip?

(A) 3 days 20 hrs. 42 mins.
(B) 3 days 15 hrs. 38 mins.
(C) 3 days 12 hrs. 2 mins.
(D) 3 days 8 hrs. 12 mins.

23. Gary bought a shirt for $15.00 and a tie for $3.95. He gave the clerk $20.00. How much change did Gary get?

(A) $2.05
(B) $1.95
(C) $1.05
(D) $ .05

24. If erasers cost 8¢ each for the first 250, 7¢ each for the next 250, and 5¢ for every eraser thereafter, how many erasers may be purchased for $50?

(A) 600
(B) 750
(C) 850
(D) 1000

25. An inch on a map represents 200 miles. On the same map, a distance of 375 miles is represented by

(A) $1\frac{1}{2}$ inches

(B) $1\frac{7}{8}$ inches

(C) $2\frac{1}{4}$ inches

(D) $2\frac{3}{4}$ inches

26. The library charges 5¢ for the first day and 2¢ for each additional day that a book is overdue. If a borrower paid 65¢ in late charges, for how many days was the book overdue?

(A) 15
(B) 21
(C) 25
(D) 31

27. A pile of magazines is 4 feet high. If each magazine is $\frac{3}{4}$ of an inch thick, the number of magazines is

(A) 36
(B) 48
(C) 64
(D) 96

28. Potatoes are selling at $1.59 for a 5-pound bag. The cost for 10 pounds is

(A) 1.59×10
(B) 1.59×2
(C) 1.59×50
(D) $1.59 \times 5 \div 10$

29. Don and Frank started from the same point and drove in opposite directions. Don's rate of travel was 50 miles per hour. Frank's rate of travel was 40 miles per hour. How many miles apart were they at the end of 2 hours?

(A) 90
(B) 140
(C) 160
(D) 180

30. A folding chair regularly sells for $29.50. How much money is saved if the chair is bought at a 20% discount?

(A) $4.80
(B) $5.90
(C) $6.20
(D) $7.40

STOP! DO NOT TURN THIS PAGE UNTIL TOLD TO DO SO. IF YOU FINISH BEFORE THE TIME IS UP, YOU MAY CHECK OVER YOUR WORK ON THIS PART ONLY.

PART 3: WORD KNOWLEDGE

Directions: This test has 35 questions about the meanings of words. Each question has an italicized word. You are to decide which one of the four words in the choices most nearly means the same as the italicized word, then mark the space on your answer form that has the same number and letter as your choice.

Now look at the two sample questions below.

S1. *Mended* most nearly means

    (A) repaired.
    (B) torn.
    (C) clean.
    (D) tied.

Choice (A) is the correct answer. *Mended* means *fixed* or *repaired*.

S2. It was a *small* table.

    (A) sturdy
    (B) round
    (C) cheap
    (D) little

Little means the same as *small*, so choice (D) is the best answer.

Your score on this test will be based on the number of questions you answer correctly. You should try to answer every question. Do not spend too much time on any one question.

When you begin, be sure to start with question No. 1 in Part 3 of your test booklet and No. 1 in Part 3 on your answer form.

DO NOT TURN PAGE UNTIL TOLD TO DO SO.

PART 3: WORD KNOWLEDGE

TIME: 11 Minutes—35 Questions

1. *Superiority* most nearly means

   (A) abundance
   (B) popularity
   (C) permanence
   (D) excellence

2. *Absurd* most nearly means

   (A) disgusting
   (B) foolish
   (C) reasonable
   (D) very old

3. Be careful, that liquid is *inflammable*!

   (A) poisonous
   (B) valuable
   (C) explosive
   (D) likely to give off fumes

4. *Conscious* most nearly means

   (A) surprised
   (B) afraid
   (C) disappointed
   (D) aware

5. *Exhibit* most nearly means

   (A) display
   (B) trade
   (C) sell
   (D) label

6. We *assumed* that Jack had been elected.

   (A) knew
   (B) wished
   (C) decided
   (D) supposed

7. *Counterfeit* most nearly means

   (A) mysterious
   (B) false
   (C) unreadable
   (D) priceless

8. *Expertly* most nearly means

   (A) awkwardly
   (B) quickly
   (C) skillfully
   (D) unexpectedly

9. *Marshy* most nearly means

   (A) swampy
   (B) sandy
   (C) wooded
   (D) rocky

10. The children pledged *allegiance* to the flag.

    (A) freedom
    (B) homeland
    (C) protection
    (D) loyalty

11. The cashier *yearned* for a vacation.

    (A) begged
    (B) longed
    (C) saved
    (D) applied

12. *Summit* most nearly means

    (A) face
    (B) top
    (C) base
    (D) side

13. The driver *heeded* the traffic signals.

    (A) worried about
    (B) ignored
    (C) disagreed with
    (D) took notice of

14. *Vigorously* most nearly means

    (A) sleepily
    (B) thoughtfully
    (C) energetically
    (D) sadly

15. *Imitate* most nearly means

    (A) copy
    (B) attract
    (C) study
    (D) appreciate

16. The *severity* of their criticism upset us.

(A) harshness
(B) suddenness
(C) method
(D) unfairness

17. *Incredible* most nearly means

(A) thrilling
(B) convincing
(C) uninteresting
(D) unbelievable

18. We made a very *leisurely* trip to California.

(A) roundabout
(B) unhurried
(C) unforgettable
(D) tiresome

19. *Gratitude* most nearly means

(A) thankfulness
(B) excitement
(C) disappointment
(D) sympathy

20. *Familiar* most nearly means

(A) welcome
(B) dreaded
(C) rare
(D) well-known

21. He had an *acute* pain in his back.

(A) dull
(B) slight
(C) alarming
(D) sharp

22. *Bewildered* most nearly means

(A) worded
(B) offended
(C) puzzled
(D) delighted

23. *Conclusion* most nearly means

(A) theme
(B) suspense
(C) end
(D) beginning

24. She likes the *aroma* of fresh-brewed coffee.

(A) flavor
(B) warmth
(C) fragrance
(D) steam

25. *Nonessential* most nearly means

(A) damaged
(B) unnecessary
(C) expensive
(D) foreign-made

26. *Amplified* most nearly means

(A) expanded
(B) summarized
(C) analyzed
(D) shouted

27. The vase remained *intact* after it was dropped.

(A) unattended
(B) undamaged
(C) a total loss
(D) unmoved

28. Penicillin is a *potent* drug.

(A) harmless
(B) possible
(C) effective
(D) drinkable

29. *Terminate* most nearly means

(A) continue
(B) go by train
(C) begin
(D) end

30. The prisoner is a *notorious* bank robber.

(A) convicted
(B) dangerous
(C) well-known
(D) escaped

GO ON TO THE NEXT PAGE

31. *Fatal* most nearly means

(A) accidental
(B) deadly
(C) dangerous
(D) beautiful

32. *Indigent* people are entitled to food stamps.

(A) poor
(B) lazy
(C) angry
(D) homeless

33. *Technique* most nearly means

(A) computed
(B) engineered
(C) calculation
(D) method

34. *Vocation* most nearly means

(A) school
(B) examination
(C) occupation
(D) carpentry

35. One should eat only *mature* fruits.

(A) edible
(B) washed
(C) ripe
(D) sprayed

STOP! DO NOT TURN THIS PAGE UNTIL TOLD TO DO SO. IF YOU FINISH BEFORE THE TIME IS UP, YOU MAY CHECK OVER YOUR WORK ON THIS PART ONLY.

PART 4: PARAGRAPH COMPREHENSION

Directions: This test contains 15 items measuring your ability to obtain information from written passages. You will find one or more paragraphs of reading material followed by incomplete statements or questions. You are to read the paragraph(s) and select the one of the lettered choices that best completes the statement or answers the question.

Here are two sample questions.

S1. From a building designer's standpoint, three things that make a home livable are the client, the building site, and the amount of money the client has to spend.

According to the passage, to make a home livable

(A) the prospective piece of land makes little difference.
(B) it can be built on any piece of land.
(C) the design must fit the owner's income and the building site.
(D) the design must fit the designer's income.

The correct answer is that the design must fit the owner's income and the building site, so choice (C) is the correct response.

S2. In certain areas, water is so scarce that every attempt is made to conserve it. For instance, on one oasis in the Sahara Desert the amount of water necessary for each date palm tree has been carefully determined.

How much water is each tree given?

(A) No water at all
(B) Exactly the amount required
(C) Water only if it is healthy
(D) Water on alternate days

The correct answer is exactly the amount required, so choice (B) is the correct response.

Your score on this test will be based on the number of questions you answer correctly. You should try to answer every question. Do not spend too much time on any one question.

When you begin, be sure to start with question No. 1 in Part 4 of your test booklet and No. 1 in Part 4 on your answer form.

DO NOT TURN PAGE UNTIL TOLD TO DO SO.

PART 4: PARAGRAPH COMPREHENSION

TIME: 13 Minutes—15 Questions

1. Numerous benefits to the employer as well as to the worker have resulted from physical examinations of employees. Such examinations are intended primarily as a means of increasing efficiency and production, and they have been found to accomplish these ends.

   The passage best supports the statement that physical examinations

   (A) may serve to increase output.
   (B) are required in some plants.
   (C) often reveal serious defects previously unknown.
   (D) always are worth more than they cost.

2. Examination of traffic accident statistics reveals that traffic accidents are frequently the result of violations of traffic laws—and usually the violations are the result of illegal and dangerous driving behavior rather than the result of mechanical defects or poor road conditions.

   According to this passage, the majority of dangerous traffic violations are caused by

   (A) poor driving.
   (B) bad roads.
   (C) unsafe cars.
   (D) unwise traffic laws.

3. Complaints from the public are no longer regarded by government officials as mere nuisances. Instead, complaints are often welcomed because they frequently bring into the open conditions and faults in operation and service that should be corrected.

   This passage most nearly means that

   (A) government officials now realize that complaints from the public are necessary.
   (B) faulty operations and services are not brought into the open except by complaints from the public.
   (C) government officials now realize that complaints from the public are in reality a sign of a well-run agency.
   (D) complaints from the public can be useful in indicating needs for improvement in operation and service.

4. In a pole-vaulting competition, the judge decides on the minimum height to be jumped. The vaulter may attempt to jump any height above the minimum. Using flexible fiberglass poles, vaulters have jumped as high as 18 feet $8\frac{1}{4}$ inches.

   According to the passage, pole vaulters

   (A) may attempt to jump any height in competition.

   (B) must jump higher than $18'\ 8\frac{1}{4}''$ to win.

   (C) must jump higher than the height set by the judge.

   (D) must use fiberglass poles.

5. When gas is leaking, any spark or sudden flame can ignite it. This can create a "flashback," which burns off the gas in a quick puff of smoke and flame. But the real danger is in a large leak, which can cause an explosion. According to the passage, the real danger from leaking gas is

   (A) a flashback.
   (B) a puff of smoke and flame.
   (C) an explosion.
   (D) a spark.

6. A year—the time it takes the earth to go exactly once around the sun—is not 365 days. It is actually 365 days 6 hours 9 minutes $9\frac{1}{2}$ seconds, or $365\frac{1}{4}$ days. Leap years make up for this discrepancy by adding an extra day once every four years.

The purpose of leap year is to

(A) adjust for the fact that it takes $365\frac{1}{4}$ days for the earth to circle the sun.
(B) make up for time lost in the work year.
(C) occur every four years.
(D) allow for differences in the length of a year in each time zone.

7. Any business not provided with capable substitutes to fill all important positions is a weak business. Therefore, a foreman should train each man not only to perform his own particular duties but also to do those of two or three positions.

The paragraph best supports the statement that

(A) dependence on substitutes is a sign of a weak organization.
(B) training will improve the strongest organization.
(C) the foreman should be the most expert at any particular job under him.
(D) vacancies in vital positions should be provided for in advance.

8. In the business districts of cities, collections from street letter boxes are made at stated hours, and collectors are required to observe these hours exactly. Anyone using these boxes can rely with certainty upon the time of the next collection.

The paragraph best supports the statement that

(A) mail collections in business districts are more frequent during the day than at night.
(B) mail collectors are required to observe safety regulations exactly.
(C) mail collections are made often in business districts.
(D) mail is collected in business districts on a regular schedule.

9. The increasing size of business organizations has resulted in less personal contact between superior and subordinate. Consequently, business executives today depend more upon records and reports to secure information and exercise control over the operations of various departments.

The increasing size of business organizations

(A) has caused a complete cleavage between employer and employee.
(B) has resulted in less personal contact between superior and subordinate.
(C) has tended toward class distinctions in large organizations.
(D) has resulted in a better means of controlling the operations of various departments.

GO ON TO THE NEXT PAGE

10. Kindling temperature is the lowest temperature at which a substance catches fire and continues to burn. Different fuels have different kindling temperatures. Paper catches fire easily because it has a low kindling temperature. Coal, because of its high kindling temperature, requires much heat before it will begin to burn. Matches are tipped with phosphorus, or some other low-kindling material, to permit the small amount of heat produced by friction to ignite the match.

The property of phosphorus that makes it ideal for use on matches is

(A) its light color.
(B) its high kindling temperature.
(C) its low kindling temperature.
(D) the fact that it contains carbon.

Questions 11 and 12 are based on the following passage.

Racketeers are primarily concerned with business affairs, legitimate or otherwise, and preferably those that are close to the margin of legitimacy. They get their best opportunities from business organizations that meet the needs of large sections of the public for goods and services that are defined as illegitimate by the same public, such as gambling, illicit drugs, etc. In contrast to the thief, the racketeer and the establishments he or she controls deliver goods and services for money received.

11. According to the above passage, racketeering, unlike theft, involves

(A) payment for goods received.
(B) unlawful activities.
(C) organized gangs.
(D) objects of value.

12. It can be deduced that suppression of racketeering is difficult because

(A) many people want services that are not obtainable through legitimate sources.
(B) racketeers are generally engaged in fully legitimate enterprises.
(C) victims of racketeers are not guilty of violating the law.
(D) laws prohibiting gambling are unenforceable.

Questions 13–15 are based on the passage shown below.

The two systems of weights and measures are the English system and the Metric system. The English system uses units such as foot, pound, and quart; the Metric system uses meter, gram, and liter.

The Metric system was first adopted in France in 1795 and is now used by most countries in the world. In the Metric system, the unit of length is the meter, which is one ten-millionth of the distance from the Equator to the North Pole.

The British have changed their system of weights and measures to the Metric system; however, in the United States, there has been much opposition to this change. It would cost billions of dollars to change all our weights and measures to the Metric system.

13. According to the passage above, the Metric system is used

(A) in all of Europe except Great Britain.
(B) in almost all countries of the world.
(C) in only a few countries.
(D) mostly in Europe.

14. The United States has not changed to the Metric system because

    (A) the system is too complicated.
    (B) the change would be costly.
    (C) the system is not accurate.
    (D) it is difficult to learn.

15. The meter is equal to

    (A) the distance from the Equator to the North Pole.

    (B) $\dfrac{1}{1,000,000}$ of the distance from the Equator to the North Pole.

    (C) $\dfrac{1}{10,000,000}$ of the distance from the Equator to the North Pole.

    (D) $\dfrac{1}{100,000,000}$ of the distance from the Equator to the North Pole.

STOP! DO NOT TURN THIS PAGE UNTIL TOLD TO DO SO. IF YOU FINISH BEFORE THE TIME IS UP, YOU MAY CHECK OVER YOUR WORK ON THIS PART ONLY.

PART 5: MATHEMATICS KNOWLEDGE

Directions: This is a test of your ability to solve 25 general mathematical problems. You are to select the correct response from the choices given. Then mark the space on your answer form that has the same number and letter as your choice. Use the scratch paper that has been given to you to do any figuring that you need.

Now look at the two sample problems below.

S1. If $x + 6 = 7$, then x is equal to

    (A) 0

    (B) 1

    (C) –1

    (D) $\dfrac{7}{6}$

The correct answer is 1, so choice (B) is the correct response.

S2. What is the area of the square shown below?

    (A) 1 square

    (B) 5 square feet

    (C) 10 square feet

    (D) 25 square feet

5 ft.

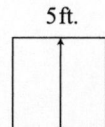

The correct answer is 25 square feet, so choice (D) is the correct response.

Your score on this test will be based on the number of questions you answer correctly. You should try to answer every question. Do not spend too much time on any one question.

When you are told to begin, be sure to start with question No. 1 in Part 5 of your test booklet and No. 1 in Part 5 on your answer form.

DO NOT TURN PAGE UNTIL TOLD TO DO SO.

PART 5: MATHEMATICS KNOWLEDGE

TIME: 24 Minutes—25 Questions

1. If you subtract $6a - 4b + 3c$ from a polynomial, you get $4a + 9b - 5c$. What is the polynomial?
   - (A) $10a - 5b + 2c$
   - (B) $10a + 5b - 2c$
   - (C) $24 + 13b - 8c$
   - (D) $2a + 5b + 8c$

2. If 50% of $x = 66$, then $x =$
   - (A) 33
   - (B) 99
   - (C) 122
   - (D) None of the above

3. If $3x = -5$, then x equals
   - (A) $\dfrac{3}{5}$
   - (B) $-\dfrac{5}{3}$
   - (C) $-\dfrac{3}{5}$
   - (D) -2

4. The first digit of the square root of 59043 is
   - (A) 2
   - (B) 4
   - (C) 5
   - (D) 7

5. A square is equal in area to a rectangle whose length is 9 and whose width is 4. Find the perimeter of the square.
   - (A) 24
   - (B) 26
   - (C) 34
   - (D) 36

6. The value of $\dfrac{27}{8} \times \dfrac{24}{9} \div \dfrac{3}{2} =$
   - (A) 6
   - (B) $7\dfrac{2}{9}$
   - (C) $8\dfrac{1}{4}$
   - (D) $9\dfrac{5}{8}$

7. If the perimeter of an equilateral triangle is $6n - 12$, what is the length of the base?
   - (A) $3(2n - 4)$
   - (B) $2(3n - 6)$
   - (C) $3n - 6$
   - (D) $2n - 4$

8. Which one of the following is a polygon?
   - (A) Circle
   - (B) Ellipse
   - (C) Star
   - (D) Parabola

9. The sum of the inside angles of a regular hexagonal (six-sided) field is
   - (A) 360°
   - (B) 540°
   - (C) 630°
   - (D) 720°

10. The area of a rectangle 12 feet by 18 feet is equal to
    - (A) 8 square yards.
    - (B) 24 square yards.
    - (C) 36 square yards.
    - (D) 72 square yards.

11. Given the formulas $d = rt$ and $A = r + \dfrac{d}{t}$, which formula below correctly expresses the value of A without using t?
    - (A) $A = dr$
    - (B) $A = r + \dfrac{2d}{r}$
    - (C) $A = 2r + d$
    - (D) $A = 2r$

12. R is what percent of 1,000?

   (A) .001R
   (B) .01R
   (C) .1R
   (D) 1R

13. The distance in miles around a circular course that has a radius of 35 miles is (use $\pi = \frac{22}{7}$)

   (A) 156
   (B) 220
   (C) 440
   (D) 880

14. The expression "3 factorial" equals

   (A) $\frac{1}{9}$

   (B) $\frac{1}{6}$

   (C) 6
   (D) 9

15. If $a = 2b$ and $4b = 6c$, then $a =$

   (A) 3c
   (B) 4c
   (C) 9c
   (D) 12c

16. Solve for x: $\frac{2x}{7} = 2x^2$

   (A) $\frac{1}{7}$

   (B) $\frac{2}{7}$

   (C) 2
   (D) 7

17. Solve the following equation for C: $A^2 = \frac{B^2}{C+D}$

   (A) $C = \frac{B^2 - A^2 D}{A^2 B}$

   (B) $C = \frac{A^2}{B^2} - D$

   (C) $C = \frac{A^2 + D}{B^2 - D}$

   (D) $C = \frac{B^2}{A^2} - D$

18. The expression, $-1(3-2)$, is equal to

   (A) $-3 + 2$
   (B) $-3 - 2$
   (C) $3 - 2$
   (D) $3 + 2$

19. The reciprocal of 5 is

   (A) 1.0
   (B) 0.5
   (C) 0.2
   (D) 0.1

20. What is the area, in square inches, of a circle whose radius measures 7 inches? (use $\pi = \frac{22}{7}$)

   (A) 22
   (B) 44
   (C) 154
   (D) 616

21. Evaluate the expression $5a - 4x - 3y$ if $a = -2$, $x = -10$, and $y = 5$.

   (A) $+ 15$
   (B) $+25$
   (C) -65
   (D) -35

22. If one book costs c dollars, what is the cost, in dollars, of m books?

   (A) $m + c$
   (B) mc

   (C) $\frac{c}{m}$

   (D) $\frac{m}{c}$

23. A purse contains 16 coins in dimes and quarters. If the value of the coins is $2.50, how many dimes are there?

   (A) 6
   (B) 8
   (C) 9
   (D) 10

GO ON TO THE NEXT PAGE

24. Solve for x: $\frac{x}{2} - \frac{x}{5} = 3$

(A) 2
(B) 3
(C) 5
(D) 10

25. If the radius of a circle is increased by 3, the circumference is increased by

(A) 3
(B) 3π
(C) 6π
(D) 6

STOP! DO NOT TURN THIS PAGE UNTIL TOLD TO DO SO. IF YOU FINISH BEFORE THE TIME IS UP, YOU MAY CHECK OVER YOUR WORK ON THIS PART ONLY.

PART 6: ELECTRONICS INFORMATION

Directions: This is a test of your knowledge of electrical, radio, and electronics information. There are 20 questions. You are to select the correct response from the choices given. Then mark the space on your answer form that has the same number and letter as your choice.

Now look at the two sample questions below.

S1.   What does the abbreviation AC stand for?

(A)   Additional charge
(B)   Alternating coil
(C)   Alternating current
(D)   Ampere current

The correct answer is alternating current, so choice (C) is the correct response.

S2.   Which of the following has the least resistance?

(A)   Wood
(B)   Silver
(C)   Rubber
(D)   Iron

The correct answer is silver, so choice (B) is the correct response.

Your score on this test will be based on the number of questions you answer correctly. You should try to answer every question. Do not spend too much time on any one question.

When you are told to begin, be sure to start with question No. 1 in Part 6 of your test booklet and No. 1 in Part 6 on your answer form.

DO NOT TURN PAGE UNTIL TOLD TO DO SO.

PART 6: ELECTRONICS INFORMATION

TIME: 9 Minutes—20 Questions

1. The core of an electromagnet is usually
    (A) aluminum.
    (B) brass.
    (C) lead.
    (D) iron.

2. An electrician should consider all electrical equipment "alive" unless he definitely knows otherwise. The main reason for this practice is to avoid
    (A) doing unnecessary work.
    (B) energizing the wrong circuit.
    (C) personal injury.
    (D) de-energizing a live circuit.

3. If *voltage* is represented by V, *current* by I and *resistance* by R, then the one of the following that correctly states Ohm's Law is
    (A) $R = V \times I$
    (B) $R = \dfrac{I}{V}$
    (C) $V = I \times R$
    (D) $V = \dfrac{I}{R}$

4. The device used to change AC to DC is a
    (A) frequency changer.
    (B) transformer.
    (C) regulator.
    (D) rectifier.

5.

The reading of the kilowatt-hour meter is
    (A) 9672
    (B) 1779
    (C) 2770
    (D) 0762

6. The device that is often used to change the voltage in alternating current circuits is the
    (A) contactor.
    (B) converter.
    (C) rectifier.
    (D) transformer.

7. Electrical contacts are opened or closed when the electrical current energizes the coils of a device called a
    (A) reactor.
    (B) transtat.
    (C) relay.
    (D) thermostat.

8. To determine directly whether finished wire installations possess resistance between conductors and ground, use
    (A) clamps.
    (B) set screws.
    (C) shields.
    (D) a megger.

9.

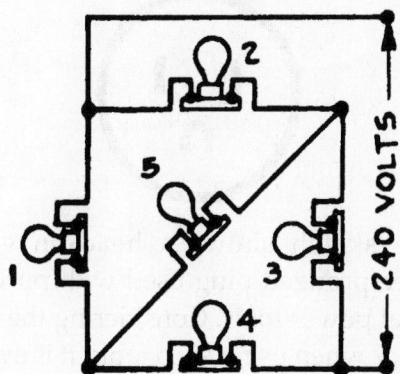

The five lamps shown are each rated at 120 volts, 60 watts. If all are good lamps, lamp 5 will be

(A) much brighter than normal.
(B) about its normal brightness.
(C) much dimmer than normal.
(D) completely dark.

10. Microfarads are units of measurement usually associated with

(A) sockets.
(B) switches.
(C) capacitors.
(D) connectors.

11. The three elements of a transistor are the

(A) collector, base, and emitter.
(B) collector, grid, and cathode.
(C) plate, grid, and emitter.
(D) plate, base, and cathode.

12. Is it proper procedure to ground the frame of a portable motor?

(A) No
(B) No, if it is AC
(C) Yes, unless the tool is specifically designed for use without a ground
(D) Yes, if the operation takes place only at less than 150 volts

13. In comparing Nos. 00, 8, 12, and 6 A.W.G. wires, the smallest of the group is

(A) No. 00
(B) No. 8
(C) No. 12
(D) No. 6

14.

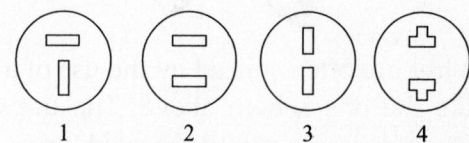

The convenience outlet that is known as a *polarized* outlet is number

(A) 1
(B) 2
(C) 3
(D) 4

15. In a house bell circuit, the push button for ringing the bell is generally connected in the secondary of the transformer feeding the bell. One reason for doing this is to

(A) save power.
(B) keep line voltage out of the push button circuit.
(C) prevent the bell from burning out.
(D) prevent arcing of the vibrator contact points in the bell.

GO ON TO THE NEXT PAGE

16.

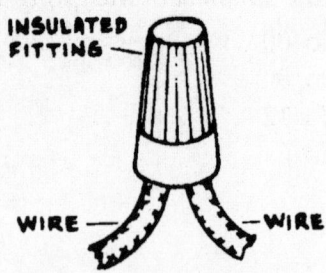

Wires are often spliced by the use of a fitting like the one shown above. The use of this fitting does away with the need for

(A) skinning.
(B) cleaning.
(C) twisting.
(D) soldering.

17. In order to control a lamp from two different positions, it is necessary to use

(A) two single-pole switches.
(B) one single-pole switch and one four-way switch.
(C) two three-way switches.
(D) one single-pole switch and two four-way switches.

18. In electronic circuits, the symbol shown below usually represents a

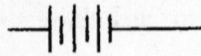

(A) resistor.
(B) battery.
(C) capacitor.
(D) transformer.

19.

The sketch shows a head-on view of a three-pronged plug used with portable electrical power tools. Considering the danger of shock when using such tools, it is evident that the function of the U-shaped prong is to

(A) ensure that the other two prongs enter the outlet with the proper polarity.
(B) provide a half-voltage connection when doing light work.
(C) prevent accidental pulling of the plug from the outlet.
(D) connect the metallic shell of the tool motor to ground.

20. A compound motor usually has

(A) only a shunt field.
(B) both a shunt and a series field.
(C) only a series field.
(D) no brushes.

IF YOU FINISH BEFORE THE TIME IS UP, YOU MAY CHECK OVER YOUR WORK ON THIS PART ONLY.
END OF FIRST SIX SUBTESTS

KEY ANSWERS AND RATIONALE
FOR ASVAB TEST ITEMS

PART 1: GENERAL SCIENCE

Key Answers

1. The correct answer is (C).
2. The correct answer is (D).
3. The correct answer is (C).
4. The correct answer is (B).
5. The correct answer is (B).
6. The correct answer is (A).
7. The correct answer is (C).
8. The correct answer is (D).
9. The correct answer is (A).
10. The correct answer is (C).
11. The correct answer is (B).
12. The correct answer is (A).
13. The correct answer is (D).
14. The correct answer is (C).
15. The correct answer is (A).
16. The correct answer is (D).
17. The correct answer is (D).
18. The correct answer is (C).
19. The correct answer is (B).
20. The correct answer is (C).
21. The correct answer is (C).
22. The correct answer is (B).
23. The correct answer is (C).
24. The correct answer is (D).
25. The correct answer is (D).

Items Answered Incorrectly: __; __; __; __; __; __; __; __.
Items Unsure Of: __; __; __; __; __; __; __; __.

**TOTAL NUMBER
ANSWERED CORRECTLY:** _____

Rationale

1. The correct answer is (C). When organic matter decays, it decomposes into its constituent elements. These elements are returned to the soil, thus increasing its fertility.

2. The correct answer is (D). The cornea, a transparent tissue, forms the outer coat of the eyeball covering the iris and pupil.

3. The correct answer is (C). The extinction of all sizes and varieties of dinosaurs all over the world can be explained neither by local phenomena nor on a one-by-one basis. The most reasonable assumption is that the dinosaurs failed to adapt and were unable to survive as climatic conditions changed radically.

4. The correct answer is (B). Combustion is a chemical process.

5. The correct answer is (B). Salt contributes to high blood pressure. The critical element in the action of salt upon the blood pressure is sodium. Iodine, or the lack of it, plays no role in raising blood pressure.

6. The correct answer is (A). Protozoa are one-celled animals. Annelida are worms; porifera are sponges; arthropoda are spiders and crustaceans.

7. The correct answer is (C). All spiders have four pairs of legs. True insects have three pairs of legs.

8. The correct answer is (D). Uranium is found in pitchblende and other rare metals. Hematite is a source of iron; chalcopyrite is an ore of copper; bauxite is a source of aluminum.

9. The correct answer is (A). The atomic weight of hydrogen is 1.0080, that of helium 4.003, and of oxygen 16.00. Air is not an element but a mixture of gases.

10. The correct answer is (C). Nitrogen constitutes about four fifths of the atmosphere by volume.

11. The correct answer is (B). Light travels at the rate of 186,300 miles per second. The sun is 92,900,000 miles from the earth, so its light arrives here in just over 8 minutes.

12. The correct answer is (A). Cirrus clouds occur at 20,000 to 40,000 feet and are made up of ice crystals. Nimbus clouds are gray rain clouds; cumulus clouds are fluffy white clouds; stratus clouds are long, low clouds, generally at altitudes of 2,000 to 7,000 feet.

13. The correct answer is (D). Group B served as the control group. If the condition of patients in Group A were to improve significantly more than that of patients in Group B, scientists might have reason to believe in the effectiveness of the drug.

14. The correct answer is (C). Vitamin A deficiency leads to poor night vision. Since carrots are high in vitamin A, they should have a positive effect upon night vision, although eating large quantities of carrots will not in itself ensure perfect night vision.

15. The correct answer is (A). Radiation cannot pass through lead.

16. The correct answer is (D). Ball-and-socket joints permit movement in almost all directions.

17. The correct answer is (D). Scurvy is a disease caused by a vitamin C deficiency. Limes are rich in vitamin C.

18. The correct answer is (C). The earth rotates 360° in 24 hours; therefore, it rotates 45° in 3 hours.

19. The correct answer is (B). The thyroid gland regulates the metabolic rate. The adrenal glands secrete hormones that regulate one's reaction to emergencies, among other things. Salivary glands secrete oral saliva. The thymus gland influences growth and development.

20. The correct answer is (C). A lizard is a reptile.

21. The correct answer is (C). Mercury is closest to the sun; therefore, it has the shortest revolutionary period around the sun.

22. The correct answer is (B). $\dfrac{\text{Distance}}{\text{Time}} = \text{Speed}$

23. The correct answer is (C). Circuit breakers serve exactly the same function as fuses. Should wires become overheated for any reason, the circuit breaker will "trip," thus breaking the circuit and interrupting the flow of electricity. Fuse burnout creates the same protective interruption of current.

24. The correct answer is (D). An electron is a negative particle. A proton is positively charged; a neutron is neutral and without charge; a meson has both positive and negative charges.

25. The correct answer is (D). Limestone, a sedimentary rock composed of calcium carbonate, can be dissolved with a weak acid.

PART 2: ARITHMETIC REASONING

Key Answers

1. The correct answer is (A).
2. The correct answer is (B).
3. The correct answer is (D).
4. The correct answer is (B).
5. The correct answer is (D).
6. The correct answer is (B).
7. The correct answer is (C).
8. The correct answer is (A).
9. The correct answer is (A).
10. The correct answer is (C).
11. The correct answer is (A).
12. The correct answer is (D).
13. The correct answer is (B).
14. The correct answer is (B).
15. The correct answer is (C).
16. The correct answer is (B).
17. The correct answer is (C).
18. The correct answer is (A).
19. The correct answer is (A).
20. The correct answer is (D).
21. The correct answer is (D).
22. The correct answer is (A).
23. The correct answer is (C).
24. The correct answer is (B).
25. The correct answer is (B).
26. The correct answer is (D).
27. The correct answer is (C).
28. The correct answer is (B).
29. The correct answer is (D).
30. The correct answer is (B).

Items Answered Incorrectly: __; __; __; __; __; __; __; __.
Items Unsure Of: __; __; __; __; __; __; __; __.

**TOTAL NUMBER
ANSWERED CORRECTLY:** _____

Rationale

1. The correct answer is (A). 8% of 75 = 6 shares; 75 shares + 6 shares = 81 shares.

2. The correct answer is (B). 60 ft. = 20 yd. The wall is 4 yd. × 20 yd. = 80 sq. yd. $10.50 × 80 = $840.

3. The correct answer is (D).

600 gallons = 2400 quarts; $\frac{2400}{120} = 20$ minutes

4. The correct answer is (B). The whole paper is 9 in. × 12 in. = 108 in.^{2} Subtract the margin:

9 in. – 1 in. – 1 in. = 7 in.; 12 in. $- 1\frac{1}{2}$ in. $- 1\frac{1}{2}$ in. = 9 in.

The paper she uses is 7 in. × 9 in. = 63 in.^{2}

$\frac{63}{108} = \frac{7}{12}$ is used for typing.

5. The correct answer is (D).

10	× $1.00	=	$10.00
9	× .50	=	4.50
8	× .25	=	2.00
16	× .10	=	1.60
25	× .05	=	1.25
			$19.35

6. The correct answer is (B). 60 minutes in one hour; 24 hours in one day; 60 × 24 = 1,440 minutes.

7. The correct answer is (C). To find the percent of increase, subtract the original figure from the new figure. Then divide the amount of change by the original figure.

$\frac{29 - 25}{25} = \frac{4}{25} = .16 = 16\%$

8. The correct answer is (A). $4 \times \frac{1}{4}$ inch = 1 inch

9. The correct answer is (A). 8 pts. in 1 gal.; 80 pts. in 10 gal.; 160 half-pints in 10 gal.

10. The correct answer is (C). Common sense will tell you that twice as many people will paint the fence in half the time.

11. The correct answer is (A). The team won 2 games and lost 10, so it played 12 games. $\frac{2}{12} = \frac{1}{6}$.

12. The correct answer is (D).

From 8:30 A.M. until noon today:

$$12:00 = 11:60$$
$$\underline{- 8:30 = 8:30}$$
$$3 \text{ hrs. } 30 \text{ min.}$$

From noon until midnight: 12 hrs.
From midnight until 3:15 A.M.: $\underline{+ 3 \text{ hrs. } 15 \text{ min.}}$
    18 hrs. 45 min.

$$= 18\frac{3}{4} \text{ hours}$$

13. The correct answer is (B). 80 cards × 7 hours = 560 cards filed; 800 – 560 = 240 cards remaining.

14. The correct answer is (B). Let x = height of tree. $\frac{60}{80} = \frac{x}{120}$; $80x = 7200$; $x = 90$ feet.

15. The correct answer is (C). Time difference between New York and Los Angeles is 3 hours. 4:15 P.M. – 3:30 P.M. = 45 minutes; 3 hours + 45 minutes = 3 hours 45 minutes for flight time.

16. The correct answer is (B).

$$\frac{2}{1\cancel{5}} \times \frac{\cancel{120}^{24}}{1} = 48 \text{ gal.}$$

17. The correct answer is (C). If 20% is deducted, the net salary is 80%. $20,000 × 80% = $20,000 × .80 = $16,000.

18. The correct answer is (A). $2,500 ÷ 100 = $25 per square yard; 25 × 5 = $125.

19. The correct answer is (A). 192 ÷ 24 = 8 gal.

20. The correct answer is (D). $21,600 + $720 + $1,200 = $23,520

21. The correct answer is (D). $29.62 × 5 = $148.10

22. The correct answer is (A).

$$
\begin{array}{r}
\text{3 days 10 hrs. 40 min.} \\
+ \qquad \text{10 hrs. 2 min.} \\
\hline
\text{3 days 20 hrs. 42 min.}
\end{array}
$$

23. The correct answer is (C). $15 + $3.95 = $18.95; $20.00 − $18.95 = $1.05

24. The correct answer is (B). 250 × .08 = $20.00; 250 × .07 = $17.50; 500 erasers cost $37.50; $50.00 − $37.50 = $12.50. Let x = additional erasers purchased.

$.05x = 12.50; x = \dfrac{12.50}{.05} = 250; 500 + 250 = 750$ erasers.

25. The correct answer is (B).

$1 : 200 = x : 375; 200x = 375; x = 375 \div 200 = 1.875 = 1\dfrac{7}{8}$ inches.

26. The correct answer is (D). 65¢ − 5¢ for the first day = 60¢ for the other days. 60¢ ÷ 2¢ = 30 other days. The book was 31 days overdue.

27. The correct answer is (C).

$4 \text{ feet} = 48 \text{ inches}; 48 \div \dfrac{3}{4} = \dfrac{\overset{16}{\cancel{48}}}{1} \times \dfrac{4}{\underset{1}{\cancel{3}}} = 64$ magazines.

28. The correct answer is (B). 10 pounds = 2 × 5 pounds, so the cost of 10 pounds is 2 times the cost of 5 pounds.

29. The correct answer is (D). Don drove 50 miles × 2 hours = 100 miles. Frank drove 40 miles × 2 hours = 80 miles. Since they drove in opposite directions, add the two distances to learn that they were 180 miles apart.

30. The correct answer is (B). $29.50 × 20% = $29.50 × .20 = $5.90 saved.

PART 3: WORD KNOWLEDGE
Key Answers

1. The correct answer is (D).
2. The correct answer is (B).
3. The correct answer is (C).
4. The correct answer is (D).
5. The correct answer is (A).
6. The correct answer is (D).
7. The correct answer is (B).
8. The correct answer is (C).
9. The correct answer is (A).
10. The correct answer is (D).
11. The correct answer is (B).
12. The correct answer is (B).
13. The correct answer is (D).
14. The correct answer is (C).
15. The correct answer is (A).
16. The correct answer is (A).
17. The correct answer is (D).
18. The correct answer is (B).
19. The correct answer is (A).
20. The correct answer is (D).
21. The correct answer is (D).
22. The correct answer is (C).
23. The correct answer is (C).
24. The correct answer is (C).
25. The correct answer is (B).
26. The correct answer is (A).
27. The correct answer is (B).
28. The correct answer is (C).
29. The correct answer is (D).
30. The correct answer is (C).
31. The correct answer is (B).
32. The correct answer is (A).
33. The correct answer is (D).
34. The correct answer is (C).
35. The correct answer is (C).

Items Answered Incorrectly: __; __; __; __; __; __; __; __.
Items Unsure Of: __; __; __; __; __; __; __; __.

**TOTAL NUMBER
ANSWERED CORRECTLY:** _____

Rationale

1. The correct answer is (D). *Superiority* is *excellence*.

2. The correct answer is (B). *Absurd* means irrational, unreasonable, or *foolish*.

3. The correct answer is (C). *Inflammable* means easily inflamed, hence *explosive*.

4. The correct answer is (D). *Conscious* means mentally awake or *aware*.

5. The correct answer is (A). To *exhibit* means to show publicly or to *display*. Often one exhibits goods that one hopes to subsequently trade or sell.

6. The correct answer is (D). To *assume* is to take for granted or to *suppose*.

7. The correct answer is (B). That which is *counterfeit* is an imitation made with intent to defraud, hence *false*.

8. The correct answer is (C). That which is done *expertly* is done *skillfully*. It might also be done quickly, but not necessarily so.

9. The correct answer is (A). *Marshy* means boggy or *swampy*.

10. The correct answer is (D). *Allegiance* means devotion or *loyalty*.

11. The correct answer is (B). To *yearn* is to have a great desire for or to be filled with *longing*.

12. The correct answer is (B). The *summit* is the *top*.

13. The correct answer is (D). To *heed* is to pay attention to or to *take notice of*.

14. The correct answer is (C). *Vigorously* means forcefully and *energetically*.

15. The correct answer is (A). To *imitate* is to *copy*.

16. The correct answer is (A). *Severity* means seriousness, extreme strictness, or *harshness*. It does not necessarily imply unfairness.

17. The correct answer is (D). That which is *incredible* is too improbable to believe.

18. The correct answer is (B). *Leisure* is freedom from pressure. A leisurely trip is an *unhurried* one.

19. The correct answer is (A). *Gratitude* is the state of being grateful or *thankfulness*.

20. The correct answer is (D). *Familiar* means *well-known*. (Think of the word *family*.)

21. The correct answer is (D). An *acute* pain may well be alarming, but what makes it acute is its *sharpness*.

22. The correct answer is (C). To be *bewildered* is to be confused or *puzzled*.

23. The correct answer is (C). The *conclusion* is the *end*.

24. The correct answer is (C). An *aroma* is a pleasing smell or *fragrance*.

25. The correct answer is (B). The prefix *non* means not. That which is not essential is *unnecessary*.

26. The correct answer is (A). To *amplify* is to enlarge by adding illustrations or details—in short, to *expand*.

27. The correct answer is (B). *Intact* means unimpaired, whole, or *undamaged*.

28. The correct answer is (C). *Potent* means powerful or *effective*. The word that means drinkable is "potable."

29. The correct answer is (D). To *terminate* is to *end*. The end of a train line is the terminus or terminal.

30. The correct answer is (C). *Notorious* means *well-known*, generally in an unfavorable sense.

31. The correct answer is (B). *Fatal* means causing death or *deadly*.

32. The correct answer is (A). *Indigent* means needy or *poor*. Indigent people might be lazy or homeless, but their indigence is their poverty.

33. The correct answer is (D). The *technique* is the *method* by which something is done.

34. The correct answer is (C). One's *vocation* is one's *occupation* or calling.

35. The correct answer is (C). That which is *mature* is fully aged or *ripe*.

PART 4: PARAGRAPH COMPREHENSION

Key Answers

1. The correct answer is (A).
2. The correct answer is (A).
3. The correct answer is (D).
4. The correct answer is (C).
5. The correct answer is (C).
6. The correct answer is (A).
7. The correct answer is (D).
8. The correct answer is (D).
9. The correct answer is (B).
10. The correct answer is (C).
11. The correct answer is (A).
12. The correct answer is (A).
13. The correct answer is (B).
14. The correct answer is (B).
15. The correct answer is (C).

Items Answered Incorrectly: __; __; __; __; __; __; __; __.
Items Unsure Of: __; __; __; __; __; __; __; __.

**TOTAL NUMBER
ANSWERED CORRECTLY:** _____

Rationale

1. The correct answer is (A). The passage states that physical examinations are intended to increase efficiency and production and that they do accomplish these ends.

2. The correct answer is (A). The passage states that traffic violations are usually the result of illegal and dangerous driving behavior.

3. The correct answer is (D). Complaints frequently bring into the open conditions and faults in operation and service that should be corrected.

4. The correct answer is (C). The vaulter may attempt to jump any height above the minimum, which is set by the judge.

5. The correct answer is (C). The last sentence in the passage states that the real danger is in a large leak that can cause an explosion.

6. The correct answer is (A). The time it takes the earth to go around the sun is $365\frac{1}{4}$ days rather than 365 days. Leap years correct for this discrepancy by adding an extra day once every four years.

7. The correct answer is (D). The point of the passage is that a business should be prepared to fill unexpected vacancies with pretrained staff members.

8. The correct answer is (D). See the first sentence in the reading passage.

9. The correct answer is (B). See the first sentence in the reading passage.

10. The correct answer is (C). Phosphorus catches fire easily. Therefore, it has a low kindling temperature.

11. The correct answer is (A). See the last sentence in the reading passage.

12. The correct answer is (A). From the second sentence in the reading passage, it may be deduced that it is difficult to suppress racketeering because so many people want services that are not obtainable through legitimate sources.

13. The correct answer is (B). See the second paragraph in the reading passage.

14. The correct answer is (B). See the last paragraph in the reading passage.

15. The correct answer is (C). A meter is one ten-millionth of the distance from the Equator to the North Pole. One ten-millionth $= \frac{1}{10,000,000}$

PART 5: MATHEMATICS KNOWLEDGE
Key Answers

1. The correct answer is (B).
2. The correct answer is (D).
3. The correct answer is (B).
4. The correct answer is (A).
5. The correct answer is (A).
6. The correct answer is (A).
7. The correct answer is (D).
8. The correct answer is (C).
9. The correct answer is (D).
10. The correct answer is (B).
11. The correct answer is (D).
12. The correct answer is (C).
13. The correct answer is (B).

14. The correct answer is (C).
15. The correct answer is (A).
16. The correct answer is (A).
17. The correct answer is (D).
18. The correct answer is (A).
19. The correct answer is (C).
20. The correct answer is (C).
21. The correct answer is (A).
22. The correct answer is (B).
23. The correct answer is (D).
24. The correct answer is (D).
25. The correct answer is (C).

Items Answered Incorrectly: __; __; __; __; __; __; __; __.

Items Unsure Of: __; __; __; __; __; __; __; __.

**TOTAL NUMBER
ANSWERED CORRECTLY:** _____

Rationale

1. The correct answer is (B). Add:

$$6a - 4b + 3c$$
$$4a + 9b - 5c$$
$$\overline{10a + 5b - 2c}$$

2. The correct answer is (D).

$$\frac{1}{2} \text{ of } x = 66$$
$$x = 66 \times 2$$
$$x = 132$$

3. The correct answer is (B).

$$3x = -5$$
$$x = \frac{-5}{3}$$
$$x = -\frac{5}{3}$$

4. The correct answer is (A). The first step to finding the square root of a number is to pair the digits to each side of the decimal point. If necessary, place 0 to the left of the first digit to form a pair and then solve with a modified form of long division. $\sqrt{05\ 90\ 43}$

As the square root of 05 is between 2 and 3, place 2 above the first pair. The first digit of the square root of 59043 is 2.

5. The correct answer is (A).

Area of rectangle = $9 \times 4 = 36$. Area of square = 36; each side = 6; perimeter of square = $6 + 6 + 6 + 6 = 24$.

6. The correct answer is (A).

$$\frac{27}{8} \times \frac{24}{9} \div \frac{3}{2} = \frac{\overset{3}{\cancel{27}}}{\underset{1}{\cancel{8}}} \times \frac{\overset{\cancel{24}}{}}{\underset{1}{\cancel{9}}} \times \frac{2}{\underset{1}{\cancel{3}}} = 6$$

7. The correct answer is (D). An equilateral triangle has 3 equal sides. $\frac{6n-12}{3} = 2n - 4$

8. The correct answer is (C). Only the star is a closed plane figure bounded by straight lines.

9. The correct answer is (D). Sum of angles of a hexagon = $180°(6 - 2) = 180° \times 4 = 720°$.

10. The correct answer is (B). Area of rectangle = 12′ × 18′ = 4 yards × 6 yards = 24 square yards.

11. The correct answer is (D).

$$d = rt; A = r + \frac{d}{t}; A = r + \frac{rt}{t}; A = r + r; A = 2r.$$

12. The correct answer is (C). To find what percent one number is of another number, create a fraction by putting the part over the whole. Then convert to a decimal by dividing the numerator by the denominator and change to a percent by multiplying by 100.

$$\frac{R}{1,000} = .001R = .1R\%$$

13. The correct answer is (B). If radius = 35 miles, diameter = 70 miles.

$$\text{Circumference} = \pi d = \frac{22}{7} \times 70 = 220 \text{ miles}$$

14. The correct answer is (C). $3! = 3 \times 2 \times 1 = 6$

15. The correct answer is (A).

$$a = 2b; 2a = 4b = 6c; a = \frac{6c}{2} = 3c$$

16. The correct answer is (A).

$$\frac{2x}{7} = 2x^2; 14x^2 = 2x; \frac{14x^2}{2x} = 1; 7x = 1; x = \frac{1}{7}$$

17. The correct answer is (D).

$$A^2 = \frac{B^2}{C+D}; A^2(C+D) = B^2; C+D = \frac{B^2}{A^2}; C = \frac{B^2}{A^2} - D$$

18. The correct answer is (A). $-1(3 - 2) = -3 + 2$

19. The correct answer is (C). Reciprocal of $5 = \frac{1}{5} = .20 = 0.2$

20. The correct answer is (C).

Area $= \pi r^2 = \dfrac{22}{7} \times 7^2 = \dfrac{22}{7} \times 49 = 154$ sq. in.

21. The correct answer is (A).

$5a - 4x - 3y = 5(-2) - 4(-10) - 3(5) = -10 + 40 - 15 = +15$

22. The correct answer is (B). 1 book costs c dollars; m books $= m \times c = mc$.

23. The correct answer is (D). Let $x = $ # of dimes; $16 - x = $ # of quarters.

$.10x + .25(16 - x) = 2.50;$
$10x + 25(16 - x) = 250;$
$10x + 400 - 25x = 250;$
$-15x = -150;$
$x = 10$

24. The correct answer is (D).

$\dfrac{x}{2} - \dfrac{x}{5} = 3;\ \dfrac{5x}{10} - \dfrac{2x}{10} = 3;\ \dfrac{3x}{10} = 3;\ 3x = 30;\ x = 10$

25. The correct answer is (C). $C = \pi d = \pi 2r$; if radius is increased by 3, $C = \pi 2(r + 3);\ C = \pi 2r + 6\pi.$

PART 6: ELECTRONICS INFORMATION
Key Answers

1. The correct answer is (D).
2. The correct answer is (C).
3. The correct answer is (C).
4. The correct answer is (D).
5. The correct answer is (A).
6. The correct answer is (D).
7. The correct answer is (C).
8. The correct answer is (D).
9. The correct answer is (D).
10. The correct answer is (C).
11. The correct answer is (A).
12. The correct answer is (C).
13. The correct answer is (C).
14. The correct answer is (A).
15. The correct answer is (B).
16. The correct answer is (D).
17. The correct answer is (C).
18. The correct answer is (B).
19. The correct answer is (D).
20. The correct answer is (B).

Items Answered Incorrectly: __; __; __; __; __; __; __; __.
Items Unsure Of: __; __; __; __; __; __; __; __.

**TOTAL NUMBER
ANSWERED CORRECTLY:** _____

Rationale

1. The correct answer is (D). Soft iron has the property of being easily magnetized or demagnetized. When the current is turned on in an electromagnet, it becomes magnetized. When the current is turned off, the iron loses its magnetism.

2. The correct answer is (C). This is a general safety question. Never assume that there is no current in a piece of electrical equipment; the results could be shocking.

3. The correct answer is (C). Using algebraic rules, Ohm's Law can be written in three equivalent ways: $R = \dfrac{V}{I}; I = \dfrac{V}{R}; V = IR$

4. The correct answer is (D). A rectifier, or diode, is a device that changes AC to DC.

5. The correct answer is (A). When a kilowatt-hour meter is read, the number that comes just before the indicator is the number that is important. The answer would then be 9672 KwHtt.

6. The correct answer is (D). Converters change DC to AC. Rectifiers change AC to DC. Contractors are remote controlled switches frequently used as part of elevator controls. Transformers change voltages in AC circuits in accordance with the ratio of the number of turns in the secondary winding to the number of turns in the primary winding.

7. The correct answer is (C). A relay works on the principle of an energized coil or an electromagnet. Another device that works by an electromagnet is a solenoid.

8. The correct answer is (D). A megger (megohmmeter) is a portable device that produces a voltage. It is used to check for high voltage breakdown of insulation. In this case, it uses a resistance measurement to determine continuity.

9. The correct answer is (D). This is the Wheatstone bridge circuit with balanced loads in each of its arms. As there is no voltage across lamp No. 5, it will not be lit.

10. The correct answer is (C). The farad is a unit of capacitance. Most capacitors used in electronics are small and their capacitance is only a tiny fraction of a farad. One microfarad is one millionth of a farad.

11. The correct answer is (A). Three common elements of the transistor are the emitter, base, and collector.

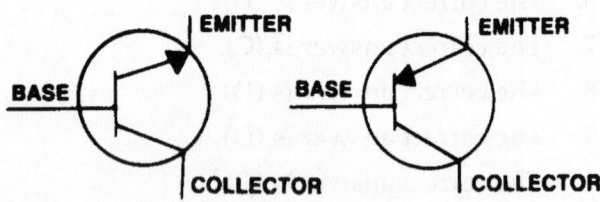

12. The correct answer is (C). This is proper safety procedure and should be followed.

13. The correct answer is (C). The number on the wires is in reverse order to the amount of current that they can carry. No. 12 is the smallest of the wires.

14. The correct answer is (A). The plug can go into the outlet in only one way in a polarized outlet. In the other outlets, the plug can be reversed.

15. The correct answer is (B). Connecting the bell to a 6- or 12-volt source on the secondary of a transformer is done as a safety precaution. Any other way would be dangerous.

16. The correct answer is (D). This is a mechanical or solderless connector. It does away with the need to solder wires and is found in house wiring.

17. The correct answer is (C). Two three-way switches will control a lamp from two different positions.

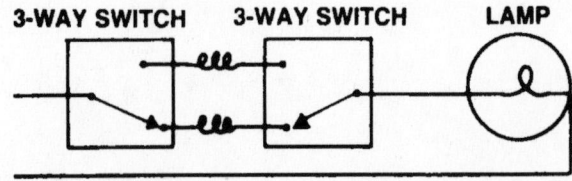

18. The correct answer is (B). A battery is an assembly of chemical cells. The common 9-volt battery found in transistor radios consists of six 1.5-volt cells connected in series to produce a total of six times 1.5 volts—or 9 volts.

19. The correct answer is (D). The third prong in the plug is the grounding wire.

20. The correct answer is (B). A compound motor has two sets of field coils. One is connected in series with the armature. The other is the shunt. It is connected in parallel across the armature.

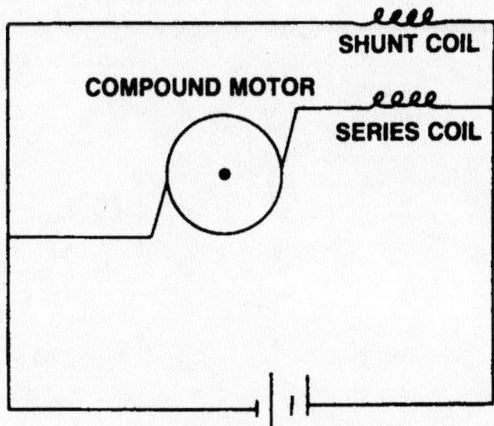

PART XI

United States Navy and Marine Corps Aviation Selection Test Battery

Specimen Subtests

Math/Verbal Test (MVT)

Mechanical Comprehension Test (MCT)

A specimen answer sheet for the Navy and the Coast Guard commissioning programs appears on page 373 and should be used in answering the questions on the Math/Verbal Test and the Mechanical Comprehension Test of the Navy and Marine Corps Aviation Selection Test Battery. In addition, this section contains key answers for determining your scores on these tests and the rationale or explanation for each key answer.

Remove (cut out) the specimen answer sheet appearing on page 373 to record your answers to the test questions. The specimen Navy and Marine Corps Aviation Selection Test Battery is similar in format and content to the actual Navy and Marine Corps Aviation Selection Test Battery. (The Math/Verbal Test was previously known as the Academic Qualifications Test.) Take these tests under real test conditions. Time each test carefully.

Use the key answers to obtain your test scores and to evaluate your performance on each test. Record the number of items you answered correctly, as well as the number of each question you answered incorrectly or wish to review, in the space provided below the key answers for each test.

Be certain to review carefully and understand the explanations for the answers to all questions you answered incorrectly and for each of the questions that you answered correctly but are unsure of. This is absolutely essential in order to acquire the knowledge and expertise necessary to obtain the maximum score possible on the tests of the real Navy and Marine Corps Aviation Selection Test Battery.

ANSWER SHEET
for
NAVY and MARINE CORPS
AVIATION SELECTION TEST BATTERY

SCHEMATIC SAMPLE

STATUS

- ○ Civilian
- ○ Officer, Navy
- ○ Officer, Marine Corps
- ○ Officer, Coast Guard
- ○ Enlisted, Navy
- ○ Enlisted, Marine Corps
- ○ Enlisted, Coast Guard
- ○ Officer Candidate—ROTC
- ○ Naval Academy
- ○ Other

NAME _____
        Last   First   M.I.

TEST
DATE ____/____/____
     Month   Day   Year

INSTALLATION OR
PLACE OF TESTING _____

EDUCATION LEVEL	RACE/ETHNIC GROUP	SEX
○ High School Graduate	○ American Indian	○ Male
○ College Freshman	○ Hispanic	○ Female
○ College Sophomore	○ Asian	
○ College Junior	○ Black	
○ College Senior	○ White	
○ College Graduate	○ Other	
○ Graduate Student		
○ Other		

SOCIAL SECURITY NUMBER

DATE OF BIRTH — MO. DAY YR.

(Bubble grids 0–9 for Social Security Number and Date of Birth)

ACADEMIC QUALIFICATION TEST

1. Ⓐ Ⓑ Ⓒ Ⓓ Ⓔ
2. Ⓐ Ⓑ Ⓒ Ⓓ Ⓔ
3. Ⓐ Ⓑ Ⓒ Ⓓ Ⓔ
4. Ⓐ Ⓑ Ⓒ Ⓓ Ⓔ
5. Ⓐ Ⓑ Ⓒ Ⓓ Ⓔ

6. Ⓐ Ⓑ Ⓒ Ⓓ Ⓔ
7. Ⓐ Ⓑ Ⓒ Ⓓ Ⓔ
8. Ⓐ Ⓑ Ⓒ Ⓓ Ⓔ
9. Ⓐ Ⓑ Ⓒ Ⓓ Ⓔ
10. Ⓐ Ⓑ Ⓒ Ⓓ Ⓔ

11. Ⓐ Ⓑ Ⓒ Ⓓ Ⓔ
12. Ⓐ Ⓑ Ⓒ Ⓓ Ⓔ
13. Ⓐ Ⓑ Ⓒ Ⓓ Ⓔ
14. Ⓐ Ⓑ Ⓒ Ⓓ Ⓔ
15. Ⓐ Ⓑ Ⓒ Ⓓ Ⓔ

16. Ⓐ Ⓑ Ⓒ Ⓓ Ⓔ
17. Ⓐ Ⓑ Ⓒ Ⓓ Ⓔ
18. Ⓐ Ⓑ Ⓒ Ⓓ Ⓔ
19. Ⓐ Ⓑ Ⓒ Ⓓ Ⓔ
20. Ⓐ Ⓑ Ⓒ Ⓓ Ⓔ

21. Ⓐ Ⓑ Ⓒ Ⓓ
22. Ⓐ Ⓑ Ⓒ Ⓓ
23. Ⓐ Ⓑ Ⓒ Ⓓ
24. Ⓐ Ⓑ Ⓒ Ⓓ
25. Ⓐ Ⓑ Ⓒ Ⓓ

26. Ⓐ Ⓑ Ⓒ Ⓓ
27. Ⓐ Ⓑ Ⓒ Ⓓ
28. Ⓐ Ⓑ Ⓒ Ⓓ
29. Ⓐ Ⓑ Ⓒ Ⓓ
30. Ⓐ Ⓑ Ⓒ Ⓓ
31. Ⓐ Ⓑ Ⓒ Ⓓ

32. Ⓐ Ⓑ Ⓒ Ⓓ
33. Ⓐ Ⓑ Ⓒ Ⓓ
34. Ⓐ Ⓑ Ⓒ Ⓓ
35. Ⓐ Ⓑ Ⓒ Ⓓ
36. Ⓐ Ⓑ Ⓒ Ⓓ
37. Ⓐ Ⓑ Ⓒ Ⓓ

MECHANICAL COMPREHENSION TEST

1. Ⓐ Ⓑ Ⓒ
2. Ⓐ Ⓑ Ⓒ
3. Ⓐ Ⓑ Ⓒ
4. Ⓐ Ⓑ Ⓒ

5. Ⓐ Ⓑ Ⓒ
6. Ⓐ Ⓑ Ⓒ
7. Ⓐ Ⓑ Ⓒ
8. Ⓐ Ⓑ Ⓒ

9. Ⓐ Ⓑ Ⓒ
10. Ⓐ Ⓑ Ⓒ
11. Ⓐ Ⓑ Ⓒ
12. Ⓐ Ⓑ Ⓒ

13. Ⓐ Ⓑ Ⓒ
14. Ⓐ Ⓑ Ⓒ
15. Ⓐ Ⓑ Ⓒ
16. Ⓐ Ⓑ Ⓒ

17. Ⓐ Ⓑ Ⓒ
18. Ⓐ Ⓑ Ⓒ
19. Ⓐ Ⓑ Ⓒ
20. Ⓐ Ⓑ Ⓒ

21. Ⓐ Ⓑ Ⓒ
22. Ⓐ Ⓑ Ⓒ
23. Ⓐ Ⓑ Ⓒ
24. Ⓐ Ⓑ Ⓒ

25. Ⓐ Ⓑ Ⓒ
26. Ⓐ Ⓑ Ⓒ
27. Ⓐ Ⓑ Ⓒ
28. Ⓐ Ⓑ Ⓒ

29. Ⓐ Ⓑ Ⓒ
30. Ⓐ Ⓑ Ⓒ

TEST 1: MATH/VERBAL TEST

TIME: 35 Minutes—37 Questions

Questions 1–20 make up the math section of the test. Each of the math questions is followed by five possible answers. Decide which one of the five options is the correct answer. Then mark the space on your answer sheet that has the same number and letter as your choice.

1. A 6-foot-tall farmer wants to determine the height of his barn. He notices that his shadow is 10 feet long and that his barn casts a shadow 75 feet long. How high is the barn?

   (A) 30 feet
   (B) 35 feet
   (C) 40 feet
   (D) 45 feet
   (E) 50 feet

2. What is the square root of 16 raised to the fourth power?

   (A) 16
   (B) 64
   (C) 128
   (D) 256
   (E) 1024

3. If the sum of the edges of a cube is 48 inches, the volume of the cube is

   (A) 4 cubic inches.
   (B) 8 cubic inches.
   (C) 16 cubic inches.
   (D) 64 cubic inches.
   (E) 96 cubic inches.

4. If the tax rate is $3\frac{1}{2}\%$ and the amount to be raised is $6440, what is the base?

   (A) $180,000
   (B) $181,000
   (C) $182,000
   (D) $183,000
   (E) $184,000

5. Each corridor contains 8 to 10 classrooms and each classroom contains 20 to 24 students. If all classrooms are occupied, what is the minimum number of students on one corridor at a given time?

   (A) 160
   (B) 170
   (C) 180
   (D) 190
   (E) 200

6. At 8:00 a.m., two trains started out from the same station. One traveled north at the rate of 60 mph; the other traveled south at the rate of 50 mph. At what time were the trains 550 miles apart?

   (A) Noon
   (B) 12:30 p.m.
   (C) 1:00 p.m.
   (D) 1:30 p.m.
   (E) 2:00 p.m.

7. How much pure acid must be added to 12 ounces of a 40% acid solution in order to produce a 60% acid solution?

   (A) 5 ounces
   (B) 6 ounces
   (C) 7 ounces
   (D) 8 ounces
   (E) 9 ounces

8. If x varies directly as y^2 and if $x = 9$ when $y = 2$, what is the value of x when $y = 8$?

   (A) 32
   (B) 130
   (C) 144
   (D) 168
   (E) 966

9. The hour hand of a clock is 3 feet long. How many feet does the tip of this hand move between 1:00 P.M. and 5:00 P.M.?

   (A) 2π
   (B) 4π
   (C) 6π
   (D) 8π
   (E) 10π

10. Find the second of three consecutive integers if the sum of the first and third is 26.

    (A) 9
    (B) 10
    (C) 11
    (D) 12
    (E) 13

11. Find the area of a square circumscribed about a circle whose radius is 10.

    (A) $31\frac{3}{7}$

    (B) $62\frac{6}{7}$

    (C) 100
    (D) 400
    (E) 440

12. An island is defended by a battery of coastal guns placed at the easternmost point of the island and having a maximum range of 10 miles. A ship, sailing due north at 24 mph along a course that will bring it within 8 miles of these guns, is approaching the position where it will be 10 miles from these guns. Assuming that the ship will maintain a straight course and the same speed, for approximately how long will the ship be within range of the coastal guns?

    (A) 15 minutes
    (B) 20 minutes
    (C) 25 minutes
    (D) 30 minutes
    (E) 35 minutes

13. A team won 25 games in a 40-game season. Find the ratio of games won to games lost.

    (A) $3:5$
    (B) $5:3$
    (C) $3:8$
    (D) $8:3$
    (E) $5:8$

14. If the entrance requirement of a certain college is 82, what mark must a student have in Geometry (weight 2) to be able to enter if his other marks are English 88 (weight 3), Spanish 78 (weight 2), and History 80 (weight 2)?

    (A) 83
    (B) 82
    (C) 81
    (D) 80
    (E) 79

15. Two planes started at the same time from the same airport and flew in opposite directions. One flew 80 mph faster than the other. In four hours they were 2600 miles apart. What was the speed of the slower plane?

    (A) 285 mph
    (B) 305 mph
    (C) 325 mph
    (D) 345 mph
    (E) 365 mph

16. One recruit can complete a certain assignment in 40 minutes; another recruit can complete the same assignment in one hour. How long would it take to complete the assignment if the two recruits worked together?

    (A) 12 minutes
    (B) 18 minutes
    (C) 24 minutes
    (D) 30 minutes
    (E) 36 minutes

17. If $(x - y)^2 = 40$ and $x^2 + y^2 = 60$, then $xy =$

    (A) 40
    (B) 20
    (C) 12
    (D) 10
    (E) −20

18. If a triangle of base 6 has the same area as a circle of radius 6, what is the altitude of the triangle?

(A) 6π

(B) 8π

(C) 10π

(D) 12π

(E) 20π

19. In the following series of numbers arranged in a logical order, ascertain the pattern or rule for the arrangement and then select the appropriate option to complete the series 5 3 9 7 21 19 ___

(A) 41

(B) 45

(C) 49

(D) 53

(E) 57

20. In the figure shown below, what is the measure of angle x?

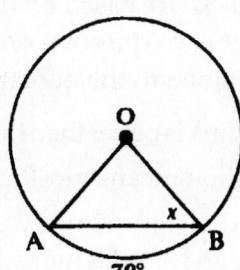

(A) 35°

(B) 45°

(C) 55°

(D) 70°

(E) 110°

The following seventeen questions numbered 21–37 make up the verbal section of the test. Each of the verbal questions is followed by four possible answers. Decide which one of the four options is the correct answer. Then mark the space on your answer sheet that has the same number and letter as your choice.

Questions 21–23 consist of a sentence in which one word or phrase is omitted. For each question, select the lettered option that best completes the thought expressed in the sentence.

21. Although he gave generously to charity, he was _____ with his family and friends.

(A) liberal

(B) polite

(C) stingy

(D) unselfish

22. _____ all the casualties sustained in combat, the troops would not surrender.

(A) Because of

(B) In accordance with

(C) In addition to

(D) In spite of

23. Cheating in deliveries of fuel oil to consumers can be accomplished by heating the oil to change the _____ of the oil in the tank truck.

(A) grade

(B) temperature

(C) volume

(D) weight

Questions 24–29 consist of quotations that contain one word that is incorrectly used because it is not in keeping with the meaning that the quotation is evidently intended to convey. Determine which word is incorrectly used. Then select from the lettered options the word that, when substituted for the incorrectly used word, would best help to convey the meaning of the quotation.

24. "A bushel of any fruit or vegetable is a standard bushel basket filled level and full; in other words, there is a standard weight for a bushel of any fruit or vegetable."

(A) certain
(B) legal
(C) no
(D) number

25. "Organization and management techniques that facilitate delegation of work should be taught to supervisors to enable them to maintain control while participating in the details of every operation."

(A) coordination
(B) instructing
(C) without
(D) working

26. "No training course can operate to best advantage without job descriptions that indicate training requirements so that those parts of the job requiring the most training can be carefully analyzed before the training course is completed."

(A) improved
(B) least
(C) meet
(D) started

27. "Our ancient ideas concerning the larger aspects of the universe are both more detailed and more consistent than those of former ages."

(A) less
(B) meaningful
(C) modern
(D) smaller

28. "The selection of managers on the basis of technical knowledge alone seems to recognize that the essential characteristic of management is getting things done through others, thereby demanding ability and skills that are essential in coordinating the activities of subordinates."

(A) executives
(B) fails
(C) improving
(D) organization

29. "It is generally accepted that when supervisors are at least as well informed about the work of their units as are their subordinates, they will fail to win the approval that is essential to them if they are to supervise their units effectively."

(A) attention
(B) poorly
(C) preferable
(D) unless

Questions 30–37 are based on different reading passages. Answer each question on the basis of the information contained in the quotation.

30. "The palest ink is better than the best memory."

This quotation means most nearly that

(A) a good memory is very useful.
(B) a written record is more dependable than a good memory.
(C) records are worth more if they are made by a person with a good memory.
(D) records must never be made in pencil.

31. "Civilization started to move ahead more rapidly when humankind freed itself from restrictions on the search for truth."

This quotation means most nearly that the progress of civilization

(A) came as a result of people's dislike for obstacles.
(B) did not begin until restrictions on learning were removed.
(C) has been aided by people's efforts to find the truth.
(D) is based on continually increasing efforts.

32. "It is recommended that the net be held by not more than 14 persons nor less than 10 persons, although under certain conditions it may become necessary to use fewer persons."

According to the above paragraph, it is

(A) best to use between 10 and 14 persons on the net.
(B) better to use 10 persons on the net rather than 14.
(C) impossible to use a net unless at least 10 persons are available to hold it.
(D) sometimes advisable to use more than 14 persons on the net.

33. "In examining the scene of a homicide, one should not only look for the usual, standard traces—fingerprints, footprints, etc.—but also take notice of details that at first glance may not seem to have any connection with the crime."

One may conclude from the above statement that

(A) one cannot tell in advance what will be important.
(B) only the usual, standard traces are important.
(C) sometimes one should not look for footprints.
(D) standard traces are not generally available.

34. "Fires cannot be fought entirely by rules or set procedures, and successful firefighters are those who study past fires and apply what they learn to their future fire fighting actions."

According to the above quotation,

(A) fires are successfully fought only through experience, but rules and procedures are valuable if based on a study of past fires.
(B) little can be learned from studying rules and procedures.
(C) studying past fires helps solve problems that may be met in future fires.
(D) the most successful firefighter is the one with the most fire-fighting experience.

35. "In order to promote efficiency and economy, it is advisable to systematize and standardize procedures and relationships insofar as this can be done, avoiding, however, the extreme routine that does not recognize individuality."

According to this quotation,

(A) a routine that does not allow some expression of individuality is, in the final analysis, inefficient.
(B) individuality is not recognized when procedures and relationships are systematized and standardized.
(C) the crushing of initiative invariably follows over-systemization.
(D) the proper recognition of individuality is best accomplished by systematization and standardization of procedures and relationships.

36. "The protection of life and property against anti-social individuals within the country and enemies from without is generally recognized to be the most fundamental activity of government."

Of the following, the one that is not an aspect of the function of government as described above is

(A) fining a motorist who failed to stop at a red traffic light.
(B) prosecuting a drug peddler who has been selling dope to school children.
(C) providing postal service.
(D) sending a delegation to a foreign country to participate in a disarmament conference.

37. "In almost every community, fortunately, there are certain people known to be public spirited; others, however, may be selfish and act only as their private interests seem to require."

This quotation means most nearly that those citizens who disregard others are

(A) community minded.
(B) fortunate.
(C) not public spirited.
(D) unknown.

END OF MATH/VERBAL TEST

STOP! DO NOT TURN THIS PAGE UNTIL TOLD TO DO SO. IF YOU FINISH BEFORE THE TIME IS UP, YOU MAY CHECK OVER YOUR WORK ON THIS PART ONLY.

TEST 2: MECHANICAL COMPREHENSION TEST

TIME: 15 Minutes—30 Questions

Questions 1–30 are designed to measure your ability to reason with mechanical terms. Each diagram is followed by a question or an incomplete statement. Study the diagram carefully and select the choice that best answers the question or completes the statement. Then mark the space on your answer sheet that has the same number and letter as your choice.

1.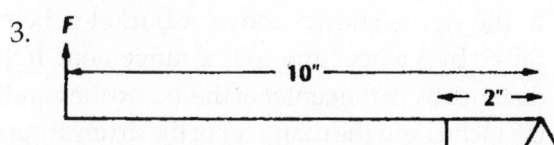

Shown above is a first-class lever. A common example of a first-class lever is

(A) a seesaw.
(B) a wheelbarrow.
(C) tongs.

2.

The force F required to balance the weight of 60 pounds on the lever, shown in the diagram above, is most nearly

(A) 210 lbs.
(B) 240 lbs.
(C) 672 lbs.

3.

The mechanical advantage of the lever shown in the diagram above is

(A) 4
(B) 5
(C) 8

4.

What effort must be exerted to the handles of the wheelbarrow shown above carrying a load of 200 pounds (neglect the weight of the wheelbarrow in your computation)?

(A) 40 lbs.
(B) 50 lbs.
(C) 65 lbs.

5.

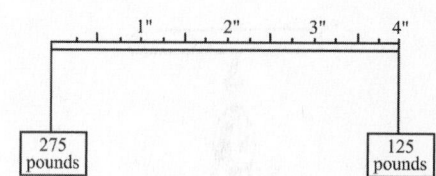

The bar above, which is exactly 4 inches in length, has a 275-pound weight on one end and a 125-pound weight on the opposite end.

For the bar to balance, the distance from the 275-pound weight to the fulcrum point should be (neglect the weight of the bar in your computation)

(A) $1\frac{1}{4}$ inches
(B) 1 inch
(C) $\frac{3}{4}$ inch

6.

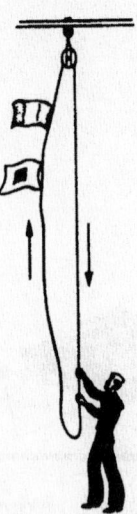

Neglecting friction, what is the mechanical advantage in using a single fixed pulley as shown above?

(A) 1
(B) 2
(C) 3

7.

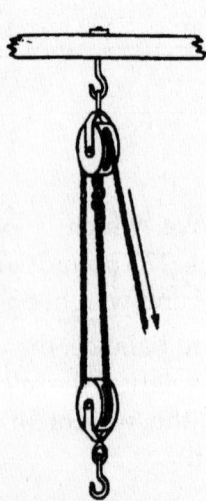

In the figure shown above, the pulley system consists of a fixed block and a movable block. Neglecting friction and the weight of the pulley system, what effort would be needed to lift a 100-pound weight?

(A) 100 pounds
(B) 75 pounds
(C) 50 pounds

8.

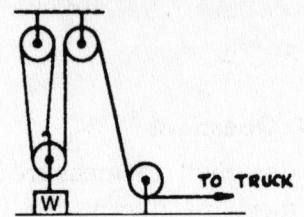

The weight W is to be raised as shown in the figure above by attaching the pull rope to the truck. If the weight is to be raised 8 feet, the truck will have to move

(A) 16 feet.
(B) 24 feet.
(C) 32 feet.

9.

In the figure shown above, the serviceperson is using a plank to roll a 300-pound barrel up to the bed of the truck. The force that must be applied is most nearly

(A) 200 pounds.
(B) 150 pounds.
(C) 100 pounds.

10.

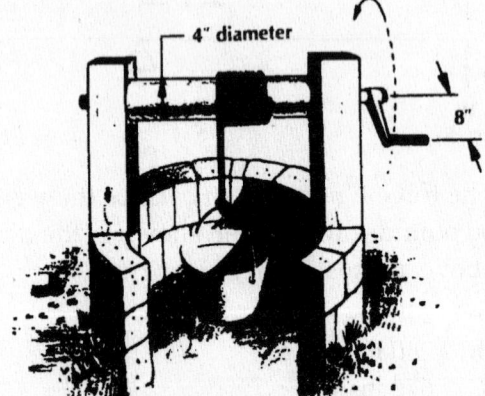

In the figure shown above, a bucket is being raised by a wheel-and-axle arrangement. If the distance from the center of the axle to the handle is 8 inches and the diameter of the drum around which the rope is wound is 4 inches, the theoretical mechanical advantage is

(A) 2
(B) 4
(C) 8

11.

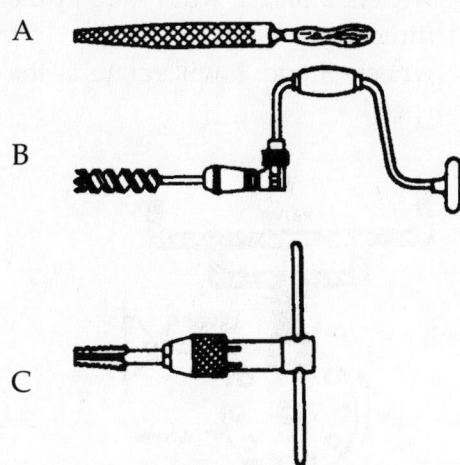

A

B

C

To make a $\frac{1}{2}$" hole in a block of wood, use tool

(A) A
(B) B
(C) C

12.

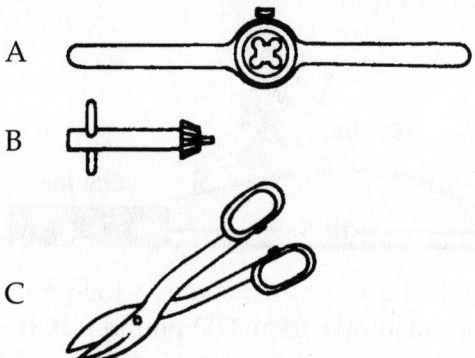

A

B

C

To cut a thread on a $\frac{1}{2}$" brass rod, use tool

(A) A
(B) B
(C) C

13.

The number 18 appearing on the tool shown above indicates

(A) depth of opening.
(B) size of opening.
(C) threads per inch.

14.

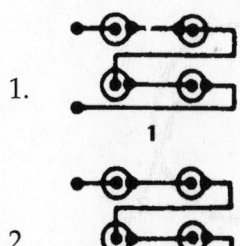

1.

2.

3.

Which one of the $1\frac{1}{2}$-volt dry cell battery connections shown above will deliver 6 volts?

(A) 1
(B) 2
(C) 3

15.

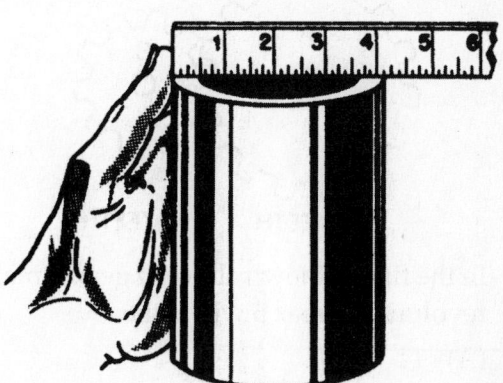

In the figure given above, if the thickness of the wall of the pipe is: $\frac{1}{2}$", the inside diameter of the pipe is

(A) $3\leq$

(B) $3\frac{1}{8}$"

(C) $3\frac{1}{4}$"

16.

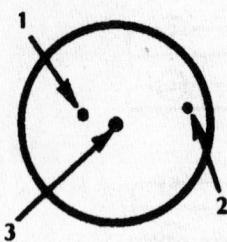

The figure above represents a revolving wheel. The numbers 1 and 2 indicate two fixed points on the wheel. The number 3 indicates the center of the wheel. Of the following, the most accurate statement is that

(A) point 1 makes more revolutions per minute than point 2.

(B) point 2 makes more revolutions per minute than point 1.

(C) points 1 and 2 make the same number of revolutions per minute.

17.

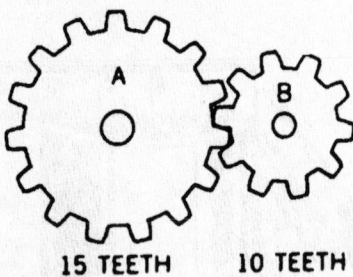

In the figure shown above, if gear A makes 14 revolutions, gear B will make

(A) 14

(B) 17

(C) 21

18.

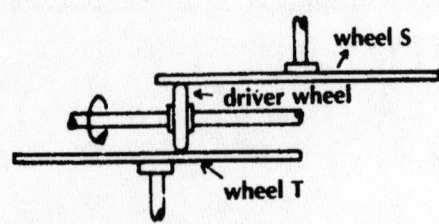

With the wheels in the position shown in the figure above,

(A) wheels S and T will rotate in opposite directions.

(B) wheels S and T will rotate in the same direction.

(C) wheels S and T will rotate at the same speed.

19.

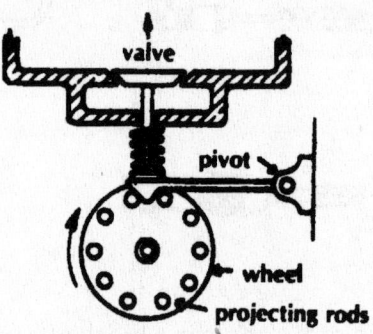

In order to open the valve four times every second, the wheel must rotate at

(A) 12 rpm.

(B) 18 rpm.

(C) 24 rpm.

20.

In the figure shown above, a 160-pound individual jumps off an 800-pound raft to a point in the water 10 feet away. Theoretically, the raft will move

(A) 2 feet in the opposite direction.

(B) 3 feet in the opposite direction.

(C) 4 feet in the opposite direction.

21.

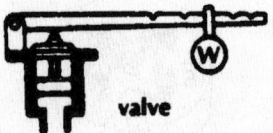

The figure above shows a lever-type safety valve. It will blow off at a lower pressure if weight W is

(A) increased.

(B) moved to the left.

(C) moved to the right.

22.

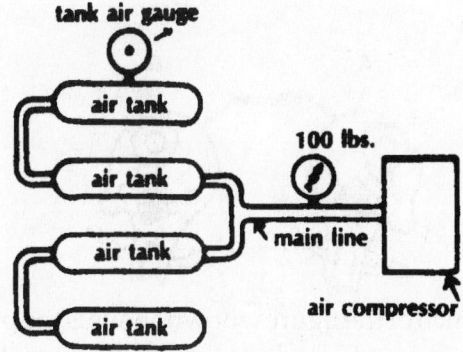

As shown in the figure above, four air reservoirs have been filled with air by the air compressor. If the main line air gauge reads 100 pounds, then the tank air gauge will read

(A) 25 pounds.
(B) 50 pounds.
(C) 100 pounds.

23.

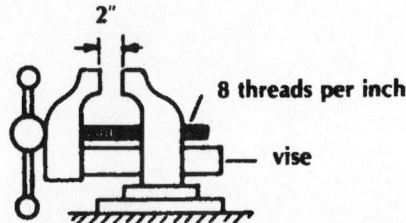

In the figure above, the number of complete turns the vise handle must make to fully close the jaws is

(A) 16
(B) 18
(C) 20

24.

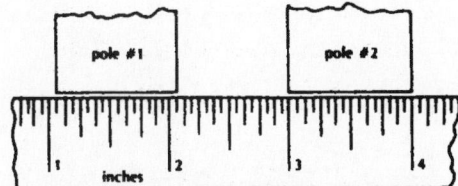

In the figure shown above, the center-to-center distance between the two poles is

(A) $1\frac{3}{4}''$

(B) $1\frac{15}{16}''$

(C) $1\frac{7}{8}''$

25.

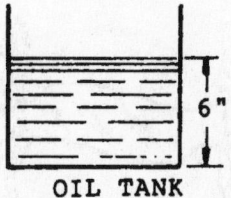

If an 8≤ level indicates 16 quarts of oil in the tank, then the number of quarts of oil to be added to raise the level from 6≤ to 8≤ is

(A) 2 quarts.
(B) 4 quarts.
(C) 6 quarts.

Questions 26 and 27 are based on the figure below showing the four strokes of the piston.

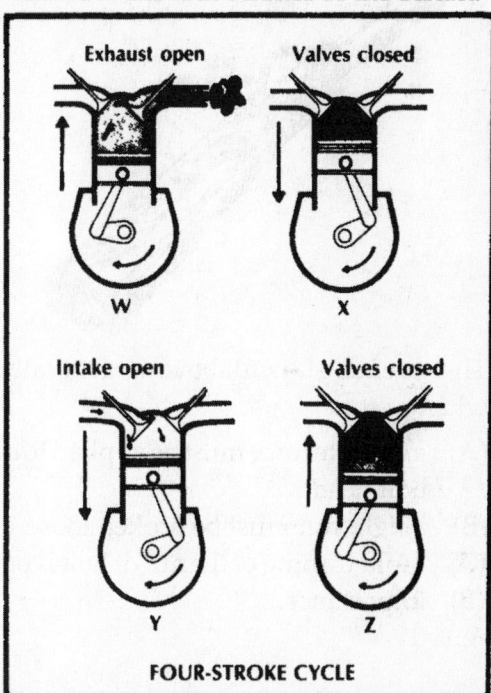

26. Which illustration depicts the compression stroke?

(A) X
(B) Y
(C) Z

27. What is the proper sequence of the four strokes of a piston in a gasoline engine?

(A) W, X, Y, Z
(B) X, Z, Y, W
(C) Y, Z, X, W

28.

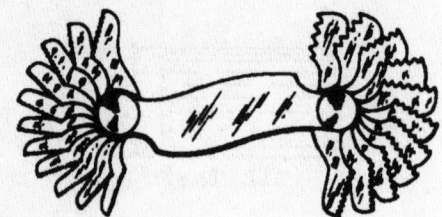

The gauge shown above is a

(A) depth gauge.
(B) feeler gauge.
(C) thread gauge.

29.

The wrench shown above is generally used when

(A) a definite force must be applied to a nut or bolt head.
(B) a tight nut must be broken loose.
(C) rapid turning of the nut or bolt is of prime importance.

30.

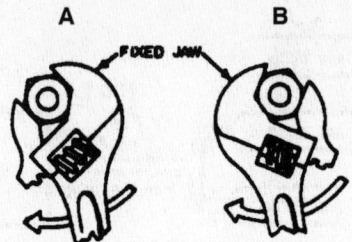

Which of the figures shown above is the proper procedure for pulling adjustable wrenches?

(A) A
(B) B
(C) Both are proper procedures.

END OF MECHANICAL COMPREHENSION TEST

KEY ANSWERS AND RATIONALE FOR NAVY AND MARINE CORPS AVIATION SELECTION TEST BATTERY

Use these key answers to determine the number of questions you answered correctly on each test and to list those questions that you answered incorrectly or which you are unsure of how to arrive at the correct answer.

Be certain to review carefully and understand the rationale for arriving at the correct answer for all items you answered incorrectly, as well as those you answered correctly but are unsure of. This is essential in order to acquire the knowledge and expertise necessary to obtain the maximum score possible on the "real" Navy and Marine Corps Aviation Selection Test Battery.

TEST 1: MATH/VERBAL TEST

Key Answers

1. The correct answer is (D).
2. The correct answer is (D).
3. The correct answer is (D).
4. The correct answer is (E).
5. The correct answer is (A).
6. The correct answer is (C).
7. The correct answer is (B).
8. The correct answer is (C).
9. The correct answer is (A).
10. The correct answer is (E).
11. The correct answer is (D).
12. The correct answer is (D).
13. The correct answer is (B).
14. The correct answer is (E).
15. The correct answer is (A).
16. The correct answer is (C).
17. The correct answer is (D).
18. The correct answer is (D).
19. The correct answer is (E).
20. The correct answer is (C).
21. The correct answer is (C).
22. The correct answer is (D).
23. The correct answer is (C).
24. The correct answer is (C).
25. The correct answer is (C).
26. The correct answer is (D).
27. The correct answer is (C).
28. The correct answer is (B).
29. The correct answer is (D).
30. The correct answer is (B).
31. The correct answer is (C).
32. The correct answer is (A).
33. The correct answer is (A).
34. The correct answer is (C).
35. The correct answer is (A).
36. The correct answer is (C).
37. The correct answer is (C).

Items Answered Incorrectly: __; __; __; __; __; __; __; __.
Items Unsure Of: __; __; __; __; __; __; __; __.

TOTAL NUMBER
ANSWERED CORRECTLY: ____

Rationale

1. The correct answer is (D). $6 : 10 = x : 75; 10x = 450;$
$x = 45$ feet.

2. The correct answer is (D).
The square root of $16 = 4$;
$4^4 = 4 \times 4 \times 4 \times 4 = 16 \times 16 = 256$.

3. The correct answer is (D). A cube has 12 edges.
$\frac{48}{12}'' = 4''; 4'' \times 4'' \times 4'' = 64$ cubic inches.

4. The correct answer is (E). Let $x =$ base.
$x \times .035 = 6440; x = \frac{6440}{.035} = \$184,000$.

5. The correct answer is (A). There is a minimum of 20 students in a minimum of 8 classrooms; $8 \times 20 = 160$.

6. The correct answer is (C). Let $x =$ time. $60x + 50x = 550; 110x = 550; x = 5$. Trains left at 8:00 A.M. Five hours later, it would be 1:00 P.M.

7. The correct answer is (B).

	No. of Ounces	Parts Pure Acid	No. of Ounces of Pure Acid
Pure Acid	x	100	$100x$
40% Acid Solution	12	40	480
60% Acid Solution	$12 + x$	60	$60(12 + x)$

$100x + 480 = 60(12 + x); 100x + 480 = 720 + 60x; 40x = 240; x = 6$.

8. The correct answer is (C).
$9 : 4 = x : 64; 4x = 64 \times 9; x = \frac{64 \times 9}{4} = 144$.

9. The correct answer is (A). The hour hand traces a circle of radius 3. The circumference of that circle $= 2\pi r = 2\pi(3) = 6\pi$. A 4-hour interval is one third of a 12-hour period or one third of a full circle. $\frac{1}{3}$ of $6\pi = 2\pi$.

10. The correct answer is (E). Represent the integers as $x, x + 1$, and $x + 2$. $x + x + 2 = 26; 2x = 26 - 2; 2x = 24; x = 12$; therefore, $x + 1 = 13$.

11. The correct answer is (D).

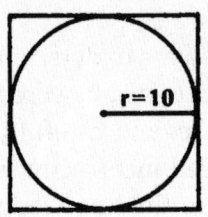

Diameter $= 20 =$ side of square;

Area of square $= 20 \times 20 = 400$.

12. The correct answer is (D).

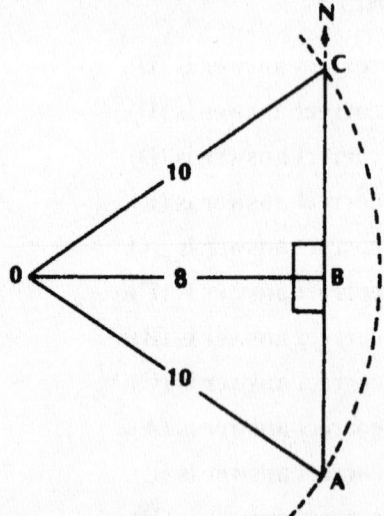

Referring to the sketch above, the ship will be within range of the coastal guns from point A to point C. Triangle OBA and triangle OBC are right triangles with one leg of 8 miles and a hypotenuse of 10 miles.

The time for the ship to travel from point A to point C must be determined. Let $x =$ the distance from A to B; $2x =$ distance from A to C. $8^2 + x^2 = 10^2; 64 + x^2 = 100; x^2 = 36; x = 6$ miles; $2x = 12$ miles.

Let $t =$ time required to travel from A to C (in minutes).
$\frac{24}{60} = \frac{12}{t}; 24t = 720; t = 30$ minutes.

13. The correct answer is (B). 25 games won; 15 games lost: $\frac{25}{15} = \frac{5}{3}$.

14. The correct answer is (E).

Eng	88×3	$= 264$
Span	78×2	$= 156$
Hist	80×2	$= 160$
Geom	$x \times \underline{2}$	$= \underline{2x}$
	9	$= 580 + 2x$

$82 \times 9 = 738$ points needed
$580 + 2x = 738$
$2x = 738 - 580 = 158$
$x = \dfrac{158}{2} = 79$

15. The correct answer is (A). Let x = rate of slower plane; $x + 80$ = rate of faster plane.

$4x + 4(x + 80) = 2600$; $4x + 4x + 320 = 2600$; $8x = 2280$; $x = 285$.

16. The correct answer is (C).

	Recruit 1		Recruit 2	
$\dfrac{\text{Time actually needed}}{\text{Time needed to do job alone}}$	$\dfrac{x}{40}$	$+$	$\dfrac{x}{60}$	$=1$

Multiply by 120 to clear fractions.

$3x + 2x = 120$; $5x = 120$; $x = \dfrac{120}{5} = 24$ minutes

17. The correct answer is (D).

$$(x - y)^2 = x^2 - 2xy + y^2$$
$$40 = 60 - 2xy$$
$$2xy = 20$$
$$xy = 10$$

18. The correct answer is (D). The area of the circle is $\pi(6)^2$, or 36π. In the triangle,

$$\tfrac{1}{2}(6)(h) = 36\pi$$
$$3h = 36\pi$$
$$h = 12\pi$$

19. The correct answer is (E). Subtract 2, multiply by 3; subtract 2, multiply by 3; etc.

20. The correct answer is (C). Arc $AB = 70°$; therefore $AOB = 70°$.
The two radii are equal.

Angle $x = \tfrac{1}{2}(180° - 70°) = \tfrac{1}{2}(110°) = 55°$.

21. The correct answer is (C). When a subordinate clause begins with *although,* the thought expressed in the main clause will not be consistent with that contained in the subordinate clause. If he gave *generously* to charity, he would not be generous with his family and friends. Of the choices given, *stingy* is the only opposite to generous.

22. The correct answer is (D). The troops wouldn't surrender because of the casualties but despite or *in spite* of all of the casualties.

23. The correct answer is (C). Oil is charged on the basis of volume (gallons). Heating the oil increases its volume. Choice (C) is the correct answer.

24. The correct answer is (C). A standard bushel basket is used to measure volume rather than weight. The critical word is *a* (standard weight), which should be changed to *no* (standard weight) to convey the true meaning of the quotation.

25. The correct answer is (C). Substituting *without* for *while* conveys the meaning of the quotation as intended. Choice (C) is the correct answer.

26. The correct answer is (D). The word *completed* does not convey the meaning intended. Analysis must begin before the training is *started* in order to have an effective training course.

27. The correct answer is (C). The word *ancient* is not consistent with the rest of the sentence. Substituting *modern* for *ancient* conveys the meaning intended.

28. The correct answer is (B). *Technical knowledge alone* is inconsistent with *ability and skills that are essential in coordinating the activities of subordinates.* Substituting *fails* for *seems* helps carry out the intended meaning of the passage.

29. The correct answer is (D). The word *when* tends to make the meaning confusing. Substituting *unless* for *when* conveys the meaning intended in the quotation.

30. The correct answer is (B). Choice (B) is the only option that rephrases the sentence without changing the meaning.

31. The correct answer is (C). By freeing itself from restrictions on the search for truth, humankind increases its efforts to find the truth. Choice (C) is the correct answer.

32. The correct answer is (A). The recommendation to use not more than 14 persons nor less than 10 persons means that it is best to use between 10 and 14 persons on the net, even if fewer can be used. Choice (A) is the correct answer.

33. The correct answer is (A). Choices (B), (C), and (D) are not valid options. To take notice of details that at first glance may not seem to have any connection with the crime implies that one cannot tell in advance what will be important.

34. The correct answer is (C). Choices (A), (B), and (D) are not supported by the quotation. Choice (C) is consistent with the meaning conveyed by the quotation.

35. The correct answer is (A). Choices (B), (C), and (D) are not supported by the quotation. Choice (A) is consistent with the meaning conveyed by the quotation.

36. The correct answer is (C). Choices (A), (B), and (D) are aspects of governmental functions for the protection of life and property against antisocial individuals within the country and enemies from without. Choice (C) is a governmental service but is not one for either the protection of life and property against antisocial individuals or protection from foreign enemies.

37. The correct answer is (C). According to the quotation, citizens who are selfish and act only as their private interests seem to require are not public spirited. Those who disregard others are concerned principally with their own selfish interests. Choice (C) is therefore the correct answer.

TEST 2: MECHANICAL COMPREHENSION TEST

Key Answers

1. The correct answer is (A).
2. The correct answer is (A).
3. The correct answer is (B).
4. The correct answer is (B).
5. The correct answer is (A).
6. The correct answer is (A).
7. The correct answer is (C).
8. The correct answer is (B).
9. The correct answer is (C).
10. The correct answer is (B).
11. The correct answer is (B).
12. The correct answer is (A).
13. The correct answer is (C).
14. The correct answer is (B).
15. The correct answer is (B).

16. The correct answer is (C).
17. The correct answer is (C).
18. The correct answer is (B).
19. The correct answer is (C).
20. The correct answer is (A).
21. The correct answer is (B).
22. The correct answer is (C).
23. The correct answer is (B).
24. The correct answer is (B).
25. The correct answer is (B).
26. The correct answer is (C).
27. The correct answer is (C).
28. The correct answer is (C).
29. The correct answer is (A).
30. The correct answer is (A).

Items Answered Incorrectly: __; __; __; __; __; __; __; __.
Items Unsure Of: __; __; __; __; __; __; __; __.

**TOTAL NUMBER
ANSWERED CORRECTLY:** ____

Rationale

1. The correct answer is (A). A seesaw is a good example of the first-class lever.

2. The correct answer is (A).

$$F \times 4 = 60 \times 14; \ F = \frac{840}{4}; \ F = 210 \text{ pounds.}$$

3. The correct answer is (B).

$$MA = \frac{10}{2} = 5.$$

4. The correct answer is (B). This is a second-class lever with the fulcrum at the end, the effort being applied at the other end, and the resistance between these points. There is an ideal mechanical advantage of 4. The application of a 50-lb. effect to the handle of the wheelbarrow 4 feet from the fulcrum will lift a 200-lb. weight 1 foot from the fulcrum.

5. The correct answer is (A). Let x = distance from the 275-lb. weight to the fulcrum point.

$$275 \text{ lbs.} \times x = 125 \text{ lbs.} \times (4 - x); \ 275x = 500 - 125x;$$

$$400x = 500; \ x = \frac{500}{400} = 1.25 \text{ inches}$$

6. The correct answer is (A). A single fixed pulley is actually a first-class lever with equal arms. The mechanical advantage, neglecting friction, is 1.

7. The correct answer is (C). The number of parts of the rope going to and from the movable block indicates the mechanical advantage. In this case, it is 2. Accordingly, a 50-pound effort would be needed.

8. The correct answer is (B). If the weight is to be raised 8 feet, each of the strands that either go around or are attached to the movable pulley must be shortened by 8 feet. $8 \times 3 = 24$ feet.

9. The correct answer is (C).

$$TMA = \frac{9}{3} = 3; \ \frac{300}{3} = 100 \text{ lbs.}$$

10. The correct answer is (B). Diameter of drum = 4″; radius of drum = 2″; $TMA = \frac{8}{2} = 4$.

11. The correct answer is (B). Tool B is a bit and brace used for making holes in wood.

12. The correct answer is (A). Tool A is a die used to cut external threads.

13. The correct answer is (C). The number 18 indicates the number of threads per inch.

14. The correct answer is (B). Circuit 2 is in series. $1\frac{1}{2} \times 4 = 6$ volts.

15. The correct answer is (B).

$$4\frac{1}{8}'' - \left(2 \times \frac{1}{2}''\right) = 4\frac{1}{8}'' - 1'' = 3\frac{1}{8}''$$

16. The correct answer is (C). The only correct choice is that points 1 and 2 make the same number of revolutions per minute.

17. The correct answer is (C). Gear A has 15 teeth; gear B has 10 teeth.

Let x = number of revolutions gear B will make.

$$15 \times 14 = 10 \times x; \ 10x = 15 \times 14; \ x = \frac{15 \times 14}{10}; \ x = 21.$$

18. The correct answer is (B). The top and the bottom of the driver wheel go in opposite directions. The driver wheel moves the left side of wheel S but the right side of wheel T, causing both wheels S and T to rotate in the same direction.

19. The correct answer is (C). Four times every second = 240 times a minute. With 10 projection rods on the wheel, the wheel must rotate at 24 rpm to make 240 rod contacts per minute.

20. The correct answer is (A). The raft will move in the opposite direction.

Let x = theoretical distance moved.

$$10 \times 60 = x \times 800; \ 800x = 1600; \ x = \frac{1600}{800} = 2$$

21. The correct answer is (B). By reducing the length of the lever arm, you are reducing the effort and will permit the valve to blow off at a lower pressure.

22. The correct answer is (C). The pressure is uniform in the system given. If the main line air gauge reads 100 pounds, the tank air gauge will also read 100 pounds.

23. The correct answer is (B). Eight threads per inch indicates that 8 complete turns of the vise handle are required to close the jaws 1". 18 complete turns are needed to close the jaws $2\frac{1}{4}$".

24. The correct answer is (B). Careful scrutiny will indicate that the center-to-center distance is 2 inches minus $\frac{1}{16}$ inches, or $1\frac{15}{16}$".

25. The correct answer is (B). If an 8" level indicates 16 quarts, a 6" level would indicate 12 quarts. Four additional quarts would be needed.

26. The correct answer is (C). Z is the compression stroke. Both valves are closed and the piston is moving upward.

27. The correct answer is (C). The proper sequence is: intake (Y); compression (Z); power (X); exhaust (W).

28. The correct answer is (C). The thread or screw-pitch gauge is used to determine the pitch and number of threads per inch of threaded fasteners.

29. The correct answer is (A). The torque is read visually on a dial mounted on the handle of the wrench. It is used when a definite force must be applied.

30. The correct answer is (A). The handle of the adjustable wrench should be pulled toward the side having the adjustable jaw. This will prevent the adjustable jaw from springing open and slipping off the nut.

NOTES

NOTES

NOTES

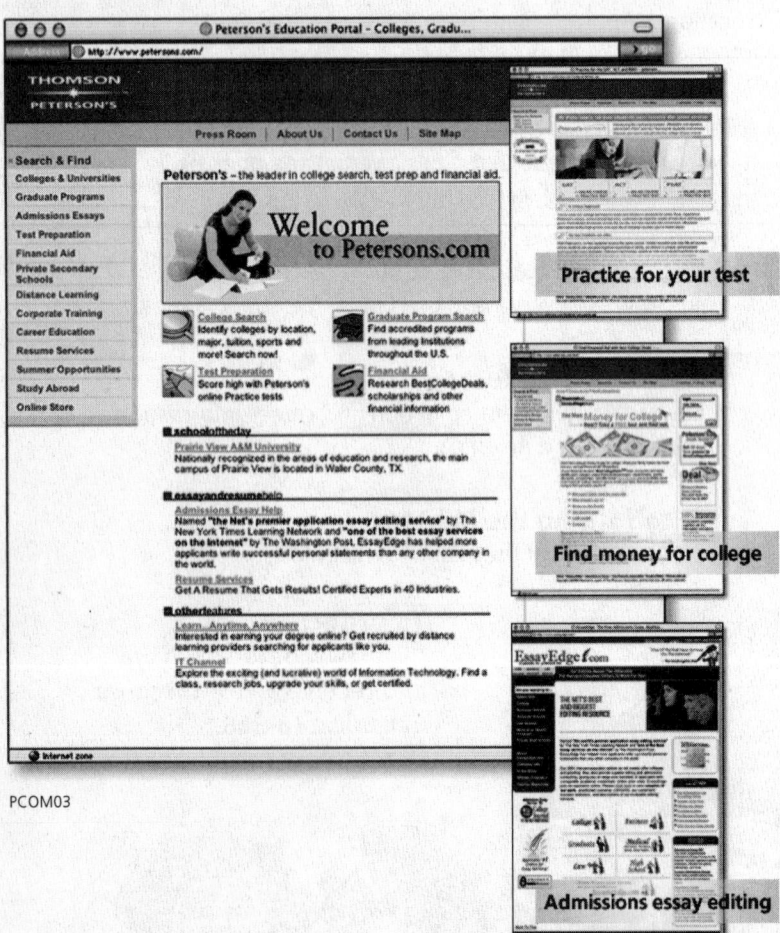